THE SCIENCE
OF POLITICS

AN INTRODUCTION

Josep M. Colomer

NEW YORK   OXFORD
OXFORD UNIVERSITY PRESS
2011

Oxford University Press, Inc., publishes works that further Oxford University's
objective of excellence in research, scholarship, and education.

Oxford   New York
Auckland   Cape Town   Dar es Salaam   Hong Kong   Karachi
Kuala Lumpur   Madrid   Melbourne   Mexico City   Nairobi
New Delhi   Shanghai   Taipei   Toronto

With offices in
Argentina   Austria   Brazil   Chile   Czech Republic   France   Greece
Guatemala   Hungary   Italy   Japan   Poland   Portugal   Singapore
South Korea   Switzerland   Thailand   Turkey   Ukraine   Vietnam

Published by Oxford University Press, Inc.
198 Madison Avenue, New York, NY 10016
www.oup.com

Library of Congress Cataloging-in-Publication Data
Colomer, Josep Maria.
  The science of politics : an introduction / Josep Colomer.
    p. cm.
  Includes bibliographical references and index.
  ISBN 978-0-19-539774-1 (pbk.)
  1. Political science.   I. Title.
  JA66.C55   2010
  320—dc22

Printing number: 9 8 7 6 5 4 3 2 1

Printed in the United States of America
on acid-free paper

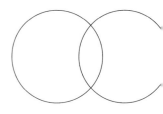

CONTENTS

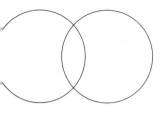

EXPANDED CONTENTS

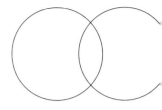

INTRODUCTION

This book is about politics, an activity that has been called a noble profession, a dismal science, or a classical art, from different views that are themselves controversial. The study of politics is addressed in this book from two points of departure. First, we understand that politics is a fundamental human activity to pursue the common interests of the members of a community—that is, in more classic words, the "public good." Second, politics, like any other human activity, can be the subject of systematic and reliable knowledge, according to the norms of what is usually called "science." If you are not particularly concerned about these two claims, you can skip the following paragraphs and go straight to the first chapter. Otherwise, you may want to spend a few minutes reading my arguments for adopting this perspective.

What Is Politics?

When the ancient Greek philosopher Aristotle said that "man is a political animal," he did not mean, of course, that to do politics, humans behave like beasts—acting only by instinct for fight and dominance. Rather, on the contrary, he meant that **politics is one of the essential activities that distinguish humans from other animals** (together with arts, religion, and science). Only human beings are able to cooperate for their common interest and abide by collective rules. Indeed, other animal species do fight to distribute resources and can have relationships in which a few individuals dominate others. Some people call this politics, although at most it would be in the roughest possible sense of the word. More important to understanding the meaning and importance of politics is the fact that no animals but humans are able to make exchanges to their mutual benefit, form coalitions and stable organizations, set up councils and assemblies, deliberate and vote, make enforceable decisions regarding collective affairs, or live in large communities under shared norms.

We should not confound the collective aims of politics with the private motivations of individuals involved in such an activity. While certain members of interest groups, political party activists, and professional politicians holding public offices may be driven by the ambition of fulfilling their private desires, including domination and the enjoyment of power, the collective aim of their activity is the provision of public goods. Think a moment about the same problem but regarding another fundamental activity of human beings, the arts. While artists can be motivated by the search for admiration and applause, the object of artistic activity is not the struggle for applause, but, obviously, the production of artwork—whether plays or poems, paintings or buildings, songs or movies—that may be enjoyed by the public. Similarly, the object of politics is, regardless of the private motivations of its actors, the provision of freedom, security, justice, means of transport, education, health care, clean air, and similar goods to the members of the community.

More precisely stated, **the stake of politics is the provision of public goods**, such as those just mentioned, by means of collective action. As we will discuss further in this book, public goods are those that cannot be divided into separate pieces or portions to be used by different individuals, and thus cannot be provided by solely market or other private mechanisms—while cars are private goods because each driver has a car, highways are public goods because all drivers share the same highway. It can be considered that the provision of public goods, which requires public institutions, draws a dividing line between the domains of public and private activities and defines the proper space of politics. Some public goods can produce near-universal benefits, as may be the case, for example, of certain natural resources, the calendar, and the world wide web, which may be provided by human **cooperation** with little institutional structure. But many public goods, such as public works, schools, social security, and other services, and the taxation policy to finance those goods, imply redistribution of resources among different members of the community, thus involving **conflicts** and **competition**.

All the different subjects presented in this book can be understood from this fundamental perspective. In the following pages we will discuss different forms of political community and regimes, including dictatorship and democracy, and different institutional formulas for democratic regimes, including the relationships between parliaments and presidents and diverse political party configurations, in turn followed by an analysis of different electoral rules and strategies for electoral competition. All these institutions, organizations, and behavior can be conceived as mechanisms for the choice and provision of public goods.

Why Science?

Politics is not a merely practical activity based on the accumulation of direct experience. The project of a science or methodical knowledge of politics is as old as politics itself. Many initiators of modern social sciences referred to the model of the sciences of nature typically with the aim of constructing some variant of "social physics." Nowadays, almost nobody believes that "natural laws" exist in society. But the outcomes of human interactions can produce regularities that are amenable to being captured, as in the other sciences, by stylized models and formulas.

Several disciplines have been taken as references for such an endeavor regarding the study of politics. The dominion of law in political studies until the early twentieth century promoted collecting data about political regimes and structures from different regions and countries of the world, thus providing a remarkable number of observations and comparisons. Nevertheless, empirical analyses were frequently mixed with normative value judgments. In a second period since the mid-twentieth century, political studies developed under the drive of empirical, inductive methods imported from sociology and psychology. This strongly fostered the adoption of quantitative techniques and statistical analyses of people's social characteristics and political behavior. In more recent decades, a new influence of economics has produced an outburst of formal models, mathematical refinements, and deductive reasoning in the study of politics. All these contributions are somehow cumulative. The scientific method indeed requires **empirical observations, quantitative measurements, and logical models** with interesting hypotheses. Both inductive and deductive reasoning may be necessary to develop a scientific analysis—a typical research moves from collecting observations to sketch a hypothesis, from the latter to amassing a higher number of more precisely identified and relevant observations, then to revising or refining the initial hypothesis, and so on.

Progress in knowledge of politics and society implies the accumulation of a set of propositions about people's behavior, the consequences of that behavior, and the relationships between institutions that should have general validity. A scientific model postulates that a relationship exists among a few clearly defined and measurable variables, such as, for instance, public goods, organized groups, public expenditure, development, dictatorship, democracy, war or peace, regime stability, assembly size, electoral rules, legislative performance, cabinet duration, political parties, electoral results, and issues on the public agenda. Do not forget that hypotheses must be both clearly spelled out, logically consistent, and supported by empirical tests and observations. Please read Box 0.1, "The Scientific Method in Politics," for further clarifications of the conditions of validity of scientific models and their capacity to predict future observations.

Often political scientists are asked to explain the causes of political events and to offer their advice for policy making or institutional choice. Although these two tasks are strongly related, actually they correspond to two different jobs: **political scientist** and **politician**. Suppose, for example, that two people make the following statements:

> GABRIEL: A high number of political parties reduces the degree of political polarization.
> MELISSA: There should be only two parties in the system to favor stable governance.

Note that Gabriel is speaking like a scientist: he is making a claim about how he see things. Melissa, in contrast, is speaking like a politician: she is making a claim about how she would like things to be. We should distinguish these two kinds of statements. A **scientific** proposition implies an assertion about **how things are**. A **normative** statement judges **how things ought to be**.

The difference between the two types of statements is that we can, in principle, validate or refute scientific propositions by examining **evidence**. We can collect data about the number of political parties in different countries, measure the party systems by taking into account the parties" relative size, estimate the policy or ideological distance among parties by scrutinizing their legislative and governmental behavior, and establish the appropriate relationships between these different sets of data. By contrast, a normative statement requires **values**. Deciding whether having many or few parties is good or bad implies a choice in favor of either faithful representation, government stability, policy consensus, or favorable opportunities for policy change.

Scientific and normative statements should be related, certainly more than ignorant and strongly opinionated people tend to suspect. As far as we know how things are, we can state our judgment on solid grounds. Gabriel's claim that a high number of parties reduces the degree of party distance and polarization (because when there are many parties, they tend to be located on relatively "close" positions to one another), if true, might lead Melissa to change her advice in favor of having only two parties accepted in the system. Yet a normative statement is not based only on scientific analysis. Instead, it requires both scientific analysis and a choice of values, so that even if the two persons agree on how things are, they can still maintain different opinions on how they ought to be.

Political scientists, thus, may agree on seeing how things are. Actually, political science has made remarkable progress in understating politics throughout the modern era, as we will see in this book. At the same time, political scientists may differ in their advice either because of as-yet-unsolved differences in scientific analysis or because of difficult-to-win arguments regarding values.

Practical politics needs science just as, to continue the analogy, even the practice of arts needs systematic knowledge. The arts of painting, playing music, or making movies are undeniably based in part on innate skills and predisposition, but also on training and practice. Artists can indeed benefit from methodical studies, and from the understanding acquired by previous practitioners. As in any other field, arts schools are not necessarily successful at producing good artists, but they can be crucial for developing the appropriate human capacities.

Likewise, political science courses, schools and textbooks should provide not only knowledge and understanding of political phenomena, but also the best foundations for applied exercises. Just as physics is the best foundation for geology and engineering, and economics has served as solid ground for the expansion of study programs in business management, a sound knowledge of political science should be the basis for the practice of organization and leadership, electioneering, public policy making, public administration, foreign affairs, and other professional activities.

The Book

This book is conceived with the aim of filling a persistent gap between developments in research and the regular teaching in the discipline. The field of political science has made a lot of progress in research and academic publications during the last few decades, but the customary teaching of political science does not match up. As one anonymous reviewer of the manuscript of this book wrote, many instructors have to "assign a textbook that has very little to do with what they talk about in lectures."

The materials presented in the following pages are only a selection of the many things that we actually know. My choices have been based on the experience accumulated by teaching this kind of course to students with varied backgrounds in three different countries on both sides of the Atlantic for more than twenty years. When selecting what to include, I tried to apply criteria of simplicity, practicality, and historical relevance. Some things that are included may need further proofs of their validity, but I bet on them because of their relevance and their consistency with other well-established postulates. Immediately after this introduction you'll find a set of "Thirty Propositions in Political Science," a summary of findings exposed throughout the rest of the book. These propositions are presented in an informal manner, although they should become more formal and better proved "theorems" in more advanced studies. Certainly much more sound knowledge could and should be taught in other courses and textbooks. But my well-grounded impression after writing this book is that, actually, we know a lot—much more than is usually acknowledged both inside and outside the academic discipline of politics.

This book should fit a regular course of introduction to political science within the semester system. It includes four parts with the following titles:

    I. **Action**
    II. **Polity**
    III. **Election**
    IV. **Government**

If the book turns out to be too long for other purposes, it can also be used according to the instructor's needs and criteria. Its partial use can be arranged in different ways:

- Parts **I and II** can be combined to provide a short introduction to the foundations of politics.
- Parts **III and IV**, and perhaps chapters from other parts, can form a course centered on the study of political institutions.

Alternatively, the book can be split as follows:

- Parts **I and III** can be studied together in a course because they share a "micro" approach in which individual decisions explain collective outcomes.
- Parts **II and IV**, by contrast, share a "macro" approach focusing on structural variables, and thus can be studied together.

These different packages may also be suitable for courses in other majors, such as political philosophy, constitutional law, political economics, and comparative or area studies.

The main body of the book is plain text with a number of boldface terms or phrases to be retained in your mind or jotted down in your notes, and only a few simple formulas. Some extensions are given in separate "boxes," which may be used at the instructor's discretion depending on the level of the course. There are also a number of disparate but intentionally relevant "cases," or examples from countries and cities

BOX 0.1 **THE SCIENTIFIC METHOD IN POLITICS**

This is an introductory book without mathematical sophistication, but it is inspired by a certain notion of what scientific knowledge of politics is and should be. The basic idea is that the complex and sometimes apparently chaotic political reality can be captured by stylized **models.**

Each model postulates that a relationship exists among a small number of variables. Let us remark that the variables in a model must be well defined with appropriate **concepts**—such as public good, interest group, leader, stability, democracy, war, decision rule, legislative performance, party, activist, policy space, and ideology—which are supplied throughout this book. The variables selected should be susceptible of precise observation and, if possible, **quantitative measurement**. Many political variables can be measured—for instance, number of individuals, area, number of governments, money, time, votes, seats, number of parties, policy "positions," or ideological "distance." You will find about a dozen indices to make quantitative measurements of political variables in this book.

A model in politics usually implies some assumptions regarding actors' motives at making decisions, that connect the variables just mentioned. Relations between variables exist precisely because people make decisions. For instance, it is usually postulated that economic development favors the stability and duration of democracy. But the relation between these two structural variables—development and democracy—is decisively mediated by people's action. A rationale may be that under conditions of relatively high average income, there is low social polarization, and political actors can accept to abide by the rules of the game because losing an election does not imply complete destitution, while undertaking a rebellion or coup d'etat would be too risky and costly. Choices such as this (to support democracy) are made under constraints and with opportunities supplied by existing structures (in this example, favorable economic and social conditions), and such choices contribute to stabilizing, changing, or creating new structural outcomes (say, a durable democratic regime). Observable relationships between structural variables can thus be hypothesized, although the mechanisms linking those variables should also be specified. Strategic **interactions** can be modeled with the help of game theory or related approaches.

For the researcher, the identification of an interesting and relevant problem for study may derive from some direct involvement in the issue at hand, a deep study of a remarkable case, or a broader research program. The formulation of hypotheses regarding the relationships among variables and people's decisions usually requires educated intuition or some effort at intellectual imagination. The criterion of **parsimony** demands the best possible ratio between the number of variables considered and the observations to be explained. If, for instance, we have a good model for explaining the effectiveness of an interest group in satisfying its demands as a function of the variable called "group size" (which is clearly measurable), and this is congruent with many empirical observations, it may be "better"—that is, more efficient and parsimonious—than trying to account for every single occurrence by a series of numerous previous events, disparate factors, and complex processes, often including unlikely episodes.

It is a common warning that models in politics, as in other social sciences, are valid only in given circumstances. But let me argue that many parts of our understanding of politics have no less strength or relevance than the accumulated knowledge in other well-established disciplines. Let us just mention one of the simplest and most popular models in economics. Any elementary textbook will tell you that in a competitive market for a private good—think, for instance, of apples or houses—an equilibrium price exists when the quantities demanded and supplied are equal. This is mainly derived from the generalized observation that people tend to buy less, or at least no more, of a good as the price rises, which is called "the law of demand." Possibly you have heard of this. By now, it has become common knowledge, although it took several centuries of thinking to formulate it with precision and insight. Just to mention a completely different field, I am sure you can remember a fundamental model in the most prized science, physics: "the law of gravity," which explains why bodies tend to fall to the ground.

Models like these form the bases of the modern "normal" sciences. But everybody knows that they are harsh **simplifications** of reality that can fit empirical observations only under specific, very well defined, but relatively rare circumstances. Equilibrium prices do not emerge in daily observations, because certain

Continued

BOX 0.1 *Continued*

goods (such as housing, just mentioned, as a particularly strong case) are not as movable or people do not have as good information about the market opportunities as is assumed in the model. Likewise, in the case of the law of gravity, bodies fall as predicted only in an idealized "perfect vacuum," but to measure and predict each specific episode, the wind, the resistance of air, or "friction," and other conditions have to be estimated. However, individual consumers, families, firms, traders, and governments would go astray if they did not know the basics of price theory, just as engineers, bricklayers, plumbers, aircraft pilots, and all of us would if we tried to ignore the law of gravity.

As in any other science, models in politics do not predict the future in an unconditional sense. They merely say that if certain **conditions** are fulfilled, then certain outcomes are likely to be expected. Forecasts are always probabilistic. For specific predictions, the models must be subjected to territorial, temporal, and other constrains on human behavior. What is more, people can change some "variables" on purpose. Under the appropriate incentives, actors' decisions on altering political situations may have an effect on structural relationships and are, therefore, indispensable to accounting for expected collective outcomes. Actually, the more knowledgeable a person is in political science, the more he or she may be able to manipulate some settings with the intention of attaining desirable results. This does not deny, however, the scientific character of models. Rather, to the contrary, well-grounded purposive behavior can be the main confirmation of their validity because it implies awareness of their potential implications.

All models should be able to be subjected to **empirical tests**. A model can be either validated or invalidated by different ways, most prominently by the following procedures, which you may want to study in more advanced courses:

- Regression analysis and other statistical techniques for large numbers of observations;
- The comparative method for a small number of appropriate observations; and
- Laboratory experiments.

Empirical tests can lead to the validation, reformulation, or rejection of hypotheses about relationships among variables and people's decisions. This permits cumulative knowledge, which is synonymous of scientific progress.

all across the world in both remote and current periods. A section on "sources" reproduces enlightening fragments of seminal texts from both classic authors and modern scholars. Each chapter ends with a "conclusion," in which the more solid findings are recapitulated and the "propositions" mentioned in the main body of the chapter are restated. There follows a "summary" and a list of "key concepts" worth studying and rereading. A few "questions for review" and "problems and applications" can help the course along.

At the end of the book, all the "key concepts" are listed in alphabetical order for further consultation. A list of bibliographical references is given for the statements presented throughout the chapters, and to entice further reading. Illustrations for part openers are by Ambrogio Lorenzetti (c. 1290-1348). *Effects of Good Government on the Citizenry*, 1338-39. Public Palace, Siena, Italy.

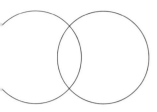

SOME THINGS WE KNOW

Thirty Propositions in Political Science

This is an informal collection of propositions and findings exposed throughout this book and specifically summarized at the conclusion of each chapter. You may want to give it a first reading now in order to realize the scope of our accumulated knowledge, although this is only a partial selection of the many things about politics we actually know. You should come back to this section after studying this course, as a kind of review of substantive things you will have had the occasion to learn.

Action

In this first part of the book, we use the concept of the public good to draw a line between the domains of political activity and private concerns. We study the conditions under which cooperation among individuals for the common interest of a group or community can emerge and hold up. In particular, we address the capacity of leaders to initiate collective action and the conditions under which efficient leadership can satisfy the public good.

1. PUBLIC GOODS.

In contrast to private goods, public goods are indivisible and cannot be satisfactorily provided by the market or other private initiatives. The provision of public goods requires cooperation or coercion, whether by means of collective action or effective government.

2. GOVERNMENT SIZE.

The demand for public goods and the relative levels of public expenditure by governments tend to increase with economic prosperity, institutional stability, and democracy.

3. COLLECTIVE ACTION.

Members of small, concentrated, and homogeneous communities or interest groups have more incentives to cooperate and participate in collective action than members of large, dispersed, and heterogeneous groups. In the public arena, small groups tend to have relatively more access to public resources at the expense of large groups.

4. VOICE VERSUS EXIT.

Collective action for the advancement of collective interests, or "voice," weakens and may fail if the rival action of "exit," in search for an alternative provider, is less costly and more likely to give access to public goods.

5. PRISONER'S DILEMMA.

The "Prisoner's Dilemma," which is the most famous model in game theory, can represent the basic structure of collective action problems for the provision of public goods. In this game, each actor has incentives not to cooperate, which may lead to an inefficient outcome in which all the participants are worse off than if all cooperated.

6. SUSTAINED COOPERATION.

In interactions of the Prisoner's Dilemma type, sustained cooperation can emerge if actors apply the strategy of cooperating and doing unto others as they do do unto yourself—also called "Tit for Tat." Mutual cooperation is more likely the greater the uncertainty as to the length of the collective relationship and the higher the number of interactions you may be involved in.

7. LEADERSHIP.

Collective action of communities and interest groups can develop thanks to leadership. Leaders distribute the costs of action among group members to provide public and private goods, while, in exchange, followers give the leaders votes or support and allow them to enjoy the benefits of power, fame, income, and a political career.

Polity

In this part, we study the fundamental forms of a political community. In addition to the classic notions of state-building and nation-building, we discuss how multiple levels of government, each with different responsibilities, can be an efficient way to provide public goods. We analyze the conditions for having a stable democratic government and its consequences regarding the provision of public goods, development, and peace.

8. SMALL IS DEMOCRATIC.

Small communities, which tend to be relatively harmonious in economic and ethnic terms, are comparatively advantageous for soft, democratic forms of government. In recent times, small independent countries and self-governed communities have proliferated, thus making the average country size decrease.

9. MULTILEVEL GOVERNANCE.

Multiple levels of government, including local, state, and global, are necessary for an efficient provision of public goods at diverse territorial scales.

10. FEDERATION NEEDS MANY UNITS.

Local democratic self-government and large-scale provision of public goods can be compatible by means of federalism. Many-unit federations, in which no unit is sufficiently large to dominate, tend to survive and endure. In contrast, two-unit-only federations tend to fail, leading to either absorption of the smaller unit by the larger one or secession of the small, likely dominated unit.

11. DICTATORSHIPS FAIL AND FALL.

Dictatorships have self-appointed rulers holding on to power by coercive and violent means. They can survive on the basis of repression and their "substantive" performance, whether economic or other. But they also tend to fall as a consequence of their failures, including military defeats, economic crises, or the dictator's death.

12. DEVELOPMENT FAVORS DEMOCRACY.

Democracy is based on freedom and regular elections of rulers. Economic development favors the viability of democratic regimes because it tends to reduce income and social polarization and lower the intensity of redistributive conflicts.

13. DEMOCRACY FAVORS DEVELOPMENT.

Democracy can favor economic development because it is strongly associated with the rule of law and is more competent in the provision of public goods.

14. DEMOCRATIC PEACE.

Democratic states are less likely to fight one another and engage in wars than dictatorships.

Election

In this part, we study how democratic representation can be organized by means of political parties and elections. Political parties are organizations that present policy proposals and candidates for leadership offices. Elections imply competition among candidates on policy proposals for different issues, which can be more or less interesting for different groups of voters. Electoral results determine the quality and contents of representative government.

15. PARTY OLIGARCHY.

Political parties are organizations that present policy proposals and compete for political power. A political organization tends to become an "oligarchy," that is, it tends to be dominated by political leaders or professional politicians seeking votes and offices.

16. EXTREME ACTIVISTS.

Voluntary political activists hold more "extreme" policy or ideological positions than party voters and even party leadership.

17. MEDIAN VOTER.

In elections in which only two major parties compete, they may have incentives to approach each other and converge in their policy positions. Once they converge around the median voter's preference, neither party has electoral incentives to move away from the other party.

18. INCUMBENT ADVANTAGE.

Electoral competition is asymmetric between the government and the opposition. The incumbent party in government can gain advantage in electoral competition by providing or hiding information on its record to obtain credibility.

19. ISSUE OWNERSHIP.

In spite of parties' convergence in their policy positions on some issues, a party can keep advantage and "own" an issue if its past record in government has given it credit for policy making on that issue.

20. NON-DEBATE CAMPAIGNS.

In electoral campaigns, rival parties and candidates tend to choose or emphasize different policy issues according to different issue ownership and the parties' or candidates' expected relative advantage.

21. POLICY CONSENSUS.

In the long term, broad policy consensus can be accumulated on an increasing number of issues. But in the short term, mediocre policies and incumbent parties with no good performance in government may survive for lack of a sufficiently popular alternative.

22. CONSENSUAL PLURALISM.

There is an inverse correlation between the number of political parties in a system and the degree of party polarization in electoral competition. High fragmentation of the party system is associated with a high number of issues on the policy agenda, which generates low polarization of political competition and more opportunities for consensus.

Government

Political institutions are the rules of the game. Typical institutional formulas for governments include a one-person office, such as a presidency or prime ministership, and multiple-person councils or assemblies. Different political regimes combine different procedures to select rulers and different divisions of power and relationships between one-person and multiple-person institutions, whether of mutual dependency or autonomy.

23. MAJORITY BIPARTISM.

Presidential and other one-office elections by plurality rule tend to be associated with single-party dominance or a balance between two parties.

24. MORE SEATS, MORE PARTIES.

In assembly and parliamentary elections, large size of the assembly and a high number of seats in each district and proportional representation are associated with a high number of political parties.

25. MICRO-MEGA RULE.

When choosing electoral rules, large parties prefer small assemblies and small districts by plurality rule, while small parties prefer large assemblies and large districts with proportional representation.

26. SMALL ASSEMBLIES, LARGE DISTRICTS

The development of multiple parties favors the adoption of large multi-seat districts with proportional representation rules. In the long term, proportional representation rules have been increasingly adopted. But in very large countries, a large federal assembly can be elected with different electoral rules, including small single-seat districts.

27. INSTITUTIONAL "DEADLOCK."

Single-party government promotes a high concentration of power, which may foster effectiveness in decision making. In contrast, separate elections for different offices and divisions of power may produce divided government, "deadlock," and policy stability.

28. MINIMUM COALITIONS.

Political parties in parliament tend to form minimum-size winning coalitions and prefer partners located in contiguous policy and ideology positions The distribution of cabinet portfolios among coalition parties tends to be proportional to the number of seats controlled by each party.

29. CABINET DURATION.

Single-party majority cabinets tend to last longer than multiparty coalition or minority cabinets.

30. TWO-PARTY STALEMATE.

In a system with division of power between the presidency and the congress, policy change is relatively more viable if there are multiple parties or individual members of congress ar not strongly tied to party votes. In contrast, a two-party system with strong party discipline may prop up confrontation and inter-institutional stalemate.

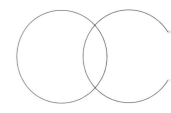

PART I **ACTION**

Politics can be distinguished from private affairs because it deals with collective or public goods. In this first part of the book, we use the concept of public good to draw a line between the domains of political activity and of private concerns. Since the provision of public goods requires coordinated, collective effort, its achievement does not depend on the cost of the goods, but on the costs of the collective action. We study the conditions in which cooperation among individuals for the common interest of a group or community can emerge and hold up. In particular, we address the capacity of leaders to initiate collective action and the conditions under which an efficient leadership can satisfy the public good.

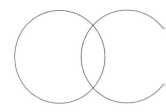

THE PUBLIC GOOD

In This Chapter You Will

- Learn to distinguish between public goods and private goods.
- Analyze why it may be so difficult to make people contribute voluntarily to the provision of public goods.
- Discover what the "tragedy of the commons" is.
- Reflect on the similarities and differences between saving the atmosphere and the oceans, making progress in research, having a common currency, and building roads and airports.
- Consider why public expenditure expands over time.
- Begin to think of politics as a compound of rules and decisions for the provision of public goods.

The stake of politics is the provision of public goods. Over centuries, many thinkers—theologians, philosophers, revolutionaries, theorists—have sought to identify the goal of living in community as "the public good" or "the common good." In the approach developed in this book, the object of politics can be conceived as the provision of a set of "public goods" to be used by the members of the community.

Think, for instance, of the road passing before your house. All the neighbors living along it may want to have it well paved and clean. However, each of them may expect to be able to use it as any other passerby would, without having to make a personal effort to maintain it. By contrast, most of those drivers using the road will probably take care of their own cars, making sure that they are well tuned and clean. The point of this example is that roads are public goods, which are usually to be provided by the government, while cars are private goods, which can be provided by the market. As Greek philosopher Aristotle observed many centuries ago, "what is common to many is taken least care of; for all men regard more what is their own than what others share with them, to which they pay less attention than is incumbent on every one."

We start this chapter by defining and discussing what a public good is. In some sense, it is something the members of the community want but cannot attain by their own individual means—including roads, as in the example, and security, justice, schools, and clean air. The provision of public goods requires coordinated collective effort, whether by voluntary or coercive means. By using the concept of collective or public good, as opposed to individual or private good, we can draw a rational line between the domains of political activity and private concerns. The most fundamental goal of politics is making the provision of public goods feasible for the improvement and well-being of the members of the community. ■

Public Goods

Any individual living in a community can obtain some goods by private means in order to satisfy basic needs such as eating, being clothed, having shelter, and obtaining means of transport. Goods such as food, clothing, houses, and cars can be used in separate units, and thus individuals can have access to them by buying and selling or by bargaining and reaching agreements with other people. These are divisible goods that can be provided and consumed by private means.

In contrast, public goods are those that cannot be divided into separate pieces or portions to be used by different individuals. Goods such as the sea, the defense of the community from external attack, a system of weights and measures, a road or a traffic signal, and a museum or a public park, just to mention a few examples, are made not to be appropriated and used in private, but precisely to provide benefits to and be shared by many people. The point is that public goods may not be obtained or maintained by individual citizens if there are no appropriate institutions leading them to contribute to their provision or preservation. Indeed, the members of a community can contribute to making public goods available by means of certain kinds of behavior, action, work, or money. But every individual can expect to have access to public goods even without contributing to their provision.

INDIVISIBILITY

Public goods are indivisible. Standard definitions of public goods emphasize that they are **supplied jointly** to all individuals interested in using them. This is in contrast to **private goods, which are supplied in separate pieces and consumed individually**. The road already mentioned as an elementary example of a public good is supplied to everybody, and it will be used by more than one person at a time. Different persons going along the road are not using different portions of the road; each and every person can use the same and the entire road. This is in contrast to the cars passing by the road: each is used by different persons. When a good, such as a road, cannot be divided into pieces or portions to be used by different individuals, private markets or bargaining cannot ensure that the good is provided at an amount people would be interested in paying for it. In this case, to satisfy people's interest in the good, there is need for cooperation or coercion, usually implying credible commitments, effectively enforced rules, or compulsory authority.

Let us assume that a band of wrongdoers is acting in a neighborhood where they break into and burglarize houses, litter the streets, and bother passersby. The neighbors may be interested in having a security patrol installed to prevent unwanted visitors from doing any kind of damage. The cost of such a patrol, either in terms of neighbors' participation in making rounds or in the amount of money to pay a selection of robust people to do the job, can be lower than the expected damage from the band of thieves. Thus, a private initiative to organize security patrols could find the job profitable. However, any private entrepreneur would have trouble recruiting neighbors to take shifts or collecting money for the service because every individual citizen can expect to benefit from collective security even without contributing to it. Public goods, such as protection and security, are collectively desirable but not privately profitable, thus they are not likely to be provided by individual means.

Let us take again the example of the road. Suppose a new factory has been established in the surrounding area of a small town and the firm is interested in installing a road suitable for trucks to deliver freight and pick up merchandise. All the residents in the town can expect to benefit from such a road for their own transport and for making other trade feasible. However, the firm will hardly be able to collect contributions from all potential beneficiaries, because each of them may expect to have access to the road regardless of their contribution. Public goods, such as transport routes, are those that people may want to have but cannot obtain at the desired level through optional private exchanges. They require wide cooperation, which is usually induced by some leadership or authority.

EXTERNALITIES

A public good is a market failure, that is, something that markets fail to provide in the desired amount. Another type of market failure, usually called an "externality" by economists, can also be understood as a public good. **An "externality" is the external effect of some people's action on other people's satisfaction or utility**. The accomplishments of the criminal gang mentioned earlier have a negative external effect on the neighborhood residents. The spread of unpredictable, threatening crime is a public "evil." In contrast, a security patrol has a positive external effect on the populace. Security is a public good. The fact that negative "externalities" can be suppressed or compensated for by some authority implies that public evils can also be suppressed or compensated for, and public goods, thus, provided and enjoyed.

A well-known negative external effect of certain industrial and transport activities is air pollution. We can think of this effect as a public evil that can be replaced with a public good. The collective evil of pollution is the smoke, while the corresponding public good is clean air. A collective effort or a compulsory authority can thus provide clean air by making producers behave in a different way, one that is able to reduce the negative external effect of their laboriousness or compensate the sufferers for their smoke-producing activity. Actually, some governments sell licenses to pollute or impose fees or fines on polluting companies and use the money collected to finance measures to refresh and protect the environment.

In an ideal model, organizations and governments can provide public goods to the desired level to the extent they can achieve the following conditions:

- Every individual in the community contributes, whether with personal effort or with money.
- The amount of the public good provided depends on the sum of the individuals' contributions.
- Everybody can use the entire public good provided.

Quick Quiz

- Define public goods and private goods, and give two examples of each.

SOURCE 1.1   Private Goods and Public Goods

Roads are public goods, which are usually provided by the government, while cars are private goods which can be provided by the market.

Most of the arts and professions in a state are of such a nature, that, while they promote the interests of the society, they are also useful or agreeable to some individuals; and, in that case, the constant rule of the authority, except, perhaps, on the first introduction of any art, is to leave the profession to itself, and trust its encouragement to those who reap the benefit of it . . . But there are also some callings which, though useful and even necessary in a state, bring no particular advantage or pleasure to any individual; and the supreme power is obliged to alter its conduct with regard to the retainers of those professions. It must give them public encouragement in order to their subsistence, and it must provide against that negligence to which they will naturally be subject, either by annexing peculiar honors to the profession, by establishing a long subordination of ranks and a strict dependence, or by some other expedient. The persons employed in the finances, armies, fleets and magistracy are instances of this order of men.

David Hume, *The History of England* (1759–62)

I explicitly assume two categories of goods: ordinary private consumption goods $(X_1, \ldots, X_n)$ which can be parcelled out among different individuals (1, 2, . . . , i, . . . , s) according to the relation $X_j = S \, X_j^i$; and collective consumption goods $(X_{n+1} \ldots, X_{n+m})$ which all enjoy in common in the sense that each individual's consumption of such a good leads to no subtraction from any other individual's consumption of that good, so that $X_{n+j} = X_{n+j}^i$ simultaneously for each and every ith individual and each collective consumptive good . . .

No decentralized pricing system can serve to determine optimally the levels of collective consumption [which are] possible for the first category of "private" goods to which the ordinary market pricing applies and which do not have the "external effects" basic to the very notion of collective consumption good.

Paul A. Samuelson, "The Pure Theory of Public Expenditure" (1954)

Types of Public Goods

The expected contributions by individuals to the provision of public goods partly depend on the characteristics of the different types of goods. For different goods, the individual utility of their users can increase, decrease, or remain the same as the number of users changes. All these goods can be collectively provided at an efficient level, but they may require putting in place different institutional means.

First, certain goods, which can be called **"network" goods, give higher potential benefits to each user the higher the number of users**. This happens, for instance, with languages, weights and measures, currencies, and the world wide web. The higher the number of people speaking a common language, the broader the opportunities for communication every speaker will have; the more numerous the communities adopting a common currency, the more frequent and varied the trade and exchanges each individual can do at low transaction cost; the higher the number of websites, blogs, and links, the larger the amount of information and potential communicators every net user may enjoy. The provision of these goods requires little governance, which may be provided by the users themselves or be borrowed from some external structure. We should be happy to have the opportunity to enjoy these public goods, although they are understudied precisely because their deliverance does not imply arduous organizational or institutional problems.

"Pure" public goods are those that can be used by one person without modifying anyone else's satisfaction or utility. Pure public goods are, for example, scientific discoveries, security, and defense, which permit increasing numbers of users to derive benefit from the same supply of the good. Indeed, a mathematical theorem does not cease to be useful or become less true as the number of learned people increases or decreases; likewise, antiaircraft warfare can defend a city from external attacks whatever the number of the city inhabitants or temporary residents may be; and so on. The provision of these goods may face the challenge of some potential users be unwilling to contribute to their costs, precisely because they can enjoy the good without being discriminated against.

Finally, **"rival" public goods suffer from potential congestion. One additional person's use of the good can diminish the utility of other people using the good**. The higher the number of users of a road, for example, the lower the utility obtained by each user, since with higher number of cars, the slower the traffic, which can even break down completely. There is rivalry among the potential users of these goods. If they are supplied to all potentially interested users, one person's use of the good can diminish the satisfaction obtained by other people using the good at the same time. Rival public goods include clean air, roads and highways, tunnels and bridges, airports, schools, and hospitals. All are vulnerable to pollution, traffic jams, overcrowding, queues, crushes, delays, congestion, and collapse. When the rival good is beyond its capacity limit, using it may be no longer possible for any individual. We discuss the problems in providing this type of good in the following paragraphs.

CLUB GOODS

A crucial mechanism to solve the problem of rivalry is the **exclusion** of certain people from accessing the public good. Think, for instance, of a concert by Diana Krall. If, on the occasion of a local festival, the concert is put on by the local government outdoors in the town's central square, free to everybody, it will be a congestible public good; too many attendants can make listening and watching arduous and can reduce each individual spectator's satisfaction. Moving the concert to a theater requiring payment for tickets, or to local cable television, which implies some degree of privatization of the public good, will reduce rivalry. But this will make a difference to people's satisfaction or utility. Some people disliking crowds may prefer the concert to be held in a theater or shown on-screen, but others may find the experience of mass spectacle more enjoyable. In any case, those excluded from the theater or the cable projection will, of course, be frustrated.

Excluding some potential users implies the introduction of a price, whether in the form of tolls, fees, or other mechanisms. A price can be introduced by establishing coercive command, creating private property rights, or transferring services to private companies under public regulations and control. The exclusion of some people from accessing rival public goods reduces congestion for the included individuals. It may involve the creation of **club goods**, that is, **public goods to be used by some people to the exclusion of others**—only for the "members" of the club.

Reductions of rivalry are attained for lighthouses, highways, and bridges by imposing tolls on ships or cars, respectively; for public schools and universities, by requiring fees; for hospitals and health care, by encouraging private insurance. At the same time, nondiscriminatory access can be given to the most interested people by offering vouchers, fellowships, subsidies, entry passes, or exemptions.

Regretfully, exclusion or privatization is also feasible for non-rival public goods, to which everybody could access without a loss of satisfaction. If anybody—for instance, the Chinese government—tries to exclude somebody from accessing the world wide web via internet, it is not to solve any problem of congestion of the public good, which does not exist in this case, but to prevent people from having certain information. For non-rival goods, such as knowledge, exclusion is just a way to provide a public evil.

THE COMMONS

A more difficult problem exists for a specific subtype of **rival or congestible good, the commons, which are not excludable**. For rival goods such as the atmosphere, certain animal species of commercial value, clean water, pools, pastureland, and woods, the number of potential users is large, but it may be impossible to exclude anyone. This configures the so-called "tragedy of the commons." Since not everybody can be required to pay for their use, these goods tend to be used excessively. However, none of the users may have an incentive to refrain unilaterally, since everyone is only a small part of the community. The tragedy emerges when the common good is exhaustible. If the air is overloaded with deleterious gases, it may become unbreathable; if fishing and hunting is not limited, shrinking numbers of fish, whales, and elephants may be unable to reproduce at a sufficient rate so as to guarantee the species' survival; if water is overused, natural cycles may be shortened and rivers and lakes may dry up.

Again, forcing some kind of divisibility, if feasible, may restore the possibility of maintaining the supply by private means. For example, certain species such as buffalos and bulls have survived and thrived thanks to having been kept on private ranches

SOURCE 1.2   The Tragedy of the Commons

The variety of animal species and plants, the atmosphere the seas and oceans, are global public goods to be preserved by means of collective action.

The tragedy of the commons develops in this way. Picture a pasture open to all. It is to be expected that each herdsman will try to keep as many cattle as possible on the commons...Explicitly or implicitly, more or less consciously, he asks, "What is the utility to me of adding one more animal to my herd?" This utility has one negative and one positive component.

1) The positive component is a function of the increment of one animal. Since the herdsman receives all proceeds from the sale of the additional animal, the positive utility is nearly +1.

2) The negative component is a function of the additional overgrazing created by one more animal. Since, however, the effects of overgrazing are shared by all the herdsmen, the negative utility for any particular decision-making herdsman is only a fraction of -1.

Adding together the component partial utilities, the rational herdsman concludes that the only sensible course for him to pursue is to add another animal to his herd. And another, and another...But this is the conclusion reached by each and every rational herdsman sharing a commons. Therein is the tragedy. Each man is locked into a system that compels him to increase his herd without limit—in a world that is limited. Ruin is the destination toward which all men rush, each pursuing his own best interest in a society that believes in the freedom of the commons. Freedom in a commons brings ruin to all.

Garrett Hardin, "The Tragedy of the Commons" (1968)

and granges instead of being allowed to run freely across savannas and deserts. Also, public authorities can distribute hunting licenses to be used only on certain lands. Privatization can make threatened collective cattle become just a set of safe individual animals.

Other solutions, beyond mere coercion, may also be feasible. If the number of persons involved in a commons problem is small, they can bargain and reach an agreement among themselves. This happens, for instance, with the classical example of neighbors on two sides of a fence regarding the use of water pool lying under properties. But for indivisible goods to be used by large groups, the costs of sharing information, bargaining, and watching over the enforcement of agreements and regulations for the appropriate distribution of the use rights may be insurmountable.

Nevertheless, coordinated self-restraint among the people involved can attain success if some favorable conditions are met. These include the establishment of clearly defined boundaries for the availability of the common good; well-distributed rights to all parts involved in participating in collective regulations; the possibility for the community to control the enforcement of agreements and punish violators; and the availability of low-cost settings to resolve disputes. There are many cases of users of meadows, forests, fisheries, irrigation communities, and other common-pool resources being able to build and sustain institutions of self-government to ensure reproduction and prevent extinction. In other conditions, especially for pooled resources on large scales without effective institutions, the provision and maintenance of common goods can fail.

Quick Quiz

• Why do interested groups and governments try to limit the use of commons resources?

The Politics of Public Goods

The list of public goods is endless. One can always think of some new potential mechanism for inducing or coercing people to cooperate or to behave in a way that could produce positive effects on themselves and on other people at the same time. Public or collective goods can be provided to the members of well-defined groups by families, voluntary labor, rural communes, patrimonial corporations, churches, guilds, workers' unions, cooperatives, professional associations, private companies, nongovernmental organizations, and foundations, as well as by fiefs, armies, guerrillas, mafias, cities, sovereign states, great empires, and international organizations. The means for making individuals contribute to the provision of public goods are varied, from mere coordination or affection to persuasion, promises, trust, mutual compulsion, coercive control, prices, threats, or organized force.

However, not all potential public goods and ways of their provision are desirable or feasible. The domain of public activity that can be socially accepted and satisfactory depends on the number of potential beneficiaries of each potential public good, the intensity of people's preference for the good, the technology available, and the costs of the collective coordination, decision making, and bureaucratic apparatus to provide the good. As Nobel Prize–winning economist Paul Samuelson suspected, any function of government not possessing the earlier defined characteristics of the public good "ought to be carefully scrutinized to see whether it is a truly legitimate function of government."

REDISTRIBUTION FIGHTS

Certain public goods can be considered global or universal, able to satisfy very large common interests and benefit many people. But many public goods involve redistributive conflicts and competition because, even if they are provided jointly to all members of the community, different people may obtain different benefits and incur different costs from them.

The most global goods for the individuals living on this planet are the variety of human beings, other animal species and plants, the atmosphere, the seas and oceans, rivers, lakes, and woods. Other worldwide public goods include the world map and pictures of Earth taken by satellite, the calendar and the time standard, many weights and measures, and the world wide web. If appropriate mechanisms for securing their survival are enforced, these goods can be accessed by virtually all members of humankind. Not so global but very broadly supplied public goods include common currencies and free-trade laws, scientific discoveries, technical inventions, and cultural products such as literary, musical, or artistic works. Their provision and maintenance require significant collective efforts and agreements, although not necessarily a state-type authority.

On other matters, the differences among public goods may reach the point where some people can consider as "good" what other people may reject as "evil." National defense, for instance, can be highly valued by many inhabitants of a country feeling threatened by foreign invasion, but some can refuse the empowerment of the military on the grounds that it is a peril for civil rule. Import tariffs and commercial protection can benefit certain industrial branches, but can harm consumers. Roads and tracks, port and airports, are very advantageous for those requiring transport, but can be a nuisance for those living in the surrounding areas. Certain artwork put at the disposal of the public in parks and museums are enjoyed by some people, but rebuffed by others as either boring or ludicrous. Thus, public goods can offer different benefits to different people, which can make their provision controversial or contentious.

Also, people can change their preferences regarding the provision and use of public goods as a consequence of technological or moral innovations. Some goods can be considered public in one community but private in another. In the late Roman Empire, for instance, family life and sexual behavior were considered to be of general interest. Even last wills that were considered wrong because of the social consequences they might have were censured in public. This dividing line has moved greatly over the centuries in different places in the world, most recently in favor of enlarging the space of privacy. At least in the West, since the second half of the twentieth century, women and siblings are considered to be entitled to have "a room of one's own" within the family house (space permitting, of course).

In fact, every collective good is public for the members of the group, but private for the nonmembers. Some house equipment and furniture, for instance, are public goods for the members of the family or the inhabitants of the household, but are private for everybody else; the garden and the swimming pool can be collectively used by the condominium residents, but they are private for other people; a public school is collective for those enrolled, but the non-enrolled are deprived of it; a law establishing a minimum wage is a public good for workers, but not for the unemployed; defense is a public good for those inside, but a private one for outsiders; guarantees for

BOX 1.1 **MEASURING GOVERNMENT ACTION**

There are several ways to measure the relative "volume" of collective action through the government in a society. A common index is the proportion of public expenditure (PEx) over total gross domestic product (GDP):

PEx / GDP

Total public expenditure includes spending by central government, public enterprises, and the Social Security system, and by regional and local governments. The weight of the different components of public expenditure reflects government's and society's priorities, while the proportion of local and regional expenditure over total expenditure reflects the degree of governmental decentralization. The amount of public expenditure may not be equivalent to total public revenue, which is the result of collecting taxes, but also of fines, fees, and charges, and of income from public enterprises and other governmental activities, and from debt and external aid. In order to compare governmental spending across countries, the values must be converted into a single unit with "purchasing power parity," that is, reflecting the relative prices in each currency of a basket of goods and services. Other measures of the volume of the government are the proportion of government employees over total waged population, or the amount of laws and regulations, which may be counted according to the number of pages of legislation.

The average proportion of public expenditure in GDP in the seventeen most industrialized countries has multiplied by four in one century due mainly to the two world wars and to redistributive services, including social security and old-age pensions. It was about 11 percent in 1900, about 30 percent in 1960 and about 45 percent in 2009.

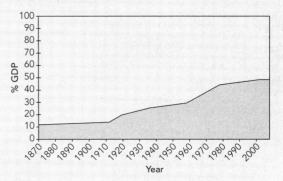

FIGURE I.1 GOVERNMENT EXPENDITURES

Sources: Author's own elaboration for seventeen countries: Australia, Austria, Belgium, Canada, France, Germany, Ireland, Italy, Japan, Netherlands, New Zealand, Norway, Spain, Sweden, Switzerland, the United Kingdom, and the United States, during the period 1870–2009, with data from Vito Tanzi and Ludger Schuknecht, *Public Spending in the Twentieth Century: A global perspective* (New York: Cambridge University Press, 2000), updated with data from the International Monetary Fund.

civil rights are public goods for citizens, but private ones for foreigners; a language is a public good for its speakers, but private for the unlearned; and the goods of nature should be considered public for Earthlings, but private for Martians and other aliens, if they existed.

In some sense, thus, all public goods are "club" goods. But different clubs have very different numbers of members; in each case, while the included may want to preserve their access, the excluded may ask for more inclusiveness. This is the basis for the politics of choosing and providing public goods.

THE GROWTH OF PUBLIC EXPENDITURE

In twentieth-century socialist countries, all "means of production" were under the control of the state, which was expected to provide everything to the members of the community, from private goods such as food, clothes, and houses, to security, national defense, instruction, and entertainment. As can be explained with the analytical tools provided in this chapter, states with such overarching ambition faced insurmountable obstacles for achieving their ends with the people's active support. Long-term results involved an increasing lack of social cooperation, little labor effort, scant technological innovation and initiative, and low availability of publicly provided goods.

In the current world, many states have reduced the scope of their intervention in order to give room to private initiatives, especially in the economic and cultural arenas, while they tend to focus on the provision of public goods that cannot be privatized. However, as can be understood from the "politics of public goods," governments have expanded redistributive services, including social security and old-age pensions, previously provided by families, churches, and other institutions. Although personal services and monetary transfers are in themselves private goods, the laws and institutions guaranteeing these services to every citizen (or to every individual belonging to a well-defined category of citizen, such as the elderly) are a patent form of public goods. On the whole, absolute and relative levels of public expenditure by non-socialist states, heavily driven by redistributive disbursements, have increased during the past few decades.

Two factors can explain the expansion of governmental interventions in certain areas. The first is economic. It is a well-known postulate that increasing per capita income and decreasing income inequalities among the population fosters social demand for public goods. The demand is particularly intense for infrastructure and labor-intensive services, which involve relatively high levels of additional public expenditure.

The second factor is political. Demands for the redistribution of resources are increasing in conditions of political freedom, which favors the organization of interest groups. The increasing availability of information makes people more aware of potential gains from collective decisions and better able to identify appropriate behaviors to obtain collective benefits. On the supply side, democratic leaders submitted to electoral accountability have more interest in providing public goods and collective benefits, in order to win or retain support from voters, than do non-democratic rulers. Once public expenditure has expanded, entrenched bureaucracies tend to resist reductions, even when economic growth decreases.

The following data fit this discussion rather well. In the seventeen most industrialized countries, the proportion of public expenditure in the countries' gross domestic product (GDP) averages about 45 percent . However, in spite of its having similar levels of economic development and political freedom, the United States dedicates lower levels of its GDP to public expenditure than the European Union. In the former, the federal budget keeps total public expenditure at about 33 percent of GDP. The tiny budget of the European Union coexists with still very heavy budgets for the states, where there are higher levels of redistributive fights, putting the average relative total public expenditure near 50 percent.

Within a country, public expenditure grows at higher rates in periods of democracy than under dictatorship. Increases are more rapid in developed countries (with Sweden having achieved the highest level, with more than 60 percent) than in underdeveloped ones. Among the latter, public expenditure grows faster in countries with democratic regimes and relatively high levels of education than in those without these elements but with comparable economic levels. For example, in recent democracies in Latin America, the proportion of public expenditure over the countries' production has moved from about 10 to about 20 percent (all, of course, roughly rounded numbers).

Quick Quiz

• Why is the World Wide Web (www) a public good?

Conclusion

In this chapter we have drawn a conceptual line between the domains of political activity and those of private concern. We have seen how the problems of guaranteeing sufficient individual contributions for the provision of public goods can explain the existence and performance of the government and other coercive devices put in place by human beings to satisfy their common interests.

The discussion on the previous pages enables us to present two fundamental *propositions*:

1. **Public goods.** In contrast to private goods, public goods are indivisible and cannot be satisfactorily provided by the market or other private initiatives. The provision of public goods requires cooperation or coercion, whether by means of collective action or effective government.
2. **Government growth.** The demand for public goods and the relative levels of public expenditure by governments tend to increase with economic prosperity, institutional stability, and democracy.

These will be sound bases for further discussion of political rules and procedures to make collective decisions throughout the rest of this book. ■

Summary

A dividing line between the domains of public activity and those of private concerns can be drawn with the help of the concept of public goods as opposed to private goods.

Public goods are indivisible and are jointly supplied to their potential users.

Individuals interested in using public goods may not have incentives to contribute to their provision because they can expect not to be excluded from access. Cooperation or coercion, whether by means of collective action or effective government, is necessary for the provision of public goods.

An "externality," or the external effect of some people's action on other people's utility, implies the production of a public good or evil.

"Network" goods are those giving higher potential benefits to each user the higher the number of users, such as languages, weights and measures, currencies, and the world wide web. They can be provided without significant institutional problems.

"Pure" public goods are those that can be used by more people without reducing other people's utility, such as national defense or advances in knowledge. They can be provided in the amount desired by the potential users, by appropriate institutional means.

"Rival" public goods are those for which the addition of users can diminish or even eliminate the utility of other users, as may happen with clean air, water, roads, and hospitals.

Rivalry can decrease and congestion can be prevented by either private provision of the good or imperative exclusion of some potential users. This involves the creation of "club" goods, which may require the payment of tolls or fees, as may be the case for roads, bridges, and hospitals.

"Common" goods are rival or congestible goods that are not excludable, such as clean air and water pools. Some common-pool resources can be provided and maintained by a small community's self-government, but for large groups, provision and maintenance of common goods may fail in the absence of coercive authority.

The provision of public goods may involve redistributive competition, because people may have varied preferences for different goods and be able to experience different benefits and costs from their provision, up to the point of differing as to whether some of them are public goods or evils.

The demand for public goods and the relative levels of public expenditure tend to expand with economic prosperity, institutional stability, and democratic government.

Key Concepts

Club good. A good to be used by some people to the exclusion of others.

Commons. Rival, or congestible, goods that are not excludable and can be exhausted.

Externality. Effect of some people's action on other people's utility, whether positive or negative.

Network good. A good that gives higher benefits to each user the higher the number of users.

Private or individual good. A divisible good that can be used individually.

Public or collective good. An indivisible good that is supplied jointly to all potential users.

Pure public good. A good that can be used by one person without reducing anyone else's utility.

Rival, or congestible, good. A good whose use by one person can diminish the utility for other people using the good.

Questions for Review

1. What is the difference between public goods and private goods?
2. What is the difference between "pure" and "rival" public goods?
3. What is a club good?
4. What are common goods?

Problems and Applications

1. Why do students walk on the grass?
2. Give examples of positive and negative externalities that can be associated with public goods and evils.
3. List goods and services provided by your local government.
   a. Discuss which are public goods, and if each is a rival or club good.
   b. Do you think your local government provides services that are not public goods?

Quantitative indices

4. Search for data on public expenditure in proportion to gross domestic product for at least five countries. The countries should have different levels of per capita income, and should include at least one old democracy, a recent democracy, and a dictatorship. Discuss.

Data sources

World Bank, Data and Research, Public Sector: www.worldbank.org.
International Monetary Fund, Government Finance Statistics: www.imf.org.

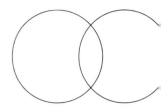

COLLECTIVE ACTION

In This Chapter You Will

- Analyze why some people do not contribute to advancing their common interests with other people.
- Learn what the problem of the "free rider" is.
- Consider the importance of private goods and selective incentives in organizations for collective action.
- Think of "voice" and "exit" as rival forms of action.
- Reflect on the advantages of small groups and countries for obtaining satisfaction in their demands for public goods.

Farmers in rich countries, including the United States, many European Union nations, and Japan, receive extensive government subsidies, while farmers in poor and mostly rural countries, such as India and China, are heavily taxed and cannot compete fairly with those in more developed ones. In rich countries that belong to the Organisation for Economic Co-operation and Development (OECD), government subsidies amount overall to about 29 percent of the farmers' revenues. They include direct payments and help for the cost of water, seed, machinery, and other farm inputs, which generally raise food prices to consumers. This is paradoxical, since in developing countries, farmers typically constitute a large fraction of the population, while in most rich countries dominated by cities and towns, they are a tiny percentage of the working population.

As we will see in this chapter, an explanation for such an unequal distribution of public resources is that small groups and their lobbies are often much more powerful politically than large groups. While small groups may be very effective in organizing themselves and advancing their interests, large and dispersed groups cannot even guarantee the development of collective action. Generally, members of small groups, including branch employer organizations, professional associations, or special interest lobbies, such as farmers in mostly urban countries, can be more effective in obtaining their desired public goods than large, disperse, and heterogeneous groups such as consumers, waged employees, low-income people, or farmers in mostly rural countries. As a consequence, the provision of public goods by means of political and institutional decisions does not depend on the cost of the goods, but on the cost of the collective action used to achieve that provision. We will see that similar relations can develop between political communities or countries of different sizes. ■

The Individual Logic

Why don't all countries cooperate in comparable proportions to the preservation of common natural resources? Some countries comply with international treaties on fishing, the exploitation of seas, or limits on gas emissions, while others do not. Why do small countries contribute proportionally less than large countries to common defense? Some countries do not defend themselves at all, but rather rely on international treaties and alliances.

Let us look now at the behavior of different groups within a society: Why are consumers insufficiently organized to ensure health guarantees and fair prices of market products? In the best of cases they can trust a public authority to do this. Why are there no such things as collective organizations of vast masses of taxpayers, low-income people, or unemployed workers? And regarding our daily experiences: Why do so many cities have traffic jams or big holdups in the business center even if public transportation is available? Why do students walk on the grass?

For quite some time, social scientists analyzing international relations, interest group pressures, class struggles, or social movements have assumed, often implicitly, that if a group could be identified by a common interest, the group would somehow get organized and seek to further their interest. But in reality, as suggested by the examples in the previous paragraphs, many people do not join an organization or act consistently to promote their collective interests. Peace, defense, security, public health, and laws regulating equitable work contracts, clean air, transportation, and a nice environment—common interests of some of the groups mentioned—can all be considered public goods. But their provision does not depend on the cost of the goods, but on the costs of the collective action able to achieve that provision.

THE COLLECTIVE ACTION FUNCTION

The problems of collective action can be analyzed from two assumptions, neither which should not surprise you very much after reading the previous chapter. These are:

- The common interest of the members of a group can be defined as a **public good**.
- Collective action to provide public goods depends on **individuals' decisions**.

In other words: **collective action is participation or contribution by individual members of a group to the provision of public goods**. As for many human decisions, whether to participate or contribute can be explained by subjectively estimated benefits and costs. In this approach, every individual decision has an expected reward, which can be called R, which depends on its benefits, let us call them B, and its costs, C. Thus, for private goods: $R = B - C$. If R is positive—that is, if the expected benefits of a good, say an iPod, are higher than its cost—it will be rational for the individual to perform such an action, for instance purchasing the good.

The point is that for all public goods such as those just referred to, including defense, security, public works, schools, clean air, transport, and so on, each individual can expect to obtain the benefits without paying its costs, since even if he does not cooperate, the individual can expect not to be excluded from accessing the good. Using the same logic for private decisions, an individual will decide to participate in a collective action leading to the provision of a public good only if his contribution is able to make a significant difference to the outcome; that is, if the marginal benefits obtained with his action (the additional benefit produced by his action in comparison with those he can expect without it) are higher than the cost of the action.

More formally, the individual logic of deciding whether to participate can be represented by this **collective action function**:

$$R = B * P - C$$

This must be read as: the reward for an individual for participating in collective action (R) equals the expected benefit from accessing the public good (B) times the probability of his action being effective for the provision of the good (P) minus the cost of participating (C). If R is positive, participating is a sound decision; if R is negative, participation may not be worth the effort.

For example, your reward for joining a students' union may equal the expected benefits—for instance, the improvement of the quality of teaching or a new student recreation camp—which can be achieved by the union's demands, times the probability that your contribution may make a difference (if you think there is risk, there can be too few fellow students in the union), minus the costs of attending meetings or paying some fee.

Note that the same function can be applied to private goods, but in this case, P always equals one, since for private goods the individual action (typically, paying a price) always makes a difference to obtain the good. In contrast, for public goods that can be obtained without paying the price, the expected benefits from the goods are weighed by the decisiveness of the individual action, P, whose values are between zero and one. In general it can be assumed that P is an inverse function of the number of people in the interest group: $P = 1/N$ (N being the number of people in the group).

WEIGHED BENEFITS AND COSTS

Let us analyze separately the components of the collective action function, which always have subjective values. The **benefits** of participating in collective action partly depend on the type of public good sought, as we discuss in the previous chapter. Specifically, for network or pure public goods, individual participation can be highly rewarding, while, in contrast, the benefits of contributing to the provision and maintenance of a rival or extinguishable good, such as a common pool or natural resource, are conditional to the contribution of other people.

Also, the benefits of a public good are not equal for everybody. Certain individuals may have higher stakes in obtaining a public good because their trade, profession, or fortune depends on it at a higher level than for other individuals. Consider, for instance, the case of the factory interested in having a road suitable for big trucks mentioned in the previous chapter. Although the road may provide collective, indivisible benefits to all neighbors in town, the owners of the factory may have greater interest, and thus be ready to pay higher costs for it than the local residents, who may have access to other means of transport. Likewise, wealthy people may have more interest than deprived citizens in an effective security system against thieves and less in public pensions; learned persons will be more interested than uneducated fellows in giving public support to the arts and public libraries, and so on.

Different forms of collective action also imply different **costs**, from the tiny ones of signing petitions to the huge costs of participating in armed struggle, just to mention two extreme forms. Also, the costs of participating in collective actions can be measured differently by different individuals, whether in terms of money, time, or effort. While for some people, attending meetings may be synonymous with wasting time, others with fewer alternative opportunities of leisure may find it an enjoyable occasion to get together with interesting people. On voting day, certain individuals may appreciate more than others the experience of being acknowledged the same dignity and value as everybody else, in contrast to the hierarchy, status, inequality, and discrimination usually experienced in daily life. While some persons may feel that attending a demonstration is embarrassing, others may enjoy the pleasure of walking freely in the middle of the street. Also, a person may change her relative evaluation of being involved in public action and devoting herself to private activities at different times of life and development.

All these different individual perceptions can induce internal disagreements and lead to different levels of provision of public goods in different groups and communities, as we discuss in the next section. But we can assume that different individual evaluations of benefits and costs can be found in comparable proportions and can counterweigh one another within each group. Thus we can make testable predictions at the collective group level.

• First, for any group, participation in collective action should be higher for the attainment of network or pure public goods, whose production positively depends on the number of individuals participating, than for the provision or maintenance of rival or common goods, whose success is subjected to other people's participation.

• Second, we should expect higher participation in low-cost actions, such as formal registration or enrolling, signing petitions or voting, than in those requiring more sustained effort, such as attending frequent meetings, paying organizational fees, voluntarily contributing to taxes, or boycotting products, and even more than in those involving some significant risk, such as parading in demonstrations, joining protests, participating in strikes, or even enrolling in voluntary militias or army units.

• Participation in collective actions should be more numerous and stable under conditions of freedom than under dictatorship, where any of the actions just mentioned may involve fines, going to jail, being deported, or worse. The demand and provision of public goods and the subsequent level of public expenditure should thus be relatively higher in democratic regimes than under authoritarianism, as stated in the previous chapter.

• Finally, if the group or community is tight and homogeneous and its members share common interests in a high number of different collective goods, the individual benefits of collective action, and thus the likelihood of the group being organized, should be higher than for sets of heterogeneous, dispersed individuals with only one common interest and many divisive issues. For relatively homogeneous groups, a single organization can pursue many beneficial goods.

THE FREE RIDER

In the individual logic of collective action presented here, any individual can expect to be a **free rider, that is, someone able to use the public good without contributing to its provision**. Abstention does not mean that the individual is not sincerely interested in having access to the collective good pursued through collective action. On the contrary, each abstainer can expect to obtain the good without participating; to "travel" for free at the expense of others paying the cost. But if everybody used the same logic and tried to free-ride, nobody would participate in collective actions, cooperate, or contribute to the provision of public goods. The interest groups would not be organized in a way able to satisfy their members' common interest.

It should be noted that the key difference between individual decisions regarding private goods and those regarding public goods derives from the P variable in the function of collective action presented earlier. P captures the belief in the likelihood of achieving the goal of the collective action, which may depend on estimates of how many other people can participate. The value of P is subjective: some people may have more resources available, more information, or more experience to be able to estimate the likely outcome of every attempt to organize the group than others, thus weighing differently the expected advantages and disadvantages of participating in collective actions. But P needs to be substantial to make the individual participate. If P is very small, the product $B * P$ will be very small, too, and a minor cost, C, can deter the individual from participating. In many cases, especially **when the group with a common interest includes many people**, which can make each individual contribution negligible, and thus P very small, **a regular individual may abstain**.

This is the collective paradox that can be produced by apparently reasonable individual decisions in favor of satisfying collective interests. Indeed, most people do not give substantial amounts of money to the collective causes they support, just as they would evade paying taxes if they were not prosecuted; some people do not bother to vote in certain elections; certain voluntary organizations crumble for lack of attendance at regular meetings; fishing companies do not refrain from over-catching certain species, risking destroying open-sea fisheries; industries pollute the air and erode the atmosphere; and so on. In other words, many public goods in which people can be sincerely interested are undersupplied for lack of participation in collective endeavors.

SELECTIVE INCENTIVES

One mechanism to make people contribute to the provision of public goods may be the **conditional supply of private goods to the participants in collective action**. This can create **selective incentives** for individuals to cooperate. Within this category one can include social recognition and moral censure, fines on abstainers and professional advantages to members of an association. In contrast to public goods, an individual can access the private, indivisible good or escape from the private evil supplied only if he contributes appropriately, in this case by cooperating or participating in the collective action. In this sense the incentives are "selective"; that is, individually, not jointly, supplied.

The addition of this variable can turn around the sign of the basic individual function of collective action presented earlier, making a negative result a positive one. Now we have:

$$R = B * P - C + D$$

Where D: selective incentives (the choice of the letter D is merely to avoid confusion with B, C, etc.).

A classic example of collective action involving heavy selective incentives for members is the workers' unions and their "closed shop" and "picket line" mechanisms. Note that the higher wages, shorter hours, better working conditions, and favorable labor legislation that unions usually demand are public goods that can be provided to all workers regardless of their membership in the union or their participation in collective actions such as demonstrations or strikes. Unions use both positive and negative incentives to attract workers interested in those goods to participate. In a number of countries, industrial workers' unions managed to make union membership compulsory just by following centuries-old traditions well established for guilds and artisanal organizations. When the union is recognized by the firm, the industrial branch, or the employers' organization for collective bargaining, it may make membership in the union a condition of employment. Employers may even deduct union dues from wages and salaries automatically. On the other hand, coercion by union activists can also be used to bring about worker participation. In the event of conflict, picket lines and moral censure can deter potential strike-breakers.

The decline of membership of workers' unions since the late twentieth century derives from several factors, which can be understood with our approach to the problems of collective action. On the affirmative side, governments took on some of the selective incentives previously provided by the unions, including unemployment insurance, which made union schemes for mutual support less attractive. On the negative side, certain governments, starting most notoriously with that of the United Kingdom as of the 1980s, facilitated individual workers' free-riding by suppressing lnks between employment and union membership not linked to employment and by introducing secret ballots for voting on strikes and in elections. Indeed, union membership decreased dramatically in the following years.

Another easily testable case refers to professional organizations. In certain countries, lawyers', physicians', and architects' associations implement restrictive licensing to exercise their profession in their respective districts. Any professional working without the association permit, which implies paying regular fees, can be prosecuted for illegal activity. In contrast, associations for other professions, such as political scientist, economist, or sociologist, may resort to more fragile positive incentives, such as the provision of job market information or social entertainment, to attract members. Of course, in the countries where different regulations are applied to different professions, the organizations with voluntary affiliation have much lower membership rates among graduates in a given field than those with a closed shop.

As suggested, incentives provided selectively by any kind of group only to those individuals participating in collective action can either be **material or moral**, as well

CASE 2.1   BENEFITS AND COSTS OF VOTING

Voting is a major form of collective action for a public good, as shown at this polling station.

Voting in mass political elections is an outstanding case of individual participation in a collective action for a public good. The electoral scores of every party and the subsequent formation of government are forced on everybody regardless of their participation. As for any public good in whose provision each individual has scarce influence, it can be argued that for an individual, abstaining can be a rational decision. However, voting is usually a "low-benefit, low-cost" action that can be easily encouraged. In fact, in mass political elections, turnout is always positive, although in different proportions, which can be explained by different benefits and costs.

At the individual level, people with higher incomes, members of the ethnic majority in the community, those who are more educated, and those who are older have a greater propensity to vote, probably because they have more information and greater stakes in the electoral outcome. Some people may also be motivated by moral incentives, such as being acknowledged as citizens with equal rights or to perform their "civic duty."

At the collective level, electoral participation is relatively higher in small countries. Turnout is higher in elections for general institutions with high potential benefits than in those for local, regional, or other relatively less influential offices. In the United States, for instance, while in concurrent presidential and congressional elections turnout is over 50 percent, in midterm congressional elections it is only about 30 percent. Turnout also tends to increase with big political crises and highly relevant and divisive campaign issues that raise the stakes of elections, and with competitive and uncertain results increasing the apparent decisiveness of every vote.

Regarding institutional incentives, electoral participation is promoted, above all, by compulsory voting, which imposes significant costs on abstention. In certain countries, people abstaining from political elections are requested to present a justification or prove their absence from their residence on election day; they may be given fines or prison terms, be deprived of the right to vote or lose other civil rights, and have difficulties getting access to public jobs or services. In Australia, Belgium, Luxembourg, and other countries with compulsory voting, turnout is usually as high as 90 percent. Positive incentives can be provided by rules that lower voting costs, such as automatic registration of electors, voting on Sunday, and ease of access to polls.

SOURCE 2.1   **The Individual Logic of Collective Action**

A lobbying organization, or indeed a labor union or any other organization, work-ing in the interest of a large group of firms or workers in some industry, would get no assistance from the rational, self-interested individuals in that industry...This would be true even if everyone in the industry were absolutely convinced that the proposed program was in their interest (though in fact some might think oth-erwise and make the organization's task yet more difficult)...The larger the num-ber of individuals or firms that would benefit from a collective good, the smaller the share of the gains from action in the group interest that will accrue to the individual or firm that undertakes the action. Thus, in the absence of selective incentives, the incentive for group action diminishes as group size increases, so that large groups are less able to act in their common interest than small ones.

Mancur Olson, *The Logic of Collective Action* (1965)

as **positive or negative**. Material, positive incentives may include gifts, perks for orga-nization members such as information on the job market, insurance, clubhouses, and discounts in shops, hotels, or car rental, while negative ones can consist of fees, taxes, or fines. Moral incentives can also be positive, in the form of prestige, good reputation, honors and awards, access to social networks, or opportunities for friendship, and nega-tive, such as collective punishments and condemnations inducing shame and guilt. It is usually estimated that negative incentives can be effective in producing short-term par-ticipation by many people (for instance, fining abstainers can make more people go to the polls), while stable participation in smaller groups may require positive incentives.

Similar to any other collective organization, governments systematically use coercive mechanisms, such as military conscription, compulsory taxes, and fines, to make people finance the collective goods in which many of them may be interested. The subsequent benefits, such as defense, public services, and order, are supplied to everyone whether or not they have served in the military or paid taxes or fines. But precisely for this reason, many people may try to skip their individual contributions while acquiescing or voting in favor of maintaining the community.

A frequent objection to this kind of model is that it can explain how an organiza-tion is maintained but hardly how or why it was created in the first place. Even if the private goods supplied can be very appealing or deterring, it seems reasonable to sup-pose that most people will join only those associations defined by a goal they share. Not many people will be willing to join a union, for example, only to have access to its summer resorts. The identification of a common interest can be, therefore, a restriction on potential membership. Thus, we can establish that most people participate only in those collective actions and organizations oriented at providing a public good in which they may be interested. But many do so only if other activities and features of the group, which can be summarily placed within the "selective incentives" category, are sufficiently engaging to break the free-riding temptation and subsequent abstention.

Quick Quiz

• What's a free rider?

The Size of Groups

Any group or community whose members have a common interest can achieve certain levels of collective action and organization. But the group's level of organization and effectiveness in promoting its interests will largely depend on the size of the group, that is, on the number of individuals who can obtain benefits from the public good and can be potentially interested in its provision. The different levels of collective action by workers and entrepreneurs, consumers and producers, urbanites and farmers, employees and unemployed, can be greatly explained by the different benefits and costs, derived from the size of the group.

At the beginning of this chapter we represented the effect of the good's indivisibility on the individual decision with the P variable in the collective action function. P captures the individual subjective estimate that his action will be influential to make the provision of the public good feasible and thus worthy of being undertaken. Generally, we can assume that P is an inverse function of the size of the group—that is, a single individual tends to be less influential in large groups than in small ones. In a large group, there are more people to whom one can let do it than in a small group.

Specifically the following can be postulated: $P = 1/S$, where S equals the size or number of people in the group. If the group size S is large, P will be small, and so will the $B * P$ product in the function. Remember the collective action equation and check that you understand that the individual reward R of participating in collective action decreases with increases in group size S. As put by political economist Mancur Olson, "the incentive for group action diminishes as group size increases, so that large groups are less able to act in their common interest than small ones."

TYPES OF GROUPS

Different groups and communities are organized at different levels and are able to exert influence on collective and political decisions to different extents. Most interest groups develop some action, but at a suboptimal level; that is, they are able to attain lower levels of provision of public goods than desired by the group members, heavily depending on the group size. Chambers of commerce, branch employer organizations, physicians' associations, agrarian lobbies, teachers' and big company workers' unions, just to mention a few examples, usually manage to combine and obtain benefits from public goods.

Besides these, it is interesting to analyze two polar types of group. On the one hand, **privileged groups are small groups in which one or few members are sufficiently interested in the good so as to pay all its cost**. In our previous example of the factory needing a road, the company may subsidize the whole public work even if it is going to be available to the entire town. Similarly, a bank can establish a private service of night surveillance at its doors capable of dissuading any thief or housebreaker from approaching the zone, thus making every inhabitant in the neighborhood more at ease. Likewise, a big naval company may put up a port lighthouse while being unable to prevent village fishermen and sporting yachts from making use of it. The army of the most powerful member of a military alliance can provide defense for all its allies even if the latter do not contribute with soldiers. In general, we can expect that those individuals, firms, or countries that obtain higher benefits from a public good may contribute more to its provision than other potential beneficiaries of the good.

On the other hand, **in latent groups there is general abstention by individuals sharing a common interest**. In such groups, which are typically very large, anonymous, and dispersed, no member can be aware of the abstention by one individual from contributing to the provision of the public good. Hence, general free-riding, a skeletal organization, fading collective action, and scanty provision of public goods are common for well-identified but vast groups such as taxpayers, consumers, low-income earners, the unemployed, and retired people. Common interests of large majorities of citizens may not be satisfied due to the difficulties of solving the free-ride problem of collective action.

The importance of size for the success of collective action may prompt members of large groups to adopt decentralized forms of organization. Within each small unit, individual members may have incentives to participate actively because their voice or their vote is likely to have an influence, and because interactions will be easy and frequent, thus preventing free-riding conduct. The costs of organization are lower the smaller the number of people who must be coordinated. Large groups, as well as great countries, can thus be better organized if they adopt a federal structure. Successful collective action can result from the union of a number of small, autonomous units.

COLLECTIVE IDENTITY

The expected influence of each individual in the group decision does not depend on group size alone. It can also depend on the internal compactness of the group and other characteristics facilitating interaction among individuals with common interests, as already noted. A density of social relationships implies that many individuals share common interests on a number of issues, which may make collective action on any one of them more beneficial.

Specifically, the spatial concentration of citizens or members of an interest group can facilitate information exchanges, discussion of criteria, and coordination for gathering together and making collective decisions, pressure, trust, and dissuasion from free-riding. Neighboring inhabitants in small towns, businesspeople located in a commercial mall, or employees working within a single big building are more likely to be able to develop collective actions for their common interest than, say, the unemployed dispersed in their homes.

Also, cultural homogeneity can favor collective action for public goods because the members of the group may share information about past actions, links, relations, principles, and interests on numerous issues, which creates opportunities to obtain higher potential benefits from their joint action. This is the case for individuals from the same tribe, relatives of an extended family, immigrants with the same origin, and for members of communities sharing similar characteristics such as religion, race, or language. They can develop more effective collective actions to promote their common interests not only in favor of their customs and traditions, but also for economic or redistributive purposes than heterogeneous individuals with some common interest on one issue but also other discordant concerns.

Individuals can use an experience of sustained reciprocity and their good reputation at being cooperative to build trust among the other members of the group. The advantages of having common ethnic traits for the provision of collective goods can also foster sentiments of identity. Subjective identification with certain cultural traits may become a tool for a more effective attainment of individuals' common interests. In general, the costs of acquiring and digesting new information may make an individual favorable to having around him people who share cultural values and references, so that he can enjoy his own allegiance to them.

Looking at it the other way around: if people actively pursue a common goal, they are likely to reinforce distinctive cultural norms. Some may join the group in order to take advantage of all the public goods that a relatively low-cost organization of the homogeneous group can obtain. Nationalist and religious movements can thrive on these incentives to attract people and achieve multiple ends.

VOICE AND EXIT

The decision to participate in collective action can also depend on the alternatives available. If an individual is interested in a public good, but the costs of joining the group or contributing decisively to the provision of the good are too high, he may choose to seek an alternative provider or move to an alternative setting in which the public good is already provided. **Action can also be called "voice,"** to suggest the existence of some unsatisfied demand that people may want to highlight. It can be replaced with **"exit," that is, a move to an alternative provider of public goods**, whether this implies leaving to join a different group, changing affiliation, voting for another party or leader, moving or emigrating (also called "voting with one's feet").

"Voice" and "exit"—or contribution and departure—**can be rival actions** on the part of the individual interested in a public good and dissatisfied with the existing state of things. An individual can choose either way depending on its costs and the likelihood of his obtaining access to the desired public goods. Paradoxically, certain governments unable to perform according to their own promises or expectations and providing very low amounts of public goods may encourage "exit"—that is, citizens' emigration—in order to prevent the outburst of "voices" of protest challenging the incumbent leaders. In an authoritarian regime, in particular, but also in certain weak states having adopted democratic procedures, ineffective leaders may prefer to facilitate potential critics going into exile.

Conversely, if the "exit" option ceases to be available because no alternative organization able to provide public goods is in place, or if it becomes extremely costly, the individual can have incentives to consider participation in collective action, or "voice." The costs of exit—which may imply moral censure against "traitors," the persecution of deserters, or restrictive decisions in migration policy—tend to be higher amon club members than among store costumers, in ethnic groups than in professional associations, and in armies than in political parties, thus creating different favorable or unfavorable conditions for collective action in different groups.

THE EXPLOITATION OF THE BIG BY THE SMALL

As discussed, small groups, and concentrated and homogeneous communities, can have an advantage, in comparison with large, dispersed, and heterogeneous groups, in gathering their members together and putting up and maintaining an organization

SOURCE 2.2   Small Groups Get Better Organized

Two neighbors may agree to drain a meadow, which they possess in common; because it is easy for them to know each other's mind; and each must perceive that the immediate consequence of his failing in his part is the abandoning of the whole project. But it is very difficult, and indeed impossible, that a thousand persons should agree in any such action; it being difficult for them to concert so complicated a design, and still more difficult for them to execute it; while each seeks a pretext to free himself of the trouble and expense, and would lay the whole burden on others. Political society easily remedies both these inconveniences…Thus bridges are built; harbors opened; ramparts raised; canals formed; fleets equipped; and armies disciplined every where, by the care of government.

David Hume, *A Treatise of Human Nature* (1740)

The inhabitants of a town, being collected into one place, can easily combine together…by voluntary associations and agreements…The trades which employ but a small number of hands run most easily into such combinations…The inhabitants of the country, dispersed in distant places, cannot easily combine together…Stockbreeders separated from one another, and dispersed through all the different corners of the country, cannot, without great difficulty, combine together…Manufacturers of all kinds, collected together in numerous bodies in all great cities, easily can.

Adam Smith, *An Inquiry into the Nature and Causes of the Wealth of Nations* (1776)

As for popular suffrage, it may be further remarked that especially in large states it leads inevitably to electoral indifference, since the casting of a single vote is of no significance where there is a multitude of electors. Even if a voting qualification is highly valued and esteemed by those who are entitled to it, they still do not enter the polling booth. Thus the result of an institution of this kind is more likely to be the opposite of what was intended; election actually falls into the power of a few, of a caucus, and so of the particular and contingent interest which is precisely what was to have been neutralized.

G.W.F. Hegel, *Philosophy of Right* (1820)

aimed at satisfying their common interest. The example of farmers in rich and poor countries, respectively, which we presented at the beginning of this chapter, can now be better understood. Likewise, employers tend to be more organized than workers, and thus better able to obtain suitable policies from governments. Producers, in general, are more organized and thus more effective at obtaining favorable governmental decisions than consumers. As observed by economist Adam Smith in the eighteenth century, as soon as a few entrepreneurs from the same branch meet together, "even for merriment and diversion, the conversation ends in a conspiracy against the public or in some contrivance to raise prices."

This may lead to what some authors have called the "capture of the government by pressure groups." Small interest groups may seek public subsidies, transfers, protective tariffs, or the establishment of other barriers against new competitors or against producers of substitutive activities, all of which may produce a kind of exploitation of large numbers of unorganized and dispersed consumers by small groups of well-organized producers.

Similar asymmetries can be observed in interstate relations. In the current world, small states obtain benefits from large areas of free trade and from international security alliances, and usually contribute to the provision of universal or large-scale public goods less than proportionally to their relative size. Specifically, in the North Atlantic Treaty Organization (NATO), the United States copes with the bulk of the load. Small states can obtain more benefits from the large states' provision of defense than from their own provision, so they choose to free-ride. Likewise, in the United Nations organization and its agencies, such as UNESCO (United Nations Educational, Scientific, and Cultural Organization), the largest and wealthiest members contribute more than proportionally to their population or product share, although decision-making power within the various UN institutions does not correspond to their contributions.

Quick Quiz

• Define "voice" and "exit" as ways of action.

Conclusion

In this chapter we have discussed the incentives for individuals interested in public goods to cooperate and contribute to the provision of the goods. We have seen how the development of cooperation or collective action can be marred by the problems of free-riding, but favored in groups with small size, internal concentration or homogeneity, as well as influenced by the availability of the alternative of leaving in search of another provider.

The previous discussion can be summarized in the following two Propositions:

1. **Collective action**. Members of small, concentrated and homogeneous communities or interest groups have more incentives to cooperate and participate in collective action than members of large, dispersed and heterogeneous groups. In the public arena, small groups tend to have relatively more access to public resources at the expense of large groups.
2. **Voice versus exit**. Collective action for the advancement of collective interests or "voice" weakens and may fail if the rival action of "exit" in search of an alternative provider is less costly and more likely to give access to public goods. ■

Summary

The existence of a group with a common interest does not guarantee the organization of the group to pursue that interest. Collective action for the provision of public goods depends on individuals' decisions to participate or to abstain.

Since public goods are supplied jointly to all members of the group, each individual can try to free-ride—that is, everybody can expect to have access to the public good without cooperating with other members of the group or contributing to the provision of the good.

People tend to participate more in low-cost collective actions than in actions involving high costs and risks, and more under conditions of freedom than under dictatorships.

Participation in collective action can be encouraged by the conditional provision of private goods or selective incentives to the participants. Collective action for public goods can be the by-product of decisions aimed at obtaining private goods.

Individual members of small groups that can expect to be relatively decisive in their group may have more incentives to cooperate and participate in collective actions for their common interest than members of large groups in which each individual contribution is negligible.

Territorial concentration and cultural homogeneity of individuals favor interactions and collective action for common interests. On the basis of the experience of cooperating, individuals can build good reputations , trust, and cultural norms favoring further cooperation.

If the costs of collective action are too high or the expectation to obtain public goods is pessimistic, people may choose to seek an alternative provider. "Voice" and "exit" are rival ways of action.

Due to the limited availability of public resources to finance or provide public goods, small groups tend to obtain more satisfaction of their demands and exploit large groups.

Key Concepts

Collective action. Participation or contribution by individual members of an interest group to the provision of public goods.

Exit. A move to an alternative provider of public goods; a rival action to "voice."

Free rider. User of a public good who does not contribute to its provision.

Latent group. A group in which there is general abstention by individuals sharing a common interest.

Privileged group. A group in which one or a few members pay the whole cost of a public good.

Selective incentives. Private goods provided conditionally to the participants in collective action.

Voice. An action usually identified with protest or a demand for public goods.

Questions for Review

1. Write the individual function of collective action and define its elements.
2. What are "selective incentives?"
3. What's a "free rider?"
4. Discuss the relative advantages of small groups and large groups for collective action.

Problems and Applications

1. Search for data on relative turnout (number of voters per number of persons entitled to vote) for local elections in your place of residence and in national or federal elections. Search also for data on turnout for elections to your school or college board. Compare data and discuss.
2. List positive and negative incentives to vote in general elections in your place of residence.
3. Choose a club, fraternity, union, or association in which you are a member. What are the public goods provided? Can you identify private goods that are supplied as selective incentives to its members?
4. Do you know any privileged group?
5. Give an example of a latent group that is not mentioned in this chapter.

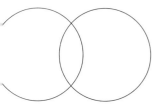

3

COOPERATION AND CONFLICT

In This Chapter You Will

- Analyze the problems of collective action in light of the Prisoner's Dilemma.
- See how people can learn to cooperate by using the "tit for tat" criterion in repeated interactions.
- Think about why cooperation is more likely to hold up in long-term relationships.
- Reflect on the advantages of and drawbacks to unilateral cooperation for the provision of environmental public goods.

Climate change has become a broad concern, leading many people to call for action to stop the planet from overheating. Yet some skepticism persists, and few governments are willing to deal with the problem by themselves. The Kyoto Protocol to put a limit on emission of greenhouse gases was formally accepted by thirty-six developed countries for the period 2005–2012. However, the United States and Australia initially refused to sign. Even some of the protocol signatories, and many developing countries, including most prominently China, continue to grow and pollute as much as they like. The holders of the global warming thesis warn that if the international response did not substantiate cooperation, the world might be condemned to catastrophic events.

However, recently, most countries seem to have found some incentive for avoiding being sanctioned for their misconduct. The Asia-Pacific Partnership on Clean Development and Climate has attained new cooperation on development and technology transfer, enabling a reduction in gas emissions. The United Nations has held talks with virtually all countries in the world to replace the Kyoto Protocol after its deadline. If things get bad enough, then cooperation may flourish.

This kind of problematic decisions on whether to cooperate or not can be analyzed with the help of game theory. In this chapter we will see more formally how, when cooperation is desirable but difficult, it can emerge and hold up for the provision of public goods such as a clean environment. ■

The Prisoner's Dilemma

Game theory studies human decisions in situations in which one's decision depends on expectations as to what others will do. They are not like individual decisions to purchase one or another good in a supermarket. They are more comparable to situations such as trying to build an international alliance among different states, such as the one regarding climate change just mentioned; negotiating between two political parties to form an electoral coalition; bargaining between a seller and a buyer to reach an agreeable price; or even playing cards with a few friends. Game theory has many applications in politics, as well as in economics, sociology, psychology, biology, and ethics.

In a strategic situation requiring collective action, each actor must decide whether to **cooperate, that is, to participate in the common action for the common benefit**, or **to compete, that is, to seek his own benefit**. When making his decision, each actor must consider how others may respond to that decision, because others' cooperation or defection can change the collective outcome. It is not isolated individual decisions but, rather, interactions among several actors that produce collective outcomes.

In game theory, different types of interactions are distinguished, especially the following:

• **Coordination games**. These imply easy cooperation among people with strongly shared interests to produce common benefit.

• **Conflict or zero-sum games**. In contrast to the previous coordination games, these include strong competition in which **gains for some participants imply losses for the others**.

• **Non-zero-sum games**. Falling in between coordination and conflict games, these are games in which the outcome is undetermined, whether in favor of cooperation or conflict, although **mutual cooperation can produce gains for all participants**.

COOPERATE AND DEFECT

A non-zero-sum game that is particularly important to the science of politics is the **Prisoner's Dilemma**. This game has **an inefficient outcome in which nobody cooperates**, which provides insight into the problems of collective action. As we have seen, on many occasions people fail to cooperate with others even if cooperation would produce a better collective outcome for all the participants. The lessons from the Prisoner's Dilemma can be applied to any group or community facing a cooperation problem among its members.

The metaphorical story of the Prisoner's Dilemma is about two burglars who have been arrested by the police as the suspects of a crime. Let us call them John and Oskar. The police chief questions John and Oskar in separate rooms and offers each of them the following deal:

"If you confess to the robbery and report your fellow-mate, your declaration will be taken as proof, and he will be condemned to ten years in prison, but as a prize for your declaration you will go free. If you both confess to the crime by denouncing each other, you both will be declared guilty and each of you will get a sentence of five years. If, however, neither of you confesses, we can lock you up for one year for illegal possession of arms."

Each prisoner has two strategies: **C, cooperate** (remain silent), and **D, defect** (denounce the other). Table 3.1 shows the outcomes associated with each prisoner's decision.

Note that John and Oskar are in separate cells and cannot communicate with each other but can only speculate about the other's likely decision. What would you expect them to do? Would they cooperate and remain silent, or denounce each other? The collective outcome—that is, the sentence for the two prisoners—depends on the strategy each chooses and the strategy chosen by the other.

Consider John's decision first. He does not know what Oskar is going to do. If he presumes that Oskar will cooperate and remain silent, John's best strategy is to denounce him, since then he will go free rather than spending one year in prison. If, on the contrary, Oskar were to denounce John, John's best strategy is still to denounce Oskar, since then he will spend five years in prison rather than ten. So, regardless of what Oskar does, John's best strategy is to denounce him.

The possible strategic choices are represented in Table 3.2. John's decisions can be approached from the left of the table, in two different rows, while Oskar is placed at

TABLE 3.1   Individual Preferences

In the game between two criminals suspected of committing a crime, each can be free by accusing the other.

		COLLECTIVE OUTCOME	
JOHN'S DECISION	OSKAR'S DECISION	JOHN	OSKAR
D defect	C cooperate	Free	10 years
C cooperate	C cooperate	1 year	1 year
D defect	D defect	5 years	5 years
C cooperate	D defect	10 years	Free

TABLE 3.2   The Prisoner's Dilemma

The sentence to be received by each prisoner depends both on his decision either to cooperate with or denounce the other fellow and on the decision made by the other prisoner.

		OSKAR	
		COOPERATE C	DEFECT D
JOHN	COOPERATE C (*remain silent*)	1 year for each	John gets 10 years Oskar goes free
	DEFECT D (*denounce*)	John goes free Oskar gets 10 years	5 years for each

the top of the table, over two columns of possible decisions. With the assumption that Oskar cooperates and remains silent—that is, if he chooses C and places the possible outcomes at the left column—then John's best strategy is to denounce, D, represented by the last row. The outcome is located in the lower-left cell: John goes free while Oskar gets ten years. If, on the contrary, Oskar denounces John and chooses D, in the right column, then John's best strategy is still to denounce Oskar, which leads to five years in prison for each of the two, as represented by the lower-right cell.

In the language of game theory, we say that John has **a dominant strategy, that is, a decision resulting in a better outcome for him regardless of the other actor's decision**. In this case, denouncing is a dominant strategy for John because he will get less time in prison if he denounces Oskar, regardless of whether Oskar remains silent or denounces John.

Now consider Oskar's decision. Since the strategic situation is symmetric for each prisoner, he faces the same choices as John, and he can reason in much the same way. Check the table again to see this. Regardless of what John does, Oskar will get less time in prison if he denounces him. So denouncing is also a dominant strategy for Oskar.

Thus the two actors may follow their dominant strategies, denouncing each other, and both will spend five years in prison. This outcome is represented by the lower-right cell of Table 3.2, as the result of the two prisoners' decisions to choose strategy D. Certainly this is a very bad, inefficient outcome. The two would have been better off—that is, they would have gotten less years in prison—had they both remained silent. By cooperating and not denouncing each other—that is, by choosing strategy C—they would have spent only one year in prison for possessing a gun, as represented by the upper-left cell of Table 3.2. But by each pursuing his individual interest in isolation from the other, the two prisoners choose a mutual betrayal on the basis of the fear that the other fellow will also choose to denounce. They reach a collective outcome that is worse for each of them.

The outcome produced by two dominant strategies is said to be an **"equilibrium,"** in the sense that it is **stable**. Consider the possibility of John withdrawing his denunciation and denying his previous finger-pointing. He would be declared the only one guilty and would have to bear the full penalty of ten years in prison. In Table 3.2, he would move the outcome from the lower-right cell to the upper-right one. Nor does Oskar have an incentive for unilaterally modifying his strategy of denouncing his partner. If neither actor were to change his strategy unilaterally, given the chance, the outcome would be considered stable, according to the concept of equilibrium coined by Nobel Prize-winning mathematician John F. Nash. **The "Nash-equilibrium" is an outcome from which no actor has incentives to move away by changing his strategy unilaterally.**

The inefficient outcome of the Prisoner's Dilemma is a representation of the free-rider problem in collective action. Each individual actor pursues his best interest by pretending to use public goods without contributing to their provision, but in the end nobody cooperates, and they cannot satisfy their common interest.

Note, however, these key assumptions in the story of the prisoner's dilemma: the actors cannot communicate, and their choices are not retractable. Once an accusation is made, one's fellow prisoner becomes irremediably guilty. It is not possible to retract the accusatory information given, just as it is not possible to deny proven facts. The non-retractability of the choices unavoidably produces an undesirable outcome. Yet this assumption may not fit some real-life situations of human interactions whose formal structure can be represented with this game, especially if they involve a low number of people who can easily communicate with each other.

In certain settings, the game may not end once the actors have made their simultaneous choices, because, on the basis of communication and the knowledge of the other actor's decision, each actor still has the chance of retracting his initial choice. A model of bargaining or negotiation between two actors, for instance, may include the possibility for one to make an offer. Yet if the other does not accept it, the initial choice does not irreversibly damage him. The bargain is not completed, and the former can listen to the latter's counteroffer or propose a new one. This can be applied to interactions between two political parties or two governments, and between a seller and a buyer, and in many other situations. The game ends only when every actor receives a response to his choice from the other actor. Then an actor can start offering conditional cooperation and expect a positive reply from the other actor if he has the possibility to change his strategy. This kind of cooperative agreement to the actors' mutual benefit is more likely to be reached in a small group with direct interactions. In contrast, in a large group with numerous actors, the chances of obtaining positive responses from the other actors and of dissuading them from defecting may still be slim.

OTHER POLITICAL DILEMMAS

As mentioned, the Prisoner's Dilemma can be used to understand the problems of collective action for the provision of public goods, including, as in our initial example, saving the atmosphere. As the players in the game have dominant strategies leading to an inefficient collective outcome, so the participants in collective action may be tempted to free-ride on the others and produce insufficient provision of public goods. In a number of cases, however, closer interaction between actors on problems involving high stakes can foster conditional cooperation and agreeable, more satisfactory outcomes. The same logic applies to many other situations, up to the point that the Prisoner's Dilemma can be considered one of the better-studied models of social interactions. Consider the following examples.

Community. What certain classical authors called "the state of nature" can be understood as a multi-actor Prisoner's Dilemma in which conflict is pervasive. If human interactions are unconstrained, anybody with the advantage of surprise can try to impose his will on the others. But if all do this, then people may find themselves living in a state of chaos in which, in Thomas Hobbes's famous words, life tends to be "solitary, poor, nasty, brutish, and short." In such an environment it is not reasonable to risk unilateral cooperation, while cooperation within groups is precarious. However, human beings can do it better. People can agree on creating a government equipped with coercion tools to enforce rules mandating those actions that individuals find beneficial to all. The government may apply sanctions against "defectors"—that is, violators of mutually beneficial rules of conduct—discourage free-riding on public goods, and craft incentives for cooperation. People can rationally accept conditional consent. By an agreed "social contract," the efficient outcome of civilization or "commonwealth," in which each can live in peace and security, can be attained.

BOX 3.1   **GOING FOR THE BLONDE**

One of the most influential contributors to game theory is John F. Nash, who was awarded the Nobel Prize in Economics in 1994 (probably the Nobel winner with the fewest pages published in his life!). In three articles, he basically introduced two concepts. The so-called Nash equilibrium is the outcome of a game in which no player can improve his results by unilaterally changing his strategy, as explained in this chapter.

Nash also introduced a normative concept, the "Nash solution," for bargaining problems in which two or more actors try to reach an agreement on how to divide a good. The classical utilitarian criterion holds that the best social solution is the one that maximizes the sum of the actors' utilities. This criterion inspires, for instance, the evaluation of the welfare of a country by its average per capita income or by the general level of citizens' political satisfaction. In contrast, the Nash solution is the one that maximizes the *product* of the actors' utilities.

An example of the Nash solution is given in the Oscar-winning movie *A Beautiful Mind* (based on the book of the same title by Sylvia Nasar) about the life of John Nash. A group of four students, including Nash, are spending some time in a bar in Princeton when five girls, including a stunning blonde, enter the room.

Nash says, "If we all go for the blonde, we block each other and not a single one of us is gonna get her." He suggests that "no one goes for the blonde," and that the four boys instead pair up with the other girls—to the bemusement of his fellow students.

A reasonable interpretation is the following. If only one person obtains the maximum prize, say with value 10, and the other three get nothing, the sum of the four actors' utilities can be relatively high in comparison with an alternative outcome in which each of the four actors gets a lower value, say of only 2 (since $10 + 0 + 0 + 0 = 10 > 2 + 2 + 2 + 2 = 8$). But the product of utilities in the first outcome is very bad (actually it is zero, since three actors get nothing and can be extremely frustrated), while the product of the latter is higher ($2 * 2 * 2 * 2 = 16$).

Generally, in comparison with the classical utilitarian "Bentham sum" solution, the "Nash product" solution favors more egalitarian distributions. For example, under the sum criterion, a distribution of values among three actors such as 3, 2, 1, is as good as the distribution 2, 2, 2 (since both imply a sum of 6 units of social utility). But under the product criterion, the former distribution (whose product is $3 * 2 * 1 = 6$) is worse than the latter one (whose product is $2 * 2 * 2 = 8$).

Democratization.   In situations of institutional regime crisis in which authoritarian rulers cannot go on as they have been accustomed to, actors with opposite political regime preferences can generate violent conflict or a civil war in which each side may fight to eliminate the other, as represented by the inefficient outcome in the Prisoner's Dilemma. Eventually, one of the sides can become a single, absolute winner, but choosing confrontation with uncertain outcome also entails the risk of becoming an absolute loser, and costs of significant destruction on both sides. In contrast, by anticipating the foreseeable consequences of their choices, either the rulers or the opposition leaders can offer conditional, retractable cooperation. Negotiations can lead to a provisional compromise, including the calling of a multiparty election not securing an absolute winner, which may open further developments in favor of either of the actors involved, as has happened in so many cases of democratization in different parts of the world since the last quarter of the twentieth century.

Deterrence.   International relations during the cold war between the United States and the Soviet Union were much like the Prisoner's Dilemma. If the Soviets chose to build new weapons, the United States did the same, and vice versa, which

---

CASE 3.1   PRISONER'S DILEMMA AT THE OPERA

The plot of the opera *Tosca*, written by Giacomo Puccini (1858–1924), is a case in point about the troubles that can be created by a Prisoner's Dilemma–type of situation. In the story, a new republic has been established in Rome under the influence of the French Revolution. Scarpia, the reactionary chief of police, captures the rebel Mario and offers him a deal: his life in return for his lover Tosca's physical surrender. Tosca has to concede, and Scarpia, to keep up appearances, gives order for a mock execution of Mario with blank cartridges. However, Tosca manages to avoid intimacy with Scarpia by stabbing a knife into his chest. Then she runs to the firing squad ceremony. After the soldiers shoot, she finds Mario is actually dead. Scarpia has double-crossed her. The interaction can be represented as follows:

Note that the initial compromise, as represented by the upper-left cell, is not an equilibrium, since the two actors have incentives to modify their decision unilaterally. Tosca has a dominant strategy: to resist Scarpia's advances, regardless of Scarpia's choice of either leaving Mario alive or executing him, while Scarpia also has a dominant strategy of operating a real execution whether Tosca concedes or resists. The inefficient outcome of the Prisoner's Dilemma is represented by the lower-right cell, although the two actors would have been better off in the upper-left cell.

		POLICEMAN SCARPIA	
		MOCK EXECUTION	REAL EXECUTION
	CONCEDE	Mario alive Tosca yielded	Mario dead Tosca yielded
TOSCA			
	RESIST	Mario alive Tosca unharmed	Mario dead Tosca unharmed

---

triggered an arms race that put both countries at risk. For each power, arming was a dominant strategy. The unrelenting logic of self-interest drove the two powers toward a conflict outcome that was worse for each of them than living in a world safe from the arms threat. The "balance of terror" without actual direct war was sustainable because, with nuclear weapons and the possibility of total destruction, the stakes were so high. Each power was able to prevent the other from ceding to the temptation of unilateral surprise attack, since each could threaten the other with massive retaliation. But the strength of mutual deterrence indirectly provoked lots of non-nuclear, limited war outbursts from local conflicts throughout the world. The United States and the Soviet Union attempted to move away from the inefficient outcome of the game—that is, to reduce and control arms through negotiations and agreements. But the arms race game stopped only with the dissolution of one of the players.

Quick Quiz

• What's an equilibrium?
• What's a dominant strategy?

SOURCE 3.1   Theory of Games

The origins of game theory were related this way by one of its inventors:

The Nazis took over in Vienna in March 1938. I [*Oskar Morgenstern*] was dismissed as "politically unbearable" from the University as well as from my Institute…While in the United States, I received a number of calls from various American universities to join their faculties…The principal reason for my wanting to go to Princeton was the possibility that I might become acquainted with [*John*] von Neumann [*also in exile from communism in Hungary and Nazism in Germany*] and the hope that this would be a great stimulus for my future work. Von Neumann and I met soon after the University opened…We were already in the midst of war, not an ideal time for work of our kind!…I recall vividly how Johnny rose from our table when we had set down our expected utility axioms and called out in astonishment: "Ja hat denn das niemand gesehen?" ("But didn't anyone see that?")…Clearly, we were convinced that it represented first of all a fundamental break with conventional economics: we demonstrated that one is not confronted with ordinary maximum or minimum problems (no matter what side conditions!), but with conceptually different situations. Though this becomes intuitively quite easily accessible for ordinary exchange, for monopoly, oligopoly, etc., the phenomenon is all-pervading…Thus the scope of the book extends far beyond economics, reaching into political science, sociology, etc.

From Oskar Morgenstern, "The Collaboration Between Oskar
Morgenstern and John von Neumann on the Theory of Games" (1976)

Arms races, such as during the Cold War between the United States and the Soviet
Union, can be analyzed with the Prisoner's Dilemma Game.

The Evolution of Cooperation

The decision to cooperate or defect may not be the same if you are involved in a single occasion to interact with unknown people or if you are going to continue to interact with the same group of individuals for a long time. If the "game" consists of only one play, many people may think that a bird in the hand is worth two in the bush. This is the kind of decision some people tend to make in a Prisoner's Dilemma situation, such as a street market in which any passerby can bargain with anonymous strangers they are not likely to meet again.

The situation is different if people are going to engage in repeated plays. Then it may make sense to try to cooperate in order to receive others' cooperation in the future. A community or institutional setting in which everybody can expect to keep interacting with the same people regularly for some time may include a household or a neighborhood, the workplace, a mall or a school, a professional organization or a political party, and the city, state, empire or world in which one is aware of living in and where one intends to stay. Reasonable behavior for repeated interactions with other individuals with some common interest can involve conditional cooperation and a positive response to the others' behavior. The possibility of cooperation in repeated plays of Prisoner's Dilemma–type situations can derive from a decision criterion called "Tit for Tat." In the long term, cooperation may spread and become the prevailing way of conduct, as we discuss in the following pages.

TIT FOR TAT

If you have to decide whether to cooperate or defect in a series of interactions, it is convenient to have a criterion for making each decision. A criterion for choosing a strategy in every interaction is called a "meta-strategy." Let us consider different possibilities for interactions that have the logical structure of the Prisoner's Dilemma or of collective action in general. First, you may choose, for instance, "always defect." This is indeed the safest meta-strategy, in which no one can possibly take advantage of you. But after a while you may get stuck in a rut of mutual punishments with your fellow "prisoners," which is likely not to produce any collective good.

A second meta-strategy may be just the opposite: "always cooperate." It works well if everybody else applies the same criterion. But it may get very bad results if others defect, since the cooperative actor can become a "sucker." It is like always turning the other cheek—and getting slapped. As philosopher Jean-Jacques Rousseau noted many years ago, "for the society to be peaceable and for harmony to be maintained," all the citizens *without exception* would have to be good cooperators; but "if by ill hap there should be a *single* self-seeker or hypocrite, he would certainly get the better of his pious compatriots...servitude and dependence."

With any of the two meta-strategies mentioned—always defect or always cooperate—you would always be running on autopilot, not taking into account what other people were doing. If you do take their behavior into account, you can improve the results greatly. Specifically, if after a few interactions you realize that the other people are always cooperating, then you can defect and gain advantage. If, on the contrary, the other people are always defecting, no matter how cooperative you are, then you should always defect, too, in order to avoid being slapped again and again and becoming a sucker. But in general you can expect that the other people will respond to your actions, too. What would be the best way for you to act if there are real interactions, that is, responsive actions by other people?

The Tit-for-Tat meta-strategy, or criterion of conduct, for repeated plays of the Prisoner's Dilemma can produce sustained cooperation. It is based on the idea of responding to the others' behavior or **doing unto others as they do unto you**, as initially identified by political scientist Robert Axelrod. As a recommendation for conduct, it includes the following elements:

- **Start nice.** Don't be the first to defect. In some real quarrels it is not even clear who started it; both sides can claim that the other started slapping and that they are just responding. This happens in situations ranging from children at play to neighboring states in conflict. The solution is, of course, to start again by making clear the initial choice of each party. Let us, therefore, start with cooperation, see what happens—that is, how the other people respond—and then do the same as they do.

- **Retaliate.** Cooperate if the others cooperate; defect if the others defect. In a series of plays, your reply should be given at the immediate next play of the game.

- **Forgive.** Don't be resentful. After you have replied to the others' defection with your own defection, be willing to start conditional cooperation again. Your negative response to the previous defection of the other actor should be a lesson, sending a message to him that he should learn to cooperate.

- **Keep it simple.** Basically, do unto others as they do unto you. Your best lemma could be: "If you cooperate, I do; if you don't, I don't." By doing this, the efficient outcome in the Prisoner's Dilemma–type of interaction can be achieved again and again. Cooperation will be met with cooperation and will feed on itself. In the same sense, the free-rider problem in collective action can be solved. People can indeed organize themselves in a stable manner and contribute to the provision of collective goods in which they are genuinely interested.

INDEFINITE PLAYS

A more pessimistic view holds that the incentive to cooperate in a series of Prisoner's Dilemma–type interactions may vanish if the participants know when the "game" is going to finish—that is, when they will cease to be members of the same community sharing some common interest. The last play of an iterated Prisoner's Dilemma is like a single play, because there will be no further opportunity to reply to any defection. Everybody will have the dominant strategy to defect—as in the one-shot interaction between John and Oskar from their cells.

Actually the problem may be even worse. If you know when the end of the game will be, then you can expect that the other actor will defect at the last play—as will you. Then you discount that play. Considering now the next-to-last play, since you have discarded any response in the last play, the next-to-last now appears as the last play on which to make a decision. Again, this will be like a single play, in which you will also defect, as will the other actor. You and every actor can reason in the same way at every play, and thus decide to defect at every "previous" play up to the beginning. By so-called **"backward induction," the repeated interaction can lead to mutual defection when the end is known**, The iteration of Prisoner's Dilemma–type interactions, if the end of the iteration is known in advance, is like a single play of the game. For all the actors, therefore, the dominant strategy is to defect in all plays of the game.

Cooperation by means of tit for tat can be achievable if the number of interactions is infinite, which is not likely to occur in this world, or if they are indefinite—that is, if the actors don't know when their interactions will finish. If nobody knows how many plays lie ahead, there is no "last" play to reason backward from. In their ignorance of the future, people will keep cooperating. Those who know, however, can take advantage at the last play. In more practical terms, we can expect that cooperation is more likely to hold up the greater the uncertainty about the length of the game and the higher the number of plays or interactions. The more repeated the cooperation strategy, the wider the spread both of information and of the actors' reputation regarding their cooperativeness.

According to this insight, we can observe that cooperation, collective action, and joint organization are indeed more intense and sustained among certain groups of people interacting for long periods of indefinite length. Cooperation should be higher, for example, among members of a condominium complex rather than among motel clients; among town residents rather than among tourists or occasional visitors; among fixed employees rather than among temporarily unemployed people expecting to find another job soon; among civil servants rather than among seasonal workers; among store owners in a commercial mall rather than among sporadic vendors in a street market; among practitioners of professions requiring costly training or implying low opportunity costs, such as miners or physicians, who are likely to stay in the job, rather than among amateurs or aficionados; among students enrolled in three- or four-year programs rather than among summer-course attendees; and among citizens in countries with a sedentary population rather than in those in which many people are likely to emigrate.

FAVORABLE CONTEXTS

Criteria of behavior such as Tit for Tat promise satisfactory results only in the long term and in average values. But no meta-strategy guarantees an efficient outcome at every play of the game. Particular results in specific circumstances may depend on the social context, that is, on what other people are doing in the particular group in which you are participating. Actually you can choose your partners—that is, you can decide to interact preferably with people with whom you can establish beneficial relations. Once you are in a particular group or community, some criteria of conduct may prove to be better than others. In general it is advisable to follow the dictum "When in Rome, do as the Romans do," although this may require some adaptation.

Self-sustained Cooperation.   Specifically, if in a group everybody applies Tit for Tat, then Tit for Tat is the best strategy for each individual. Cooperation is universal and permanent. In such a context, even the meta-strategy "always cooperate" can survive and obtain the same result, since people using Tit for Tat reply to cooperation with cooperation.

In certain contexts, slightly different meta-strategies might produce even better results. **"Tit for Two Tat,"** for instance—which implies not responding with defection to the other actor's first defection but only to the second one, or, in other words, being more forgiving—may help prevent the quick diffusion of defective behavior in communities in which most people are prone to behaving cooperatively.

Even in an adverse context in which people using the "always defect" criterion abound, a set of people applying Tit for Tat may obtain some success. After the permanent defectors have proven their advantage, the population of exploited "suckers" cooperating unilaterally tends to disappear. Then the defectors may find themselves with nobody to exploit, thus mutually defecting with everybody, which produces mediocre results. In the long term, people with the Tit for Tat criterion can obtain better results than defectors by responding with defection to the defectors and developing numerous cooperative interactions among themselves. This may make Tit for Tat advantageous and eventually the most common strategy in the group.

Trust.   If people reciprocate with cooperation to cooperation in repeated interactions, they can build a good reputation for themselves that may move other people to cooperate with them. Feelings of trust may emerge among people having information about others' past action and among new participants obtaining regular positive retribution for their conduct. In the mid- or long term, increasing and sustained cooperation among members of a community may induce them to construct institutional environments that limit individual competition and tend to homogenize the population. Internal sanctions against defectors can go together with the promotion of values such as honesty and empathy for others' distress, thus reinforcing social cooperativeness.

Indeed a sense of reciprocity and a capacity for empathy seem to have developed over time among human beings. In fact, there are numerous groups and communities in which broad conditional cooperation prevails, although with some degree of diversity, including both good unconditional cooperatives and evil defectors—after all, there are always saints and sinners in the world.

Intergroup Conflict.   The development of cooperation among members of a community or interest group requires some mutual commitment to stay within the contours of the group. If, conversely, people living within the same institutional setting consider themselves to belong to two different groups with opposite goals, asymmetric relations can develop. The difference between groups can be based on family or tribal traditions, contrary economic interests, adversarial preferences for the location of public goods, or alternative ethnic allegiances such as language, race, or religion.

People can then apply "discriminatory Tit for Tat." When interacting with members of the same group, as it is perceived by the individuals themselves, they can start cooperating and develop the afore-mentioned kind of evolution favoring collectively efficient outcomes to their mutual benefit. People may be more cooperative toward others the more closely related they are. But when two individuals from clearly different groups interact, they can defect. This arrangement can be stable. In this context, an individual who tries to use the nondiscriminatory criterion of Tit for Tat will be worse off because his cooperative strategy with members of the other group will be regularly responded to with defection. If this is observed, most people may tend to start any interaction with members of the other group with defection, just to prevent being the sucker from the beginning.

In this type of situation, the larger group may obtain relatively better results than the smaller group. Even if each individual interacts randomly with members of any of the groups, the members of the larger group interact more often with other members of the same group, thus having more opportunities to develop cooperative strategies leading to efficient outcomes. The members of the smaller group, by contrast, are likely to have more interactions with members of the larger group, thus receiving higher proportions of inefficient results produced by mutual defection.

In the long term, members of the small, disadvantaged group may want to split off and create a separate community, whether another family, tribe, company, organization, union, coalition, municipality, state, or alliance. This may be beneficial for members of all groups, since each will then have better opportunities to interact within their own group and to develop cooperation as a consequence of iterated plays.

Quick Quiz

• What's a meta-strategy?
• Define the "Tit for-Tat" meta-strategy in two sentences.

Other Games of Collective Action

Although the Prisoner's Dilemma can be considered as representing the most basic structure of the problems of collective action for the provision of public goods, other game structures can clarify certain other situations. People can play different "games"—that is, they can develop different strategic interactions, depending on the opportunities, incentives, and constraints supplied by given structures and institutions. To put it in terms of critical political economist Karl Marx, "Men make their own history, but they do not make it as they please…but under circumstances existing already, given and transmitted from the past." Structural conditions do not determine human behavior, but usually shape a distinct set of feasible choices. Human beings can also try to modify certain elements of a given situation, especially rules, institutions, and organizations, in order to have the capacity to develop the interactions in which they are interested.

Game theory can help to model specific problems for the provision of different types of goods and in different settings in which individuals can organize collective action, which we have addressed more informally in the previous two chapters. In the following pages we discuss two well-known games that correspond to different sets of incentives and opportunities: "Chicken" and "Stag Hunt" (curiously, both with animal names). For the Prisoner's Dilemma and for each of these two additional types of situations, different outcomes—that is, different levels of cooperation among members of an interest group—can be expected.

CHICKEN

Besides the Prisoner's Dilemma, another important model for a diverse range of human interactions is "Chicken." It can enlighten, among many other situations, some challenges of the global warming problem mentioned at the beginning of this chapter. The origin of the model's name is a real Saturday night game played by some teenagers in American cities in the 1950s and popularized across the world by movies such as *Rebel Without a Cause*. One variant of the game consists of two boys simultaneously driving cars toward the edge of a cliff and either putting on the brakes or jumping out at the last possible moment. The one exiting the car closest to the edge wins, and the other is declared the "chicken."

In this game it is not difficult to identify the preferences of the players, let us call them James and Dean. First, the best thing that can happen to James is to keep driving ahead and jump out and let Dean stop. James wins, and Dean is a chicken. The second best thing is that both boys stop in good time; both are chickens but save their lives. Finally, James's stopping first while Dean continues driving implies that he is a chicken, but it is less bad than if no car stops and both boys fall over the edge of the precipice. Dean has analogous preferences.

Let us call braking the car "cooperating" and driving ahead "defecting." Note the difference between the structure of this game and that of the Prisoner's Dilemma, which is apparently minor but has significant consequences. The actors in the two games switch only their last and next-to-last preferences. In the Prisoner's Dilemma everybody prefers to defect if the other actor defects. Cooperating when the other defects would make one the sucker—the worst possible outcome. In contrast, in Chicken, unilateral cooperation while the other defects—putting on the brakes and saving his life—is less bad than mutual defection, which implies that both players go over the cliff.

What would you expect the outcome of the game to be? Consider James's decision. He does not know what Dean is going to do. If he sees that Dean is stopping, he should drive just a little farther ahead and jump out of his moving car. If, in contrast, James thinks that Dean is going to drive ahead, it is better to stop—better a chicken than dead. In contrast to Prisoner's Dilemma–type situations, here the actors do not have dominant strategies. In one assumption about the other player's decision, it is better to drive ahead, while in the other assumption it is better to stop. Thus there are **two possible outcomes of the game in which some actors cooperate and others defect**. In Chicken, in one outcome James wins and Dean stops; while in the other, James stops and Dean wins. But which of the two possible outcomes will occur is uncertain—that's precisely the allure of the game. Check the players' possible strategic choices in Table 3.3. The two outcomes of the game are located in the upper-right and the lower-left cells.

One way to try to select one of the two possible outcomes of the game may imply pre-commitment by one of the players not to stop. If at the beginning of the challenge James announces out loud before his fans that he will not stop, he may force Dean to stop early (or just quit the game). But any actor's pre-commitment must be credible and rely upon reputation built on previous plays of the game. Otherwise, announcing a valiant strategy and not fulfilling it may aggravate the humiliation of the loser of the game. To commit or not to commit oneself at the beginning of the game can thus be another game of Chicken with an uncertain outcome.

Another way to deal with the result of the Chicken game is to assume that every player will choose the least-risky strategy, with the criterion called **maxi-min, in order avoid the worst possible outcome**. Since every strategy can produce a minimum value

TABLE 3.3 Chicken

The outcome of the game depends on the decision made by each boy on the basis of his expectation as to what the other boy will do.

		DEAN	
		COOPERATE C	DEFECT D
JAMES	COOPERATE C (*stop*)	Both chicken	James chicken Dean wins
	DEFECT D (*drive ahead*)	James wins Dean chicken	Both fall

(being a chicken if one cooperates, and falling into the precipice if one does not), it is assumed that the actor will choose **the strategy that guarantees the "maximum minimum" result**—in the metaphorical story: to save his life.

Note that this is also the criterion of choice that we assumed would be used by the players in the Prisoner's Dilemma game: by trying to avoid the strategy that could produce the worst possible outcome (ten years in prison), they chose to defect. In the Chicken game, in contrast, this criterion would lead the two players to cooperate—placing the outcome in the upper-left cell of Table 3.3.

In any of the possible readings of the game structure, we should expect, therefore, that there will be at least some degree of cooperation—although it is not clear who will cooperate. Note again that the worst possible outcome in which both players defect is not an equilibrium, because each player has incentives to unilaterally modify his strategy (and brake).

The Chicken game is a representation of collective action problems when unilateral cooperation is worthy because it is presumed to be able to provide *some* collective good. Logically this strategic interaction can be appropriate only for the provision of collective goods that can be provided in incomplete amounts.

Let us think about different types of collective goods from the perspectives provided by the Prisoner's Dilemma and Chicken games. In Prisoner's Dilemma–type situations, neither individual finds it beneficial to cooperate unilaterally because he would be unable to provide any amount of the collective good by himself. This assumption may fit collective goods that must be provided in entire units, such as highways, bridges, tunnels, canals, harbors, airports, schools, and hospitals. These are also called "lumpy" goods—in contrast to "continuous" goods, similar to different ways of providing sugar. To have half a bridge or a portion of a tunnel is like not having one at all. Goods of this type require some significant amount of provision—a lump—to be able to benefit their potential users, rendering partial cooperation not helpful.

In contrast, for continuous collective goods, such as certain environmental goods, unilateral cooperation can provide some amount. Partial cooperation and provision can exist. Saving the atmosphere, seas, oceans, rivers, lakes, and woods from global

BOX 3.2   **BASIC GAMES**

The structure of the three basic games of collective action can be represented by the following table. One actor is located in the row and the other in the column. Each actor can choose between cooperating (C) or defecting (D). The strategy of each actor leads to a collective outcome that is represented by each of the four cells in the table. If the two actors choose mutual cooperation, each receives a reward (R). If the two actors choose mutual defection, each receives a penalty (P). If one cooperates while the other defects, the cooperative actor is a sucker (S), while the defector cedes to the temptation (T).

In each game the actors prefer the outcomes in a different order. See the actors' orders of preference and the subsequent equilibrium outcomes.

GAME	ACTOR'S PREFERENCE ORDER	COLLECTIVE OUTCOMES IN EQUILIBRIUM
Prisoner's Dilemma	T > R > P > S	PP: mutual defect
Chicken	T > R > S > P	TS, ST: partial cooperation and defect
Stag Hunt	R > T > P > S	PP: mutual defect RR: mutual cooperation

		COLUMN	
		COOPERATE C	DEFECT D
ROW	COOPERATE C	RR	ST
	DEFECT D	TS	PP

warming, mentioned earlier, or the reproduction and maintenance of some animal species and plants can be done at different rates. But each of these goods can have a critical level of provision to guarantee its preservation.

Consider now the case of a river surrounded by factories polluting its water by discharging their detritus into it. The river waters can absorb rubbish from a certain number of factories and still remain usable, but when the waste from many factories surpasses some critical threshold, it results in an ecological catastrophe. Since this would be the worst result for every company making use of the river, some of them may unilaterally restrain from polluting it, even if others continue to pollute it. In this outcome some companies cooperate and others free-ride, and the subsequent benefits are suboptimal and unevenly distributed, but all are better off, including the unilateral cooperators, than if the waters ceased to be usable. Similarly, an international agreement on limiting the hunting of certain species—whales or elephants, for instance—are frequently fulfilled by some of the signatory parties to the agreement, in order to permit the reproduction of the species, while being contravened by others–in the knowledge (and righteous anger) of the former.

In some cases the real actors involved in a conflict may not be sure of whether the structure of their interaction more closely resembles the Prisoner's Dilemma or Chicken. For instance, in the previous chapter we depicted the Cold War and arms race between the United States and the Soviet Union in the second half of the twentieth century as a Prisoner's Dilemma. However, some pacifist groups in the West, fearful of the risk of massive destruction of the globe, put mutual defection at the

SOURCE 3.2   **Chickens and Stags**

The catchy metaphors giving ground to some basic games of collective action originated in old political speeches:

Since the nuclear stalemate became apparent, the Governments of East and West have adopted...a policy adapted from a sport which, I am told, is practiced by some youthful degenerates. This sport is called "**Chicken!**." It is played by choosing a long straight road with a white line down the middle and starting two very fast cars towards each other from opposite ends. Each car is expected to keep the wheels of one side on the white line. As they approach each other, mutual destruction becomes more and more imminent. If one of them swerves from the white line before the other, the other, as he passes, shouts "Chicken!", and the one who has swerved becomes an object of contempt...When the game is played by eminent statesmen, they risk not only their own lives but those of many hundreds of millions of human beings.

Bertrand Russell, *Common Sense and Nuclear Warfare* (1959)

If a **stag** was to be taken, every one saw that, in order to succeed, he must abide faithfully by his post. But if a hare happened to come within the reach of any one of them, it is not to be doubted that he pursued it without scruple and, having seized his prey, worried very little if by so doing he caused his companions to lose theirs...[Over time] men may have imperceptibly acquired some rough ideas of mutual commitments and of the advantages of fulfilling them, but only to the extent that present and perceptible interest could demand it.

Jean-Jacques Rousseau, *Discourse on the Origin of Inequality* (1754)

TABLE 3.4   Stag Hunt

Two hunters may either catch a hare each or cooperate to chase after a stag—a collective good to share.

		JACQUES	
		COOPERATE C	DEFECT D
	COOPERATE C *(chase stag)*	Stag to share	Jean gets nothing Jacques catches a hare
JEAN			
	DEFECT D *(catch hare)*	Jean catches a hare Jacques gets nothing	A hare for each

bottom of their preferences, and advocated unilateral cooperation—that is, unilateral disarmament of the United States and Western Europe even at the risk of surrendering to Soviet expansion. Along the lines of a boy in the Chicken game, afraid that his competitor would drive ahead anyway, they coined a euphonic saying: "Better red than dead." Finally, however, the West ended up neither red nor dead.

STAG HUNT

Still more likely to succeed in producing individuals' mutual cooperation are situations outlined by the game structure called Stag Hunt, or "Assurance." In this case the original story of the game refers to the attempt to organize collective action for hunting some edible animals in the woods. The basic assumption is that no individual can catch a stag by himself—that is, nobody can provide the whole collective good to be shared—but by defecting from the team, anyone can catch a hare and get some private good to eat. For the two hunters playing the game, it is also assumed that getting half a stag is better than getting a hare—that is, the individual share of the big collective item is better than what one can attain by oneself. So for each actor, it is better to cooperate and obtain the big collective good than to go out on his own, but to get something on his own is better than cooperating unilaterally and getting nothing at all (facing the stag alone).

What would you expect the outcome of the game to be? Let us call the two actors Jean and Jacques. In the fear that Jacques will go his own way to chase after a hare, Jean can do the same and obtain some good. In this outcome there would be **mutual defection**. This result can last for a long time—with lonely individuals walking through the woods each chasing after their own food. But even if this is the first, provisional outcome, **achievement of mutual cooperation should be relatively unproblematic** because all actors prefer their share of the collective good to any other outcome. Table 3.4 represents the possible strategic choices. If everybody defects, each gets a hare, but if somebody starts chasing the stag, he can expect that the other may join in the effort, and the two will obtain the collective good. The structure of this game might enlighten interactions between people with some common interest in which the participants can develop effective mutual pressure and dissuasion, leading them to cooperate. Initially, mutual defection can be an equilibrium. But some individual initiative can obtain the efficient outcome.

Quick Quiz

• Is mutual defect an equilibrium outcome in the Chicken game?

Conclusion

Game theory has helped us to analyze diverse strategic situations in which people interact to promote their common interests. From the previous discussion we can establish two basic *propositions*:

1. **Prisoner's Dilemma.** In this game, which represents the basic structure of collective action problems for the provision of public goods, each actor has a dominant strategy not to cooperate, leading to an inefficient outcome in which all the participants are worse off than if all cooperated.
2. **Tit for Tat.** The strategy of starting to cooperate and doing unto others as they do unto you can lead to sustained cooperation. Mutual cooperation is more likely the greater the uncertainty as to the length of the collective relationship and the higher the number of interactions.

Different conditions for the provision of public goods, which can be stylized with the Prisoner's Dilemma, the Chicken, or the Stag Hunt games, can entail different degrees of cooperation and defection. Nevertheless, success or failure in attaining cooperative interactions within an interest group does not necessarily correspond to socially efficient or inefficient solutions. Remember the moral ambiguity implied by the foundational story of the Prisoner's Dilemma, in which successful cooperation—among suspects of a crime—may lead them to escape punishment, while justice would most likely be implemented if they defected. The collective strength of some groups may indeed provoke conflict with other groups or favor asymmetric and biased redistributions of resources, hindering more satisfactory outcomes for greater numbers of people. ∎

Summary

Game theory helps to analyze human interactions in strategic situations in which individual decisions depend on what each participant expects the others will do.

The Prisoner's Dilemma represents the most basic structure of the problems of collective action for the provision of public goods. Each actor has a dominant strategy not to cooperate. In the inefficient equilibrium outcome of the game, all participants are worse off than if all cooperated. This can be considered to be a representation of the free-rider problem.

The Tit for Tat meta-strategy or criterion of decision for repeated plays of the Prisoner's Dilemma is based on the idea of responding to the others' behavior. It consists of starting cooperating and doing unto others as they do unto you: cooperate when the others cooperate, and defect when the others defect. It can produce sustained cooperation when the number of interactions is indefinite.

Cooperation is more likely to hold up in certain groups the greater the uncertainty as to the length of the collective relationship and the higher the number of interactions. Iterated reciprocity may build good reputation and trust among members of the group and the building of institutions favoring further cooperation.

The Chicken game can lead to two possible outcomes, each involving some degree of cooperation among the participants. This result can be a representation of the advantages of unilateral cooperation for the provision and reproduction of "continuous" goods, such as those in question in certain environmental problems with a catastrophe threshold.

In the Stag Hunt, or "Assurance," game, mutual defection is an equilibrium outcome, but mutual cooperation is also an equilibrium outcome that should not be difficult for the participants to attain for their mutual benefit.

Key Concepts

Backward induction. Reasoning leading to mutual defection when the end of the interaction is known.

Chicken. Game with two possible outcomes in which some actors cooperate and others defect.

Competition. Action among several players each for his own benefit.

Conflict or zero-sum game. An intercation in which the gains for some people imply losses for others.

Cooperation. Action for the common benefit.

Coordination game. An interaction in which there are efficient results for all participants.

Dominant strategy. The best actor's decision regardless of the other actor's decision.

Equilibrium. Stable outcome of a game. In Nash's concept, an outcome from which no actor has incentives to move away by changing his strategy unilaterally.

Maxi-min. Criterion of decision to prevent the worst result and guarantee the "maximum minimum."

Positive or non-zero-sum game. An interaction in which mutual cooperation can produce gains for all participants.

Prisoner's Dilemma. Non-zero-sum game with an inefficient equilibrium outcome and in which nobody cooperates.

Stag Hunt. An assurance game with mutual defection and mutual cooperation equilibrium outcomes.

Tit for Tat. Meta-strategy for repeated plays of the Prisoner's Dilemma that can produce sustained cooperation.

Questions for Review

1. What's the equilibrium outcome of the Prisoner's Dilemma game?
2. What's "Tit for Tat?"
3. What's the outcome of the Chicken game?
4. What's the outcome of the Stag Hunt game?

Problems and Applications

1. Play this coordination game: After being separated during a term break, you are to meet a fellow student on campus on the first day of classes at twelve noon. You did not make an arrangement regarding where to meet and your cell phone has been stolen. You both have to guess where to meet and try to make your guesses coincide. Note that the two of you have identical interests, but you will succeed only if you make identical choices. You win only if you do what the other expects you to do.

    Collect the written responses and match each student's response with those of the others.

2. Represent the following strategic situation with the help of game theory: At a beach resort in California is the Hotel Flamingo which produces waste and refuse polluting the waters of the sea. Usually Mr. Grant, a hotel employee, quite successfully does the job of filtering the waste. Since about a year ago, a new tourist resort, PalmHouse, which opened just a few yards away, has been producing similar waste, polluting the waters as well. Initially, Mr. Grant did his best to filter everything he could. The result was not optimal, however, since it would have been better for PalmHouse to have organized its own filtering mechanisms. Some visitors noticed dirty waters at the beach, but there was no visible decrease in the number of customers. However, Mr. Grant retired a few weeks ago, and now nobody does his job. There is much concern regarding the visible water pollution. The tourist season

seems to be in danger. Everybody thinks that somebody should do something about it.

   a. Define the public good as provided by actors' cooperation.

   b. Order actors' preferences regarding all possible outcomes.

   c. Draw a table representing the possible outcomes.

   d. Discuss the actors' strategies and identify the outcome of the game. What may it mean in terms of the provision (or not) of the public good?

3. Represent the following strategic situation with the help of game theory: One individual is assaulting female residents in suburban Town. The police are not acting appropriately. The victims think that just two men would be sufficient to apprehend the criminal. A voluntary night patrol is organized by the president of the residents' association. Three men from Town will be called each night, at random. About eight thousand families live in the area. The president sends a letter to each family head explaining the plan and allocating one patrol night to each addressee. On the first day, three family heads are called. Each of them has to decide whether to attend.

   a. Define the public good as provided by actors' cooperation.

   b. Order actors' preferences regarding all possible outcomes.

   c. Draw a table representing all possible outcomes.

   d. Discuss actors' strategies and identify the outcome of the game. What does it mean in terms of provision or not of the public good?

4. Play the repeated Prisoner's Dilemma game and register your scores by using any of these websites:

   www.gametheory.net/Web/PDilemma

   www.people.bath.ac.uk/mk213/ipd

   www.paulspages.co.uk/hmd

5. Working in pairs, play the repeated Prisoner's Dilemma. Two of you can sit at the front of the classroom, backs to each other, and at successive indications from the instructor, you can raise either a green card, indicating cooperation (C), or a red card, indicating defection (D). Both players should raise their cards simultaneously, without being able to see the other's action in anticipation. The game must be played multiple times until the instructor ends it. The scores are the following:

   • One player chooses D (5 points) while the other chooses C (0 points).

   • Both choose C (3 points each).

   • Both choose D (1 point each).

   • First, make the following decisions:

   • Start with either C or D.

   • Retaliate (or not) to the other player's decision at the next play.

   • Remember past grievances or forget and forgive. Remember that to win the match you need not win every play.

   • Show a clear criterion of conduct or, rather, be confusing and unpredictable.

   At the beginning of the game you can announce what you are doing to do (or what you intend the other player to believe you are going to do). Remain silent throughout the rest of the game, taking into account only the other player's decisions.

   Somebody should record the scores of each play and make the final sum at the end of the game. Observe whether mutual cooperation emerges and becomes more frequent with the play of the game. The results may be different if the players know how many times they are going to play their interaction or not.

Discuss

Indicative results: For every ten plays of the game, the maximum score is 50 and the minimum is 0. Likely scores at the first round may be between 10 and 30. For each actor, less than 15 points is a bad score; between 16 and 22 is poor; between 23 and 29 is good; 30 or above is excellent. Consider individual scores as well as collective ones based on the sum of the two players' scores.

For a term paper

6. In cases of disputes or negotiations, certain algorithms enable the parties to find fair and equitable outcomes. Steven Brams's formulas of fair division have been applied to conflicts ranging from divorce to international border disputes. If you plan to write a term paper, consider these analytical tools. You may visit www.FairOutcomes.com.

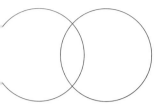

4

LEADERSHIP

In This Chapter You Will

- Consider what the motivations of political and social leaders are to engage in collective action.
- Consider which personal qualities and skills leaders may need.
- Learn what the "critical mass" is.
- Think of a "chain reaction" making different people follow leaders at different moments.
- Discuss the different degrees of effectiveness achieved by different leaders.
- Reflect on why some countries and groups have effective leaders, while in others, people accept low-quality leadership.

Nelson Mandela is one of the few political leaders to have achieved almost universal respect around the world. He was imprisoned for twenty-seven years for his opposition to apartheid in South Africa. Mandela came out of prison in 1990 championing reconciliation between blacks and whites and was recognized as the most credible negotiator. However, he had to win the support of his own followers and at the same time allay white people's fears. His leadership resulted in the country's first democratic elections and his selection as president. Mandela himself argued that he "was not a messiah, but an ordinary man who had become a leader because of extraordinary circumstances."

All organized societies and durable movements have leaders. These are people who, like Mandela but to different extents, somehow have the capacity to provide collective goals, group identification, and incentives to followers. They include presidents, prime ministers, and party chiefs in modern democracies; kings, dictators, popes, and emperors in other settings; and small-scale union organizers, employer organization bosses, professional association entrepreneurs, religious prophets, and agrarian lobbyists, obviously all of them with different degrees of support and success.

In the following pages, first, we discuss what a leader is and what personal qualities and skills a leader may need, including vision or the ability to identify common goals, communication skills, and organizational capacity. Second, we approach the mechanisms by which leaders and followers interact and by which a following may be achieved. Finally, we analyze different "circumstances," in Mandela's words—that is, different institutional and social contexts—favoring efficient leadership. ■

What Is a Leader?

In the previous chapter we left unexplained the origin of organized groups and communities. In this chapter we will analyze how collective action for the common interest of a group or community can be initiated by some people able to collect resources from the members of the group and make the provision of public goods viable. In contrast to the "horizontal" interactions among members of a group with common interests, we will analyze a "vertical" interaction between people with different motivations. Collective action can develop and communities can be formed and endure thanks to a division of labor between those people leading and those following the leaders. In order to create and maintain an organization, both leaders and followers need to receive sufficient benefits from their relationships to accept their different, asymmetric roles.

Think of the role of the sports coach, if you have the experience of playing on a team. When somebody leads, you can benefit from following the leader. The leader determines the team's strategy, selects resources by choosing the appropriate players for each match, and tries to motivate and train the members to cooperate with the team. The coach or the leader himself is more motivated and feels better when he has a successful following.

Let us put forward a definition: leaders are those people who are able to coordinate the members of an interest group or community, set up an organization or institutional construction, initiate an action, and make viable the provision of public goods in which the group is interested.

More specifically, effective leaders should achieve the following aims:

- **Identify public goods** and common goals to pursue by the group, such as, the suppression of apartheid, the achievement of better wages or trade protection, or the preservation of fishing banks.
- **Mobilize collective resources** by the members of the group, including time, money, and organizational efforts.
- Create and reinforce collective trust, the **group identity and cohesion** to support sustained cooperation.

The motivations of leaders must be different from those of the typical member of the group. They can be based on the possibility of achieving benefits for themselves from the public goods whose provision they can make possible and from the private goods they supply. Leaders are also gratified with other rewards, especially power, and satisfying their vanity with fame and praise, receiving an income, and pursuing a professional career.

Remember that benefits and costs are always subjective, for potential leaders as for anybody else. Valuations of power, fame, or money, as compared to, say, alternative professional success, free time, or family life, can differ for different people depending on personal skills and opportunities. On the basis of expected collective and personal benefits, social and political leaders can found and expand organizations and communities and seek collective benefits for the group. In return, group members may be willing to give resources to leaders in exchange for saving organization costs and making collective action feasible. If the members of the group enjoy the public and private goods that leaders provide, they may be willing to accept and contribute to the special position of the leaders, giving them their support or their votes, as usually happens, for example, with elected politicians, unions organizers, or agrarian lobbyists.

LEADERS' BENEFITS AND OPPORTUNITY COSTS

Leaders can either share personally the interests and goals of the group they are leading, especially if the group is simple and has clearly identified priority interests, or not, if the group is complex and leading it requires some professionalization. In any case, to be a leader is a kind of a job, which may imply holding public office, running as a candidate, or working as an aide, a consultant, or in public relations. Holding a leadership position requires a decision to accept it, which basically depends, as for any other job, on the likelihood of being successful and on the opportunities available.

Since leading is a form of participating in collective action, we can present the individual logic of deciding whether to lead or not in analogy with the collective action function presented in chapter 2, with this **leadership function**:

$$R_L = B_L * P_L - C_L$$

This must be read as: the reward for an individual by becoming a leader, R_L, equals the expected benefit from leading, B_L, times the probability of leading, P_L, minus the opportunity cost of leading, C_L. The **opportunity cost** is the value of the rewards missed from some other professional, social, or private activities that might have been obtained instead. Also, in this case, if R_L is positive, trying to become a leader is a sound decision; if R_L is negative, it may not be worth the effort.

According to this, the individuals more likely to choose to become social or political leaders should envisage a positive balance of benefits and costs, which can derive either from a high identification with the common goals of the group (which is a component of the B variable) or from lacking a sufficiently gratifying alternative profession or activity (as reflected in C). Leadership may also be helped by open and inclusive institutional environments offering likely rewards (which is captured by the P variable). In contrast, leadership should not be expected to be a frequent choice in less cohesive communities by people with satisfying alternative professional or private devotions. In other words, if the probability of successful leadership is low and the opportunity costs of leading are too high, candidates for leadership will be quick to quit when facing adverse events.

LEADERS' PERSONAL SKILLS

The appropriate personal qualities of leadership can be different for different types of groups, from children in the school playground, to neighborhood gangs of youths, to interest group organizations, to political parties, to international diplomacy. Personal skills may derive both from natural traits and from learning and experience (at least the existence of so many courses and programs on leadership would suggest that some aspects of leadership can be taught).

CASE 4.1 SOME TOP LEADERS

Some might think it an insult to call a president an actor. It was certainly intended that way when [United States president] Ronald Reagan was dismissed as "just an actor." But all politicians need some of an actor's abilities. They must feign a welcome to unwanted constituencies' attentions, cooperate with despised party allies, wax indignant at politically chosen targets. This is not the work of inferior politicians, but of the masters. The three presidents normally at the top of historians' lists—Lincoln, Washington, and Roosevelt—all had strong histrionic instincts…An actor is not, as such, a leader. The appreciation of an audience is not motion toward some goal shared with the actor. Fans are not followers. But a popular leader must use some tricks from the actor's stock. Above all, the leader must be sensitive to the followers' reactions, must know when he or she is "losing the audience"…A good leader must know what is appealing to followers, and what risks that appeal…Great leadership is not a zero-sum game. What is given to the leader is not taken from the follower. Both get by giving. This is the mystery of great popular leaders like Washington, Lincoln, and Roosevelt.

Garry Wills, *Certain Trumpets: The Call of Leaders* (1994)

The trajectory of postwar Japan was to an extraordinary extent set during Yoshida Shigeru's tenure as Prime Minister (1946–47 and 1948–54)…Yoshida presented a unique combination of background, character, and skill that were useful and effective in dealing with the [American] occupation, marshalling the talent of Japan's policy elites, and manipulating power for the implementation and perpetuation of his vision…In many ways Yoshida's leadership closely resembled that of Konrad Adenauer in postwar Germany. Both enjoyed long tenures in office, and left a decisive imprint on postwar democracy and the international posture of their countries—countries which faced many similar conditions in the course of defeat, occupation, and reconstruction.

Terry Edward MacDougall, "Yoshida Shigeru and the Japanese Transition to Liberal Democracy" (1988)

Nelson Mandela overthrew apartheid and created a nonracial democratic South Africa. He offered eight "lessons of leadership":

1. Courage is not the absence of fear—it's inspiring others to move beyond.
2. Lead from the front—but don't leave your base behind.
3. Lead from the back—and let others believe they are in front.
4. Know your enemy.
5. Keep your friends close—and your rivals even closer.
6. Appearances matter—and remember to smile.
7. Nothing is black or white. What is the most practical way to get your end?
8. Quitting is leading too—leaders lead as much by what they choose not to do as what they do.

In general, it may seem logical to expect that effective leaders will be preferably recruited from among people who have relatively high levels of certain resources. The essential talents for leadership can be summarized as follows:

• **Vision:** The ability to identify common goals and provide collective goods to the members of a group or community. This may require some professional qualification or at least the capacity to recruit experts in the field.

• **Communication:** This includes verbal and nonverbal skills, especially through the media. This also requires some personal talents, although it may be helped by advisers and aides.

SOURCE 4.1   Effective Leadership

The elaboration and approval of the United States Constitution in 1787 was an outstanding example of efficient leadership.

The fundamental characteristics of leaders, which can be assessed for their success in responding to their followers' expectations and demands, are identified in similar manners by authors using different intellectual approaches, as can be noted in the following quotes.

Charisma is a certain quality of an individual personality, by virtue of which he is set apart from ordinary men and treated as endowed with supernatural, superhuman, or at least specifically exceptional powers or qualities....On the basis of them the individual concerned is treated as a leader...as long as it receives recognition and is able to satisfy the followers or disciples...[*But*] if proof and success elude the leader for long, if he appears deserted by his god or his magical or heroic powers, above all, if his leadership fails to benefit his followers, it is likely that his charismatic authority will disappear.

Max Weber, "Types of Domination" (1922)

A political entrepreneur is an individual who invests his own time or other resources to coordinate and combine other factors of production to supply collective goods."

Norman Frohlich, Joe A. Oppenheimer, and Oran R. Young,
Political Leadership and Collective Goods (1971)

Leadership over other human beings is exercised when persons with certain motives and purposes mobilize, in competition or conflict with others, institutional, political, psychological, and other resources so as to arouse, engage, and satisfy the motives of followers.

James MacGregor Burns, *Leadership* (1978)

Leaders are those who help a group create and achieve shared goals.

Joseph S. Nye, Jr., *The Powers to Lead* (2008)

- **Organizational capacity:** This includes communication at short distance and in small groups, and the management of information flows, resources, and the incentives structure of the group or institution.

As is usually remarked on in the literature on leadership, certain leaders appear particularly able to raise new issues and propose new alternatives. When they are exceptionally communicative, self-confident, and strongly motivated to attain and assert influence, people can expect that they will be more effective. These personality traits are considered to be foundations of "charismatic" or "transformational" leadership. But, as has also been noted, any leader also needs "transactional" skills and effectiveness to some degree. In general, it is a leader's power and his success in delivering public goods to his followers that can create charisma—rather than the other way around.

Since leaders cannot have the same motivations as their followers to participate in collective action, they may need to hide or at least disguise somewhat their driving purposes. If leaders demonstrate too evident an ambition and desire for power or if they act as if they are something special, they can be considered to be self-serving and could be subjected to private resentment and public disrespect, or even to derision and hostility. In order to be effective and durable, leaders must, above all, be able to adapt to changing situations and be sensitive to their followers' demands and reactions. Although leaders need to be motivated by some power ambition, they can be more accepted and respected if they show little or no desire for personal benefits from their leadership position. Think, for example, of the effective style of rhetoric in politics that has been attributed to U.S. president Barack Obama. A potent way to win over opponents is to accept that they have legitimate concerns, for that triggers an instinct to reciprocate.

Quick Quiz

- What's a political leader's opportunity cost?
- What's the opportunity costs of Barack Obama for being president of the United States?

Leaders and Followers

The role of leaders is to initiate collective action. But their success depends on whether other people follow their initiative and join the initial group. Let us focus here on the mechanisms by which leaders can achieve a following. First of all, a leader needs to listen to and understand his followers. In order to succeed at mobilizing them, leaders can supply well-selected information to persuade group members of the value of their participation and the likely success of their actions. They can also provide private goods in the form of selective incentives, such as awards or fines, social recognition or moral censure, for individual contribution to the collective effort and to dissuade potential defectors. Crucially, leaders need to be able to collect contributions, whether from themselves, the government subsidies, or the members of the group, to make the provision of collective goods viable.

THE CHAIN REACTION

In a large group, most people can be, to some degree, leaders and followers. An individual can follow a leader with strong skills and motivation and, at the same time, lead other people with reluctance to undertake collective action. Depending on the different intensity of people's commitment, there can be diehards, activists, affiliates, accomplices, sympathizers, eyewitnesses, recalcitrants, free-riders, and traitors in a group.

Let us assume, as in the previous chapter, that people decide whether to participate in collective action depending on what other people do, which can be taken as an indicator of the likelihood that the action will succeed in obtaining its aims. The crucial point is that the the amount of people participating provokes a reaction that may be different for different individuals. For each person there can be a **threshold, or minimum participation level,** necessary for him to think that his own participation is worthy, which is based on subjective evaluations of the likelihood of the group's common goal being achieved. Depending on the distribution of different thresholds among the members of a group, there can be a chain of decisions regarding participation in collective action.

Let us imagine a group of people who, having come out of a night spot, wish to cross a busy street. Assume there are no pedestrian crossings or traffic lights. If this group is small in number, those involved will hesitate; they will look around at one another, and only a cluster of the most daring may take the initiative of stepping out into the street. As they do so, others may feel that there are now enough pedestrians to discourage the drivers and ward off danger, and they, too, follow suit. Then others will follow, and in the end the crowd will win out and traffic will come to a standstill. However, if at the outset there are only one or two persons attempting to cross, it may be that they will not succeed in stopping the cars and will be forced to turn back.

Something similar happens at certain formal gatherings when there is no set rule regarding the appropriateness of applauding at the end of the presentation or speech by the guest of honor. If, after a few moments of silence, only one or two people begin to clap, then theirs may be a solitary and even ridiculous action. However, if a larger group joins in right at the beginning, it is likely that there will be a unanimous ovation.

Let us again compare participation in collective action with "voice," now in a literal sense. At any party where people get together in groups in a large room, it is easy to see that some guests feel the need to raise their voices as soon as they start to hear the chatter of the group around them. By so doing, they only raise the noise level of the room, causing other people, who had been chatting at a perfectly normal volume, to have difficulty hearing one another. They, too, will begin to raise their voices, and in the end the party will turn into an uproar. There is a chain, but along the chain each individual has a different level of tolerance to others' noise and starts shouting at a different moment.

"Leaders" are those who first try to cross the street, start applauding, or begin to raise their voice. They need to be followed closely by other people within the community or interest group. A stable organization is usually formed of people with different levels of commitment to the group, but all of them can be necessary to attain broad collective action. General participation can be achieved after reaching a **critical mass,**

You can see a graphic representation of the dynamics between leaders and followers in Figure 4.1, which is a variant of the model initially proposed by Nobel Prize–winning economist Thomas Schelling. The horizontal axis represents the number of people expected to participate in a collective action, and the vertical axis represents the number of people who do, in fact, participate. The diagonal forty-five degree dotted line represents a hypothetical situation in which the number of expected participants is always equal to the number of actual participants. The curve rises to the right, but, in general, since different people have different thresholds of participation, it can be assumed that it has an *S*-shape.

In the graph on the left, the starting point of the curve at the bottom-left corner indicates that some people always participate: the "leaders." At the upper-right corner the solid line of the curve flattens out, since not even an expected participation of 90 percent can move the recalcitrant remaining 10 percent. As an example, for an expected participation of thirty, only twenty participate, which triggers a demobilization process. In contrast, for an expected participation of sixty, eighty actually participate, which generates a participatory process. There are two points of equilibrium, implying, respectively, general demobilization and general action, as indicated by the points near the two extremes of the curve.

The graph on the right, with curve B representing the original curve, shows what can happen if the number of people always participating increases. This can produce a massive mobilization, as represented by the new curve C, which is always above the forty-five-degree line. In contrast, if a few leaders disappear, the curve starts at zero. The new curve A is always below the forty-five-degree line, which indicates that the number of people participating will always be lower than the number expected, and thus collective action will fail.

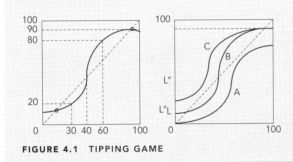

FIGURE 4.1   TIPPING GAME

which is a concept borrowed from nuclear engineering and is equivalent to the mass that **causes a chain reaction**. Here the critical mass is the number of people crossing the street, applauding, or speaking loudly at which others are induced to do the same and that triggers a process toward a general participation in collective action.

THE TIPPING GAME

In the interactions between leaders and followers there can be several equilibrium outcomes, each implying a different level of mobilization. In any collective action, there can be a small proportion of group members who always participate, even when a poor turnout is expected, whom we call "leaders." In general, the higher the number of actual participants, the higher the number of people who can think the group will succeed and who will be attracted to take part in the action.

Let us imagine that the action consists of a protest held on a regular basis in the same place, which might be a neighbors' association rally to demand better security in the city, a periodic assembly of a professional organization, or a student meeting to be held each week. For an individual to participate in collective action, his threshold, or subjective evaluation of what is a "sufficient" number of participants to move one to join in, should match the actual mass of participants. If, say, sixty people are expected to attend, many people may find this number appealing and there may be a real participation of eighty, which will make all those present happy to have taken part. There will also be those who, when they hear how successful the action was, will be sorry not to have gone along. The next time, these people will also attend, and thus a maximum number of people ready to participate on some level in the collective action will be **mobilized** to participate in the action. Once the critical mass of participants is achieved, a chain of participation gradually involving additional people will be assembled.

If, contrary to the previous example, we suppose that a turnout of only thirty is expected on the first gathering, it may be that fewer than thirty feel that this is a sufficient number and thus the real participation may be only twenty. This will cause some disappointment among some of the twenty participants, because they expected a greater turnout, and the real figure will be considered inadequate. On the following occasion, those disappointed the first time around will not go, causing attendance to drop, which will provoke further disenchantment. In the end, only a handful of people always willing to go will bother to participate. Note that this chain of **demobilization** depends on the distribution of individual thresholds, or subjective evaluations of how many people will make a difference to achieving the goal, not on people's interest in the collective good sought. A small spark can start a prairie fire, as the Russian revolutionaries said. But also a few drops of rain (or repression) can extinguish the fire, and eventually become a tempest and provoke an overflow.

Quick Quiz

• What's the critical mass?

Institutions for Leadership

What are the circumstances that can make an ordinary man a leader, as mentioned at the beginning of this chapter? Different leaders can be more or less efficient in providing public goods depending on different institutional and social contexts and not only on their individual skills.

Generally, the relationship between leaders and followers can solve the free-rider problem of collective action and make a community or interest group organized. The leaders can make arrangements guaranteeing to all members of the community or group that if all contribute a share of the costs lower than their individual benefits from using the good, the good will be provided. For instance, if all neighbors pay their share, there will be a security patrol able to prevent burglaries and damages of higher value than that share. But leaders may have different degrees of efficiency in the provision of public goods. The members of the group can receive greater amounts of a good than the scarce or nil amounts they would get as free-riders, but still smaller than could be provided with their individual contributions.

A leader can be considered **inefficient**:

• First, for their lack of appropriate skills, collecting fewer resources and providing less than the amount of public good the followers desire; and

- Second, for exploiting the followers by absorbing some extra benefits (kickbacks, for instance) and returning a lesser share of the good than corresponds to their contributions.

In either of these situations, the members of the group can engage in collective action because the benefits of contributing can be higher than those of free-riding. But obviously the degree of efficiency of the leadership in providing public goods varies.

WILLING LEADERS

Efficient leaders should emerge more consistently in institutional systems in which public leaders are well rewarded and prestigious and in social contexts in which there are scarce professional opportunities in the private sector. In brief, where being a leader is better than being a follower, relatively well qualified people can be attracted to leadership, as tends to happen in many democratic societies. However, the absolute level of quality of those people may depend on the general contextual level, which may not be so high in a society with low levels of economic and social development and little private opportunities.

Competition among numerous professionalized candidates can help to produce efficient cost-sharing arrangements among the members of the group for contributing to the provision of the public good in which they are interested. Usually, professional organizations, workers' unions, college and university departments, political parties, democratic states, and international organizations all hold periodical assemblies, conventions, and competitive elections to renew or replace incumbent leaders—in classical terms, to promote the "circulation of elites." Usually they have written or common rules to facilitate the renewal of leaders, such as limited mandates or the common advice of not presenting oneself for candidacy again after a failure in providing the expected collective goods.

RELUCTANT LEADERS

The situation is different when there are low incentives to become leader. Public leaders can be more difficult to engage if they receive little power, a bad reputation, or low wages, in exclusionary institutional systems and in societies providing robust private and corporate alternatives. In this kind of situation, some members of the group can agree to lead basically for the possible rewards of providing the public good in which all the group members, including themselves, are interested. These can be called "sacrificed" leaders or "heroes" because they can benefit from the public good, but to a lesser extent than if others had chosen to lead, due to the opportunity cost of leading with low rewards.

This situation involves a higher risk, and the most qualified people may be reluctant to engage in such leadership, while people choosing to lead may have relatively few gifts and could be motivated only because they have inferior alternatives. Relatively skilful leaders, if they ever obtain support, can be more prone to resigning or withdrawing from leadership positions if they gain evidence of the competitive advantages of being simply a regular group member, such as opportunities for professional success, the disposal of free time, or family life. If frequent temptations of the leaders to resign are not counterweighed with additional institutional incentives, the subsequent need to search for candidates can push group members to accept relatively low quality leaders, as may happen in weak organizations and new democratic regimes.

GROUP ASYMMETRIES

Some asymmetries among different groups regarding their availability of resources for collective action and their capacity to obtain collective goods, which we studied in chapter 2, may be reinforced by the role of leadership. In settings with institutional incentives for leading, competition among candidates for leadership can produce efficient cost-sharing arrangements among the members of the group to contribute to the provision of the public goods in which they are interested.

In contrast, in contexts with scarce resources and weak incentives for leading, there can be lack of candidates. In that case, leadership by some poorly qualified people or some inefficient cost-benefit arrangements for the followers may be accepted. However, in relatively deprived interest groups, candidates for the leadership can use their own resources—and previously existing organizations or social networks originally conceived for other purposes, such as churches, guilds or clubs—to create favorable conditions for more reluctant people to participate in low-cost collective actions.

The discussion about the size of the group can thus be revised. The theory of collective action suggests that large groups can have relatively big problems in organizing themselves. However, if we consider the crucial role of leadership, even for large groups just some people participating can be considered "sufficient" to induce other people to join, as explained with the model of the "critical mass." The critical mass able to generate a large mobilization may be not a proportion of potential members of the group, but an absolute number of participants. This number can be relatively more easily achieved within large groups with many potential members than in small groups.

Consider the extreme case of a guerrilla or violent insurgent movement. A large country can be more prone to suffer this kind of collective action because it contains a higher number of potential rebels than a small country. Even if those engaged in action are a small proportion of the total population, they can be a sufficient number to threaten the status quo, challenge the government, and produce some political consequences along the lines of their objectives.

Comparable analysis can be made for interest groups using peaceful means to launch their demands. Just a small proportion of people in a large community can be a multitude, which may be found sufficient for many other people to accept their initiative. If there are enough people who have the motivation and resources to initiate an action—those whom we call "leaders"—and to attract a few followers beyond other people's participation threshold, they can generate a sufficient level of collective action for the group to be able to achieve its common goals.

In fact, for an interest group to be successful it is not necessary to mobilize every single person who would benefit from a collective good. The identification of large pools of passive sympathizers, even if they are potential free-riders, does not necessarily hurt the movement. It may, on the contrary, help its organization, especially if these inactive members can be reached through social influence chains. Small groups of activists promoting new causes—such as suppression of the death penalty, environmental protection, or animal rights—if they are able to organize just some demonstrations to spread their message, they can find themselves in that situation.

Quick Quiz

• What does "circulation of elites" refer to?

Conclusion

The problems of developing sustained collective action can be solved by a small subset of individuals acting on behalf of the group's interest. If a group contains some people who can make a significant contribution to the group, and if members are connected to one another so that they can coordinate their decisions, collective action for collective goods can develop. This can be presented in form of a *proposition*:

> • **Leadership.** Collective action of communities and interest groups can develop thanks to leadership. Leaders distribute the costs of action among group members to provide public and private goods, while, in exchange, followers can give the leaders votes or support and allow them to enjoy the benefits of power, fame, income, and a political career.

In reality, many organizations and social movements originate in the actions of a relatively small number of extremely active participants, who think they can make a difference. The crucial element for a community or a group seeking their common interest can be the presence of a cluster of people with sufficient ambition, vision, communication skills, and personal character to initiate an action. They can use their own resources, and existing organizations or social networks originally conceived for other purposes, to create favorable conditions for more reluctant people to participate in low-cost collective actions. Leaders can be conceived as the minimum "critical mass" able to cause a chain reaction. ■

Summary

Collective action can develop thanks to the role of leaders, that is, people able to coordinate the members of an interest group or community, set up an organization, and collect resources to make the provision of public goods viable.

Effective leadership implies that, in addition to "horizontal" interactions between members of the group, there are "vertical" interactions between leaders and followers. Both leaders and followers can receive sufficient benefits from their relationship and accept their different roles.

Leaders can obtain benefit from the public goods they provide, and from exerting power, satisfying their vanity, and getting income and other private goods.

The basic personal talents for successful leadership, which may derive from both natural traits and learning and experience, include vision, which requires information and expertise, communication skills, and organizational capacity.

Followers can be motivated to participate in collective action by the leaders' supply of persuasive information, selective incentives, and dissuasion of potential defectors. In exchange for the provision of public goods, they can give leaders their support or their votes.

The critical mass is the minimum amount of participation necessary to make the group appear capable of achieving its common goal and induce additional people to participate.

A participation chain is the process of involving people with different participation thresholds in the group's collective action.

Institutional incentives for leading can facilitate the emergence of and careers for highly motivated leaders, while in contexts with scarce resources and weak incentives for leading, there can be more reluctant, scarce, or low quality leadership.

Key Concepts

Critical mass. Number of participants required to generate additional participation.

Efficient leadership. The provision of the amount of public goods desired by the followers, at optimum cost.

Follower. Member of a community or interest group giving the leader his support or his vote.

Leader. Provider of public and private goods to the members of a community or interest group.

Mobilization. Bringing together people and resources for action.

Opportunity cost. Benefit from alternative activities.

Participation chain. The process of involvement of people with different participation thresholds once the critical mass is achieved.

Participation threshold. The minimum participation level necessary for an individual to participate.

Questions for Review

1. Write the leadership function.
2. What are "opportunity costs?"
3. What's the "critical mass?"
4. Discuss the incentives for effective leadership and the conditions that may produce high-quality leaders.

Problems and Applications

1. Mention at least five groups in which some people initiate an action and other people follow. Do not include political parties, presidents, or governments. Try to think of actions in which you participated or witnessed closely.
2. List positive and negative incentives to be a political leader. How should the decision to become a leader be weighed against other professional and private alternatives? Do the ways in which these incentives vary depend upon the type of leadership position you are considering? Would they be different for an elected position as political representative than for leadership of a professional organization? Compare these different situations.
3. Identify the main party leaders, presidential candidates, or parliamentary group speakers in your country or community—between, say, two and ten. Do some research about their professions before they entered politics. Try to obtain official data on their public office salaries. Discuss.

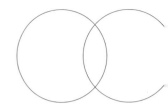

PART II

POLITY

In this part, we study the fundamental forms of a political community whose members cooperate for their common interests and are bound by collective decisions. In addition to the classic notions of state-building and nation-building, we discuss how multiple levels of government, each with different responsibilities, can be an efficient way to provide public goods. Efficient provision of public goods and democratic self-government can be made compatible through the union of small governments in a large federal structure. But for most of history, most human beings have lived in dictatorial political regimes in which political power is strongly concentrated and held by non-elected, self-appointed rulers. We analyze the conditions for having a stable democratic government and its consequences regarding the provision of public goods, development, and peace.

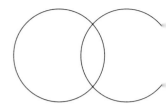

5

COMMUNITY

In This Chapter You Will

- Learn what "multilevel governance" means.
- Reflect on the concept of sovereignty and its relevance in the current world.
- Analyze the relation between state-building and nation-building.
- Consider the differences between "national state" and "multinational state."
- Distinguish between city, state, and empire.

About twenty years ago I spent some happy times at the University of Chicago, located in the neighborhood of Hyde Park (formerly an independent township), on the South Side of the city of Chicago, in Cook County, the metropolitan area covering several counties and commonly called Chicagoland, in the state of Illinois, in the Midwest of the United States, in the Western Hemisphere. At the moment of writing these words, I am in the neighborhood of Gavà-Mar, in the town of Gavà, in the county of Low Llobregat, in the metropolitan area of Barcelona, in the province of Barcelona, in the autonomous community of Catalonia, in the state of Spain, in the euro region of the Pyrenees-Mediterranean (which encompasses regions across the border between France and Spain), and within the European Union, just to mention those institutional structures with more visible consequences on people's life. I am sure you have comparable experiences at hand.

These examples suggest that the organization of political communities to make enforceable collective decisions may indeed require **multiple levels of government**. Each unit of government and administration can have specific responsibilities to deal with different policy issues and public goods and to be able to have elected and accountable rulers. While certain traditional states claim exclusive powers to make decisions regarding all the issues or "sovereignty," multiple levels of local, state, and federal government, each with different responsibilities, may be an efficient way to provide public goods.

In this chapter we pay attention to the fact that each public good can be provided efficiently at a particular territorial scale and for a specific group of human beings. Collective decisions can be enforceable if people within some territorial boundaries think or accept that they share enough with the others to abide by the outcomes. Building a political community, whether a small city, a midsize region, a large state, or a vast empire, can create the conditions for the identification of different public goods and their consumers or beneficiaries. ■

Multilevel Governance

The efficient provision of public goods may require diverse territorial scales. On one extreme, certain public goods can be considered **global**, able to satisfy very large common interests and benefit many people, and thus the larger the scale at which they can be provided, the better. For example, the protection of the atmosphere, the seas, and oceans; the organization of security; the prosecution of financial crimes, arms trade, and terrorism; and access to scientific and artistic works, among other amenities, can be considered global goods requiring universal maintenance. Trade agreements and common currencies would be better the larger the scale at which they were enforced. Broad transport routes and communication networks may be well provided, perhaps, at a **continental** level.

In contrast, provisions such as roads and highways, the management of the waters of a river basin, or the administration of civil law and justice, seem to require **midsize** territorial ranges. Finally, services such as garbage removal and parks, schools and hospitals, libraries and museums, can usually be well supplied at the **local** level, while for many services for personal assistance, the smaller the scale, the better they can be provided.

In an ideal world, each public good could be provided by a specific governmental and administrative unit encompassing the territory of its efficient scale and be financed with taxes and other resources collected from the citizens who would benefit from its provision. With differentiated territorial scales for each public good, benefits and costs would be clearly identified and negative externalities would be reduced to minimum levels. This would imply a complete development of what is usually called "fiscal federalism."

PROVISION AND PARTICIPATION COSTS

The proliferation of governmental jurisdictions may make the election and control of rulers a too costly task. Too many separate offices on different issues, each with their candidacies, campaigns, deliveries, and past records to account for, may make the collection of information and the action of participation too costly for many potential voters. A plural but moderate number of institutional levels can strike the right balance. Some offices can be elected by the citizens' vote, while others can be indirectly appointed by elected representatives. A citizen can be involved in a set including, for instance, an urban district; a city, town, or borough; a county or a metropolitan area; a region (also called a province, nation, or state); a state (that is, a unit represented in

---

BOX 5.1   **THE SUBSIDIARITY CRITERION**

Governance at multiple levels requires decisions regarding the allocation of powers to the several institutional bodies involved. A democratic criterion may favor the "small" or "lower" levels of government.

"The powers not delegated to the United States by the Constitution, nor prohibited by it to the States, are reserved to the States respectively, or to the people."

United States Constitution, Amendment X (1791)

"Under the principle of subsidiarity, in areas which do not fall within its exclusive competence, the European Union shall act only if and in so far as the objectives of the proposed action cannot be sufficiently achieved by the member states, either at central level or at regional and local level, but can rather, by reason of the scale or effects of the proposed action, be better achieved at Union level."

Treaty of Maastricht on European Union, Article 5.3 (1992)

---

the United Nations); a trans-frontier region or a league of local or regional governments; and a continental organization or institutionalized treaty, as illustrated at the beginning of this chapter.

In fact, each of these or similar institutional bodies may deal with several issues at the same time, but they can also create internal departments or agencies specialized in each specific issue, as an ideally efficient provision of public goods and services would require. With a limited number of separate governments (between three and eight), a citizen can reasonably contribute to and take part in a diversity of collective affairs. Note that this kind of structure does not necessarily imply only a series of concentric levels, such as city, region, and state. It can also include transversal arrangements, such as metropolitan areas and trans-frontier regions, thus with diverse forms of overlapping over the same population groups. Multiple levels of governance go together with a polycentric world.

Quick Quiz

• What is the aim of having multiple levels of government?

Sovereignty

Living in a small community together with people sharing similar characteristics and interests is of course the oldest form of human conviviality. The first human beings lived in autonomous bands, tribes, and villages made up of families and clans. Some villages began to aggregate into larger units, perhaps around 5000 BC. But still in 1500 BC, it is estimated that there were about six hundred thousand autonomous communities on earth, in general not exceeding a few dozen or one hundred people each.

In contrast to other animals, human beings can form a political community also through the union of different tribes and villages, that is, by placing people without direct blood ties and living within a territory under a common authority able to provide some public goods. For the provision of primary public goods such as the

CASE 5.1   LOCAL SELF-GOVERNMENT IN RENAISSANCE ITALY

Late medieval and Renaissance Florence and Venice, and many other cities in the north of the Italian peninsula, such as Genoa, Pavia, Pisa, and Siena, were outstanding examples of the capacity of democratic self-government of a small community. From the mid-thirteenth century onward, several dozen northern Italian cities elected their rulers with broad popular participation. The assembly of all the citizens, or "harangue," was an open, inclusive, and popular event, in which participants were able to make decisions on the basis of broad social consensus. It was also an occasion of public spectacle, processions, and festivities. Regular elections to numerous offices were held with the participation of most adult men.

However, as new economic interests developed and social complexity increased, the pattern of the relatively peaceful fusion of old and new elements in society weakened. New institutional rules and procedures were designed with the aim of promoting the rotation of rulers, preventing the concentration of power into a single group, and accommodating varied social demands. These included lots to select public officers, several stages of indirect election of candidates, and shorts terms of only six months or a year for officeholders.

However, the association between popular participation in increasingly complex communities and rising instability was inescapable. Elections, factions, or parties, and institutional stability became a difficult combination. Lacking appropriate rules for consensus-making, factionalism, family feuds, and class conflicts weakened democratic self-government. Northern Italian self-governed cities, deprived from protection by the fading Empire, entered into frequent conflicts with their more powerful neighbors—the duchy of Milan, the Papacy, and the kingdom of Naples—and among themselves. In most cases, the republican form of government was eventually replaced with authoritarian, aristocratic rule.

maintenance of internal order and defense from other communities, the community needs leaders able to collect resources, recruit men for work and war, and decree and enforce collective norms and laws. The most outstanding individuals among the winners in battle tended to be appointed for offices of authority. In some communities, military, administrative and political power went together with religious authority. Then, with the collected resources and the mobilized personnel, the authority could also build fortresses, roads, irrigation, palaces, and temples. This early kind of political community was the outcome of a cultural process that developed in different places across the planet at different times.

The primitive territorial scope of human relations was strongly constrained by the early concentration of population, the availability of natural resources, and natural barriers such as mountains, seas, and deserts, which thwarted the alternative of leaving. Through fights to obtain scarce resources, especially agricultural land and energy sources, villages were enlarged into chiefdoms and counties, usually encompassing a well-defined valley. At a later stage, multi-valley kingdoms were formed by military conquest. At a more complex juncture, vast and complex empires were built. The most ancient empires were formed around the Nile, especially in Egypt, as of 3000 BC; in Asia, with China around 2000 BC and later India and Persia; and Mesopotamia in the Middle East. More recently, the Roman Empire was built in Europe about eight centuries before our era. In America, there existed mainly the Aztecan and Incan empires, within the second millennium of our era.

SOURCE 5.1   **Small is Democratic**

The association between the small size of a community and its capability to develop self-government by soft or democratic means has been observed for a very long time.

What, I said, will be the best limit for our rulers to fix when they are considering the size of the community and the amount of territory which they are to include, and beyond which they will not go? What limit would you propose? I would allow the community to increase so far as is consistent with unity; that, I think, is the proper limit.

Plato, *Republic* (c360 BC)

A very populous city can rarely, if ever, be well governed; since all cities which have a reputation for good government have a limit of population…If the citizens of a community are to judge and to distribute offices according to merit, then they must know each other's characters; where they do not possess this knowledge, both the election to offices and the decision of lawsuits will go wrong. When the population is very large they are manifestly settled at haphazard, which clearly ought not to be.

Aristotle, *The Politics* (c325 BC)

In a small republic, the public good is more strongly felt, better known, and closer to each citizen.

Montesquieu, *The Spirit of Laws* (1748)

The larger the country, the less the liberty…Generally, democratic government suits small countries, aristocratic government those of middle size, and monarchy great ones…How many conditions that are difficult to unite does such a [*democratic*] government presuppose! First, a very small community, where the people can readily be got together and where each citizen can with ease know all the rest…

Jean-Jacques Rousseau, *Social Contract* (1762)

The sizes of national states or countries are due to trade-offs between the benefits of size [*or economy of scale*] and the costs of heterogeneity of preferences over public goods and policies provided by the government…which in the modern world tend to be connected to linguistic, ethnic, and cultural differences…As the world economy becomes more integrated, the trade-off "tilts" in favor of small size, as in a world of free trade even small countries can prosper.

Alberto Alesina and Enrico Spolaore, *The Size of Nations* (2003)

As small communities regularly fought one another, the imperial structure was a kind of umbrella for imposing order. But in Europe, there was a sustained, huge rivalry between the Emperor of the Holy Roman Empire and the Pope of Rome and head of the Christian Church. While the pope sought to invest the emperor with divine-right legitimacy, the emperor acted as arbiter in the election of the pope, a frequently controversial episode and a source of conflicts and schisms. After the twelfth century, the emperor finally renounced the privilege to appoint or confirm the pope, but the kings of the great powers continued vetoing certain candidates in the conclave until the early twentieth century. On his side, the pope maintained jurisdictional claims over Catholic countries even until modern times.

The notion of **sovereignty** was formally adopted in Europe in an attempt to put an end to jurisdictional disputes and establish **a single source of legitimacy holding the monopoly of organized violence**. The French jurist Jean Bodin forged the most influential doctrine on this topic in the late sixteenth century. Sovereignty was conceived as an **absolute, perpetual, inalienable, and indivisible** power, the supreme source of authority within a well-defined territory.

Soon thereafter, the so-called Peace of Westphalia, signed in 1648, ended both the Thirty Years' War fought by most European powers in German territory and the Eighty Years' War between Spain and the Netherlands. The Holy Roman and German Empire—which still contained Austria, together with about three hundred autonomous territories in German land, including republics and free cities, independent duchies and lordships, abbeys and bishoprics—was almost nullified. The new sovereign states attempted to put cities, principalities, courts, monasteries, cathedrals, and universities under their exclusive jurisdiction. In the new Westphalian order, the territory of the larger states was broadened, and new borders were established, especially for France, Prussia, and Sweden. Also, the Dutch Republic and Switzerland were formally recognized as independent units. The treaties of Westphalia consecrated the notion of territorial sovereignty for each state, which implied a doctrine of both internal monopoly of power and noninterference in the affairs of other states.

STATE-BUILDING AND NATION-BUILDING

The earliest political units in Europe deserving to be called states were England, France, Spain, and Sweden, which were formed on territories located on the periphery of the fading Holy Roman and German Empire. Out of the reach of imperial control, each of the states mentioned could organize a new, highly centralized command over its territory from a new privileged capital city—London, Paris, Madrid, Stockholm. The modern states, which were initially organized as absolutist monarchies, tried to absorb vast numbers of traditional autonomous territories under a single centralized power, whether by military conquest, dynastic combinations, or mutual agreement. New states were also formed later, in late nineteenth century, in the core territory of the Holy Roman and German Empire —that is, Italy and Germany—although in a more decentralized way, based on the aggregation of networks of middle-size cities and regions.

Building an effective state requires an extremely costly initial accumulation of resources into the hands of the public authority. The larger European states achieved some efficiency through long, violent, and cruel processes of internal and external warmongering and concentration of power at the expense of many of their subjects. Within its territory, the sovereign state organizes and holds the monopoly of violence, with the aim of providing the basic public goods of **defense and security**, which implies the internal policing, surveillance, and protection of citizens. States obtained such a monopoly by outlawing private armies and the public display or even possession of weapons of self-defense by private citizens. This subsequently permitted the state to use armed agents to confront unarmed civilians. The concentration of military power advanced together with an increase in the administrative, technical, and financial resources of the states.

Each state also tried to excel in providing internal standardization of weights and measures, a common currency within its territory, and civil law, by these means helping to consolidate relatively **large markets**. Thanks to this effort, the territorial scope of certain private activities and exchanges was enlarged, which enabled many economies to take off. Economic prosperity fostered and reinforced a sense of statewide community and the allegiance of different people to common institutions, customs, and rules.

The states asserted themselves against not only the declining empire, but the universal claims of the Christian church. The right of each king was instituted to determine the religion of his subjects. The religion of the ruler would become the religion of the people under the motto "Whose rule, his religion" (*Cuius regio, eius religio*, in Latin). Then modern states sought to absorb social and personal services traditionally administered by the Church, starting with the education of children.

In contrast to the typical internal variety of traditional empires, the model of national state aimed for all public goods to be provided within the same territory and homogeneously for the whole population. Its slogan could have been "one size fits all"—with, as in the case of Procrustus's bed, those parts not fitting being amputated. Typically, each state attempted to create a **"nation," that is, a culturally unified community regarding religion, language, and a sense of common interest,** by means of repression and coercion, new symbols, forced military service, and compulsory schooling. Certain newly peripheral regions, given the increasing costs of secession, acquiesced to integration, but in exchange, they developed innovative demands for participation and power sharing within the state, thus resisting the homogenization design.

The establishment of territorial borders of a state is an essential element of it sovereignty.

In a model **national state** there a majority, homogeneous group initially faces a number of small, weak, or internally heterogeneous groups that are in time annihilated by and assimilated into the patterns of the largest group. Then, the large centralized state is viable and may be relatively efficient for a while. The most prominent case of this path was, of course, France. Great Britain was also very successful, although it attained lower degrees of internal homogeneity; actually most of Ireland seceded, and England, Scotland, and Wales are recognized as different nations.

In spite of these and further numerous attempts, which are reviewed later in this chapter, almost nowhere is there a complete fit between the "state" and the "nation." A significant number of **large states are "multinational."** In these cases the majority or largest group may not be strongly homogeneous, while a second or further group is sufficiently large and homogeneous to try to rule, or at least influence, the ruling of the state. Some internal rivalry may develop, which may lead to power sharing or decentralization. Cases include, for instance, heavily polarized Belgium, between Flemish and Walloons; Canada, where an English-speaking majority, unevenly distributed across the territory, coexists with a vast French-speaking minority; Spain, where there is a blurred, inconclusive Castilian predominance across several differentiated regions; Switzerland, with a majority of German speakers coexisting with robust linguistic minorities; and the predominantly black but multiracial South Africa. We will consider these and other cases in the next chapter.

STATE WAR-MAKING

Internal protection of domestic assets by each state has come hand in hand with external rivalry with other states to accumulate resources and potential markets. To this end, the largest modern states tended to organize heavy military apparatuses and fight numerous lethal wars. The costs of fighting, conquering territories, defending oneself, and making war dramatically increased after the invention of gunpowder in the mid-sixteenth century. From that moment onward, engaging in war required a standing army made up of well-trained troops. Permanent, volunteer and professional armies gave way to state-owned, centralized military organizations. The spreading of railways permitted the introduction of the compulsory military service for adult men, a formula that had been adopted by several countries by the late nineteenth century.

There were successive attempts to build a system of collective security based on the so-called "balance of power" among territorially bounded, heavily armed states with mutually exclusive sovereignties. However, these states entered into almost permanent conflict and increasingly frequent interstate wars. Specifically, during the eighteenth century there were 68 wars (counting only those having produced at least one thousand deaths in battle per year) that killed in total about 4 million people. During the nineteenth century, the number of major wars rose to 205, producing 8 million deaths. The twentieth century established itself as the most bellicose in human history. From 1900 to 1989, there were some 237 civil and interstate wars, with 115 million deaths in battle (to which a similar number of civilian deaths should be added). These include: the First and the Second World Wars, fought mainly among European states; the Sino-Japanese War; and a number of local wars promoted by the Cold War between the United States and the Soviet Union or China, including the Korean and Vietnam wars.

In contrast, current relative levels of armed personnel and military expenditure per total population and total public expenditure are the lowest they've been for several centuries. Military strength is heavily concentrated in the United States, followed by Britain, France, and China. Most states of the world do not even possess effective military equipment. In many cases, they are not even able to provide actual control of their borders or real defense of their "sovereign" territory and population. This general demilitarization corresponds to a situation in which the world scene is no longer one of sovereign states trying to maintain some balance of military power. Due to technological developments in transport, communications, and weaponry, state or national defense is nowadays strongly linked to international security. The most prominent security tasks include the prosecution and prevention of terrorism and the formation of international peacemaking and peacekeeping missions. Due to this, traditional patriotic, state-owned, rival armies have become obsolete. In most democratic countries, compulsory military service has been abolished; in many places, the professional soldier is also a less admired figure than in the past.

STATE FAILURE

The larger nation-states in Western Europe could survive as independent polities in the international arena only thanks to having colonial empires. When colonial empires disappeared, the West European states created a new "empire" among themselves, the European Union, able to provide new large common markets and mutual security.

Outside Europe, the Westphalian model of the sovereign state has been largely unsuccessful. Most of Asia, North America, and Russia have been unacquainted with the Westphalian model of sovereign states. In particular, the United States was created from the beginning as a "compound republic" (rather than as a national state) formed by previously existing units retaining their constituent powers. Instead of concentrating power around a single center, as in European-style states, the American empire was organized as a federation, a "checks and balances" regime based on division of power, negotiation, and jurisprudence, as we will study in chapter 6. In Asia, a few very large, overpopulated empires have also escaped from the project of "statization": China, India, Indonesia, and Japan have maintained certain traditional imperial characteristics of internal complexity, not adopting the centralizing and homogenizing features of modern European states just mentioned.

Attempts to replicate the typical European "state" form of government have been made in Hispanic America, Africa, and the Middle East as a consequence of the colonial expansion of European states and the further independence of their colonies. Several accounts of failed states in the current world are continually being revised by some international organizations. These include between thirty and fifty "collapsed or failing states," and others in permanent internal conflict. They are mostly located in the Andean region, Central America, and the Caribbean, Central and West Africa, and the Middle East. In the countries at the bottom of the scale of statehood, the central rulers have no control over most of the state's territory; they are very ineffective at collecting taxes; they do not provide even the most basic goods and services (not even coinage, for instance); and there is persistent violence, widespread crime, ethnic civil wars, frequent interstate border conflicts, and massive emigration.

Quick Quiz

• Define "sovereignty."

City, State, Empire

The numerous and highly diverse forms of political communities that have existed in the history of humankind or that currently exist can be grouped into three very general categories: cities, states, and empires. Cities and other small political units with high degrees of autonomy or independence—called principalities, republics, or just "nations"—have always been a basic form of collective organization in human history. Sovereign states have succeeded mainly in Europe, within a historical period that began about three hundred years ago, as we reviewed in the previous section. Finally, there have always been large—in fact, as new transport and communication technologies have developed, increasingly large—empires. We define these basic concepts—city, state, and empire—in the following paragraphs.

CITY

There is a very old tradition of local self-government in many places in Europe, Asia, and the Americas. In ancient, medieval and early modern times, there was an array of small units where many collective decisions were made by the vote of a broad electorate, including villages, communes, municipalities, republics, provinces, counties, towns, boroughs, colonies, or other communities of small size.

The better known cases of self-governing cities include a number of cases in Mesopotamia; the poleis of Greece; the German territories; the Swiss cities, rural villages, and cantons; and a number of medieval Italian communes that have existed since the late Middle Ages. In Europe, other well-governed small or middle-size kingdoms and principalities existed in Bohemia, Brittany, Catalonia, Scotland, and Sicily, among other places. On the basis of these and many other similar experiences, medieval assemblies summoned by the kings were formed with representatives not only of diverse social categories but also of well-defined small territories. Even the largest kingdoms, such as England and France, somehow relied upon county and borough elections, town assemblies, and provincial estates.

The typical medieval city, commune, canton, county, rural town, or village was formed from private associations of households organized to provide public goods such as the maintenance of a food supply, the administration of justice, and military defense. Many old cultural communities and self-governing units were absorbed by the new, large states.

However, in recent developments, classical building of large sovereign states implying the unification of varied territories under a single source of power has been mostly replaced with a proliferation of small countries. Since the late nineteenth century, the number of independent countries in the world has almost quadrupled. Specifically, while there were only fifty independent countries in the world in 1870, and about the same number in 1900, there are almost two hundred members of the United Nations in the early twenty-first century.

With the modern proliferation of countries, the average country size decreases. Among the current members of the United Nations are forty-one microstates with fewer than one million inhabitants, and seventy mini-states with a population of between one and ten million inhabitants (such as Botswana, Estonia, Ireland, or Uruguay). The median country size nowadays is about seven million inhabitants.

In addition, there are more than 500 non-state political units with governments and assemblies with legislative powers located within a couple dozen large states or federations. There are also about 20 "territories" that were formally linked, but are physically noncontiguous, to some large state, and that are, in fact, quite independent; and about 15 other territories that have de facto seceded from recognized states. About 150 of these small, non-state units are in Europe (with outstanding cases including the Basque country, Bavaria, Catalonia, Corsica, Flanders, Kosovo, Lombardy, and Scotland), nearly 200 in the Americas (such as Greenland, Puerto Rico, and Quebec), about 150 in Asia (including Aceh, Hong Kong, Kashmir, Kurdistan, Palestine, and Taiwan), and about 40 in Africa (such as Western Sahara).

Most of these small political units share the following defining characteristics:

- **Small size** in terms of both territory and population;
- **High degrees of internal harmony,** as defined by the economic and ethnic characteristics of their members; and
- **Simple and soft forms of government** based on the ease with which they form a social majority supporting collective, enforceable decisions.

STATE

The "state" is a form of government that has achieved wide appeal in modern history. As mentioned, the current world is officially organized into almost two hundred states. But only a relatively limited number of these political units can be considered to be successful states in the strict sense of the word.

The state as a form of government, as we sketched out in the previous section, "Sovereignty," when analyzing its origins, can be defined by the following characteristics:

- **Large or medium size** in terms of both territory and population.
- **Fixed territory and formal borders**. The clear establishment and foreign recognition of the territorial limits of a state are intended as protection from external attack, invasion, immigrants, and imports.
- **Sovereignty**. The state has supreme authority over a territory and population. It recognizes no other source of jurisdiction but itself. The state's power to take ultimate decisions is recognized by other sovereign states.
- **Monopoly and homogenization**. The state has reserved functions with exclusive jurisdiction within its territory. Whether dictatorial or democratic, it is organized with an internal hierarchy of powers. In order to facilitate the exercise of its functions and consummate its exclusiveness, it tends to establish a uniform administration over the territory, and to promote the homogenization of important social and cultural characteristics of its subjects or citizens.

Since the period of the foundation of states in Europe, four waves of "statization" of the world can be distinguished, each of them punctuated by major wars and the dissolution of large empires. At the time of the congress of the greater powers in Vienna in 1815, after the Napoleonic wars, there were barely a dozen states in Europe, together with numerous traditional small political units. The first wave of state formation started with the dissolution of the Spanish Empire in the Americas. The four large

Spanish colonial viceroyalties had, by 1840, become fifteen republics of disparate size and composition. The second wave of state formation arose during the First World War and with the fall of the Austro-Hungarian, Ottoman, and Russian empires. The so-called "principle of nationalities," which sought the formation of ethnically homogeneous units, led to the creation of ten new states in Europe by 1920.

The third wave of state formation occurred after the Second World War out of the dismantling of the European colonial empires, especially the British and the French (but also the Belgian, Dutch, German, Italian, Portuguese, and Spanish) in Southeast Asia, Africa, and the Middle East. No fewer than forty new independent states were created between 1945 and 1960, and about thirty more by 1975. The number of states in the world thus more than doubled within a period of thirty years. The fourth wave of state development was a consequence of the end of the Cold War, which brought about the Soviet disunion of the Russian Empire, the disintegration of the multiethnic Yugoslavia, and the split of Czechoslovakia. After 1991, within a couple of years, twenty new independent republics were created in Central and Eastern Europe and Central Asia.

Nowadays, the better-established large "states" are the few units that have been accepted as members of the Organisation for Economic Co-operation and Development, which, according to its own criteria, must share a commitment to democratic government, good governance, and a market economy. In total, they are thirty states, of which twenty-three are in Europe, three in North America, two in Asia, and two in Oceania.

EMPIRE

The notion of "empire" can account for more than two dozen cases of ancient, medieval, modern, and current experiences of human government. They include the ancient Assyrian, Chinese, and Persian empires; the classical Roman and Byzantine empires; the Arabian empire of the Caliphate; the Ottoman Empire; the Indian empires; the colonial empires of Spain, Britain, and France; modern Russia; the historical development of the United States of America; and, in some sense, the ongoing process in the European Union. Most of the population in the current world lives in vast units of such "imperial" dimensions, including the United States, the European Union, Russia, China, India, and Japan.

Over time, the size of the empires tends to increase, thanks to technological advances in transport and communications. Roads, canals, harbors, railways, and highways have always formed the skeleton of empires. But things changed dramatically in the nineteenth century with the invention of the telegraph, later followed by the telephone and the Internet, which created the age of instant communication. The art of government at a distance has multiplied the size of viable empires.

Another historical trend is toward an increasing number of simultaneous empires, so that the imperial form of government includes increasingly higher proportions of the world's population. Virtually none of the territories of the existing states in the world has been alien to or outside some large modern empire.

An empire can be defined as a political unit with the following characteristics:

- **Very large size**, in terms of both territory and population.

SOURCE 5.2   National and Multinational States

> The British multinational state was built up through a process of step-by-step incorporation of culturally distinctive territories on the Atlantic periphery...The Celtic west and north peripheries were gradually brought under the English crown but were never fully integrated into the political system...The forces of resistance grew in intensity in the nineteenth century and reached a first peak with the Irish uprising and the civil war over the boundary dividing the Republic and the six counties of the North. The next wave of nationalism was triggered by the decline of the economic power of the English centre and the dismantling of the overseas empire...
>
> "France was the first country self-consciously to call itself an état-nation, a culturally unified, centrally controlled territory...The revolutionary policy of ideological equalisation served first to centralise decisions further: by preaching equality the Jacobins reduced the people of the peripheries to subjects or at least second-class citizens...There was definitely a phase of cultural colonialism in France, assisted by the unification of the labour market, with the more backward peripheries treated not very differently from the overseas colonies acquired during the nineteenth century...
>
> "Spain had been built up through a slow process of military-administrative unification, but this process at the elite level had not produced a corresponding cultural integration at the mass level...Spain has to this day remained a state and not a nation: the Catalan and the Basque peripheries for centuries refused to identify with the power centre in Castile and have on several occasions been on the brink of secession.
>
> Stein Rokkan, *State Formation, Nation-Building, and Mass Politics in Europe*
> (ed. by Peter Flora, 1999)

- **Absence of fixed or permanent boundaries**. Empires tend to expand across the territory, up to the point of conflict with other empires, and when in decline, they may also contract. In general, "territory" is not considered a strong defining element of an empire.

- **A compound of diverse groups and territorial units.** In ancient and medieval times, an empire could be comprised of cities, republics, counties, principalities, bishoprics, and a variety of other forms of political organization. Today, multiethnic federations can be arranged with less heterogeneous institutional regimes. But they may develop their own rules and be linked to the center by diverse institutional formulas.

- **A set of multilevel, often overlapping jurisdictions.** Within an empire, no authority typically rules with exclusive powers on all issues. Rather, the central government may rule indirectly through local governments; the latter develop self-government on important issues; and division of powers is widespread.

These definitional characteristics of the "imperial" form of government—very large size, no fixed boundaries, territorial diversity and multilevel jurisdictions—contrast

BOX 5.2 **COUNTRY-BUILDING, 1870–2009**

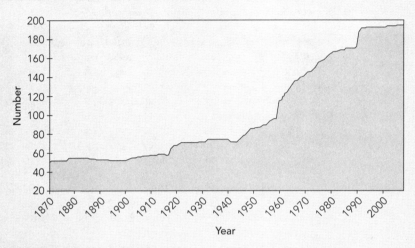

FIGURE II.2   NUMBER OF COUNTRIES

In recent worldwide developments, the Westphalian model of building large sovereign states initiated in the seventeenth century has been replaced by a proliferation of small countries. The unification of various territories under a single source of power was enforced most notoriously in France, the United Kingdom, Spain, and Sweden, followed later by Germany and Italy. Since then, the number of countries in the world has almost quadrupled. While there were only 50 independent countries in the world in 1870 and about the same number in 1900, there are 192 members of the United Nations in 2009. With the proliferation of countries, average country size decreases. Nowadays, the median country size is about 7 million inhabitants.

Source: Data from Josep M. Colomer, *Great Empires, Small Nations* (London: Routledge, 2007).

with the basic characteristics of the "city" and 'state' forms of government presented in the previous paragraphs.

Some soft, lasting empires have emerged as confederations of previously existing, largely respected political units on which a new central power was superposed. If stable borders are established and an institutional design is consolidated, an empire can evolve into a democratic federation, as was the case, most prominently, of the United States.

A very large empire implies that no exclusionary borders exist within its territory and, therefore, the occasions for inter-territorial conflicts are lower than in a setting of numerous sovereign, mutually hostile states. The empire is an umbrella for the territories included, which may prevent their mutual belligerency. Certainly, external imperial borders tend to be conflictive, especially if they border other empires. But a world organized into a few empires implies a shorter total length of borders and, therefore, fewer lines of potential conflict than one organized into many sovereign states.

Quick Quiz

• What are the differences between "state" and "empire?"

Conclusion

In this chapter we have discussed the importance of size for building a viable political community. Different public goods can be provided at different scales of efficiency, which can be associated with multiple levels of governmental structures. Cities, states, and empires are the basic categories of political communities that permit classifying all cases in history and in the current world.

On this subject, at least the following *propositions* can be stated:

• **Size and democracy.** Small communities, which tend to be relatively harmonious in economic and ethnic terms, are comparatively advantageous for soft, democratic forms of government, while large-scale units can be efficient for the provision of certain public goods. In the current world, small independent countries and self-governed communities proliferate, thus making the average country size decrease.

• **Multilevel governance.** Multiple levels of government, including local, state, and global, are necessary for an efficient provision of public goods at diverse territorial scales.

We follow up this subject in the next chapter. ■

Summary

An efficient provision of public goods can require multiple territorial scales, from global to local, and many intermediate sizes.

A state is characterized by having a fixed territory and formal borders, making a claim for sovereignty, and making an attempt at monopoly and homogenization. Modern sovereign states in Europe have provided internal security and favored the consolidation of large markets.

A large state usually attempts to create a culturally unified "nation." However, nowadays many states are "multinational."

An empire can be defined by its very large size, the absence of fixed or permanent boundaries, and a compound of diverse groups and territorial units having a set of multilevel, often overlapping jurisdictions.

Stabilizing the territorial boundaries of an empire and its internal institutions may imply its transformation into a democratic federation.

Key Concepts

Community. A set of people accepting to make enforceable collective decisions on issues of common interest.

Empire. A vast compound of diverse territorial units with a set of multilevel jurisdictions.

Multilevel governance. The covering of different, overlapping territories by a set of institutions to provide different collective goods.

Multinational state. A state in which power is shared by people of multiple religions, races, or languages.

Nation. A culturally unified, relatively harmonious community.

National state. A culturally unified community within a sovereign state.

Sovereignty. A single source of legitimacy holding the monopoly of organized violence.

State. A sovereign power over the population within a fixed territory with clear borders.

Questions for Review

1. What's the aim of having multiple levels of government?
2. Define "sovereignty."
3. What are the differences between "nation," "state," and "empire?"
4. Define a "national state" and a "multinational state."

Problems and Applications

1. List and count the different levels of government with jurisdiction over your place of residence (municipal, state, etc.). Mark those supported by a direct popular election and those indirectly elected or appointed by other bodies. Comment.
2. Which of the institutional structures just identified:
   a. Has legal powers on education?
   b. On the police?
   c. On railways?
3. Search for a list and number of member states of the United Nations Organization when it was founded in 1945, and the number now. Comment.
4. Is your country a member of a regular international military alliance? What other members are in it?

Data sources

Correlates of War project: www.correlatesofwar.org
United Nations: www.un.org

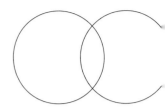

FEDERATION

In This Chapter You Will

- Ponder the benefits and costs of small and large countries.
- Analyze how ethnic variety may either help or hinder political stability.
- Consider the advantages of having many units in a federation.
- Learn how political decentralization can be measured.
- Study the essential institutional elements of federalism.

The long and hazardous process of building the United States of America during the late eighteenth and nineteenth centuries has found some recent replication in the still-uncertain process of building the European Union since the mid-twentieth century. Building the United States involved a gradual expansion from the thirteen initial members to the present fifty, which provoked territorial tensions and a lethal civil war between formerly independent states. Only the establishment of neat external borders for the American union, which are not fixed in the Constitution, permitted the achievement of internal institutional stability and the consolidation of federal formulas at the beginning of the twentieth century. Analogous to the American experience, the construction of the European Union has implied a gradual enlargement of its territory. During several decades after the lethal Second World War, which was also a kind of civil war between European states, the European Union has expanded from its initial six members to the current twenty-seven. But there are still a number of additional and in some cases controversial candidates, including in the Balkans, some former republics of the Soviet Union, and Turkey.

The union of small governments in a large federal structure, such as that of the United States and to some extent the European Union still in process, can make community's self-government and the provision of large-scale public goods compatible.

Federalism is just the technique to achieve, simultaneously, the advantages of small-scale democratic government and broad-scale governmental services. This chapter is divided into two parts. First, we analyze the benefits, costs, and opportunities of governments of different sizes. Second, we discuss the essential elements of federalism. ■

The Size of the Community

Communities of different sizes can be viable if they attain a positive balance between benefits and costs. On the one hand, small size may favor collective decision making close to citizens' preferences, thanks to relatively high degrees of internal harmony. On the other hand, small communities can be deprived of large-scale markets and public goods. Likewise, a large and varied country may find difficulties making decisions supported by a broad majority of its citizens. However, large size can be advantageous for the provision of public services on a large scale. Let us address these two sides of the question in turn.

DEMOCRATIC BENEFITS

The relevance of the size of the community for democratic government is both procedural and substantive. This means, first of all, that size matters for the process of making collective decisions. In general, small groups have relatively favorable conditions for collective action, self-organization, and the promotion of the common interests of their members, as we discussed in chapter 2.

Specifically, small political communities may work better at each of the three stages of the decision-making process that forms the democratic procedure: **deliberation, aggregation,** and **enforcement.** First, in a small community, citizens have more opportunities to gain knowledge on collective issues by direct observation and experience. Thanks to territorial proximity, they can deal more directly with political leaders, and the latter can easily gain information about citizens' demands and expectations. At the same time, it is likely that members of a small community will have relatively harmonious interests, shared values, and a common culture, which will induce consensual preferences and shared criteria of choice. This may make them able to identify priority public goods with relative ease and make generally acceptable collective decisions. Finally, small communities are more likely to generate loyalty. People will tend to comply with collective rules and decisions, while leaders may be more responsive regarding their own decisions and activities.

We already know the other side of the question, that is, that within a large and heterogeneous community, collective action for the common interests of its members may be blurred and highly unequal for different individuals and groups, as we also studied in chapter 2. Specifically, in a large country, people may receive more deficient information on the set of policy issues submitted to collective decision making and feel more distant from government than in a small community. Since the costs of aggregating citizens' preferences and making compelling and enforceable collective decisions tend to increase with the size of the political unit and the heterogeneity of the population, aggregating citizens' disparate preferences by fair procedures is more costly in large communities.

TABLE 6.1   Separated Winners

With separate elections in each of the three communities, A, B, and C, the winners are supported by a total of 180 voters; while in a unitary election a winning majority made of only 160 voters emerges.

		PARTIES	
		X	Y
Communities	A	_60_	40
	B	_60_	40
	C	40	_60_
Outcome	Unitary:	_160_ > 140	
	Separate:	_180_ (60 + 60 + 60)	

Note: The winners in separate elections are set in italics.

Regarding substantive outcomes, different sizes of the community may imply that different numbers of people are identified with collective decisions. Small political units enable different groups of people, each with relatively consistent preferences, to obtain somewhat satisfactory decisions. In contrast, within a large political unit where different interests, values, and opinions are likely to exist, a collective decision made on a set of different policy issues in bloc is likely to produce a high number of losers. Specifically, within a large, heterogeneous, but unitary state, local majorities may become global minorities and see their preferences excluded from binding collective decisions. The total number of individuals whose preferences fit collective decisions in a set of many small units is higher than in a single large unit.

To see this, consider the example presented in Table 6.1. We take the very simple case of three small communities—let us call them A, B, and C—in which only two groups (whether political parties, social classes, or ethnic categories) compete; call them X and Y. Each community has a majority of 60 to 40 in favor of one of the groups, but the winning group is not the same in all the communities; there is some diversity. As can be easily seen, if each community makes its own decisions, the total number of people voting for the winning group is 180 (as there are three majorities of 60). In contrast, if the three small communities are included into a single large unit making enforceable decisions for all its members, a group wins with the support of only 160 voters. The number of people whose preferences correspond to the collective outcome is lower with a unitary structure. Then not only are the minorities in communities A and B defeated, but also the majority of people in community C becomes a global minority and is excluded from the winning group.

SIZE AND DEMOCRACY

There is a positive correlation between the proliferation of small-size countries and the diffusion of democracy in recent periods. Specifically, at the beginning of the twenty-first century, there is democracy in almost all recognized micro-countries with fewer than three hundred thousand inhabitants, in more than two thirds of those with fewer than one million inhabitants (including the former group), and in more than one half of all small countries with fewer than ten million inhabitants (including the two former groups). In contrast, only a little more than one third of large countries with more than ten million inhabitants enjoys democratic regimes. As a result, the number of small democracies is twice the number of large democracies (specifically, by 2009 there was democracy in 63 of 111 countries with fewer than 10 million inhabitants, and in 30 of the 81 countries with a larger population).

Rates of success in democratization are even higher for large federations. Nowadays, of all the large countries in the world with more than ten million inhabitants, those with local legislatures or a federal structure are democratic in more than three fourths of the cases, including, in particular, Argentina, Australia, Brazil, Canada, Germany, India, South Africa, Spain, and the United States. In contrast, in large centralized and unitary states, democracy exists in only one fourth of the cases. Specifically, there is democracy in fourteen of the eighteen large federal countries, but in only sixteen of the sixty-three large centralized states. Decentralization and federalism, which give small groups means of self-government, consolidate democracy. No backsliding toward authoritarianism has existed in recent times in plural federations that have adopted democratic formulas.

ECONOMIC EFFICIENCY

The main advantages derived from the large size of a nation are broad markets and large-scale collective goods. Traditional big states protecting large markets offer positive opportunities to different groups with economic specialization to develop extensive exchanges with people in other territories within the state to their mutual benefit. In doing so, the groups can overcome isolation and the perils of parochialism. Economic links and interdependence may also favor acquiescence to the state authorities and allegiance to a broad nation.

However, in the current world, small communities have new opportunities to exist and survive as a consequence of the development of vast commercial and communication networks extending beyond the limits of traditional states. Transnational circulation of people, goods, services, capital, and information, which was already high at the end of the nineteenth century and the beginning of the twentieth century, has increased substantially again during the last few decades. Massive migrations, trade over long distances, transnational capital investments, and information and cultural messages are promoted by the reduction of transport and communication costs. In the current period, they are also facilitated by the diffusion of a few common currencies, numerous free-trade agreements, and a network of international institutions binding state governments and able to provide some large-scale public goods.

In general, the larger states, which are able to protect internal trade, are relatively more closed to the exterior, while the smaller countries are outwardly more open. Indeed, large states facilitate the development of "domestic" trade among people and firms located in their different internal regions, which can foster prosperity and mutual ties. But with the building of broad interstate or trans-national networks, state protection has become less necessary. People and firms located in a small community have the opportunity to develop similar amounts of trade with traders located at similar distances, but across borders, which counts as "international."

Quick Quiz

- What relation exists between the size of a country and the likelihood of its having a democratic regime?

Union

How is it possible to attain the democratic advantages of a small-size community and the economic and communication advantages of large-size one? Naturally, by establishing a large territorial scope of public activities and by building broad protective umbrellas for small groups. But, then, is it possible to organize the efficient provision of large-scale public goods and prevent the emergence of big bureaucracies not subjected to democratic control? One modern institutional invention was crucial for making democracy workable for large populations. When, in the late eighteenth century, thirteen small, highly homogeneous communities in North America began to gain independence from the United Kingdom, they invented a federation of small republics, thus making large size and democracy compatible for the first time. In this way, the United States of America was actually created not as a large unitary state, but as a large federation of small republics.

A federation implies self-rule by the local units and shared rule on a large scale by the union. Building a federal union usually implies political exchanges between communities of different size and power. In general, a federation can be built if the leaders of a large, relatively powerful community accept to expand the territorial scope of their potential control or influence by renouncing violence and imperial command and use peaceful, institutionalized procedures of decision making. In turn, relatively small or weak community leaders can replace independence with union in the aim of achieving access to broad markets and protection from external threats. A well-institutionalized federation can attain both the efficiency of large spaces for the provision of public goods and the advantages of small-size democratic government.

ETHNIC VARIETY

In almost no case in the current world is there a complete fit between the limits of the "state" and the boundaries of the "nation," as we mentioned in the previous chapter. We refer to "national," or "ethnic," characteristics as those including religion, race, or language.

Fragmentation versus Polarization. According to the most attuned data and calculations, the average country today has about five ethnic groups, and most have between three and six (counting only groups larger than 1 percent of the country's population). In only about two thirds of the countries does one ethnic group includes

Religious conflicts have been relatively frequent in human history, such as between Christians and Muslims.

an absolute majority of the population. The average size of the largest group within a country is about two thirds of the total population, while the average size of the second largest group is about one sixth.

Within this notable internal variety, three types of countries can be distinguished. First, there are medium-size, relatively homogeneous national states. These are mainly in Europe, including Britain, France, Germany, Hungary, Italy, Poland, and Sweden, but there are a few in some other regions, such as Egypt and Japan.

Second, there are large federations with significant ethnic variety. These include Brazil, Canada, and the United States in the Americas; Belgium, Spain, and Switzerland in Europe; India and Indonesia in Asia; and South Africa, to mention some of the most currently successful in democratic terms.

Finally, there are varied countries in which the attempt to build a unified national state has been the occasion for frequent conflicts, failures, and lasting instability. These include Bolivia, Colombia, Ecuador, and Peru along the Andes in South America; Congo, Ethiopia, and Sudan in Central Africa; and Afghanistan, Iraq, and Lebanon in the Middle East.

Thus, different degrees of ethnic variety seem to require different institutional forms of division of power to achieve effectiveness. Among the most peaceful and stable political communities there are those that are highly homogeneous, that is, countries in which one ethnic group has become strongly dominant and most people share values and wide common interests—a successful national state. But peace and stability are also likely to exist in communities that are **highly varied or "fragmented," that is, those including many small ethnic or national groups**, if they have sufficiently inclusive institutions. In these situations no group can expect to become absolutely dominant over the others, and as a consequence, coexistence and tolerance spread and federalism appears as a feasible agreement.

In contrast, the highest levels of ethnic conflict exist in countries with **high "polarization," where two groups of similar size and marked differences face each other**. The maximum polarization thus corresponds to an intermediate, moderate level of fragmentation, since it implies that only two large groups exist. Typically, in situations prone to conflict, an ethnic group that claims to be the majority tries to dominate, but a large minority is able to develop vigorous resistance.

Religious polarization appears to be more prone to generating conflict than are differences based on race or language. This is probably due to the categorical and exclusionary character of religious affiliation, for which mixtures comparable to racial crossbreeding or multilingualism are not usually conceivable. However, religious pluralism in a society seems to foster more tolerance and freedom than not only bipolar affiliations but also a single religious allegiance.

Many Is Better Than Few. A high number of small communities provides a more solid ground for a federation than a low number. As just explained, the existence of many small groups implies high fragmentation, while two or a few groups is associated with high polarization. The problem is that in federations formed of only two groups, one of them can reasonably expect to dominate the center and develop the subsequent ambition. This can lead either to the absorption of the other group into a unified structure, or to conflict and secession, the two alternatives both implying the dissolution of the federation.

Let us observe a stylized representation of this type of conflictive situation, as presented in Table 6.2. Let us assume that the three possible alternatives are: (1) the dominance of one single group; (2) a federal arrangement with parity of powers, thus usually implying some overrepresentation of the small unit; and (3) the split of the

TABLE 6.2 The Secession Game

In a federation with only two groups, the larger, likely dominant group prefers a unitary structure, while the smaller group prefers parity of powers, but both can converge on the split of the union. The figures in parentheses suggest the share of power that a group can control in each formula.

	LARGE GROUP	SMALL GROUP
First preference	Unitary (100%)	Federal parity (50%)
Second preference	Separation (own group >50%)	Separation (own group >0%)
Least preference	Federal parity (50%)	Unitary (0%)

union, typically by secession of the smaller unit. On the one side, it seems logical that the large national or ethnic group may prefer dominance to separation, since in the former situation it would control not only its own resources but also those of the other group. Then the typical federal arrangement to share powers with some overrepresentation of the minor group can be the last preference of the large group.

In contrast, the small, likely dominated group can develop exactly the opposite order of preferences. It may prefer, first, a federal arrangement with parity of powers, which implies its own overrepresentation. But then separation, which will give it control over its own resources, may be preferred to subordination to the larger group. The small unit can relinquish to subordination if the cost of separating is too high or if there is no favorable international context. But separation appears to be the intermediate preference for both groups. In certain circumstances, such as an imperial dissolution or the aftermath of a war, separation can be the converging outcome of a bilateral relation.

Many two-unit federations have failed as a consequence of the large group's attempt to dominate and the small group's choice of secession. Cases of failed dominance of a large group since the nineteenth century include: Argentina with the separation of Paraguay and Uruguay after independence; Colombia with the separation of Ecuador, Venezuela, and later Panama; Peru with the split with Bolivia; Mexico with the separation of Guatemala and, immediately afterward, the rest of Central America in dispersion; the United Kingdom with secession by Ireland, followed by prolonged conflict with Northern Ireland; India with separation by Pakistan after independence; Pakistan with secession of territorially separated Bangladesh later on; South Africa with secession by Namibia; Rhodesia (which became today's Zimbabwe) with secession by Zambia and Malawi; Ethiopia with secession by Eritrea; Czecho-Slovakia with secession of the latter; and the Serbian-dominated Yugoslavia, which split into another six republics. The outstanding case of the dissolution of the Russian-dominated Soviet Union is the subject of Case 6.2. Other highly polarized conflicts still exist, such as that in Belgium between Flemish and Walloons and in Cyprus between Greeks and Turks, although in these cases the umbrella provided by the European Union may prevent a full split of the countries.

In contrast to the frailty of two-unit, polarized federations, successful experiences usually encompass high numbers of units. With territorial pluralism, none of the units can reasonably feed its ambitions of becoming the single dominant one, thus leaving the small communities to develop their own ways within the union. Cases of relative stability and duration include: the United States (with 50 units), Mexico (32), India (28), Brazil (26), Switzerland (26), Argentina (24), Italy (20), Venezuela (20), Spain (17), Germany (16), Malaysia (13), Canada (11), Austria (9), South Africa (9), Australia (8), and the process in the works in the European Union (with 27 members so far).

DIVIDED INSTITUTIONS

Federalism requires "vertical" division of powers between central and non-central governments. Different institutional formulas create differently balanced relationships among the units of a federation, which may produce different distributions of relative winners and losers. A balanced federation may result from the holding of separate elections to different territorial governments, and from interinstitutional cooperation, especially through a second federal chamber in parliament. In the following paragraphs we analyze these basic institutional elements of a successful federation.

Vertical Division of Powers.   In a federal country, **different powers are allocated to the central and local governments**. The central government is usually allocated powers on issues related to the interests of large groups, including defense, foreign affairs, foreign trade, money, and credit; as well as over some redistributive policies; together with the accompanying taxation powers. Non-central governments, in contrast, focus on economic issues related to territorial scale or location, such as local commerce, agriculture, urban planning, and public works, and on issues linked to the interests of small groups, including education and the management of religious, racial, or language differences.

The ideal model that we discussed in the previous chapter, by which each collective good could be provided by a specific governmental unit, can be difficult to establish due to the high costs of administration and participation in a very complex structure. In the practice of federal states, there are fewer institutional levels than territorial scopes of public goods. Since each institutional level deals with public affairs somewhat diversely distributed across the territory, there is some degree of overlapping and power sharing among several units. Federal, state, and local governments can have concurrent jurisdictions over certain domains.

Federalism requires that each governmental level have exclusive powers to make final decisions on some issues. But power sharing on some other issues can require interinstitutional cooperation and agreements in order to complete the process, which starts with the approval of legislation to specific policy decisions and their implementation. Interinstitutional cooperation through "vertical" division of powers tends to produce consensual outcomes.

Fiscal federalism also implies divided taxation powers. Generally, the allocation of taxation powers to different institutions according to their policy powers can produce efficient results. Governments that collect their own taxes and are fiscally accountable to voters have incentives to provide public goods that can indirectly foster economic growth and favor the government's own revenue. In contrast, local governments that rely on transfers of revenue from the central government can create the "fiscal illusion" to voters that their services are for free and use resources from redistribution and patronage rather than investment. To paraphrase the leaders of the American independence, "no representation without taxation" is a good principle of fiscal federalism.

Separate Elections.   The actual division of powers between the central and non-central governments can be measured by the legal powers in the hands of each institution, and by the fiscal resources they can collect or spend, as just reviewed in the previous paragraphs. Another important measurement refers to political party control of separate governments. Even if jurisdictions and money are highly decentralized, if a single, internally centralized party controls all the governments, the country tends to work as a unified political structure. This is exactly what happened, in an extreme case, in the formally federal Soviet Union, which was in fact controlled by the centralized Communist Party. On the other hand, if only local parties exist it is likely that secession will eventually be pursued. A stable federation thus requires an appropriate balance between federal, internally decentralized parties, which can be based on accords among local groups and independent local parties.

On the basis of economic, social, and ethnic differences, different structures of the party system can contribute to either unity and cooperation or rivalry and conflict. In some cases, the federal parties are relatively loose coalitions of local organizations maintaining high levels of cooperation, as in Australia, Brazil, Germany, Mexico, Switzerland, and the United States. Alternatively, a few large national or federal parties with relatively high degrees of internal cohesion can coexist with independent territorially based parties in less balanced relationships, as in Argentina, Canada, India, Indonesia, Italy, and Spain. Finally, all political parties may have a clear territorial or ethnic affiliation, which tends to promote higher levels of interterritorial competition, as in Belgium and South Africa, among other countries.

Political decentralization, whether in favor of the federal opposition party or of local parties, is facilitated by separate elections. If federal and local elections are held at the same time it is likely that the federal campaign will dominate, local issues will not be salient in the electoral agenda, and the political party winning the federal election will also take control of many local governments. In contrast, non-concurrent, staggered elections for local governments favor the emergence and salience of different issues in the different types of elections, the voters' revelation of their varied preferences in different fields, and subsequent opportunities for parties that are not in central government to obtain support.

The degree of actual **political decentralization can be measured by the proportion of local chief executives whose party is not in federal government**. In the United States many states have replaced two-year state governor terms, which half of the time produced concurrent elections with the presidential election, with four-year terms, usually scheduled for non-presidential election years, which has favored an increase in the proportion of governors from parties not holding the presidency. In large federal countries holding separate elections for the federal and local institutions, such as Argentina, Australia, Brazil, Canada, Germany, India, Mexico, and Spain, most regional, provincial, or state governments are usually ruled by a party that is not in central government. Over time it can be observed that the federal prime minister's or president's party tends to lose votes in the regional elections following the federal election, even if the party wins again in the following federal election.

Bicameralism.   In federal countries **two chambers exist: one representing the whole population and the other representing the people in the different territories**. While the seats in the lower chamber are usually apportioned among different districts in correspondence to their numbers of inhabitants, in the second or upper chamber, in contrast, each of the different territories can elect equal or similar numbers of seats, thus giving overrepresentation to the smaller units. Overrepresentation in the upper chamber is frequently a condition for the citizens of small units to accept to participate in collective decisions in a large and varied country or federation, since they are more likely to be in a minority in a chamber in which seats are based only on total population numbers.

BOX 6.1   MEASURING ETHNIC VARIETY

The ethnic variety of a country can be measured quantitatively in order to compare countries and test relationships with other variables.

Number of Groups

The number of ethnic groups in a country can be measured using any of these indices:

$$\text{Fragmentation: } F = 1 - \Sigma\, P_i^2$$
$$\text{Effective number: } N = 1\, /\, \Sigma\, P_i^2$$

Where:
F: Fragmentation
N: Effective number
P_i: Size of group *i* (in share of inhabitants)

The fragmentation index has values between 0 and 1, where 0 corresponds to a country where all inhabitants belong to a single group and 1 to a hypothetical situation in which each individual belongs to a different group. An example approaching zero fragmentation—that is, maximum ethnic homogeneity—is Japan, while the extreme case of high fragmentation in the current world is Papua–New Guinea, inhabited by several thousand communities, most formed by just a few hundred people. The effective number of groups has values from 1 upward, the higher the number of groups of

a similar size. The values of the two indices are strongly correlated, since $N = 1\, /\, (1 - F)$.

Ethnic Polarization

The degree of ethnic polarization in a country can be measured with this index:

$$\text{Polarization: } Pol = 1 - \Sigma\, [(\tfrac{1}{2} - P_i\,)/\, \tfrac{1}{2}]^2\, P_i$$

Where:
Pol_2: Polarization
P_i: Size of group *i* (in share of inhabitants)

The index captures how far the quantitative distribution of ethnic groups is from the ½–½ bipolar distribution, which has the highest level of polarization. An example of a highly polarized country is Belgium, which is divided between Dutch-speaking Flemish and French-speaking Walloons. The index does not measure "distances" between ethnic groups, but assumes that the identification of differentiated groups is arranged in a way that each group can be considered to be roughly equally distant from each other; for instance, in a certain community, Christians can be considered to be as distant from Jews as Jews are from Muslims and as Muslims are from Christians.

The members of the upper chamber can either be chosen directly by the citizens in territory-based elections or be appointed by the territorial assemblies or governments. In the United States, for example, the citizens of every state elect two senators despite the fact that the larger states may have up to seventy times more population than the smaller ones (as in the case of California versus Wyoming). A more common formula is the allocation of a minimum number of seats to all units while the rest are allocated on the basis of population. For instance, in the federal upper chambers of Argentina and Brazil, each state is initially allocated three seats, and the rest are allocated in correspondence to population.

The typical upper chamber in a federal country has significant legislative powers on issues involving the territorial redistribution of resources. The requirement that a bill be approved by the two chambers of the assembly is equivalent to the requirement of a supermajority in a single chamber. Even if each of the chambers can make decisions by simple majority, if they have different political majorities after being elected by different procedures, joint decisions will be negotiated and supported by a broad, inclusive supermajority. We will return to this point for other formulas of division of powers in chapter 15.

CASE 6.1   CONSENSUAL SWITZERLAND

The Swiss Confederation is one of the most successful experiences in federal government, which is based on wide pluralism and broad government consensus. Its origins can be traced to the fourteenth century, when a few "forest" democratic cantons, later followed by several self-governed cities, began to break away from the Austrian monarchy and the Holy Roman Empire and formed a league to preserve their local autonomy. After a short civil war in 1847–48, a more formal federation was formed. Today, Switzerland is composed of twenty-six cantons, each relatively homogeneous in economic and ethnic terms, with its own constitution and institutions of democratic self-government.

In all of Switzerland, there is a majority language group, German, spoken by about 65 percent of the total population; followed by French, with 23 percent; Italian; and Romansh. Swiss people are quite evenly balanced in religious affiliation between Catholics and Protestants, with a patchwork of majorities across most of the country. A complex set of institutions prevents any ethnic group from imposing its dominance over the others. All powers not explicitly reserved for the federal government, such as defense and trade, lie under the control of the cantonal governments. The federal Assembly has two chambers, the first elected in cantonal districts and the second formed by two representatives per canton, regardless of its population size. The citizens can collect signatures to challenge federal legislation in popular referendums. While any bill must be confirmed by a majority of Swiss voters, constitutional reforms and international treaties need both a federal majority and a majority of voters in a majority of cantons.

The possibility that federal legislation can be defeated in popular referendum moves legislators to build very large majority coalitions. The executive Federal Council, which is appointed by the two chambers of the Assembly, is usually formed by members from different cantons, both German-speaking and French- or Italian-speaking. Four-party coalition governments have been consistently formed since the late 1950s, always including the Radical, the Conservative-Christian, the Socialist, and the Populist (formerly Agrarian) parties, which usually encompass more than 80 percent of popular votes. The Swiss Confederation is still mainly an instrument for preserving local, popular self-government.

THE CHOICE OF FEDERALISM

A democratic federation can ultimately derive from a confederative or imperial process of putting disparate units across a vast territory under the jurisdiction of an aggregative center. As we discussed in the previous chapter, both a confederation of previously existing political units and the expansion of a previously existing center can result in an "empire." But when the empire cannot assimilate more territories, population, or variety, and it ceases expanding, or it even contracts, a more stable formula based on neat division of powers at different levels can be established. In this sense, an empire may be a federation in the making, as a federation can be conceived as a democratic, stable kind of empire.

In the building of a federation, there seems to be a strong relationship between the setting up of fixed territorial limits of the union and its internal consolidation and institutionalization. As we've mentioned, both the building of the United States of America in the past and the ongoing process in the European Union suggest that the establishment of a relatively permanent number of member units and of neat external frontiers is a condition for attaining a predictable balance of powers within the union

CASE 6.2 THE SOVIET DISUNION

The failure of the Soviet Union is a foremost example of the implausibility of a multinational federation when one of the groups is large enough to try to become dominant. The Union of Soviet Socialist Republics (USSR) was created in 1922, after the Russian Revolution and the First World War, initially as a federation of four republics: Russia, Ukraine, Belarus, and Transcaucasia. Other territories of the former Russian Empire had declared their independence, but most of them were reintegrated during the Second World War, including three Baltic republics and lands from Czechoslovakia, Finland, Germany, Japan, Poland, Romania, and Tuva. The USSR was then the largest political unit in the world in territory. By 1956, it was organized into fifteen republics—to which the constitution recognized the sovereign right "to freely secede from the Union"—and numerous autonomies, regions, and areas. Several dozen nationalities and ethnic groups were also officially acknowledged.

However, Russia was always the dominating unit of the USSR. The synecdoche "Russia" continued to be commonly used. In the 1920s, ethnic Russians constituted 53 percent of the total population, while the Russian Soviet Republic contained nearly 70 percent of the population and more than 90 percent of the territory; in the 1980s, after a long decline of the Russian ethnic population, Russia still contained 51 percent of the total population and two thirds of the territory. The formally federal structure of the country was nullified by the monolithic and strongly centralized structure of the Communist Party, which was in control of all public life. The party's official doctrine was that eventually nationalities and ethnic distinctions would disappear and a single language would be adopted. At the end of World War II, Josif Stalin proclaimed that Russia was "the leading force of the Soviet Union among all the nationalities of our country." Cultural and linguistic Russification was intensified.

The building began to tremble in the second half of the 1980s, when Mikhail Gorbachev, pressured by the economic breakdown of the socialist experiment, introduced political liberalization. As the costs of collective action decreased, local groups used local and republican institutions and elections, and the official right to secede, to proclaim their sovereignty. By late 1991, the Soviet Union was disbanded. Russia, now an independent republic, replaced the Soviet Union in most of its previous international commitments.

and the subsequent consolidation of democratic federal formulas that can be accepted by all members.

"Vertical" and "horizontal" divisions of powers may support each other. An effective federal structure with multiple levels of government and political decentralization is more likely to exist and survive in the framework of divided central government, whether in the form of multiparty coalition cabinets or coexistence and cooperation between different party majorities in the presidency and the assembly. This can be explained by certain processes triggered in situations of horizontal division of powers. If no party controls all the central institutions, and power sharing exists, the competing parties in the center may have an interest in negotiating and compromising with other parties in the local governments in order to expand their shares of power to the local institutions. At the same time, the parties in local governments can protect their powers if they become pivotal in the federal assembly, especially in the upper chamber, thus preventing a single party in the center from controlling all powers. An independent judiciary not controlled by a single party, whether in the

SOURCE 6.1   **Self-Government and Union**

[S]mall wards and townships…have proved themselves the wisest invention ever devised by the wit of man for the perfect exercise of self-government, and for its preservation. We should thus marshal our government into, 1, the general federal republic, for all concerns foreign and federal; 2, that of the state, for what relates to our own citizens exclusively; 3, the county republics, for the duties and concerns of the county; and 4, the ward republics, for the small, and yet numerous and interesting concerns of the neighborhood. In government, as well as in every other business of life, it is by division and subdivision of duties alone, that all matters, great and small, can be managed to perfection.

Thomas Jefferson, "Letter to Sam Kercheval" (1816)

We shall generally find more persons in easy circumstances, more contentment and tranquility, in small nations than in large ones…Small nations have always been the cradle of political liberty; and the fact that many of them have lost their liberty by becoming larger shows that their freedom was more a consequence of their small size than of the character of the people…The federal system was created with the intention of combining the different advantages which result from the magnitude and the littleness of nation.

Alexis de Tocqueville, *Democracy in America* (1835–40)

Separation of powers necessarily involves fragmentation of authority. Federalism necessarily involves overlapping jurisdictions.

Vincent Ostrom, *The Political Theory of a Compound Republic* (1971)

Among the units most needed in the world as it has been evolving lie several at the extremes: we need some very small units and some very large units…Thus one task of democratic theory may be to specify not an optimal unit but an optimal number of units with comparatively fixed boundaries.

Robert A. Dahl and Edward Tufte, *Size and Democracy* (1976)

Federal principles involves the combination of self-rule (or self-government) and shared rule (or federal government).

Daniel J. Elazar, *Exploring Federalism* (1987)

Federalism is the main alternative to empire as a technique to aggregating large areas under one government…The essential institutions of federalism are, of course, a government of the federation and a set of governments of the member units, in which both kinds of governments rule over the same territory and people and each kind has the authority to make some decisions independently of the other.

William Riker, *The Development of American Federalism* (1987)

form of supreme court or constitutional tribunal, can also help to keep the balance of decentralization.

Quick Quiz

• What relationship exists between ethnic fragmentation and ethnic polarization?

Conclusion

In this chapter, we have analyzed federalism as a formula for making self-government of small communities and the provision of large-scale public goods compatible. A successful and stable union requires "vertical" division of powers between the central government and the local governments, usually implying different political parties' control of different governments, and power sharing and interinstitutional cooperation, especially in the federal upper chamber representing the territorial governments.

A clear, logical, and empirical finding can be enunciated in the form of a *proposition*:

• **Multi-unit federations.** Many-unit federations in which no unit is sufficiently large to dominate tend to survive and endure. In contrast, two-unit federations tend to fail, leading to either absorption of the small unit by the large one or secession of the small, likely dominated unit. ■

Summary

Small-scale communities have democratic advantages, thanks to relatively high degrees of internal harmony, at the stages of deliberation, aggregation, and enforcement.

In turn, large-scale political units can facilitate access to broad markets, collective security, and open communication networks.

In large unions or federations, both high internal homogeneity and high heterogeneity or fragmentation among many national or ethnic groups favor peace and stability.

In contrast, high polarization between two consistent groups fosters attempts to dominate and likely conflict. Two-unit federations tend to fail.

A federal union implies division of powers between governments having the right to make final decisions on some issues, and power sharing on other issues.

The degree of political division of powers, or decentralization, can be measured by the proportion of local governments controlled by parties that are not in the central government.

A federal upper chamber gives overrepresentation to the smaller units as protection from a federal homogeneous majority.

A democratic federation can be formed from an empire by adopting stable territorial and institutional formulas.

Federalism, or "vertical" division of powers, is favored by "horizontal" division of powers and power sharing at the center, whether in the form of multiparty coalition cabinets or cooperation between separate institutions.

Key Concepts

Bicameralism. The lower chamber in the assembly represents the entire population while the upper chamber gives overrepresentation to the people in small territories.

Federation. Local self-government and large-scale union, implying self-rule and shared rule.

Fragmentation. Number of different ethnic groups, as can be defined by religious, racial, or language affiliations, weighted by their size.

Polarization. Relative sizes of different ethnic groups.

Political decentralization. Share of local governments controlled by parties not in the central government.

Vertical division of powers. Allocation of different powers to the central and local governments.

Questions for Review

1. Is there any relation between the size of a country and the likelihood of its having a democratic regime?
2. What's the relation between ethnic fragmentation and ethnic polarization?
3. How could you measure the degree of political decentralization in a country?
4. Argue how "vertical" and "horizontal" divisions of powers can be compatible.

Problems and Applications

1. For the federal Senate of the United States, calculate the ratio between the number of senators and the populations in California, North Dakota, Texas, and Wyoming. Comment.
2. For the federal upper chamber of Germany (Bundesrat), calculate the ratio between the number of members and the population in Baden-Württemberg, Bavaria, Bremen, and Hamburg. Comment. Compare with the previous question.

Quantitative indices

3. Look at the ethnic composition of the following four countries in terms of percentage of population. The data presented here are simplified and based on race, religion, or language depending on the major division in each country (also the percentages are rounded).
   a. Calculate the fragmentation index and the effective number of ethnic groups for each country.
   b. Calculate the polarization index for each country.

ESTONIA	IRAQ	JAPAN	SWITZERLAND
Estonian 69	Arab Shi'a 52	Japanese 98	German 65
Russian 31	Arab Sunni 28	Koreans 1	French 23
Kurdish 20	Chinese 1	Italian 11	Romansch 1

4. Compare the results in the previous exercise. Can you see any correlation between fragmentation and polarization?

Data sources

World Christian Database: www.worldchristiandatabase.org
Ethnologue, Languages of the World: www.ethnologue.com

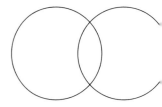

7

DICTATORSHIP

In This Chapter You Will

- Distinguish among the different types of dictatorship.
- Reflect on the conditions for a dictatorship to endure.
- Consider some factors of revolutions and civil wars.
- Compare different ways of democratization.

Nondemocratic government existed in the Southern states of the United States, which had slavery and a plantation economy during most of the nineteenth century. But in contrast to processes in other countries, a slow process of gradual allocation of voting rights to different groups of the population developed during a long period all across the United States. Initial requirements of land ownership or real estate property for voting were replaced with personal property, tax qualifications, and literacy tests. In most states, African Americans were legally enfranchised after the Civil War, although they remained actually disfranchised in the South. Residence requirements prevented the massive introduction of new immigrant voters. Women's suffrage was established in all states in 1920. Poll taxes and literacy tests, used in the southern states to exclude African Americans, were suppressed only in 1964.

A comparably gradual and relatively peaceful process of democratization developed in Britain during the nineteenth century, and in a few former British colonies in different periods. But in other countries, establishing democratic elections and governments has required more dramatic change. Indeed, for most of history, most human beings have lived under dictatorships. In a dictatorship, an individual or a group "dictates," or orders, enforceable policy on a number of matters and excludes large groups of the population from participating in decision making. Most countries in the Middle East and in Central Africa, and others in Asia and Latin America, still live with nondemocratic regimes. In this chapter we study the conditions for the existence and survival of dictatorships, and the characteristics of their different forms. We also approach the different ways of regime change and democratization. ■

Forms of Dictatorship

The most elementary form of dictatorship can be developed by the head of a family if he acts as the owner and unchallenged chief of his spouse and children. In primitive communities, a dictator was the tribal chief or a bandit who had beaten other bandits, knights, or warlords and set himself up as the only boss. On a larger scale, dictatorial forms of government were created by some armed leaders exerting effective violence over diverse, small groups and communities across a large territory. In general, **dictatorship, or "autocracy," is a form of government in which the political power is held by non-elected, self-appointed rulers**.

A major favorable condition for dictatorship is the large size or isolation of the country, as we suggested in chapter 5. A large, heterogeneous society with several lines of conflict and lower internal cohesion may create more opportunities for a dictator to rise and win than would a small, harmonious community with dense networks of human relations. Also, for a potential dictator motivated by confiscatory aims, a very large colonial dominion or a very large territory under a single jurisdiction may be a relatively appealing setting, since he can have access to a higher total volume of resources from a large population than in a scarcely populated country. However, the larger the country, the more costly the administrative and police apparatus needed to keep the dictator in control, so effective dictatorships should also be limited in size.

All dictators have a common primary goal, which is to hold on to power by coercive or violent means. But dictatorial rulers can uphold different relationships of force with their opponents and the different groups in society, depending on the depth of the conflicts on which they are based and the process that led them to power. While strong dictators facing an anomic society can rule arbitrarily, relatively weaker rulers may need to rely not only on repression and command, but on some other exchanges with their subjects. Different combinations of "carrots" and "sticks" can produce different forms of dictatorship. In modern times we can distinguish, at least, between **despotism**, **authoritarianism**, and **totalitarianism**, to be put in order ranging from lower to greater degrees of social support and ruler control over the society. Please bear in mind that different words have been used to refer to different forms of nondemocratic rule, but in order to obtain fine analytical insights, it is always convenient to look at substantial differences between the several categories presented rather than nominal discrepancies. Some definitions and discussion follow.

DESPOTISM

Despotism, or **personalistic** rule, is an old form of dictatorship **deprived of ideology and prone to arbitrariness**. Traditional despots can be motivated by tight, self-interested motives, both of power and wealth, and by fear of revolution by their subjects, workers, or slaves. Traditional despotic regimes exert wide control but apply repression just up to the limits necessary to prevent or curtail rebellions and survive.

Usually they do not need to build sophisticated political institutions, but merely mechanisms of coordination to give the rulers and the privileged class the capacity to secure their interests and make enforceable decisions. Some of these regimes may become depredatory if they are seriously threatened. Whenever a dictator expects a brief tenure, he can have incentives to confiscate assets for his own gain, thus setting up a so-called "sultanistic" regime.

A relevant factor for a despotic regime to emerge and endure is the existence of a single-crop economy, which, by its very nature, is resistant to social, cultural, and political pluralism and relatively easy to control. Specifically, despotism can flourish and endure in countries where the main economic activity involves large agrarian possessions or the extraction of natural resources. In traditional, extensive agricultural economies—such as those producing sugar, cotton, cereals, opium, coca, or certain tropical fruits—there tends to be great economic and social polarization between a tiny minority of landowners and a vast majority of workers or peons. Likewise, if the economy of a country can focus on extracting and exporting a single profitable natural resource, such as oil, gas, metals, or diamonds, a dictator or a small set of rulers may expect to obtain sufficient assets and exert control, whether in collusion with the foreign owners of wells, mines, or beds or through state ownership. If most of the population were given freedom and participation rights, the proprietors might fear massive expropriation. Then they could not emigrate with their assets as they are "fixed." At the same time, in such simple and transparent societies, the exertion of control, vigilance, and repression against potential leaders and rebels can be relatively easy to enforce. Thus there exist favorable conditions for a dictator in coalescence or fusion with big owners.

In the past, absolute monarchs in large countries—including most of the Tudors in England, the Bourbons in France and Spain, the Romanovs in Russia, and the Qings in China—did indeed rely on extensive agrarian economies. The emblematic "banana republic," a satiric term originally coined in reference to Honduras in the early twentieth century, also belongs to this category. A paramount example of this today is the ruling of sultans and emirs in oil-producing countries in the Persian Gulf. In general, the availability of certain valuable natural resources can help to explain the current resilience of dictatorial regimes and the fragility of democratic experiences in areas including Russia, the Middle East, most of Central Africa, and the Caribbean and Andean regions.

AUTHORITARIANISM

An authoritarian regime is a form of dictatorship typically corresponding to a relatively complex situation in which the rulers face a variety of groups in society. In order to be durable, an authoritarian regime may need to rely not only on control and repression, but also on the deliverance of collective and private benefits able to gain acquiescence and prevent rebellion by its subjects. Authoritarian regimes usually establish certain institutional rules to settle competition among different groups of rulers. We address these two aspects in the following paragraphs.

Economic Performance.   Authoritarian rulers can be interested in some degree of deliverance of private and public goods in order to attract collaborationists, thwart rebellion, and obtain broad assent and obedience. In the typical exchange under an authoritarian regime, the citizens renounce the right to choose or control the rulers, thus attracting less control and repression, in return for some favorable economic or other performance.

At low levels of wealth, fast economic growth can be facilitated by merely opening the country to foreign investment and international trade, which can increase mass consumption and produce almost universal benefits for the population. An authoritarian regime can also extract people's resources by substituting theft with taxes, which may make the regime able to deliver some public goods. The government's economic policy may protect domestic producers from foreign competition in order to gain their support. While there can be exclusion and arbitrariness in politics, a certain degree of rule of law in the economy may be enforced, especially regarding property and contract rights favoring private activity. In general, economic growth can be used temporarily to strengthen nondemocratic regimes.

Institutionalization.   A durable authoritarian regime may need to adopt some institutional rules to coordinate internal decisions, co-opt new adherents, and convey a certain air of stability and predictability. By accepting a certain degree of pluralism and promoting a limited degree of social organization, the dictatorship may attain both some degree of inclusiveness and the intimidation of potential foes.

Specifically, some authoritarian ruling parties have organized several branches addressing different social groups in order to coordinate sectoral economic interests. A number of authoritarian regimes also set up assemblies and elections, although the former have no real legislative or control powers and the latter are usually won by the rulers' candidacies by overwhelming supermajorities. Even if a single party exerts broad control, several political parties or groups may be accepted in a subordinate position.

For example, in Franco's Spain, an "organic democracy" was set up by means of an assembly, named after the medieval "Courts," which was formed of representatives of families, municipalities, and unions, and in fact including fascists, monarchists, and technocrats. In postrevolutionary Mexico, the ruling party, tellingly named "Revolutionary" and "Institutional," or PRI, was initially created as a coalition of previously fighting warlords; it was organized into three "sectors" representing workers, peasants, and the military. IThe regime held regular congressional and presidential elections in which several opposition parties from both the right and the left were recognized, gaining, in total, about one fourth of popular votes and seats on average. In the "people's democracy" in Poland and East Germany, the ruling Communist Party held periodical elections in which a single list of candidates included members of peasant, liberal, and christian parties, sometimes under the labels of "national" or "patriotic" fronts. In the current "people's democratic dictatorship" of China, the ruling Communist Party is no longer defined as the party of workers and peasants, but of "three represents," including intellectuals and entrepreneurs.

TOTALITARIANISM

A totalitarian regime aims, as its name suggests, to be an all-embracing, total state. A totalitarian regime exerts control over all the public and private activities of its

CASE 7.1   THE DICTATOR'S SUCCESSION

A major institutional problem for any dictatorship is the succession of the leader. In the ancient Roman republic, dictators were nominated by the Senate and the consuls to perform extraordinary tasks in situations of war or other emergencies for a maximum of six months. But most dictators are appointed or self-appointed for life. The death of the dictator is usually a moment of major crisis and uncertainty. A traditional formula for succession is, of course, the hereditary monarchy. Yet nobody can bet on the personal leadership qualities of somebody's descendants. In the current world, hereditary dictatorships still exist in a few countries, including Brunei, Saudi Arabia, and the United Arab Emirates, de facto ruled by the emirs of Abu Dhabi and Dubai (while it seems that new authoritarian dynasties are also being tried in North Korea and Syria).

An alternative, more skillful formula for the orderly succession of leaders was established in Mexico by the Revolutionary Institutional Party (PRI), with the principle of "non-reelection" and the rotation of numerous offices. Over a period of about sixty years, each Mexican president was in office for only one six-year term, and during his last months in office, he appointed his own successor with "the big finger" (*dedazo*) after a process of consultation with party and sectoral leaders, which generated varied expectations. The procedure not only solved the problem of succession, but also triggered faithful support for the incumbent president during his mandate by all potential candidates for nomination to the presidency or other relevant posts. Due to the success of this experience for the stability of the regime during several decades, novelist Mario Vargas Llosa called PRI's Mexico "the perfect dictatorship."

The last-minute appointment is a kind of rediscovery of a procedure used in early eighteenth-century China. When the successor to the emperor was appointed openly, long before the time of succession, the emperor's other siblings fought him. In reaction, emperor Yongzheng set up the "Heir Apparent Box" system, by which the name of the successor was written on a document sealed within a box placed behind the throne; the emperor always carried a copy with him. After the emperor passed away, the secretly appointed crown prince would ascend the throne.

In post-Mao China, the Communist Party established unwritten rules to rotate the leader every ten years, that is, every two party congresses. This induces preliminary negotiations among potential rivals in the intermediate congress to nominate the future candidate. But as in other experiences mentioned, an agreement is not likely to be reached much before the last minute.

subjects, including education, occupation, residence, travel, communication, migration, recreation, and religion. The state control can be organized by a single party with an all-encompassing ideology or by a state church. It appears to be incompatible with the regular activity and influence of any independent or autonomous organization, whether local governments, business or trade associations, labor unions, churches, or political parties.

Typical totalitarian states can be characterized, in particular, by two distinctive elements: ideology and terror.

Ideology.   For a totalitarian state, an ideology is not only an instrument of legitimization. It must also provide a comforting, single answer to the dilemmas of life and history in order to serve as a pedagogical arm that can easily be spread widely among the subjects, and bring about a transcendental or revolutionary message able to generate mass mobilization.

Terror.   In totalitarian regimes, control by the secret police, purges, torture, murder, and concentration camps are instruments of government, while education and the

SOURCE 7.1   Authoritarian and Totalitarian Dictatorships

Fascist dicatorships in Western Europe were overthrown by the Allied armies in the Second World War, as represented by the Liberation of Paris in 1945.

The emergence of a new type of dictatorship with the rules of Adolf Hitler in Germany and Josif Stalin in the Soviet Union captured the imagination of a number of scholars, who elaborated on the concept of "totalitarianism."

Totalitarianism is never content to rule by external means, namely, through the state and a machinery of violence; thanks to its peculiar ideology and the role assigned to it in this apparatus of coercion, totalitarianism has discovered a means of dominating and terrorizing human beings from within.

Hannah Arendt, The Origins of Totalitarianism (1951)

A totalitarian regime has eliminated almost all pre-existing political, economic, and social pluralism, has a unified, articulated, guiding, utopian ideology, has intensive and extensive mobilization, and has a leadership that rules, often charismatically, with undefined limits and great unpredictability and vulnerability for elites and nonelites alike. [*In contrast*] an authoritarian regime is a political system with limited, not responsible, political pluralism, without elaborate and guiding ideology, but with distinctive mentalities, without extensive nor intensive political mobilization, except at some points in their development, and in which a leader or occasionally a small group exercises power within formally ill-defined limits but actually quite predictable ones.

Juan Linz and Alfred Stepan, Problems of Democratic Transition and
Consolidation (1996) media are supervised, censored, and intensively used. The repression of dissidents and resisters is justified as serving the state's ideological aims. Certain social or ethnic categories identified as enemies of the ideological project (whether aristocrats, the bourgeoisie, peasants, the clergy, Jews, homosexuals, or foreigners) can be victimized without consideration of individual guilt for specific acts.

Some totalitarian aims can be perceived in past absolute monarchies inspired in the doctrine of the divine right of kings, including Charles I of England, Louis XIV of France (who allegedly declared, "The State, It's me"), and Russian tsar Peter the Great. Modern cases more in accordance with our definition include Hitler's Third Reich, Stalin's Soviet Union, and Mao's People's Republic of China, and their replicas in occupied or neighboring countries. All these regimes developed an extreme concentration of power and cult of personality. They also engaged in external expansion and subsequent wars.

The experience of modern, revolutionary totalitarianism, which involves an extreme degree of people's mobilization from above, is not long-lasting. In fact, it tends to be rather ephemeral, enduring for one generation at most. The totalitarian regime may be defeated by foreign powers. Alternatively, it can internally evolve into softer forms of "post-totalitarian," authoritarian rule, especially at the disappearance of the dictator or due to its inability to maintain people's permanent mobilization and attain the initial aims of absolute social control.

Quick Quiz

• What is a dictatorship?
• Define a totalitarian regime.

The Fall of Dictatorships

Dictatorships tend to fall as a consequence of their own failures. But different ways of regime change can come about partly depending on the existing type of regime and partly on certain economic and social structures. A process of regime crisis and change can lead to the establishment of a new dictatorship, a semi-democratic regime, or a new democratic regime.

In particular, as we will review in the following pages, a despotic regime may be deposed by an internal rebellion, coup, or revolutionary movement, which sometimes establishes a new dictatorship, as has happened repeatedly in certain countries in Africa and Latin America. In contrast, in the case of authoritarian regimes with a relatively more balanced relationship of forces, it is possible for processes without major violence and based on exchanges between the rulers and the opposition to develop, as was the case of existing democracies, especially in Southern Europe, Eastern Asia, Latin America, and Eastern Europe, during the last few decades. Finally, a totalitarian regime can either be defeated by an external army or evolve into an authoritarian regime. As is well known, the Nazi regime of Adolf Hitler in Germany was overthrown by the Allied armies in the Second World War, while, in contrast, the Communist regimes in the Soviet Union and China evolved into softer, "post-totalitarian" forms after the deaths of Josif Stalin and Mao Zedong, respectively.

REVOLUTION AND CIVIL WAR

Certain dictatorial regimes can be overthrown by means of **violence**. A violent conflict within a country can be considered to be a civil war if it causes at least one thousand deaths, although some of the best accounts available include conflicts that produced more than a thousand casualties *per year*. **As most civil wars are eventually won by one side, they are indistinctly called "revolutions."** Some major cases are the English Civil War in the mid-seventeenth century, the French Revolution in the late eighteenth century, the American Civil War in the late nineteenth century, the Russian and the Mexican revolutions in the early twentieth century, and the Spanish Civil War and the Chinese Revolution in the mid-twentieth century. Other instances of the overthrow of authoritarian rulers by violent means have taken place in Latin America, Africa, and the Middle East in modern times.

The strategic human decision to engage oneself in armed struggle can be facilitated by a number of structural factors that create a favorable relationship between expected benefits and costs. As happens with other forms of collective action, violence, guerrilla fighting, and warfare can be relatively appealing options for people making a high evaluation of the gains at stake and having low opportunity costs. In addition, a prolonged violent conflict is more probable if the incumbent rulers are relatively too weak to maintain control.

More specifically, major violent conflicts and civil wars are relatively more likely to be fought in countries under the following conditions:

• An extensive agrarian economy or the availability of natural resources. These resources can entice the ambition of rebels to expropriate private owners or take control of the state itself.

• Low per capita income. Low income diminishes the opportunity costs of people engaging in armed action. This may create a vicious circle. Poverty fosters war, but war destroys assets and impoverishes people, further reducing the availability of alternative opportunities for the fighters, who can find themselves trapped in their actions with no exit option available.

• Large size of the country. A large population increases the number of potential rebels. Also, an extended territory may make it difficult for the government to keep control over certain local environments, even more so if they contain mountainous terrain or other physical features facilitating safe havens for combatants.

• State weakness. State corruption and incompetence may trigger popular distress, indignation, and protests. At the same time, weak states lack administrative, police, or military capability to persecute and defeat insurgents. They may also have a commitment problem and be not sufficiently credible to implement their own decisions, inducing rebels to mistrust reforms, rebuff compromises, and prolong the conflict.

• Semi-democratic regime. A partly dictatorial, partly democratic regime may result from the opening or softening of the dictatorship, sometimes as a temporary stage. An intermediate regime is both less inclusive than a democracy and less effective at exerting control and repression than a dictatorship. It can thus foster demands from outsiders and at the same time lower the costs of their collective action.

Communist dictatorships in Eastern Europe were replaced by processes of democratization without major violence, as with the fall of the Berlin Wall in 1989.

DEMOCRATIZATION

From authoritarian and "post-totalitarian" regimes, processes of regime change can develop that do not involve major violence. In fact, most existing democracies have been the result of reforms and pacts, rather than of revolutions or civil wars. While the incumbent rulers can accept broad suffrage rights and the inclusion of opposition movements in the political system, they may request guarantees that they will not be massively expropriated or generally persecuted, but will also have opportunities to share or compete for power under the new institutional framework.

Reform from Above.   Relatively peaceful processes of democratization developed in the United Kingdom, the United States, and, to some extent, former British colonies such as Australia, Canada, and New Zealand, throughout the nineteenth and twentieth centuries, as mentioned at the beginning of this chapter. In these countries, voting rights were successively allocated to different minority groups through a slow, lengthy process of moderate reforms, while the available political alternatives were reduced to a two-party system by institutional means. In this way, each small step in the enfranchisement of a new minority group forced its members to enter into collaboration with one of the two existing larger parties, thus giving the incumbents the possibility of maintaining significant control over the political agenda and retaining some winning positions. This process seeks to prevent the sudden formation of a new alternative political majority for the incumbent electorate. Soft authoritarian, partly free, or liberal, but nondemocratic regimes can exist for a while during this kind of long-term process.

A different pattern was being followed in northern Europe, especially in Finland, Norway, and Sweden, by the early twentieth century. In these countries, a sudden massive enfranchisement of voters was implemented. But this was in conjunction with the establishment of proportional representation electoral rules permitting multiparty coalition politics to consolidate. This was conceived to be a device protecting the incumbent rulers from being expelled from the system as they might have risked with the old electoral system by plurality rule in which a single winner takes all. The number of voters was multiplied almost overnight, but under the new electoral rules, the conservatives and liberals shared power in multiparty coalition governments, often with the agrarians or centrists, and alternating with the social democrats.

Transition. Alternatively, an authoritarian regime may be precipitated into a process of collapse and replacement by unexpected triggering events that reveal its failures and relative weaknesses. Democratic transitions completed within a short period by means of negotiations and pacts among political elites proliferated during the third wave of democratization, undergone in different parts of the world since the mid-1970s. In these situations, there is some balance of forces between the authoritarian government and the opposition movements, usually entailing significant internal divisions among the rulers. This may make the government no longer able to rule regularly with the existing formulas, and the opposition not sufficiently powerful to replace entirely the incumbent regime by its own means. For instance, the last leader of the Soviet Union, Mikhail Gorbachev, launched his policy of "restructuring" and "openness" in the late 1980s on the basis "we cannot go on living like this"—even if he acknowledged the uncertainty of the outcome, as frequently shown with his elusive "life will tell" forecast.

If there has been a prolonged civil war in a country, both the regime and the insurgents may recognize that neither can win by military means and open negotiations for pacification, as happened in some countries in Central America. The mere fear that confrontation may lead to a civil war can be sufficient. For instance, Adolfo Suárez, Spanish prime minister and leader of the transition to democracy in the 1970s, mused, in retrospect, that he had obtained broad popular support not because "the Spanish people, in general, had dreams and eagerness for freedom, but for fear of a confrontation [between the minority yearning for freedom and the authoritarians] after [dictator] Franco's death; because I was pulling people away from the bull's horns."

Most of the world's existing democratic regimes were established as the result of processes including different forms of bargaining and negotiations between the incumbent rulers and the opposition leaders, especially since the late twentieth century. In certain countries, a formal "round table" was formed, as in Brazil and Chile, Poland and Hungary, and South Africa and Indonesia; while in other cases, former persecutors and the recently persecuted met suddenly and unexpectedly, as in Greece and Portugal, Argentina and Czechoslovakia.

Quick Quiz

• Which conditions may favor revolutions and civil wars?
• Define a democratic transition.

CASE 7.2 MUST ISLAM BE ASSOCIATED WITH DICTATORSHIP?

A minimal democracy based on freedom and elections does not require an ideological commitment by the citizens, and should thus be compatible with any religion or creed. However, there seems to be a factual association between Islam and dictatorship in the current world. The vast majority of countries with a majority of Muslims, which are mainly located in North Africa, the Middle East, Asia, and the former Soviet Union, have dictatorial regimes. Actually, more than half of all nondemocratic countries in the world have a Muslim majority.

However, the apparent incongruity between democratic politics and Muslim religion may not be more solid than the traditional wisdom that denied democratic capacity to the countries with a Catholic majority. A succession of democratic failures in Latin European and Latin American countries with a Catholic majority during most of the nineteenth and twentieth centuries gave some ground to the suspicion that a redeeming and proselytizing religion such as Catholicism could not acknowledge legitimacy to governments not committed to its morals and doctrines. In fact, the Popes prohibited the participation of Catholics in elections and political parties until as late as 1931. There were a few previous experiences of parties and movements of Catholic inspiration that participated in liberal politics in France and Italy, but Christian-democratic parties were widely diffused only after the Second World War. From that moment on, however, not only did those parties become important components of democracy in a number of countries, but the Catholic Church itself helped processes of democratization in places such as Spain, Central America, and Poland.

At a second glance, one can see that the most brutal political regimes in the Muslim world are not religious governments, but military or personalistic dictatorships, occasionally using interpretations of the Muslim doctrine in some of their policies. In contrast, new Muslim democratic parties, somehow comparable to the old Christian-democrats, have competed in democratic elections and participated in governments in certain countries, such as Indonesia and Turkey. If, together with these, we count the Muslim minorities living in India and other countries, about one third of the 1.5 billion Muslims of the world may be living under democratically elected governments. If anything, this fact suggests that there may not be intrinsic incompatibility between individual Muslim faith and collective democratic rule. A viable democracy requires religion to be a private affair and the source of one opinion among others in the public debate and political contest.

Conclusion

For most of history, most human beings have lived under self-appointed rulers who have used different combinations of carrots and sticks. In this chapter we have analyzed different types of dictatorships involving various combinations of repression and deliverance of public and private goods.

Depending on the characteristics of the incumbent dictatorial regime and on certain economic and social conditions, a process of political change can go in different directions, leading either to another dictatorship, an intermediate regime, or an alternative democratic formula. In general, the following *proposition* stands:

• **The fall of dictatorships.** Dictatorships can survive on the basis of both repression and their "substantive" performance, economic or other. But they also tend to fall as a consequence of their failures, including military defeats, economic crises, or the death of the dictator. ■

Summary

Dictatorship, or "autocracy," is a form of government in which the political power is held by non-elected, self-appointed rulers.

"Despotic" rule by a personalistic tyrant or a military junta is deprived of ideology and prone to arbitrariness. It is more likely to exist in countries with a single-crop economy and great social polarization.

"Authoritarian" regimes can survive on the basis of repression and control together with good economic performance and a certain degree of internal institutionalization.

"Totalitarian" regimes with a single-party rule intend to control all the public and private activities, are incompatible with autonomous social organizations, use an official mobilizing ideology, and implement widespread terror.

Dictatorships tend to fall as a consequence of their failures, including military defeats, economic crises, or the death of the dictator.

Revolutions and civil wars are more likely in large countries with available natural resources, low per capita income, state weakness, and a semi-democratic regime.

Democracy can be established by processes not entailing major violence through exchanges between the rulers and the opposition. In particular, democracy can be the outcome of a process of broadening suffrage rights within an existing institutional setting, in which the rulers permit inclusiveness while reducing political competition.

Alternatively, a democratic transition can develop from a more balanced relationship of forces between the authoritarian rulers and the opposition through bargaining and negotiations to prevent or eliminate violence and call multiparty elections.

Key Concepts

Authoritarianism. Control and repression plus economic performance and limited institutionalization.

Civil war. Prolonged violent conflict within a country.

Democratization. Replacement of dictatorship with democracy.

Despotism. Personalistic, non-ideological, and arbitrary dictatorship.

Dictatorship. Government by non-elected, self-appointed rulers.

Revolution. Regime change by violent means, which can produce a civil war.

Totalitarianism. All-encompassing regime, distinctively using ideology and terror.

Transition. Democratization without major violence by means of negotiations between incumbent authoritarians and the opposition.

Questions for Review

1. What is a dictatorship?
2. Indicate the differences between a totalitarian regime and an authoritarian regime.
3. List a number of conditions that may favor revolutions and civil wars.
4. Define a democratic transition.

Problems and Applications

1. Which is currently the most populated country in the world with a dictatorial regime?
2. Define "despotism," "authoritarianism," and "totalitarianism."
3. Read Case 7.2, "Must Islam Be Associated with Dictatorship"? Discuss.
4. Search the most recent report at any of the sources cited in the Data Sources that follows.
   a. Which countries are classified as the worst on the scale of freedom and democracy?
   b. Of all in the bottom category of "not free, "autocracy," or "authoritarian" regimes (depending on the survey), how many are in Africa? How many are in Asia?
   c. Discuss.

Data sources

Freedom House: www.freedomhouse.org
Polity IV Project: www.systemicpeace.org/polity/polity4.htm
The Economist: www.economist.com/media/pdf/Democracy_Index_2007_v3.pdf

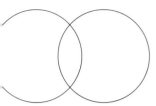

8

DEMOCRACY

In This Chapter You Will

- Consider the utility of a "minimalist" definition of democracy.
- Learn what "civic culture" means.
- Analyze the relations between political democracy and economic development.
- Discuss whether democracies are more inclined to engage in wars than dictatorships.

Probably the least demanding argument in favor of democracy ever made is the famous quip by British prime minister Winston Churchill that "democracy is the worst form of government, except all the others that have been tried from time to time." Churchill said this in late 1947, shortly after the defeat of fascist and military dictatorships in Europe and Japan and at the beginning of the Cold War between Western democracies and Soviet communism. His comment can be taken as a warning that a democratic regime may not guarantee efficient policy outcomes. "No one pretends that democracy is perfect or all-wise," Churchill noted. But it can be preferred to any form of dictatorship, particularly fascist and communist ones, due to other advantages, including individual freedom and the opportunities for government's change.

Other people hold, nevertheless, that in spite of its advantages, democracy is a luxury that poor countries cannot afford. Holding regular political elections may require costly investments in citizen's education, party organization, open media, and the like. Successive failures at attempts of democratization in the Middle East, Africa, and other regions of the world have been used to argue this. However, democracy with high levels of civil liberties and competitive elections for rulers exists nowadays in about half of the countries, inhabited by about half of the world's population, including some at relatively low levels of economic development. In this chapter we study the essential elements of democracy, its relationship with political, economic, and social development, and with war and peace. Different political regimes can produce different performances. But the analysis and discussion show that indeed democracy can be preferred, in a global balance, to dictatorial regimes. ■

What Is Democracy?

The ideal of democracy should include effective citizens' participation, voting equality, and well-informed choices on both the agenda of issues and the policy proposals for each issue. Different institutional formulas may produce different performances in democratic quality, as we will study in later chapters. In practice, however, the minimum elements that make democracy better than dictatorship are **freedom and elections**. In this "minimalist" perspective of what democracy is about, Johan Skytte Prize–winning political scientist Robert Dahl coined the concept of "polyarchy." Its components, which focus on the procedures to make collective decisions, can be restated as follows:

- Freedom of association;
- Freedom of expression and information;
- Broad suffrage rights;
- Right to form candidacies for public offices and compete for votes;
- Free and fair elections; and
- Government policies depending on electoral results.

The relations between these democratic procedures and their substantive performances, including their capacity to foster efficient policy making, economic development, people's well-being, and peace, will be discussed later in this and other chapters. But these performances do not need to be included in the preliminary definition of democracy. Precisely, a merely "procedural," "minimalist," or "thin" definition of democracy is necessary to be able to analyze its relations with other political, economic, social, and cultural variables.

OVERTHROWING THE RULERS

A test on whether a democratic regime works according to some minimal requirements is the possibility that incumbent rulers can be peacefully overthrown and replaced as a result of elections. Philosopher Karl Popper stated that, to have democracy, "the ability to vote a bad government out of office is enough." However, for this to be fulfilled, a demanding behavior by both the winners and the losers of elections is required.

In a well-established democracy, the winners in government should follow established procedures for making policy decisions, which should be reversible, and they should be committed to calling a further election by collectively accepted rules. For this behavior to be guaranteed, the rulers should value the costs of suppressing the opposition as being higher than those of tolerating it, which may imply some capacity for potential resistance from the opposition.

On their side, the losers of the election should step down if they are in government and not try to rebel if they are already in the opposition. Acquiescence and consent can be expected if the costs of rebelling are higher than the costs of complying. This can be facilitated by the existence of appropriate electoral and institutional rules that make the results acceptable and by relatively low losses for passing to the opposition.

Thus, favorable conditions for political leaders to comply with the basic rules of democracy include the presence of relatively robust political and social organizations, fair electoral and institutional rules for achieving power, and the fact that being out of government does not imply complete destitution with regard to political rights and influence. More specifically, the losers can be relatively more prone to consent if the existing political institutions favor power sharing or division of powers, whether by means of proportional representation, separate elections to different offices, or federalism, or if they create reasonable expectations of alternations in government, as we will study in further chapters. Losing an election can also be relatively more acceptable if clear boundaries are drawn between the public and the private domains of activity, if certain social relations are not submitted to enforceable collective decisions, and if some divisive issues are settled not by majority decision but by proportionate distribution of resources to different groups.

The crucial achievement is consensus on the rules of the game. Groups with opposite interests and aims should agree to disagree, and no group should attempt to dominate or repress another.

CONSOLIDATION

A democracy can be considered **consolidated if** it is self-enforcing, that is, if **the main actors routinely play according to the rules of the game**. To achieve this may take some time. Indeed, democracies are more vulnerable when they are young. This can be shown by the fact that the average duration of the thirty-four democracies established since the Second World War and subsequently replaced by dictatorships was only about ten years. In countries where democratic institutions have existed for more than twenty years, breakdowns and replacements by dictatorships provoked by internal crises are rare (the exceptions are the Philippines, which returned to democracy, and Lebanon, Sri Lanka, and Venezuela, which are still in the process). The vast majority of the new democracies established since the 1970s, which are now the majority of the really existing democracies, have so far managed to survive. The longer a democratic regime endures, the less likely it is that it will be replaced by a dictatorship.

After a period of habituation, consensus among political leaders and citizens on the basic criteria of decision-making can be created. This process can be associated with the development of a **"civic culture,"** or a "civic virtue," which is formed of relations of **trust, cooperation, and engagement in collective activities**. Such collective behavior implies a shared set of values and beliefs that the basic political rules are appropriate and worth defending.

At some point, democracy can be valued in itself, even if it can produce some adverse policy outcomes. As put by philosopher Bertrand Russell, "A democrat need not believe that the majority will always reach a wise decision. He should however

BOX 8.1   **MEASURING DEMOCRACY**

There are several methods for measuring democracy, whether as a continuum implying different "degrees" of freedom or with categorical classifications entailing a dividing line between democratic and nondemocratic regimes.

A widely used source is Freedom House's annual survey, "Freedom in the World," which is based on experts' opinions. It uses ten indicators of political freedom and fifteen indicators of civil liberties, derived to a large extent from the Universal Declaration of Human Rights; their average values produce a scale from 1 to 7. Countries are classified as "free" (scoring from 1 to 2.5), "partly free" (3 to 5), and "not free" (5.5 to 7). Freedom House also measures "electoral democracy," which requires free and competitive elections with universal adult suffrage. "Electoral democracies" include all "free" and some "partly free" countries. The survey, which covers all countries, has been published annually since 1972. It is available at www.freedomhouse.org.

The Polity Project on "political regime characteristics and transitions" provides scores from –10 to +10. Countries are classified as an "autocracy" (–10 to –6), an "anocracy" (–5 to +5), and a "democracy" (+6 to +10). The Polity IV dataset covers countries with more than half a million inhabitants from 1800 on, It is available at www.systemicpeace.org/polity/polity4.htm.

The Economist Intelligence Unit's "index of democracy" is mainly based on the "World Values Survey." It uses sixty indicators broken up into five categories: electoral process and pluralism; civil liberties; the functioning of government; political participation; and political culture. Their averages produce a scale from 0 to 10. Each country is classified as a "full democracy," "flawed democracy," "hybrid regime," or "authoritarian." The survey covers all but the microcountries. It is available at: www.economist.com/media/pdf/Democracy_Index_2007_v3.pdf.

The classifications of countries with these three indices are highly correlated. Comparative rankings can be found at: www.en.wikipedia.org/wiki/List_of_indices_of_freedom.

believe in the necessity of accepting the decision of the majority, be it wise or unwise, until such a time that the majority reaches another decision."

As we studied in chapter 3 with the model of a repeated Prisoner's Dilemma, actors can accept to comply in the short term, in spite of the possibility of obtaining immediate benefits from not obeying, if they can expect higher total benefits in the long term. Mutual cooperation is more likely to hold up the longer and more durable the citizens' relationships are under the same type of rules. When there are no powerful anti-system groups, all significant groups participate in elections, and both the winners and the losers accept the electoral results and abide by the rules, especially when they alternate in government, democracy stabilizes and becomes **"the only game in town."**

Now we can identify the opposite circumstances that may hamper the likelihood of democratic consolidation. In economically poor, polarized societies in which people develop heavy redistributive demands, place high stakes in politics, and expect a lot from government, it may be difficult to achieve consensus on the rules because it may greatly depend on their capacity to produce "good" substantive outcomes. In those conditions, losing an election may be highly costly because there can be a large policy distance between the winners and the losers on some important issues, distances that can be amplified by expectations encouraged by ideological radicalism. Even if institutional incentives for cooperation exist, people with strongly opposed interests may choose not to comply. Some individuals may be motivated to think like

BOX 8.2   **DEMOCRACY AND DICTATORSHIP, 1870–2009**

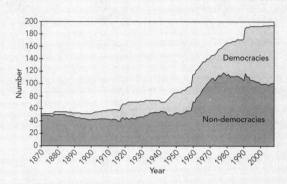

Democratic regimes are widely diffused across the world. In the late nineteenth century, there was electoral democracy in only one fifth of the recognized countries, while 90 percent of the world population lived under monarchies, dictatorships, or colonial domination. In contrast, by the early twenty-first century, about half of the countries and about half of the population of the world live in countries with democratic regimes and the other half live under dictatorships.

Sources: Author's own elaboration, with data from Freedom House series (1972–2009), Polity IV, and Josep M. Colomer, *Political Institutions* (Oxford University Press, 2001).

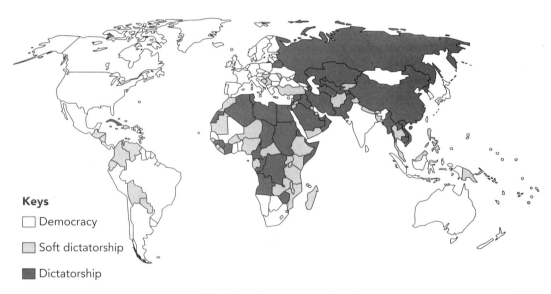

Keys

☐ Democracy

☐ Soft dictatorship

■ Dictatorship

FIGURE 8.1 DEMOCRACY AND DICTATORSHIP IN THE WORLD
Source: Adapted from Freedom House, "Freedom in the World 2008."

SOURCE 8.1   Civic Culture

A stable democracy may require a balance between competition and consensus. The acceptance of the rules of the political game by all significant participants may feed a culture of cooperation and civic duty, which, in turn, helps stabilize the institutions.

The most democratic country on the face of the earth is that in which men have in our time carried to the highest perfection the art of pursuing in common the object of their common desires, and have applied this new science to the greatest number of purposes...In democratic countries the science of association is the mother of science; the progress of all the rest depends upon the progress it has made. Amongst the laws which rule human societies there is one which seems to be more precise and clear than all others. If men are to remain civilized, or to become so, the art of associating together must grow and improve in the same ratio in which the equality of conditions is increased.

Alexis de Tocqueville, *Democracy in America* (1835–40)

Constitution makers have designed formal structures of politics that attempt to enforce trustworthy behavior, but without these attitudes of trust, such institutions may mean little. Social trust facilitates cooperation among the citizens in these nations, and without it democratic politics is impossible...If there is no consensus within society, there can be little potentiality for the peaceful resolution of political differences that is associated with the democratic process. If, for instance, the incumbent elite considered the opposition elite too threatening, it is unlikely that the incumbents would allow a peaceful competition for elite position.

Gabriel Almond and Sidney Verba, *The Civic Culture: Political Attitudes and Democracy in Five Nations* (1963)

The civic community is marked by an active, public-spirited citizen, by egalitarian political relations, by a social fabric of trust and cooperation...[*Some countries and regions*] are blessed with vibrant networks and norms of civil engagement, while others are cursed with vertically structured politics, a social life of fragmentation and isolation, and a culture of distrust. These differences in civic life turn out to play a key role in explaining institutional success.

Robert D. Putnam, *Making Democracy Work: Civic traditions in Modern Italy* (1993)

revolutionary Vladimir I. Lenin who, in early twentieth-century poor Russia, retorted to Spanish social-liberal Fernando de los Ríos, "Liberty, for what?"

The losers' disaffection can be propelled by institutions favoring the concentration of power in a single absolute winner. Politicians may also be motivated to resist complying if enjoying power entails great advantages in comparison with few alternative professional or private opportunities. In short: social polarization, exclusionary concentration of power, and lack of consensus on rules among leaders can facilitate some political entrepreneurs without appealing alternatives to try to gain support from certain groups against others in order to establish a dictatorial rule.

WAVES OF DEMOCRACY

Democratic regimes have been widely diffused across the world, and at an increasing pace in recent times. In the late nineteenth century, competitive elections to legislative assemblies were regularly held in only nine of about fifty empires and states existing at the time. These were France, Switzerland, the United States, the United Kingdom, New Zealand, Canada, Spain, Norway, and Belgium (in chronological order). In all these cases, adult male suffrage (and woman suffrage in only one case) was established within previously existing institutional regimes between 1871 and 1900. By the turn of the century, electoral democracy existed, thus, in less than one fifth of the extant states, an area inhabited by less than 10 percent of the total population, while most humankind lived in authoritarian monarchies or empires or under colonial domination.

Democracy expanded, first, in the aftermath of the First World War, when several old empires in continental Europe fell and new states were created. The number of democracies doubled in twenty years. However, virtually all of these new democratic regimes disappeared as a consequence of revolutions, counterrevolutions and coups d'état. At the beginning of the Second World War, the number of democracies was about the same as forty years before. Democratization spread more widely after World War II with the liberation of Western Europe, including France, Germany, and Italy, and Japan. It was followed by the independence of many colonies, starting with India, and the formation of new countries in Africa and Asia, a period in which the number of democratic regimes doubled.

Finally, the so-called third wave of democratization started in the mid-1970s in Southern Europe, including Portugal, Greece, and Spain; moved to Latin America, starting with Argentina and Brazil; to some countries in Africa and Asia, including South Africa, South Korea, and Indonesia; and more dramatically to Central and Eastern Europe, starting with Poland and the Baltic republics, where the number of new countries also rose, globally multiplying the number of democracies again, this time by more than two and a half. There have been a few cases of retreats from democratization, but most new democracies have stabilized.

By the early twenty-first century, democracy characterized by high levels of civil liberties and competitive elections in which both men and women can vote exists in about 90 countries. This is the highest number ever and represents almost half of the 192 currently recognized countries, inhabited by about half of the world's population. In fact, these numbers might imply some undervaluation of the spread of freedom. Some form of "electoral democracy" exists in two thirds of the independent countries. If the intermediate category of "partly free" countries were accepted in the classification, then non-free countries, or strict dictatorships, would currently encompass only about one third of the world's population, mostly concentrated in North Africa and the Middle East.

Quick Quiz

- What's a democracy?
- What's civic culture?

Electoral democracy can be established in any country when a dictatorship fails, although precarious economic conditions of live can hinder its stabilization and performance.

Democracy and Development

Political democracy and economic and social development maintain complex and mutually reinforcing relationships. On one direction, economic growth and social complexity tend to reduce the likely levels of conflict when a democratic regime is established, and thus favor its viability and endurance. On the other direction, democracy can also create favorable conditions for economic and cultural development. We study these relationships in two separate sections here.

DEVELOPMENT FAVORS DEMOCRACY

At low levels of economic and social development, the rulers and the members of dominant social groups may fear the introduction of elections with broad voting rights to select the government. The risks of sudden enlargements of the electorate and, in particular, of giving the vote to workers and other economically dependent groups were the subject, for example, of a seminal, enlightening discussion in early nineteenth-century Britain. The moderate liberal Thomas B. Macaulay avowed that a radical reform of the franchise would undermine the security of private property. He suspected that under universal suffrage, a numerical majority, a poor majority, would govern, and this majority, following its immediate interests, would seek to dispossess the rich minority. Accordingly, Macaulay thought that those without property should be excluded from suffrage, especially "in countries in which the great majority live from hand to mouth." His fear seemed to be confirmed from the opposite side, for instance, when revolutionary socialist Karl Marx considered that "universal suffrage [would be] the equivalent of political power for the working class in England, where the proletariat forms the large majority of the population." Similar discussions took place in other countries during the nineteenth century.

A logical inference from the correlations just mentioned is that a sustained process of economic development may produce a more diversified economy, foster demands for education, and craft a more complex society. High levels of collective wealth may reduce income and social polarization, and thus lower the intensity of redistributive conflicts. This can facilitate the acceptance of peaceful legal mechanisms for making collective decisions on the basis of votes.

Specifically, if the working and lower classes go beyond the level of subsistence (or of "living from hand to mouth") and have "something to lose" besides their chains, or, better put, if they have access to "a quantity of necessaries of life habitually required," as also formulated by Karl Marx (admittedly for the opposite hypothesis), they may want to avoid risky revolts and revolutions entailing significant degrees of violence and destruction.

Then, in the absence of a revolutionary threat, the upper class can accept opening the system to some degree of political pluralism. The risk that a relatively deprived majority can impose a moderate redistribution of income and wealth by democratic means may not discourage the wealthy classes from accepting electoral democracy if they can still retain a significant amount of absolute welfare and if the costs of reestablishing a harsh dictatorship appear too burdening. The development of financial means (in contrast to an economy based on the exploitation of extensive agriculture or natural resources) can also create a last-resort escape for the privileged, since, should the events not develop as expected, they could move their assets elsewhere.

The members of the educated middle class can act as a moderating cushion and prevent a polarized clash. But they can also push for further liberalization and inclusiveness as they can expect to obtain benefits of their own from socially balanced democratic decisions due to their crucial intermediate situation. Thus, in general, economic development and the subsequent social changes favor the viability and the duration of democratic regimes.

All this does not prevent the establishment of a democratic regime when a dictatorship in a less developed country fails. In fact, a number of poor countries currently enjoy political freedom and democracy. Democracy is not a luxury. If, in spite of its poverty, a country has a relatively egalitarian income distribution, a homogeneous or a highly varied (that is, a non-polarized) ethnic structure, and a balance of forces among groups that makes none of them capable of dominating absolutely, democracy can survive. But, in terms of general probability, "once they are established, democracies are more likely to endure in more highly developed countries," as formulated by political scientist Adam Przeworski and his associates.

DEMOCRACY FAVORS DEVELOPMENT

Even if economic development favors the viability of political democracy, it might be the case that, once established, democratic decision making may hinder economic growth. Actually some economists point out that there is a contradiction between the market and democracy as alternative principles for making collective decisions and allocating resources. An argument is that a market economy can create income and wealth inequalities that may be difficult to render harmonious with the egalitarian principle of one person, one vote. On its side, democratic decisions by majority rule may favor high taxes and redistributive policies with negative effects on economic productivity. As we studied in chapter 2, the opportunities for collective action supplied by a political regime of freedom may indeed favor the formation of lobbies and interest groups putting pressure on the government to benefit minority interests at the expense of the many. But whether growing collective action in society deters productive economic activity or empowers citizens is a question for discussion.

Economic and Political Institutions.   Let us start by noting that economic growth and development are not a direct result of democracy or of any other form of political regime. The expansion of economic activity and production depends, first of all, on technological changes and innovations, which derive from the effort of scientists and inventors, the ingenuity of entrepreneurs, and the hard work of ambitious pioneers. But certainly some initiatives in favor of innovative economic activity, production, and exchange can be helped, stimulated, and protected by the appropriate institutions.

The key institutions favoring economic development are those usually put under the umbrella of **"rule of law,"** which includes **protection of property rights, guarantees for the enforcement of contracts, effective administration, and an independent judiciary**. These institutions can prevent the fulfillment and diffusion of confiscatory attempts, depredatory behavior, widespread corruption by the rulers, and the dissemination of cheating and fraud among traders and in the relations between employers and employees.

Efficient economic institutions can be compatible with political dictatorship, that is, with the persecution of adversaries of the existing rulers. But under a dictatorial regime, the future of economic institutions can be menaced by the arbitrariness of the rulers and by the uncertainty of their succession. In contrast, political freedom—that is, civil liberties of association, expression, and information—can give economic freedom and institutions more solid ground. Democratic political institutions entrench economic institutions, making them more stable and credible. Information and transparency, in particular, enable people to predict the conditions of their future activity and invest in the long term. Rule of law and democracy tend to be mutually reinforcing.

Democracy tends also to be more competent for the provision of public goods, as we have remarked from the beginning of this book. Authoritarian rulers may prefer to abstain from giving economic and social strength to people who can move beyond

BOX 8.3 **ECONOMIC WEALTH AND POLITICAL REGIME**

New democracies have been established in countries with very different levels of per capita income. For instance, Switzerland, the United States, and the United Kingdom enforced broad male suffrage in the late nineteenth century at comparable levels of per capita income of, say, present Azerbaijan or Egypt, which are persistent dictatorships. Likewise, when Norway and India democratized many decades ago, they were as poor as today's Burma and Guinea, which maintain nasty authoritarian regimes. The few democracies that were established in poor countries in the nineteenth century and have survived experienced later processes of economic growth that helped democracy to stabilize. But without political initiatives, economic prosperity in itself is not a guarantee of democracy. Some dictatorships that have reached high levels of affluence in recent periods have managed to survive. As extreme examples, authoritarian Singapore and the United Arab Emirates are among the richest countries in the world, several times wealthier than most countries when they democratized.

Per capita GDP in international dollars

POOR DEMOCRACIES		POOR DICTATORSHIPS (2003)	
Switzerland (1874)	2,397	Algeria	3,133
United States (1879)	2,909	Angola	871
U. Kingdom (1885)	3,574	Azerbaijan	3,394
Norway (1890)	1,709	Burma	1,896
New Zealand (1890)	3,755	Cambodia	1,550
Canada (1891)	2,409	Congo	2,006
Australia (1900)	4,013	Cuba	2,569

Per capita GDP in international dollars (*Continued*)

POOR DEMOCRACIES		POOR DICTATORSHIPS (2003)	
Finland (1907)	1,834	Ethiopia	595
Sweden (1910)	2,980	Egypt	3,034
Ireland (1921)	2,533	Guinea	601
India (1947)	618	N. Korea	1,127
Israel (1950)	2,817	Laos	1,322
Japan (1952)	2,336	Libya	2,427
Costa Rica (1953)	2,353	Pakistan	1,881
Jamaica (1962)	2,722	Sudan	1,080
Botswana (1966)	473	Turkmenistan	2,489
South Africa (1994)	3,623	Vietnam	2,147
Indonesia (1999)	3,161	Zimbabwe	1,070

Per capita GDP in international dollars

RICH DEMOCRACIES		RICH DICTATORSHIPS (2003)	
Portugal (1974)	7,048	Bahrain	5,589
Greece (1975)	7,722	Belarus	7,387
Spain (1977)	8,833	China	4,803
Brazil (1979)	4,892	Eq. Guinea	13,562
Argentina (1983)	7,383	Iran	5,539
S. Korea (1988)	7,621	Kazakhstan	7,655
Chile (1990)	6,402	Kuwait	10,145
Poland (1991)	4,738	Qatar	8,915
Hungary (1991)	5,694	Russia	6,323
Czechoslovakia	7,439	S. Arabia	7,555
Estonia (1991)	9,799	Syria	7,698
Latvia (1991)	8,707	Singapore	21,530
Lithuania (1991)	8,154	Thailand	7,195
Taiwan (1996)	13,985	U.Arab Emirates	17,818

Note: For democracies, data are for the first year of the most recent democratization. For all countries, per capita GDP is given in 1990 U.S. dollars with purchasing power parity, as in Angus Maddison, Historical Statistics, www.oecd.org (updated in 2007)

their control. In contrast, the appropriate supply of public goods such as roads, infrastructure, and schools, which can be crucial for the propulsion of economic growth, is higher in democratic regimes with accountable rulers. Demands for education, in particular, typically soar as people can foresee peace and institutional stability.

We again need to specify the mechanisms by which some rules and institutions create favorable conditions for certain people's behavior, which is the proximate cause of any collective outcome. It is not that rules and institutions can promote economic growth or depression by themselves. But if the appropriate institutional incentives exist, people are more likely to behave in favor of innovation and growth. Innovators, entrepreneurs, and hard workers can be more ready to follow their own motivations if they can predict mid- and long-term rewards for their efforts and investments.

Institutions are thus a favorable and sometimes necessary condition for development. However, they are not a sufficient condition. In fact, under certain conditions, poverty and underdevelopment can be relatively stable. For instance, in a poor country, the members of the educated minority may not be interested in the diffusion of education, because it would reduce the competitive advantage of having a school degree and erode their relative positions. Alternatively, a populist coalition may reject the introduction of market institutions due to the risk of being left out as a consequence of people's general inefficiency and low productivity. Even if some institutions supply a favorable environment, people motivated by particular short-term interests may not take the opportunity to alter their behavior if doing so might prompt a risky change.

Resilient Democracy.   Empirical observations show that in countries with stable democratic regimes, evils such as infant mortality tend to decrease, while goods such as life expectancy and secondary school enrollment tend to increase. In general, people deprived of civil and political rights are more likely to be left behind regarding health care, education, and other social goods.

A remarkable observation is that no independent and democratic country has ever experienced a famine. Famous famines were produced, among other places, under alien British rule in Ireland; under communist dictatorships in the Soviet Union, with the collectivization of agriculture; in China, with the failure of the so-called "Great Leap Forward"; and more recently, under dictatorial regimes in failed states such as Ethiopia, North Korea, Somalia, and Sudan. Dictatorial rulers tend to attribute these failures to natural disasters such as floods, drought, and crop failure. But famines have "never materialized in any country that is independent, that holds elections regularly, that has opposition parties to voice criticisms and that permits newspapers to report freely and question the wisdom of government policies without extensive censorship," as pointed out by Nobel Prize–winning Indian economist Amartya Sen. India, in particular, was the subject of a natural experiment when the series of famines it had routinely undergone until the early 1940s simply disappeared with the arrival of independence and the establishment of a multiparty democracy and a free press.

During the last decades, no significant statistical difference has been convincingly reported between the annual rates of economic growth in countries with democracy and those with a dictatorship, whether rich or poor. However, this can be due to a statistical fallacy disguising a crucial difference between the two types of political regimes with regard to their compatibility with both economic growth and depression. Some dictatorships may permit or support free-market relations and economic growth, as already mentioned. They can even seek legitimacy through good economic performance. But they are vulnerable to crises and external shocks. The vulnerability of the dictatorship is higher if the model of economic growth is based on the extensive exploitation of some factors and is alien to public goods and technological change. In general, dictatorships can fail, and may then fall. When the dictatorship ceases to deliver on its own promises

CASE 8.1 DEMOCRATIC INDIA, DICTATORIAL CHINA

China and India are the two most populated countries of the world. Recently, the two economies have been growing at impressive annual rates. However, while India is a democracy, China is a dictatorship.

When India became independent from British colonial domination in 1947, the general opinion was that a democratic regime could not last in such a huge, poor, illiterate, and ethnically varied country. Most prospects were as grim as that of the British tea planter who predicted, "Chaos would prevail in India if we were so foolish to leave the natives to run their own show." Indeed, independence was immediately followed by war, provoked by the separation of Pakistan, which caused more than one million deaths. The rule of the dominant Congress Party, under the strong leadership of Jawaharlal Nehru, managed to achieve some stability. But the Congress's governments, which implemented protectionist and interventionist economic policies, presided over a long period of economic stagnation, derisively referred to as the "Hindu rate of growth." In fact, democracy broke down. In 1975, Prime Minister Indira Gandhi (Nehru's daughter) declared a state of emergency. Civil rights were suppressed, thousands of opposition members were imprisoned, and hundreds of journalist were arrested. However, two years later, Gandhi reestablished legal guarantees and called a new election, which she and her party lost. Back in power at the following election, she was killed by her own guards. Since the late 1980s, the political system of India experienced

significant transformations. Single-party dominance was replaced with a multiparty system, federal coalition cabinets became the norm, and an increasing number of state governments were ruled by local and opposition parties. Although some ethnic and territorial conflicts were persistent, especially in Punjab and Kashmir, at the borders with Pakistan, violent riots became routine incidents. Open now to foreign trade and investment, the Indian economy began to burgeon.

The communist-dominated People's Republic of China was established just two years after India's independence. For almost three decades, Mao Zedong led a dictatorship with major totalitarian trends, including campaigns of permanent mobilization, such as the Great Leap Forward and the Great Proletarian Cultural Revolution, which caused several million deaths and big economic disasters. Since 1978, shortly after the dictator's death, the new leader Deng Xiaoping promoted economic liberalization and opening up to foreign investments, under the motto "To get rich is glorious," which fostered rapid growth. However, rising social unrest could not be channeled through integrative institutions. The slaughter of protesters in and around Tiananmen Square in 1989 became a bloody warning for future dissidents. Relatively minor conflicts have threatened to shake the stability of the regime, as shown in the tensions around the vindication of Taiwan, demands for autonomy in Tibet, religious persecutions, and other protests.

and in line with people's expectations, protests tend to arise, as do doubts about the regime's future spread, and eventually the regime loses ground.

A case in point is the so-called "Asian tigers," a set of countries with authoritarian regimes in which high rates of economic growth developed during the 1970s and '80s. A sudden clash and recession in the second half of the 1980s precipitated processes of major political change, including in South Korea, Taiwan, and Indonesia. In many countries, democracy has replaced authoritarianism in conditions of economic decline. In contrast, democracies are more compatible with both economic growth and depression. Some responsibility for economic recessions can be attributed to a specific team of rulers, who can be overthrown by means of regular elections and institutional procedures without putting the political regime in question.

Thus, dictatorships are more vulnerable than democracies to economic failures. In fact, the periods of high economic growth under dictatorships tend to be relatively

SOURCE 8.2   Socioeconomic Correlations with Political Democratization

The relationship between economic and social processes and political democracy has been discussed largely by political scientists, sociologists, and economists. Many analyses focus on structural variables, such as the level of economic development or income inequalities, which can create constraints or incentives for conflicts and coalitions between groups and for individual strategies and decisions.

Perhaps the most common generalization linking political systems to other aspects of society has been that democracy is related to the state of economic development. The more well-to-do a nation, the greater the chances that it will sustain democracy...Economic development, producing increased income, greater economic security, and wide-spread higher education, largely determines the form of the "class struggle"...A larger middle class tempers conflict by rewarding moderate and democratic parties and penalizing extremist groups.

Seymour M. Lipset, *Political Man: The Social Bases of Politics* (1960)

A key feature in bourgeois revolutions is the development of a group in society with an independent economic base, which attacks obstacles to a democratic version of capitalism that have been inherited from the past...The allies this bourgeois impetus has found, the enemies it has encountered, vary sharply from case to case. The landed upper classes were either an important part of this capitalist and democratic tide, as in England, or if they opposed it, they were swept aside in the convulsions of revolution or civil war. The same thing may be said about the peasants...No bourgeoisie, no democracy.

Barrington Moore, Jr., *Social Origins of Dictatorship and Democracy* (1966)

Capitalist development is related to democracy because it shifts the balance of class power, because it weakens the power of the landlord class and strengthens subordinate classes. The working and the middle class—unlike other subordinate classes in history—gain an unprecedented capacity for self-organization due to such developments as urbanization, factory production, and new forms of communication and transportation.

Evelyne Huber, Dietrich Rueschemeyer, and John D. Stephens, "The Impact of Economic Development on Democracy" (1993)

Dictatorships may die for so many different reasons that development, with all its modernizing consequences, plays no privileged role...After all, many European countries became democratized because of wars, some dictatorships have fallen in the aftermath of the death of the founding dictator, some have collapsed because of economic crises, some because of foreign pressures, and perhaps some for purely idiosyncratic reasons...[But] Even if the emergence of a democracy is independent of the level of development, the chance that this regime will survive will be greater if it is established in an affluent country...One possible account for the durability of democracies in wealthy countries...is that wealth lowers the intensity of distributional conflicts.

Adam Przeworski, Michael E. Alvarez, José A. Cheibub, and Fernando Limongi, *Democracy and Development: Political Institutions and Well-being in the World* (2000)

Continued

> The middle class plays an important role in the emergence of democracy in a number of ways: 1) it can be the driving force for democracy, especially for the emergence of partial democracy, 2) it can be in favor of the poor being included in the political arena, facilitating a move from partial to full democracy, 3) perhaps most interesting, it can act as a buffer between the rich and the poor by ensuring that democracy will not be very anti-rich and, therefore, dissuading the rich from using repression or mounting coups; and 4) when it is in power together with the rich, it can play the role of soft-liners arguing against repression and in favor of a transition to democracy, which is less costly for the middle class than for the rich.
>
> Daron Acemoglu and James A. Robinson, *Economic Origins of Dictatorship and Democracy* (2006)

short, encompassing at most one generation. The statistical correlation between political regimes and economic performance mentioned earlier may therefore be due to the fact that dictatorships are unable to bear deep recession and economic failure, while democracies are more resilient to them. In the very long term, relatively modest rates of annual growth in conditions of democratic institutional stability may produce significant accumulated wealth.

This is the long-term result that is usually captured by the snapshot in which wealthy countries appear associated with democracy, and poor ones with dictatorship. In certain countries, some people are still ready to give up political freedom and democracy in the expectation of getting food, public security, or services. But this expectation is likely to be frustrated. If dictators made countries rich, Africa would be an economic colossus, as *The Economist* once said.

Democratic Peace

Democracies are less likely to fight each other and engage in wars than dictatorships. This has been common knowledge at least since the late eighteenth century, when German philosopher Immanuel Kant identified the conditions for "universal peace." In his words, since in democracy "the consent of the citizens is required to decide whether or not war is to be declared, it is very natural that they [the rulers] will have great hesitation in embarking on so dangerous an enterprise." In contrast, in a nondemocratic regime, "it is the simplest thing in the world to go to war; for the head of state is not a fellow citizen, but the owner of the state, and a war will not force him to make the slightest sacrifice."

Together with political freedom, two other conditions favor international peace. One is economic interdependence among countries, which is usually built by ties of international trade and investment. The other is international law and institutions, including treaties for mutual cooperation among democratic states. We review some of these relationships here.

PEACE FOR VOTES

The idea of democratic peace implies an extension of domestic democratic norms for resolving conflict without violence, that is, by means of negotiations and votes, and by establishing relationships among states. However, this international behavior of states can in fact be the result of governments' foreign policy driven by domestic motives. Several crucial elements distinguish the processes of going to war in a democratic as opposed to a dictatorial regime.

First of all, political leaders in a democracy, if they are interested in obtaining popular support and winning elections, are relatively likely to adopt foreign policies that can be accepted by voters. Citizens can reject war for fear of its casualties and the diversion of resources from other priorities. Leaders, in turn, may fear that a military defeat will become a political failure and put them at risk of losing power.

Second, institutions of free opinion and information can facilitate public debate about the expected consequences of going to war. For political leaders to be confident of a military initiative, the voters must be sufficiently convinced that the cause is just, the war is winnable, and the costs are not going to be disproportionate. Otherwise, apart from self-defense against aggressors, people may not find a motive valuable enough to justify the human costs of going to war. Finally, a democratic regime requires following specific institutional procedures in order to declare war, which are usually shaped in the intention to prevent the rulers' arbitrariness.

All these factors favor democratic leaders' abstention from undertaking aggressive wars. The fact is that democratic regimes rarely start a war of aggression, virtually never fight each other, and, in general, minimize political violence. The more democratic a political regime, the lower is the probability that it will exert violence, whether inside or outside the country, and the more peaceful its foreign relations are likely to be.

On the other hand, one can suspect that democratic leaders facing dwindling political fortunes due to other failing policies may feel impelled to resort to war, perhaps even fabricating an international incident with some detestable dictatorship, in the expectation that winning the conflict might increase their chances of retaining power. Anecdotal occurrences of this sort can surely be identified. But, most commonly, democratic leaders can argue, rather contrarily, in favor of the advantages of peace. In the words of U.S. president William Clinton's, which echo the correlations between peace and democracy just presented, "Ultimately, the best strategy to ensure our security and to build a durable peace is to support the advance of democracy elsewhere. Democracies don't attack each other."

Of course, many people can be mistaken sometimes and approve or give support to a war that may turn out to be a disaster. But it is more likely that a few people will make this kind of decision more often if they act in conditions of secrecy and unrestrained ambition—that is, the typical setting for decision making in dictatorships. Mistakes in democracy can also be corrected by the regular replacement of rulers through elections and other legal mechanisms. In general, democratic governments find relatively great difficulty in obtaining a social consensus to go to war. They face a high probability that the suffering inflicted by war on their citizens will lead to their peaceful electoral overthrow.

According to this line of reasoning, democracies are unlikely to initiate wars or disputes, but are more inclined to reach peaceful settlements; they fight only when they are confident of victory, tend to avoid disastrous wars, and when they do fight, they try to do it quickly and at relatively low cost. In the well-informed words of another U.S. president, Ronald Reagan, "History teaches that wars begin when governments believe the price of aggression is cheap."

In contrast, dictatorships can usually coerce their subjects into participating in a war and can also expect to obtain direct benefits from the subsequent military gains. Dictatorial leaders may feel freer to adopt unpopular policies, knowing that public anger is less likely to cause them to lose office. They can thus give little weight to the costs in human lives to their people in comparison with their motives of self-aggrandizement. Some dictatorial rulers can be misled by their own advisers and by distorted intelligence reports about the presumed feasibility of victory. They can also try to transform a military defeat into a political success by attacking internal enemies and manipulating patriotic sentiments. Dictatorships are more inclined to engage in risky wars. It is the dictatorships that tend to undertake conquest and looting wars producing mass slaughter and destruction, including so-called "democides" (the slaughter of more than one million people), both within and outside the dictators' countries. They may even seek to exploit the reluctance of democratic governments to engage in military fight by threatening, blackmailing, or attacking countries with democratic regimes. After all, dictators and tyrants of all persuasions have repeated again and again that democracies are too cowardly to venture into certain feats of aggression.

PEACE FAVORS DEMOCRACY

It is not only that democracy favors peace, but also peace favors the opportunities for democracy to be established and survive. Major wars were fought by European powers in their conquest of foreign territories and populations in Africa, Asia, and the Americas, especially from the seventeenth to the nineteenth centuries. Note, however, that the existence of very large colonial empires was traditionally considered incompatible not only with freedom for the colonized peoples, but also with the liberalization and democratization of the metropolitan state.

Already in the eighteenth century, the liberal Adam Smith dreamed that "Great Britain should voluntarily give up all authority over her colonies, and leave them to elect their own magistrates, to enact their own laws, and to make peace and war as they might think proper," in order to save military expense and develop more advantageous free trade. The radical democrat Jeremy Bentham, who had also favored relinquishing the British colonies in North America, sent a message to the French National Convention proposing, "Emancipate your colonies!" Later on, he advised the Spanish liberal constituents to "Rid themselves of Ultramaria," that is, of the Central and South American colonies, in the cause of adopting a more democratic regime in Spain. Even the socialist Karl Marx, although he was more ambiguous regarding the "civilizing" effects of colonialism in Asia, hoped that the "emancipation of the English working class" would be greatly favored by the independence of Ireland from Britain. Indeed, both Great Britain and Spain, although at very different paces, introduced stable universal suffrage and competitive elections only when they began to rid themselves of most of their colonies, and in so doing, reduced their involvement in this kind of war.

By one account, the major interstate wars, which are defined as those producing at least one thousand deaths in battle per year and excluding civil wars, from 1816 to

1991 (that is, between the end of the Napoleonic Empire and the dissolution of the Soviet Empire) were fought in 198 cases between dictatorships and in 155 between democracies and dictatorships. After decades of continuous warfare in Europe, especially around the rivalry between France and Germany, and the most lethal Second World War, European political leaders acknowledged that, in order to prevent new interstate wars, democratization was a fundamental condition. This has indeed been the permanent message and requirement presented by the European Union to the successive and numerous candidates wishing to join the "club." Building the EU has enabled most states to save building their own armies. More broadly, all across the world after the Cold War, the number of interstate wars has dramatically decreased at the same time that democracy has expanded in all regions of the world. The higher the number of stable democracies there are in the world, the fewer potential enemies democracies may have and the wider the zones of peace may be.

Quick Quiz

• What relationship exists between democracy and war?

Conclusion

A minimalist definition of democracy based on freedom and elections allows us to establish a clear dividing line between the political regimes of the world. In this chapter we have studied the conditions in which a democratic regime can be established and those that favor its stabilization and consolidation. We have seen that, in comparison with dictatorships, democracies are more resilient to crises. The longer a democratic regime endures, the less likely it is that it can be replaced by a dictatorship.

Several well-established findings are captured by the following *propositions*:

• **Development favors democracy.** Economic development favors the viability of democratic regimes because it tends to reduce income and social polarization and lower the intensity of redistributive conflicts.

• **Democracy favors development.** Democracy can favor economic development because it is strongly associated with the rule of law and is more competent in the provision of public goods.

• **Democratic peace.** Democratic states are less likely to fight each other and engage in wars than are dictatorships.

While the number of democracies expands across the world, more favorable conditions for economic prosperity and international peace also are established. ■

Summary

A minimal definition of democracy includes freedom of association and expression, broad suffrage rights, the right to compete as candidates, free and fair elections, and a government dependent on electoral results.

The consolidation of democracy implies that both winners and losers accept the electoral results and abide by the rules. A consolidated democracy can be associated with a civic culture favoring trust, cooperation, and engagement in collective activities.

The longer a democratic regime endures, the less likely it is that it will be replaced by a dictatorship.

Economic development favors the viability of democracy because it reduces income and social polarization and lowers the intensity of redistributive conflicts.

Democracy favors economic development because it is strongly associated with the rule of law and is more competent in the provision of public goods.

Dictatorships are more vulnerable to economic failures than are democracies.

Democracies are less likely to fight each other and engage in wars than dictatorships. They fight only when they are confident of victory; while dictatorships are more inclined to engage in risky wars.

Key Concepts

Civic culture. Values of trust, cooperation, and engagement in collective activities.

Consolidation. A situation in which democracy is, for both winners and losers, "the only game in town."

Democracy. Government by means of freedom and elections.

Democratic peace. Democracies are less inclined to engage in wars than dictatorships.

Rule of law. Property rights, guarantees of contracts, and an independent judiciary.

Questions for Review

1. What's a democracy?
2. What's civic culture?
3. What relationship exists between economic development and political democracy?
4. What relationship exists between democracy and war?

Problems and Applications

1. Which are the three most populated countries in the world with a democratic regime nowadays?
2. Search for the per capita income of the three countries identified in the previous question. Comment.
3. For your own country, search for:
   a. Total population;
   b. Total number of legal voters in the census; and
   c. How many people voted in the last general election.
   Comment.
4. Read Box 8.3, "Economic Wealth and Political Regime." Discuss.

Data sources

Same as for the previous chapter.

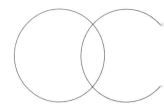

PART III ELECTION

In this part, we study how democratic representation can be organized by means of political parties and elections. Political representation implies people in public offices acting in the interests of others and being responsive to them. Political parties are organizations that present policy proposals and candidates for leadership offices. Democratic elections entail competition among candidates on policy proposals for different issues, which can be more or less interesting for different groups of voters. Electoral results determine the quality and contents of representative government.

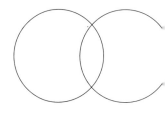

9

POLITICAL PARTIES

In This Chapter You Will

- Examine what a political party is.
- Discuss why parties exist.
- Examine how a political party can become an "oligarchy."
- Learn that party activists hold more extreme political positions than voters and leaders.
- Consider the political consequences of different types of political parties.

During the United States primary elections for president in 2008, Mark Penn, chief strategist for candidate Hillary Clinton, said that the Democratic Party's other major candidate, Barack Obama, was "unelectable." Clinton's supporters argued that Obama, in spite of his success among participants in party caucuses and primary elections, was the weaker candidate against the Republicans because of his inexperience and inability to attract white workers' support, which would be crucial for winning the general election. Actually, examples abound where the winner of a party primary is not the stronger candidate to win the general election. At some moment, Hillary Clinton relied upon the support she expected from "superdelegates," that is, professional politicians and other non-elected delegates in the party convention, to become the Democratic candidate for president. Indeed, any candidate faces the challenge, first, of attracting the support of party activists and registered voters, and of party leaders and public officers, and then of persuading moderate, independent, swing, and undecided voters, who rarely vote in the primaries or participate in party activities.

If a person wants to become a political leader or have influence in politics, it is likely he or she will have to join a political party. Political parties are organizations that present policy proposals, select candidates for leadership offices, whether by primary elections or other procedures, and play a significant role in shaping governance within institutional rules. In this chapter we study political parties as a special form of collective action and leadership, which we analyzed from a more general perspective in the first part of this book. First, we discuss why parties exist, how they are formed, and what advantages they can provide to the community. Second, we consider different types of political parties by examining the goals and motivations of different party members and their relationships. ■

Why Parties?

A political party is an organization of individuals formed to compete for political power and provide public goods in the form of public policy. Certain members of political parties are interested in attaining power as a means of promoting their preferred public policy, while others may use collective interests and policy proposals as instruments to seek power for its own sake. In general, political parties facilitate governance by participating in competitive elections in democracy and helping to form governments. Let us first consider how political parties are formed, before discussing their potential advantages.

FORMATION OF POLITICAL PARTIES

Political parties do not always have good fame. Opinion polls in democratic countries typically relegate parties near the bottom on the scale of reputation (usually near the mass media; while universities rocket to the top). From the beginning of their formation, political parties, which were initially called "factions" in some places, were associated with bad intentions and the introduction of divisiveness to the disadvantage of broad collective interests. In the mid-nineteenth-century United States, for example, the National Municipal League complained that "while many voters find sentiments which they disapprove in each [party] platform, they can see no alternative but to cast their ballots for one or the other, and thus seem to endorse and support ideas to which they are really opposed." This is a sentiment that some people can still resent nowadays. However, as freedom and democracy are established in a community, political parties eventually tend to be acknowledged as unavoidable evils.

We can distinguish between "endogenously" formed political parties, which emerge from existing elections and assemblies, and "exogenous" parties, created at the initiative of some people who intend to enter into competition with established parties.

Endogenous Parties. The earliest modern political parties emerged from the eighteenth century on, at different moments depending on the country, within the framework of traditional elections and representative assemblies as **collective candidacies and legislative coalitions.** Individual candidates found incentives to form closed lists of candidates to be voted for "in bloc" by the citizens. Forming or joining a coordinated candidacy may increase the prospects of winning additional votes and the likelihood of winning a seat. Also, coordinating individual representatives' initiatives and votes within an assembly may increase the opportunities of approving a bill or a motion.

Thus, early political parties adopted the form of electoral committees and parliamentary groups. An organizational link between the two was then added. Improvised clubs, or temporary coalitions, tended to become permanent organizations. For those excluded from coordinated candidacies and votes, the best reaction was to counter-or-ganize, thus transforming elections and assemblies with traditions of individual rep-resentation and consensual agreements into the scene of political party competition.

Exogenous Parties. New political parties have been formed in more recent times as suffrage rights have expanded and societies have become increasingly complex. A political party can be formed from outside the existing elections and assemblies on the basis of a new proposal on some collective issue, with the intention of changing the established policy. As a policy proposal usually implies some unequally distributed advantages or costs for the members of the community, a party of this kind may be **based on the support of previously existing interest groups.**

For instance, liberal parties can be formed around a free-trade policy proposal, with corresponding support from merchant and consumer organizations; some social-ist parties were formed around the proposal of taking collective control over private property, with the support of previously existing workers' unions and guilds; a chris-tian democrat or neoconservative party can be formed in defense of traditional family values, with support from a church or religious groups; a green party may be formed with policy proposals aiming at protecting natural resources with support from agrar-ian and environmentalist organizations. New parties can also be formed from splits in existing ones.

FUNCTIONS OF PARTIES

Organizing a successful political party implies a few basic tasks:

- Proposing innovative **policy** on some selected collective issues;
- Developing collective action by means of **leadership** and other organizational incentives; and
- Competing in elections and exerting influence and power in **assemblies** and **governments.**

Policy Making.   Regarding the first goal, political parties need to promote the design of innovative public policies. It has been said that politicians, even if they believe they are exempt from any intellectual influences, are usually the slaves of some defunct scholar. "Madmen in authority, who hear voices in the air, are distilling their frenzy from some academic scribbler of a few years back," in economist John M. Keynes's attuned words. But in mature democracies, politicians are increasingly aware of the importance of ideas for designing public policy. Political party leaders regularly resort to advisors, think tanks, and research institutes for policy analysis and design. (Some of them even graduated with degrees in political science!)

The choice of policy proposals strongly depends on which issues can obtain salience in public opinion and electoral campaigns and move people to vote for one or another party. Political parties select only a few issues, among the huge number of potential collective goods and divisive questions arising in any complex society, to deal with them in the short- or midterm agenda. A party agenda can reduce the number of potentially prominent issues and facilitate stable decision making. But, although the formation of the public agenda enables identifying priorities in the provision of public goods, it also implies self-interested calculations by political parties who wish to give salience to those issues in which they can present advantageous proposals.

Leader Selection. Parties select candidates to stand in elections for seats on councils and assemblies, and for the offices of mayor, governor, prime minister, president, and other elected or representative offices. Would-be leaders usually have to be accepted not only by voters but also by party members and activists, as we mentioned before and will discuss later in this chapter.

Government Formation. Political party members typically provide individuals to fill executive offices. The claim of "partocracy" refers to the frequent choice of persons who may not be the most qualified ones for public office, but who are more faithful to party leaders or more embedded in the party organization. However, party government allows making rulers responsive and accountable to voters in democracy. Even if some individual officeholders do not run for reelection, the continuity of political parties allows voters to reward or punish previous incumbents' records in government by voting or refusing to vote for the subsequent party candidacies.

Political parties are not the only way to promote satisfactory policy making and broad social support for collective decisions. Other arrangements—such as loose coalitions of individual representatives, pressure groups and associations, issue networks, popular legislative initiatives, or referendums—may be superior for certain issues and under different conditions. In certain cases, the party may even become part of the problem. Party finances, in particular, are a frequent subject of suspicion and controversy. Although the mechanism of political parties has proven useful for the main tasks just listed, a high-quality democracy may require a refined combination of parties and other means.

Quick Quiz

- What is a party?
- How can political parties facilitate collective decision-making?

Types of Parties

A political party is an **organization**, that is, a group of individuals with a common purpose in its external activity of competing for votes, political power, and policy making. A political party, however, can also be conceived as an **institution** that enforces rules for its internal process of decision making. As electoral candidacies, legislative coalitions, or politicized interest or opinion groups endure, they can be "institutionalized" into a political party by the adoption of internal rules and procedures. These are, however, relatively more variable than those usually enforced in other formal institutions such as assemblies, governments, or courts, which will be analyzed in later chapters in this book. Informal methods and customs tend to be more relevant within a party. They are basically useful for making compromises between its members, especially regarding the adoption of policy proposals and the selection of candidates.

BOX 9.1 EXTREME ACTIVISTS

Regarding the normal configuration of major and semi-major parties operating where overt, organized, electoral competition for governmental offices is institutionalized...I am suggesting these uniformities:

1. Top leaders and non-leaders [*voters*] are more nearly congruent with one another, in median positions on substantive issues, than are the intermediate cohorts of sub-leaders [*activists*] with either the top party leaders or the non-leaders [*voters*]. This might be dubbed the General Law of Curvilinear Disparity.
2. Sub-leaders [*activists*], relative to top leaders and non-leaders [*voters*], are substantive extremists. In a generally Left-of-Center party they are the most leftist cohort: in a generally Right-of-Center party they are the most rightist cohort. From this it follows, at least for two-party systems, that the sub-leaders [*activists*], relative to the top leaders and the non-leaders [*voters*], are most estranged from public opinion at large.
3. Accordingly, the top leaders occupy an intermediate position (but not an exact mid-way position) between the median opinions of their sub-leaders [*activists*] and their non-leaders [*voters*]. From the standpoint of inter-party relations, top leaders are more polarized than their respective non-leaders [*voters*]. But the contrast is small in scale and the top leaders are not the most extremist echelon.

...I shall dub the last two propositions the Special Law of Curvilinear Disparity.

John D. May, "Opinion Structure of Political Parties" (1973)

In order to distinguish different organizational types of political parties, we focus on the goals and motives of different types of party members, which are just one special case of the relationship between leaders and followers studied in a previous chapter.

PARTY MEMBERS

The members of a political party can be classified into **two categories: (1) leaders, or professional politicians; and (2) followers, or voluntary activists**. The first category encompasses those who make or aim to make a living off politics, including public officeholders, party leaders, and electoral candidates. It can also include their direct employees and appointees, either within the party bureaucracy or at certain levels of the public administration under their control. **Professional politicians are usually considered as being "vote-seekers" and "office-seekers."**

The second category of party members includes all those activists or militants, adherents or affiliates, who give their time, effort, or money to the party not in the expectation of getting into office but to promote their preferred policy, ideology, or values. Members of interest groups or movements closely related to a party in pursuit of specific legislative or governmental decisions can also be included in this category. **Party activists can thus be called "policy-seekers."** We now examine these two categories of party members.

Politicians. Professional politicians are those people who lead a party, promote new policy proposals, run as candidates in elections, and hold assembly seats, governmental portfolios, or other offices. They may embrace certain values or a spirit of public service, but they need to be motivated to undertake collective action by

SOURCE 9.1   **The Political Oligarchy**

> The consciousness of power always produces vanity, an undue belief in personal greatness…When the leaders are not persons of means and when they have no other source of income, they hold firmly to their positions for economic reasons, coming to regard the functions they exercise as theirs by inalienable right…It is organization which gives birth to the dominion of the elected over the electors, of the mandataries over the mandators, of the delegates over the delegators. Who says organization, says oligarchy.
>
> Robert Michels, *Political Parties* (1911)

selective incentives, especially the ambition for public office. Since the likelihood of success in politics is always uncertain and remote, professional politicians need to enjoy the day-to-day exercise of power—that is, the capacity to make other people do things—and have high potential vanity to satisfy. This may be achieved through frequent appearances in the media and other public exposure, having a high status, receiving compliments, being bestowed titles, given preferential seating, and enjoying numerous spoils and perks from public office, including the use of governmental assets and the warm atmosphere created by solicitous secretaries, assistants, and pages.

A pure professional politician can conceive a policy proposal as a means of winning office—the reason for which so many are considered to be "opportunist." However, politicians competing in elections need to win voters' support, which induces them to choose policy stands that the voters may back and, if they are running for reelection, to deliver what the voters can find sufficiently satisfactory. The dominance of party leaders or professional politicians within political parties tends to create a **political "oligarchy."**

Activists. Party activists are supposed to be a link between party leaders or governmental officers and the electorate. They should have the opportunity to participate in deliberative arenas for policy making, and spread the party's policies and candidacies among potential voters. However, as political activists are typically motivated by the promotion of a specific policy, value, ideology, or interest for which they have an intense preference, they are not necessarily representative of the political tastes of the electorate. Voluntary activists tend to hold more "extreme" positions than most party voters and even party leaders.

If activists are willing to pay relatively high costs to participate in collective action, they can logically aspire to obtain greater benefits than those any citizen could reasonably expect from the simpler act of voting. Activists and lobbyists may give work, money, or other resources to a party or candidate, expecting to obtain favorable policy decisions—for example, ethnic minority rights, export subsidies, environmental safety. Members of interest- or value-organized groups may also belong to this category if they are stably attached to a party, as frequently happens with corporate associations, labor unions, certain churches, and social movements. In contrast to rather flexible or ambiguous professional politicians, party activists are frequently labeled

Political parties can mobilize activist with intense preferences on policy and ideological issues.

"true believers," Some activists can also seek access to public officials, jobs, contracts, or individual favors, or simply value membership as a source of information, social, or psychic rewards.

TWO-LEVEL GAMES

Party members always play a "two-level game:" one outside, at the electoral and institutional level; and another inside, at the level of internal party decision making. Politicians and activists need each other. They may pursue different goals, but they have a common interest: winning votes leading to power, whether as an end in itself or as a necessary condition to see their goals fulfilled. This moves them to seek agreements. Politicians and activists may be pulled together by some common policy, value, or ideological allegiance, but also by mutual threats of "exit" and "voice"—remember these concepts from chapter 2? Relevant candidates or officeholders may be willing to leave the party if it does not stay in potentially winning positions, while activists disappointed with the party positions can launch internal protests, disturbing the party's regular business. Internal tensions between differently motivated members plague all political parties.

On one side, politicians may face the following dilemma: If they present a policy proposal able to obtain broad electoral support but likely to alienate the favor of activists or interest groups, they may lose organizational and campaign resources to make their message available to potential voters. If, however, politicians rely too much on the beliefs of activists and the interests of lobbies, they risk being placed at extreme policy positions not likely to be embraced by broad sectors of the electorate.

Similarly, activists may have to choose between holding their preferred policy positions while staying in the opposition and accepting relatively less satisfactory policies enacted by vote- and office-motivated party leaders. A crude formulation of this alternative was given, for example, by British prime minister Anthony Blair, at the first Labour Party annual conference held after arriving in government in 1997, following a very long period in opposition to conservative ("Tory") governments. Addressing grass-roots party members who were beginning to show their discontent with "new center" government policy decisions, Blair said, "The choice is not between the government you have and the government you would like. The choice is between the government you have and a Tory government."

Two main variables shape the internal relations between party members and the subsequent types of political parties:

- **the number of members**; and
- **internal rules and procedures** creating different opportunities for member participation in decision-making.

The relative number of members in a party can be measured with the ratio M/E, where M is the number of party members and E is the number of party electors. On the one hand, we could expect that this value would increase over time, as it is a form of cooperation and participation that is expected to broaden within stable institutional settings, according to our discussion in chapter 3. On the other hand, a tendency toward low levels of permanent organization can be perceived in many countries, partly as a consequence of new forms of communication and technological changes, among other factors. While old democracies still retain some of the networks built in past periods, new ones may have missed the chance to reproduce some traditional enticements for party affiliation, membership, and participation.

The second variable, internal party rules and procedures, is relevant regarding the size and structure of the central party bureaucracy at the service of party leaders; the degree of decentralization; and the role of basic or local units of party organization formed by grass-roots activists. The degree of participation by activists or party voters in selecting candidates for public office, for instance, through primary elections, convention voting, or other expressions of opinion, can be especially influential on the party's policy stands before the public.

PARTY TYPES

Within each party, several types of equilibrium, or stable solutions, can be distinguished as resulting from the proportions of different types of party members and the enforcement of relatively more participatory or restrictive internal party rules. Traditionally three organizational types of political parties have been distinguished:

- **Cadre party**, implying low membership and restrictive internal rules;
- **Mass party**, involving large membership and participatory rules; and
- **Militant party**, a combination of low membership and participatory rules.

Cadre Party. A party may be **dominated internally by party leaders, or professional politicians**, either by discouraging mass affiliation or through restrictive internal rules favoring hierarchical, top-to-bottom processes of information diffusion and decision making. This implies high autonomy for what has been called the "political oligarchy," "inner circle," or "dominant coalition" within a party. This type of internal relation, corresponding to the traditional so-called "cadre party," typically emerged in early elections and parliaments in countries such as Britain. But is has also been maintained or reproduced as a regular organizational model for certain parties in more recent times, especially for conservative and liberal parties. If the party leaders are electorally motivated and sufficiently skillful, the cadre party can be adapted to adopt policy proposals able to obtain broad electoral support and compete successfully for leading positions in assemblies and cabinets.

Mass Party. Conversely, **a party can have numerous affiliates and activists**, able to provide abundant organizational and campaign resources, and apply internal rules giving its members **significant opportunities to intervene in the party's decision making**, not only through party branches, but also at open assemblies and general conventions or conferences. This model of "mass party" was typical of early socialist and christian-democratic parties in several countries in Europe. The diffusion of primary elections in the United States and other countries also enlarged the number of participants in the choice of candidates.

Generally, party affiliates and primary voters tend to favor relatively more extreme or outsider candidates and have different issue priorities than the electors. But the candidates can obtain certain legitimacy before the general public by being elected by a high number of participants. At the same time, party leaders and the bureaucratic apparatus can exert some control over the process, for example, by endorsing pre-candidates and by emphasizing that those chosen in the internal process should also be "electable" in the real contest.

Militant Party. This was the traditional model in the past for communist and fascist parties with a **reduced but actively mobilized membership**—as "militant" is related to "militia." In more recent times a new kind of "militant" party with different ideological persuasions has emerged, as a consequence of a general decrease in party affiliation, when the party keeps open internal rules for participation, as is the case of some green and radical-left parties. They are likely to adopt relatively extreme policy proposals on a few selected issues, which may make them relatively unpopular among voters. However, they may keep a stable core of faithful voters intensely interested in the issues in question, whose support may allow party leaders to negotiate favorably the corresponding specialized legislative decisions or cabinet portfolios in multiparty coalitions.

Firm, or Cartel, Party. Parties corresponding to the different types just mentioned can coexist and compete. But over time, distinctions among political parties acting within the same polity tend to blur, as they operate under similar incentive structures. In recent times, the benefits of party membership have steadily declined in many countries as a consequence of generally changing incentives for collective action.

On the demand side, party leaders can replace fund-raisers with state subsidies or big donors, while electoral campaigns are put in the hands of marketing and

---

CASE 9.1   HOW THE BRITISH LABOUR PARTY CHOSE CANDIDATES

The long period during which the British Labour Party was in opposition, during the 1980s and early '90s, was attributed partly to the way the party selected candidates for Parliament and prime minister. While in the winning Conservative Party, leaders and members of Parliament kept control of nominations, in Labour, all party members and trade union affiliates had voting rights.

Since then, 'the party which has done most to change the way it chooses its aspirant members of parliament [MPs] is the Labour party. In 1999, it began to require aspiring MPs to be screened by party headquarters. Candidates were obliged to attend training weekends, to submit standardized CVs, and to be interviewed by a panel which included at least one member of parliament. The intention, according to a senior party figure, was to "weed out of the charlatans" who might have somehow sneaked through the old selection system in which constituencies chose their own representatives. He was frank about what this meant. People who "appeared not to have a pragmatic line on policy disagreements" or could "not avoid sounding divisive and combative if disagreeing with party policy", or who 'showed an unpreparedness to listen to the whips" would be eradicated. In theory, the final choice of candidate remained the responsibility of the local constituency. But headquarters also made it harder for constituency radicals to deselect MPs they felt were too slavishly obedient to London.

From: Jeremy Paxman, *The Political Animal* (2002)

---

electioneering professionals and the mass media rather than those of traditional campaign volunteers. Party leaders therefore have new channels for addressing the broader public directly, which may make them think party members are less necessary, and even a nuisance.

On the supply side, the appeal of party membership has also decreased. The increasing complexity of public agendas in advanced societies makes certain traditional parties with an ideology encompassing a package of policy proposals on disparate issues less adapted to attract followers with strong motivations on specific issues. This indirectly fosters the emergence of nonpartisan, single-issue movements (including, for instance, immigration, abortion, antiwar, environment protection, and animal rights). People also have greater opportunities to obtain political information thanks to new communication technologies, especially television, the telephone, and the internet, without paying the costs of collective action in a party. Finally, citizens usually have a greater range of leisure alternatives than party meetings for obtaining social or psychological gratification.

As a consequence of declining party membership, political parties have increasingly become a label for a **team of political entrepreneurs**, mostly officeholders and candidates, **presenting policy proposals to compete in elections**. In many countries, parties are heavily protected by state resources and finances, which make them "cartels" or inefficient, deficiently competitive "firms." They address citizens through the mass media rather than through the affiliates' links.

All this could be seen as a return to the cadre party model. However, some parties try to maintain the appearance of numerous affiliates corresponding to the mass party model. In fact, parties tend to work with internal hierarchies facilitating top-to-bottom internal decision making, while activists and close followers work in service to their candidates. Electoral meetings and events, even party conventions and conferences, are increasingly designed to match television news. Unpaid activists can still have some effect in local-level electoral campaigns in mobilizing the electorate. But, above all, the pool of nonprofessional party members is the chief source for recruitment of candidates and future leaders making a living off politics.

Quick Quiz

- How could you distinguish professional politicians from voluntary activists?
- What are the differences between a cadre party and a mass party?

Conclusion

In this chapter we have presented some advantages and risks of making collective decisions by means of political parties. Political parties are means to promote new policy proposals and make decisions on collective issues, although they are usually suspected of introducing divisions among citizens. Parties select leaders and candidates to be voted for in competitive elections, but most parties are beleaguered by internal tensions among their members. On the basis of their advantages, political parties have managed to convince many people of their inevitability and expediency, although not everybody is persuaded of political parties' desirability.

Two *propositions* are well established in political science regarding parties:

- **Party oligarchy.** A political organization tends to become an "oligarchy," that is, it tends to be dominated by political leaders, or professional politicians, seeking votes and offices.
- **Extreme activists.** Voluntary political activists hold more "extreme" policy or ideological positions than party voters and even party leadership. ■

Summary

A political party is an organization competing for political power and providing public policy.

Political parties can be formed "endogenously," from within elections and assemblies, as collective candidacies and legislative coalitions, which may become permanent organizations.

Alternatively, parties can be formed "exogenously," from outside existing institutions, on the basis of new policy proposals on some issues and with support from previously existing interest or value groups.

Political parties provide mechanisms for facilitating collective decision making, especially regarding policy design and agenda setting, and leader selection and government formation.

The dominance of party leaders, or professional politicians, within political parties tends to create a political "oligarchy" alienated from the vast majority of citizens.

Voluntary activists, typically motivated by the promotion of a specific policy or interest for which they have an intense preference, hold more "extreme" positions than most party voters and even party leaders.

Party positions result from compromises between voter- and office-seeking party leaders and policy-seeking activists. The main variables of internal party interactions

are: the number of members and the opportunities created by party rules for participation in internal decision making.

"Cadre" parties have low membership, and dominion by party leaders. They can
be relatively advantageous for adopting policy proposals able to obtain broad electoral support.

"Mass" parties have a broad membership and rules facilitating member participation in party decisions and candidate selection.

In recent times, party membership has declined in many countries as a consequence of generally changing incentives for collective action. Political parties increasingly rely on public resources and the mass media.

Key Concepts

Activists. Voluntary contributors to the party; also called "militants."
Cadre party. Party with low membership dominated by professional politicians.
Endogenous party. A party formed from inside elections and assemblies.
Exogenous party. A party formed from outside existing institutions with support of
   previously existing groups.
Firm, or cartel, party. Party with low membership relying heavily on state resources
   and the media.
Mass party. Party with broad membership with high internal participation.
Militant party. Party with low membership with high internal participation.
Office-seeking. A politician's motivation for running for office.
Oligarchy. Dominating professional politicians within a party.
Policy-seeking. An activist's or interest group's motivation for supporting a party.
Political party. An organization to compete for power and provide public policy.
Politicians. Candidates and officeholders making a living off politics.
Vote-seeking. A politicians' motivation for running for election.

Questions for Review

1. What is a party?
2. How can political parties facilitate collective decision-making?
3. How could you distinguish professional politicians from voluntary activists?
4. What are the differences between a cadre party and a mass party?

Problems and Applications

1. Search for data on political parties in your country by visiting the parties' websites.
   Try to respond to these questions:
   a. Do they highlight their policy proposals more or less than they do the character-
      istics of their candidates?
   b. Do they give numbers of affiliates or participants in some of their activities? Try
      to establish the ratio between parties" activists and parties" votes in the most
      recent election.
   c. Are there significant differences between parties on the two aspects referred to
      in questions a and b?

2. In light of the data collected for the previous question and your own knowledge and reflection, list positive and negative incentives for becoming a party member.
3. Can you name a politician whose driving force is the fulfillment of a policy or ideological aim rather that the quest for power? Now name one with the opposite hierarchy of motivations? Which personal, contextual, and institutional factors can explain these differences?

Data source

Wikipedia "political parties:" www.wikipedia.org/List_of_political_parties_by_country

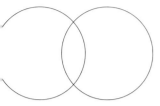

10

ELECTORAL COMPETITION

In This Chapter You Will

- Examine what determines the party an individual votes for.
- Analyze why political parties hold similar policy proposals on some issues and differ on others.
- Discuss the electoral strategy of adopting the "median voter's" preference.
- Consider the electoral advantage of parties in government versus those in the opposition.
- Reflect on how some people can become "identified" with a party.

In many democratic elections, candidates from different parties assert that their proposals fit, above all, the center, middle-class, moderate, or independent voters, who are sometimes specifically named as "soccer moms," "hockey moms," "Joe Six-pack," "Joe the Plumber," "Joe (or Jane) Public," or "John (or Jane) the Citizen." Indeed, electoral competition between two large parties may produce a "convergence" of the two parties around a similar moderate position. But when this happens, some people blame the parties for being irresponsible, not giving real opportunities of choice to the citizens, and being like the "Tweedledum and Tweedledee" twins (or like two brands of cola).

In order to make a difference, political parties and candidates not only make policy promises, but also remark upon their higher credibility in comparison to that of their competitors, especially on the basis of their governmental record. Sometimes electoral competition looks as if political parties are talking the same blah, blah, blah, while on other occasions they attack each other mercilessly.

In order to make sense of all these and other aspects of electoral competition, in this chapter we begin by analyzing voters' preferences on different policy alternatives. Then we discuss parties' electoral strategies. Finally, we consider the credibility factor, which can lead some voters to choose a party or candidate in spite of their relative distance in matters of policy or ideology. ■

The Voters

Democratic elections have been compared to markets. Political entrepreneurs lead parties supplying policy alternatives, and voters choose among them by means of their votes. Electoral markets, however, are different from economic markets in that they do not deal with private goods, but, as emphasized in the first part of this book, mostly with collective or public goods and redistributive policy decisions. In contrast to private exchanges between firms and consumers, electoral exchanges between parties and voters produce collective decisions that are enforceable on all members of the community.

INDIVIDUAL PREFERENCES

Different proposals on an issue can be analyzed with a "spatial" model such as the one in Figure 10.1. As suggested by this simple graph, different policy proposals and voters' preferences can be represented as positions along a continuum. Imagine, for instance, that the issue is taxes, and the different positions represent increases or reductions in income tax. Alternatively, you may prefer to imagine that the horizontal axis refers to the family issue, with different positions encompassing, say, official support to traditional families and support for the legalization of gay marriage. **The**

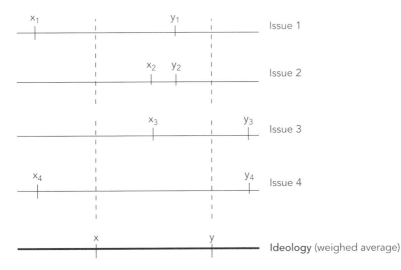

FIGURE 10.1 IDEOLOGY

On the ideology axis, the positions of parties X and Y are derived as an average of their positions on the issues 1, 2, 3, and 4—that is, of x_1, x_2, x_3, x_4 for party X, and of y_1, y_2, y_3, y_4 for party Y. In spite of holding synthetic ideological positions, parties can maintain different relative distances from each other on different issues.

spatial "distance" between positions represents the differences between policy proposals or voters' preferences. On many issues, as in these examples, the measurement of this distance implies both monetary and regulatory aspects.

In the spatial theory of voting it is assumed that **each voter has a preferred position, or "ideal point," on each issue**. The individual can estimate distances from the voter's ideal point to different policy proposals, including **the status quo policy, which is typically identified with the incumbent party in government**. In principle, a given voter will vote for the "closer," or less distant, alternative to his ideal point.

Political parties tend to present their policy proposals in consistent ideological packages. An ideological dimension can be represented by a single line, covering "left" and "right" or "liberal" and "conservative" positions. As illustrated in Figure 10.1, a party's ideological position can be conceived as a weighted average of the party's positions on a high number of issues. Note that the ideological "average" position can be weighted according to the different importance given by the party in question to different issues. As can be seen in the figure, two parties' ideological positions may be moderately distant from each other, but this may be compatible with parties' close positions on some issues and more distant positions on some others.

At a glance, the degree of ideological consistency in voters' preferences may be overvalued, since it can be due partly to restrictions imposed by the institutional system on citizens' choice. Indeed, most democratic elections do not permit voters to choose specific policies on different issues—say, on defense, security, taxes, trade, and education. This is in contrast to the kind of decisions you make when purchasing consumer goods in a private economic market, where you can choose different amounts of products from different brands. The electoral choice is usually restricted to only one party or candidate carrying a set of policies on different issues. Choosing one party is akin to acquiring a pre-wrapped package of products of a single brand in a supermarket, instead of making up your own basket of products. Or, put another way, in political elections you are not offered optional courses, as is probably the case in your college or university; you must take the whole package from a single department.

This means that, although every voter chooses a single party or candidate, many voters are not ideological in the sense of having a set of policy preferences that completely coincide with those of the candidacy for which they vote. An implication of this is that many voters can be sensitive to changes in policy proposals introduced by political parties on certain issues, as we will discuss further on.

THE VOTER'S UTILITY FUNCTION

We can also use simple geometry to represent voters' preferences in the policy or ideology "space." Specifically, the utility function of each voter can be represented as a **curve of preference**, as in Figure 10.2. The horizontal axis represents the set of policy alternatives on a single issue, dimension, or encompassing ideology. The vertical axis represents the individual's utility. So, for individual A's ideal point on the horizontal axis, the curve reaches its maximum on the vertical axis. Since the voter's utility is lower for less preferred, or more distant, alternatives, the curve decreases the farther away the alternatives on the horizontal axis are from the voter's ideal point. As the examples of A and B in the figure suggest, the curves of individual preference on

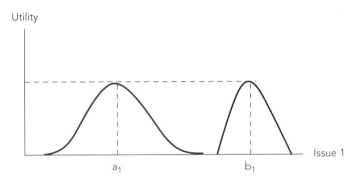

FIGURE 10.2   INDIVIDUAL PREFERENCES

a single-issue or dimension space can have different, more or less sharp or smooth, shapes. But they are all:

- **Single-peaked** on the voter's ideal point; and

- **Symmetrical** around the ideal point. This implies that if two alternatives are equidistant from the voter's ideal point on different sides of the policy space, one on its right and the other on its left, the voter will be indifferent between them. Although this is a disputable assumption, it makes analysis operative and is able to produce reasonable analytical results.

COLLECTIVE DISTRIBUTIONS OF PREFERENCES

In an electorate, different voters have different policy preferences or ideologies. **The collective distribution of individual preferences can be represented just as the number of individuals with the same ideal points**. But since communities are of different sizes, which may encompass from a few dozen to many million individuals, in order to compare them and establish generally valid postulates, it is better to use proportions of individuals. For each position, we take the number of voters with that ideal point divided by the total number of voters in the community. This can also be called "density" of preferences, representing, for each position, the probability that a voter, chosen at random, prefers that position as his ideal point.

In reality, a collective distribution of preferences can take any shape. If the space is defined, for example, along the left-right axis, a community can be considered to be collectively more leftist, more centrist, or more rightist, depending on the density of individual preferences on each position. If the space is alternatively defined along a cultural axis (say, based on religion, race, or language), very different shapes can exist depending of the relative size and distance of each group.

A unimodal distribution implies a high consensus on the policy attracting the highest number of voters—the mode. A bimodal distribution, in contrast, implies high polarization between two different groups of voters preferring distant alternatives. This can correspond to a deeply divided society, for instance regarding income distribution between rich and poor, or on ethnic characteristics. It can also represent

BOX 10.1   PARTY VOTING AND ISSUE VOTING

Observe the following paradox, which can arise when voters are given the option to vote for a political party "package" of issue policies instead of voting separately on each issue. Let us assume that there are three voters (or three homogeneous groups of similar size): A, B, and C. The public agenda is formed of three issues, 1, 2, and 3—for instance, taxes, education, and foreign policy. For each issue, there are only two alternatives, x and y. The two competing parties, X and Y, hold those alternatives for all the issues.

See the table in vertical columns: A prefers alternative x on issue 1, so x_1, alternative y on issue 2, y_2, and alternative y on issue 3, y_3. Since he coincides with the alternatives of party Y on most issues he can consider important (although not in all), he votes for Y (at the bottom of column A). Analogously, voter B votes for party X, and voter C votes for party Y on the basis of their preferences on most issues, which we may presume are more important for them. So party

Y wins with two thirds of the votes. The winner will implement the policies y_1, y_2, y_3.

But what would have happened if the voters had voted separately on each issue, say, for example, by means of a few referendums? As seen in the table, by reading it horizontally, the winning alternatives would have been x_1, x_2 and y_3, each with a majority support from voters, as shown in the right column. Observe, thus, that on most issues, the winning party holds policy positions not having the majority support of voters.

	VOTERS	A	B	C	WINNER
ISSUES					
1 (taxes)		x_1	x_1	y_1	x_1 (A+B)
2 (education)		y_2	x_2	x_2	x_2 (B+C)
3 (foreign policy)		y_3	y_3	y_3	y_3 (A+B+C)
Party votes		Y	X	Y	
Winning party: Y (y_1, y_2, y_3)					

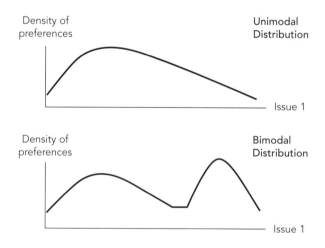

FIGURE 10.3   COLLECTIVE PREFERENCES

preferences on an issue on which a new, highly controversial proposal challenging the status quo has been presented and a consensual policy has not been settled.

To read Figure 10.3, note that while the horizontal axis represents policy or ideological positions, the vertical axis represents proportions or densities of people (not utility, as for individual preferences in Figure 10.2).

SOURCE 10.1   **Elections as Markets**

> Democracy does not mean and cannot mean that the people actually rule in any obvious sense of the terms "people" and "rule." Democracy means only that the people have the opportunity of accepting or refusing the men who are to rule them. But since they might decide this also in entirely undemocratic ways, we have had to narrow our definition by adding a further criterion identifying the democratic method, viz., free competition among would-be leaders for the vote of the electorate…And we define: the democratic method is that institutional arrangement for arriving at political decisions in which individuals acquire the power to decide by means of a competitive struggle for the people's vote.
>
> Joseph A. Schumpeter, *Capitalism, Socialism, and Democracy* (1942)
>
> My hypothesis implies that, in a democracy, the government always acts so as to maximize the number of votes it will receive. In effect, it is an entrepreneur selling policies for votes instead of products for money. Furthermore, it must compete for votes with other parties, just as two or more oligopolists compete for sales in a market. Whether or not such a government maximizes social welfare…depends upon how the competitive struggle for power influences its behavior. We cannot assume a priori that this behavior is socially optimal any more than we can assume a priori that a given firm produces the socially optimal output.
>
> Anthony Downs, *An Economic Theory of Democracy* (1957)

Quick Quiz

• How you can represent policy positions on an issue space?
• What is a voter's "ideal point?"

Convergence on the Median Voter

The idea of fighting for the political "center" has been fashionable in electoral politics in many democratic countries since the mid-twentieth century. Let us see why this is so. Assume that two political parties (or candidates) are competing for people's votes on the basis of their positions on only one policy issue or on a single encompassing ideological axis. This situation can be represented as in Figure 10.4. If everybody votes for the party that is "closer" to their ideal point, the electorate will be split by the intermediate position, which is exactly at the same distance from each of the two parties. In the figure, all those voters to the left of the dotted line are closer to party X, while the voters to the right of that line are closer to party Y; each group will vote for the closer party.

To see what the electoral result will be, let us now consider the **"median point."** As you will recall from high school maths , **the median is the point having less than half the total points on one side and less than half on the other side**, as indicated by the vertical line in the figure. If everybody votes for the party that is closer to his or her ideal point, party Y will receive all votes from the voters on the right side of the vertical line between the two parties; but since this line lies to the left of the median, party Y will receive the votes from half the electorate on the right of the median plus those in the shaded area, who are closer to party Y than to party X. In other words, the party closer to the median voter will receive more than a half of the votes and will win.

ELECTORAL EQUILIBRIUM

We have seen that the party that is closer to the median voter's preference wins the election by majority. But if parties can alter their positions—that is, if they can "move" along the space—this result may not be stable, since the losing party will have incentives to approach the median point for the following election, in order to attract intermediate voters to its side—as suggested by the arrow in Figure 10.4. This move may not be easy, especially if the losing party has traditionally been associated with a rigid policy or ideological position. Further changes toward more "centrist" positions might not be understood or might be mistrusted by the voters, and resisted by policy- or ideology-motivated activists within the party.

But only when **the two parties converge in their positions in the policy-ideology space around the median voter's preference** can the electoral outcome be considered stable, or in **"equilibrium."** Once there, no party would have electoral incentives

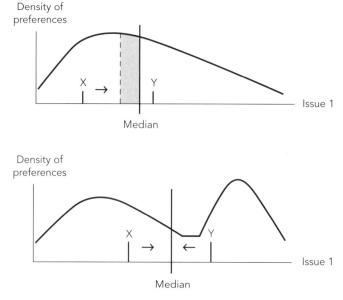

FIGURE 10.4 CONVERGENCE ON THE MEDIAN VOTER

Two parties or candidates competing on a single issue space have incentives to adopt converging positions around the median voter's ideal point. The vertical line indicates the median point. In the top graph, with unimodal distribution of preferences, the dotted line is at the same distance from the two parties, X and Y. The shaded area lies closer to party Y, which wins more than half the votes. The losing party, X, has incentives to approach the median, as indicated by the arrow. Note that the same reasoning applies to the bottom graph, in spite of its having a bimodal distribution of preferences.

to alter its positions—that is, to move away from the other party. Indeed the median voter's position wins in a two-party competition because, by definition, any majority of voters with contiguous locations along the policy space must include the median voter. The party unilaterally moving away from the median would be defeated at the following election.

Observe that the same reasoning applies to bimodal distribution of preferences, as represented in the bottom graph in Figure 10.4, in spite of implying polarization among the voters. At the expense of losing affection from relatively distant voters, not only at the extremes but also at the two modes of the distribution, parties seeking to win elections with majority support can approach the median to dispute the intermediate, decisive voters.

THE EFFICIENT MEDIAN VOTER

There has been some discussion about the social efficiency of governmental policies if they approach the median voter's preference. Some people may prefer more differentiated, alternating policies and governments, which may be refreshing in the long term. But the median voter's preference, if it becomes an enforceable policy, minimizes the sum of distances from all voters' preferences, and therefore it can be considered as maximizing social utility.

That the median point minimizes the sum of distances is a well-established mathematical property. As an example, let us examine the simplest case of an electorate composed of three voters with differentiated preferences (or three voters' groups with the same preferences and a similar number of members) located on a single issue-dimension, such as A, B, and C, as in Figure 10.5. Assume, for instance, that the distance between voter A and voter B is half the distance between voter B and voter C, as suggested in the figure. If B, which is the median voters' preference, wins and becomes public policy, the total distance from the voters' preferences to the winner can be measured as the distance from A to B (let's call this one unit) plus the distance from B to B, which is zero, plus the distance from C to B (two units), so the sum of distances from voters' preferences to the winner equals three units. In contrast, note that if the winner were A, the sum of distances from the voters' preferences to the winner would be four units; and if the winner were C, it would be five units. This shows that the median voter's alternative (B in the example) minimizes the sum of distances and, therefore, maximizes social utility.

Note, however, that the result of convergence should produce a tie in votes between the two parties. It may be logical that party leaders do not resign themselves to this result and seek other means to break or prevent that tie and win the election.

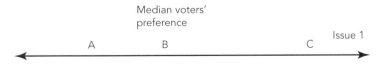

FIGURE 10.5 THE EFFICIENT MEDIAN VOTER

On a single issue, three voters have their ideal points at A, B, and C. The ideal point of the median voter, B, if it becomes enforced policy, minimizes the sum of the distances to all voters' ideal points.

SOURCE 10.2   The Median Voter Maximizes Social Utility

What is the best regime and the best way of life for most citizens and most human beings? The political community that is based on those in the middle is best. The best legislators come from the middle citizens.

Aristotle, *The Politics* (c. 325 BC)

Only if we make a precise and unified plan and follow the [*Confucius's*] doctrine of the mean, can we rule the country well. When we handle matters properly and harmoniously without leaning to either side, all things on Earth will flourish.

China's emperor Qianlong (1735–96), quoting Confucius from *Book of Rites*:
"*He took hold of their two extremes, determined the Mean, and employed it in his government of the people.*"

The class which is universally described as both the most wise and the most virtuous part of every community, the middle rank...which gives their most distinguished ornaments to science, to art, and to legislation itself, to every thing which exalts and refines human nature, is that part of the community of which, if the basis of representation were now so far extended, the opinion would ultimately decide. Of the people beneath them, a vast majority would be sure to be guided by their advice and example.

James Mill, "Government" (1820)

Consider, as an example, a situation in which the society is governed by an omniscient and beneficent dictator faced with the task of selecting the "best" policies for his country...The dictator accomplishes this objective by selecting a position identical to the average desires of the population, so he selects the mean. Hence, competitive conditions which cause the two parties to converge toward the mean result in the electoral process producing the kind of result that a beneficent dictator should choose.

Otto A. Davis, Melvin J. Hinich, and Peter C. Ordeshook, "An Expository Development of a Mathematical Model of the Electoral Process" (1970)

[*Robert*] Dahl's "reasonable justification of democracy" [Democracy and Its Critics, 1989]...directs our attention to identifying the policy position that is in some sense "most preferred" by the voters. We believe that the position that has the best claim to represent this "most preferred" policy is the position of the median voter. On a single issue or a single-issue dimension, if we assume that the preferences of voters are single-peaked, the position of the median voter is the only policy that is preferred to all others by a majority of voters.

John D. Huber and G. Bingham Powell, Jr., "Congruence between Citizens and Policy Makers in Two Visions of Liberal Democracy" (1994)

In reality, some parties tend to converge and other parties maintain distant positions from each other. A two-party system can imply proximity in some countries, but it can be associated with polarization in others, as we will discussed in a later chapter. More frequently, parties tend to converge on some issues, but then they choose to give salience to new issues on which they have distant positions. That is, they converge on some issues and at the same time hold distant positions on other issues

ELECTORAL CAMPAIGN POSTERS IN JAPAN

by offering contrasting policy proposals—in spite of "average" ideological distances between them.

What the "median voter theorem" predicts is not that all pairs of parties will always converge—although this was once a rather common reading of the theorem. More accurately, we can establish the following postulates:

- In a two-party system, the party at the median position wins a majority of votes against a party at any other position.
- For any two parties' positions, the party that is closer to the median position wins a majority of the votes, whatever their relative distances.

Quick Quiz

• Define the median voter's position as an equilibrium.

The Incumbent's Advantage

Consider this comment by former U.S. president Bill Clinton, as voiced outside the sessions of the Democratic Party convention in 2008, for which there were two major candidates, Senator Barack Obama and Clinton's wife, Senator Hillary Rodham Clinton: "Suppose, for example, you're a voter, and you've got candidate X and candidate Y. Candidate X agrees with you on everything, but you don't think that person can deliver on anything. Candidate Y disagrees with you on half the

BOX 10.2   **MEASURING ELECTORAL CHANGE**

Changes in voters' support for political parties can be measured using the volatility index:

$$\text{Volatility: } V = \tfrac{1}{2} \Sigma \, |P_{it} - P_{i(t+1)}|$$

Where:

V: Volatility

P_{it}: share of votes for party i in the election at time t

$P_{i(t+1)}$: share of votes for party i in the following election at time t+1

The volatility index captures the minimum number of voters changing the party they vote for from one election to the next (the real number can be higher, since changes in opposite directions cancel each other out). This index has values between 0 and 1, where 0 corresponds to a sequence in which all parties obtain the same proportion of votes in two successive elections, and 1 corresponds to a complete replacement of all the parties in the system with new ones.

issues, but you believe that on the other half, the candidate will be able to deliver. For whom will you vote"?

Candidates and political parties with past records of good performance in government can have an advantage in the eyes of the public, in comparison with those who did not fulfill their previous promises, which may make them appear unreliable. In certain elections, the personal characteristics of the candidates, including moral and physical, are also highlighted. Some of the most loudly voiced scandals in democratic politics are provoked by politicians' lies and private behavior, sometimes about business involving public money and resources, sometimes regarding love or sex affairs. There can indeed be differences in candidates' reputation for honesty and competence on the basis of their records in public office or in private professions or merely in their personal appearance and way of speaking. These differences can be independent of policy or ideological positions, although some people tend to associate, for example, candidates from parties with a good record on moral values with good morals and those with an emphasis on social policy with compassion or empathy. In general, this suggests that the candidate's character is used as a credibility weight of policy promises, as an element of reliability. Actually, the shorter the distance between the voter and the party, the more important the credibility factor can become in the voter's function. In other words, the closer the voters to the parties' positions or the higher the level of policy and ideological consensus among parties (which implies low differences in their distances to voters' preferences), the more important these non-policy factors can be in the voters' deciding for whom to vote. Conversely, the greater the distance between party policy positions, the less relevant the candidates' personal character or even the party's reliability may be.

Specifically, if the candidates' policy proposals are sufficiently close to one another on the most salient issues in an electoral campaign, a candidate with personal qualities that can be highly appreciated by the public may win an election that he might otherwise have lost. Similarly, a candidate considered corrupt, inept, or unpredictable may lose an election that he might have won on the basis of his policy positions.

BOX 10.3 MATHEMATICS OF VOTING

The "spatial" models of electoral competition have been elaborated by using some elemental algebraic symbols. If you have some familiarity with this language, you may grasp the following notation, which will be helpful to introduce you to more advanced academic literature.

First, observe that we are using different symbols for different variables:

For issues: 1, 2, 3…m.
For voters: A, B, C…N, being any voter $i \in N$.
For parties or candidates: X, Y, Z…
Then, voter A's ideal point on issue 1 will be represented as: a_1.
And voter A's global or ideological ideal point on issues 1 and 2, as: A (a_1, a_2).
In turn, party X's policy position on issue 1 will be: x_1.
And party X's package of policy proposals or ideological position on issues 1 and 2: X (x_1, x_2).

Now you can address some basic concepts which have been presented in the text in a more informal manner.

Voter's utility function

$$U_A(X) = -(A-X)^2$$

This must be read as: Utility for voter A of alternative X is a decreasing function of the distance between the ideal point of A and the position of X. That the function is decreasing means that as the distance increases, the utility decreases, and vice versa.

The voter's decision can be made by comparing the distances from the voter's ideal point to different political parties:

$$|A-X| \lessgtr |A-Y|$$

Candidate's credibility

We can introduce the "credibility" variable into the voter's utility function. Let us call $\alpha_{A(X)}$ the evaluation by voter A of the character of a candidate from party X (after α, the following Greek letters can be used for further candidates: β, χ, δ…). The voter's utility function just presented becomes the following:

$$U'_A(X) = -[\alpha_{A(X)} * (A-X)^2]$$

Observe that we multiply the evaluation α by voter A of party X's candidate's character by the function

of their distance. This suggests that the candidate's character is used as a weight of policy promises, as an element of reliability that can change the voter's decision when comparing the distances to different parties:

$$|A-X| > |A-Y|$$
$$\alpha_{A(X)} > .\beta_{A(Y)}$$
$$U'_A(X) > U'_A(Y)$$

This must be read as: Even if voter A's ideal point is more distant from party X than party Y, if the candidate characteristics α of party X are sufficiently better evaluated than those β of party Y, the weighted utility for voter A of party X can be higher than the weighted utility of party Y.

Incumbent's advantage

The evaluation by voters of non-policy characteristics of candidates of the party in government, which can be called X, can be higher than those from parties in opposition, such as Y:

$$\alpha_{A(X)} > .\beta_{A(Y)}$$

Additionally, recent performances can be given higher weight than those more remote in time:

$$\alpha_t > \alpha_{t-1} > \alpha_{t-2} > \alpha_{t-3}$$

where α_t is the evaluation of candidate or party performance in the current period t, α_{t-1} is the evaluation in the previous period t–1, and so on.

Party identification

For a voter with sufficient experience of voting and observing the performance of parties in government in successive periods, the choice can be made by comparing two parties according to these equations:

$$U''_A(X) = U_{At}(X) + \alpha_{At-1} * U_{At-1}(X) + \alpha_{At-2} * U_{At-2}(X) + \ldots$$
$$\gtreqless U''_A(Y) = U_{At}(Y) + \beta_{At-1} * U_{At-1}(Y) + \beta_{At-2} * U_{At-2}(Y) + \ldots$$

which must be read as: Utility for voter A of party X equals the sum of utilities for voter A of party X in successive periods of time t, t–1, t–2…weighted by the evaluation α for voter A of candidate or party X's performance in those periods. Analogously for party Y.

Continued

BOX 10.3 ⋈ *Continued*

Multidimensional space

In a two-dimensional space, the distance between voter A's ideal point and party X's position can be found by using Pythagoras, which you should know from high-school math:

$$(A - X)^2 = (a_1 - x_1)^2 + (a_2 - x_2)^2$$

which implies:

$$|A - X| = \sum_{}^{2} [(a - x_i)^2]^{1/2}$$

Generalizing for a number of issues, the distance between voter A and party X in a multidimensional space is:

$$|A - X| = [\sum_{}^{M} (a - x_i)^2]^{1/m}$$

GOVERNMENTS WIN AND LOSE ELECTIONS

Italian former prime minister Giulio Andreotti, who had an extremely long record in public office, said that "power erodes…especially those who don't have it." There is indeed **asymmetry between political parties in electoral competition, depending on whether they are in government or in opposition**. An incumbent party can have an advantage because it can give selected information to the public about its actions in government. It can also present actual policies implemented from government, with the policies' concrete consequences on citizens' wellbeing, in contrast to dubious hypothetical results of policy proposals presented from the opposition. The evaluation of the incumbent can be based on facts, while estimation of the opposition can derive only from speculative hypotheses and expectations about what it could have been or it could be.

Incumbent parties tend to win reelection, which makes people think that elections that produce a change are lost by the government rather than won by the opposition. Consider these data. In the United States, due to term limits for reelection of the president, there are two types of elections, those in which the incumbent president runs for reelection, and elections with new candidates. Since 1948, the incumbent president has run for reelection in ten elections and won in seven, while, in contrast, when no incumbent president was running, the opposition party won in five out of six elections. In the United Kingdom since 1950, the incumbent prime minister ran for reelection leading his or her party in all sixteen elections and won in ten. In Germany, although there is a multiparty system and coalition governments, the leaders of the two larger parties are seen as candidates for chancellor; since 1953, the incumbent chancellor ran for reelection in all sixteen elections and won in thirteen. Comparable proportions can be found in many democratic countries.

PARTY IDENTIFICATION

In the first democratic election in Spain in the 1970s, a cousin of mine living in the country told me that she had voted for a certain center-left party, although she confessed to not knowing much about the turnabouts the party was then undergoing.

She explained that, in the previous democratic period in the 1930s, a government of the party in question—one of the few that was running again after such a long period without elections—had effectively distributed cultivable land to small peasants, including her grandfather, in whose house she was still living.

Although this may be a rather extreme case, it is relatively common that some voters decide their vote not only by comparing the candidacies' relative distance to their ideal point on the current policy or ideology continuum, but also by estimating the candidates' or parties' level of credibility on the basis of previous governmental performance. This can be called "retrospective voting."

Political pundits and advisors often remark that people have limited memory and a tendency to remember recent things better than remote ones. Cognitive psychologists confirm that this is certainly the case for most people. Thus, the recent performance of the incumbent party can be given higher weight in voters' evaluation than that of other parties in previous periods. In the long term, however, some voters may accumulate those evaluations in favor of the party in government (as in the case of my cousin). If the advantage is sufficiently high as to make the voter always vote for the same party, we can say that the voter is "identified" with the party. **Party identification can lead voters to vote for a party on past performance rather than current issues**. Even if some old party policies lose ground, certain voters can remain stuck to the party, the way some consumers remain loyal to a commercial brand, due to the costs of collecting new information on potential alternatives.

This approach can account for a number of observable facts, such as the following:

- In new democracies, voters can be relatively volatile, that is, prone to change their vote from one election to another, and party systems not consolidated, since voters have to rely only on recent government performance and have no opportunities to develop party "identification."

- Current issues and electoral campaigns are more important for the electoral decision of young voters than for older ones, since the latter can include memories of past performances in their evaluation of parties and candidates.

- Young voters can be more volatile as a consequence of parties' new policy proposals, new politicized issues, or changing ideological positions, since these voters give less weight to non-policy issues.

- The fidelity of voters to a party can increase over time. In the long term, it can become party "identification."

- In many countries, most—but not all!—democratic elections are won by the incumbent party, especially if the leading candidates run for reelection.

- In a well-established democracy, a significant voting change may require a sudden event introducing either a dramatic change in the agenda of public issues or new adverse information on the character of the candidate or the reliability of the party.

Quick Quiz

- What is party identification?

Conclusion

In this chapter we have addressed two-party electoral competition on the basis of a simple "spatial" model in which voters' preferences and parties' or candidates' policy proposals can be represented as points at different distances from each other. Two *propositions or theorems* of political science can be stated:

- **Median voter.** A two-party convergence around the median voter's position is an electoral equilibrium outcome. In two-party competition on a single dimension, electorally motivated parties have incentives to adopt a policy around the median voter's preference, approaching each other and converging in their policy or ideological positions. Once they converge, neither party has electoral incentives to move away from the other party.

- **Incumbent advantage.** Electoral competition is asymmetric between the government and the opposition. The incumbent party in government can gain advantage in electoral competition by providing or hiding information on its record to obtain credibility. ■

Summary

Political elections can be compared to economic markets in that political parties supply policy alternatives and voters choose from among them by means of their votes.

In "spatial" models, every voter has a preferred position or ideal point on each salient issue. The voter's decision is made by comparing the distances from the voter's ideal point to different political parties' or candidates' proposals.

A party's ideology can be conceived as the weighted average of the party's positions on a high number of issues.

In a two-party competition, the party that is closer to the median voter's position wins a majority of the votes. The two parties have incentives to converge around the median voter's position, which may produce a tie in votes.

The incumbent party can have an advantage in providing information on its past record and obtaining credibility.

In the long term, voters can develop a sense of identification with one party on the basis of cumulative past performances.

Key Concepts

Convergence. A strategy by which parties approach each other around the median voter's position in the policy or ideology space.

Distance. Spatial representation of difference between voters' preference and policy proposals or "positions."

Distribution of preferences. A set of probabilities of having a voter at every ideal point.

Ideal point. A voter's preferred policy position.

Incumbent advantage. Asymmetry in electoral competition between the government and the opposition.

Median voter. The voter with fewer than half of voters' ideal points on each side in the policy space.

Party identification. Voter's motivation to vote for a party on past performance rather than current issues.

Status quo. The existing policy, which is the usual reference for alternative proposals.

Voter's curve of preference. On a single dimension, a single-peaked, symmetrical shape around the voter's ideal point.

Questions for Review

1. What does the median voter theorem stipulate?
2. Why can the incumbent party have an advantage in electoral competition?
3. What is party identification?

Problems and Applications

1. Imagine that you are an ice-cream vendor arriving in the middle of the summer to a long, linear beach, where people, your potential consumers, are randomly distributed.
   a. Where would you locate your ice-cream cart in order to minimize the distance to the swimmers?
   b. Let us figure out that a second ice-cream seller appears with the same product quality and prices. He can make a difference to you only by reducing the distance to the potential consumers. Where would he locate his cart?
   c. Imagine that a third ice-cream seller arrives, also bargaining only with distance. Where would he be located?
   d. Can you suggest a comparison between this problem and that of electoral competition between political parties along a single, linear policy or ideological dimension? Identify similarities and differences.
2. Look at the bimodal distribution of preferences in Figure 10.3.
   a. Mark approximately the median point, which should lie around the center, in an area with few voters.
   b. Estimate what would be the result if two parties adopted distant positions, for example, around the two modes. Draw the dividing line splitting the distance between the two parties.
   c. Consider whether any party would be able to attract more voters by moving its position toward the median point.
   d. Think about what the losing party would do in order to gain more votes.
   e. Compare the results with those previously discussed for a unimodal distribution of preferences.
3. Assume a uniform distribution of preferences with the same density of preferences on each point. You can label different party positions along the axis by using percentages of voters on its left. For example, a party a quarter of the way from the extreme left would be at 25, a center party would be at 50, and so on. Suppose that two parties collude and decide to coordinate their positions in order to guarantee that one of the two will always win the election, block the system, and make it impossible for any third party, whatever position it may take, to win more votes than the initial two. Where should the two initial parties place themselves?

Quantitative measurements

4. For a given issue dimension on a scale of 1 to 10, let us consider the following distribution of voters' preferences:
   a. Which is the median position?

Scale:	1	2	3	4	5	6	7	8	9	10
No. of voters:	3	5	15	20	15	12	10	10	7	3

   b. Assume that voters with positions from 1 to 5 can be called on the "left," while those from 6 to 10 are on the "right." Are there more people on the left or on the right?
   c. Suppose that this electorate votes for two alternative parties, X on the left and Y on the right, placed respectively at X = 2 and Y = 7. Which party wins a majority?
   d. Suppose that a third, centrist party, Z, is created and adopts a position at 5. In a three-party competition, which party wins the most votes?
   e. Suppose that now the two parties created earlier get to move toward more centrist positions, X = 3 and Y = 6. Meanwhile, Z remains at 5. In the new three-party competition, which party wins the most votes?
   f. Suppose that Y's move away from its traditional rightist position causes a radical branch to leave the party and create a new party placed at the extreme rightist position, W = 10. The other three parties stay at their positions as in question e. In a four-party competition, which party wins more votes?
   g. Do you have any comments about these moves and results?

Scale:	1	2	3	4	5	6	7	8
No. of voters:	7	11	15	16	18	16	11	6

5. For a given issue dimension on a scale of 1 to 8, let us consider the following distribution of voters' preferences:
   a. Which is the median position?
   b. Suppose that this electorate votes for two alternative parties, X on the moderate left and Y on the right, placed respectively at X = 3 and Y = 7. Which party wins a majority?
   c. If a third party wants to enter the competition and win the election against the other two parties, where ought it locate itself?

For a term paper

6. The median voter's theorem has been applied to settings in which there are no formal elections, but where a decisive actor with the median properties can be identified. If you plan to write a term paper, consider using this analytical tool: Bueno de Mesquita's website offers the possibility of analyzing a situation of potential conflict among groups or countries by estimating three parameters: the relative positions of the actors, their potential influence in producing an outcome, and the importance of the issue for each actor. Visit Bueno de Mesquita Policy Forecaster at: www.bdm.cqpress.com/policy forecaster.asp.

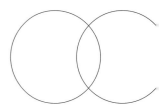

11

AGENDA FORMATION

In This Chapter You Will

- Analyze how electoral competition on multiple issues fosters instability, while single-issue decisions can produce stable outcomes.
- Learn what the "win-set" is.
- Examine how political parties choose issues in electoral campaigns.
- Distinguish between position issues and valence issues.
- Consider how different values and arguments can be used in support of policy proposals.
- Discuss how policy consensus can be created, and why electoral competition concentrates on divisive issues.

On the occasion of a U.S. election, former president Bill Clinton, who was not running as a candidate, pondered, "The presidential elections in the United States always turn around three questions. First, there is the candidate's position on certain issues…As a second element, how one would feel at having that person as president?…The third factor is the following: What is this election about? Is it about the United States having a multilateral attitude on foreign policy? Or is it whether taxes should be lowered for the rich or more should be done for the poor?"

In the previous chapter we analyzed two of Clinton's questions: the candidate's positions on policy issues and the influence of candidates' credibility. In this, we analyze the third question: What are elections about? Consider this comment by a leading Republican strategist in early September 2008, when, after the two parties' conventions, the presidential campaign for the election on November 4 was about to start. "If in October we're talking about Russia and national defense and who can manage America in a difficult world, [Republican] John McCain will be president. If we're talking largely about domestic issues and health care, [Democrat] Barack Obama probably will be president. Events, however, can affect that conversation. If Russia invades another country [after Georgia] on Oct. 20 or Iran detonates a nuclear weapon, advantage McCain; if there's another Bear Stearns meltdown, or a stock market crash, put a few points on the Obama side" (from *The New York Times*, September 7, 2008).

As we study in this chapter, indeed the selection of issues and the formation of the public agenda can be the arena in which political parties, leaders, and candidates have more room for maneuvering. Government information and electoral campaigns focus largely on this. ■

Multiple Issues

Political parties can run in elections with a set of policy proposals on many issues, typically wrapped in an ideological label or value, as a single "package" for voters to take or leave. Such a package may include policies on taxes, security, the market, social spending, family, race, and foreign relations. This may prevent voters from choosing their most preferred policy position on each issue. The voter might have to choose, for instance, between one party's package, which might include lower taxes, toughness on crime, the free market, family values, and external isolation; and another's including higher taxes, government regulations, universal health care, affirmative action, and foreign multilateralism. Remember, it's like purchasing the products by a single brand in the supermarket.

Setting the agenda or selecting the issues to be given salience in an electoral campaign is one of the key strategic decisions for a political party or candidate in order to try to win an election. We first examine how restrictions on voters' choices can produce dissatisfaction and unpredictable electoral outcomes. Then we discuss how a few issues can be selected to be the focus of the public agenda and electoral campaigns.

INDIVIDUAL INDIFFERENCES

When policies on several issue dimensions have to be decided on the basis of a single vote, we say that voters are placed in a **"multidimensional"** space. In order to understand how this works, let us begin by reminding you of the analysis of individual voters' preferences in the previous chapter. Remember this "spatial" approach: Every voter has a preferred position or "ideal point" on each issue, and estimates the relative "distances" to different policy proposals in comparison to the "status quo" policy.

For the purposes of simplification, let us now assume that we are dealing with only two issue dimensions at the same time: for instance, dimension 1, on socio-economic issues, and dimension 2, on moral and family issues. As in our previous discussion, a straightforward line can represent the set of policy alternatives on each issue dimension, say, along the social spending/economic market axis and along the moral freedom/family values axis, respectively. But in a two-dimensional space, there is an area shaped by the two linear dimensions on which voters' ideal points can be placed, as in Figure 11.1. Note, therefore, that voter A's ideal point on one issue can be located at any point along a **line**, such as a_1 on issue 1 and a_2 on issue 2, but voter A's ideal point on the two-dimensional space can be located at any point in the **area**. Specifically, voter A's ideal point on the two-dimensional space formed by issues 1 and 2 is the crossing point of A's ideal points on each of the two issues, as represented by A (a_1, a_2). Similarly, the party X's package of policy positions on the same space of two issues can be represented as X (x_1, x_2).

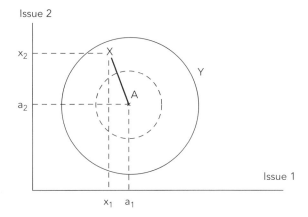

FIGURE 11.1 CURVES OF INDIFFERENCE

On two issue dimensions, 1 and 2, voter A's ideal points are a_1 and a_2, respectively. Voter A's ideal point on the two-dimensional space is the crossing point of the two ideal points: A (a_1, a_2). Party X's package of policy proposals on issues 1 and 2 is the crossing point of the two policy proposals: X (x_1, x_2). The same holds for party Y. The utility function of voter A can be represented by curves of indifference centered on A's ideal point. Voter A is closer to party X than to party Y.

The voter's utility function can also be represented with simple geometry as a **curve of indifference including all policy positions at equal distance from the voter's ideal point**, as can be represented by a circumference. As shown in Figure 11.1, voter A's preference or ideal point is at equal distance from any point on the circumference. Thus, voter A prefers any policy located inside the circumference to any policy located outside, since voters prefer the "closer," or less distant, alternatives from their ideal points to the more distant ones.

Then how would the voter vote? If party X's package of proposals on the two issues is located at a point inside voter A's curve of indifference, and party Y's package of proposals is located outside that curve of indifference, A will prefer X to Y. Any set of party proposals can be compared by drawing the appropriate curves of indifference, which may take the form of concentric circumferences, as suggested by the dotted line in the figure.

THE WINNING SET

Electoral outcomes in a multidimensional space of issues can be explained with the help of the kind of spatial models we are using in this part of the book. Let me introduce the concept of **"win-set,"** which is a fancy term for **the area including all the potential electoral winners in a multidimensional space**. The simplest possible case to consider is a competition between two parties, which necessarily produces a winner by a majority of votes and a loser with a minority of votes (except in the improbable case of a tie, which we do not consider here). The analytical tools you will learn here are also valid for more than two dimensions in the space, higher numbers of voters, and more parties in competition.

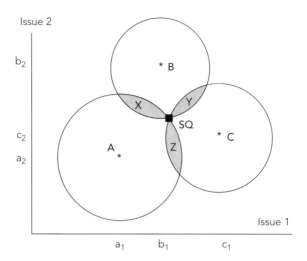

FIGURE 11.2 WIN-SET

On a two-dimensional space with three voters, A, B, and C, any point inside the intersection of two voters' curves of indifference will be preferred by the two voters to the status quo, SQ, and will win by majority. The shaded area includes the set of all possible winning points, or "win-set."

Three curves of indifference around voters A, B, and C's ideal points are drawn in Figure 11.2. Each curve crosses the status quo policy, SQ. This permits each voter to compare any new policy proposal with the existing, or status quo, policy for their relative distances to the voter's ideal point. Any policy located inside the voter's curve of indifference will be preferred to the status quo policy.

Suppose the incumbent party in government, which is identified with existing policy position SQ, is challenged by another party located at X in the figure. As you can see, X is closer to A's ideal point than is the status quo (because it is inside A's circumference) and also closer to B's ideal point than is the status quo (because it is inside B's circumference). Both voters A and B will, therefore, prefer X to the status quo. C, in contrast, will prefer the status quo, which is on C's circumference, to the more distant X. If there are only three voters, A and B can form a majority of two out of three, and by voting for X, they can make X the winner over the status quo party.

There would be a similar occurrence if the status quo party were challenged by a party at Y or by a party at Z. For each of these alternatives, two out of three voters will prefer the challenger's position to the status quo because the challenger is inside their curves of indifference (B and C for Y, and A and C for Z, as you can see in the figure). In fact, a party could win by a majority against the status quo if it were located at any point inside the trefoil, the shaded area, in the figure. This area displaying several petals is called the "win-set," that is, the area of all potentially winning points in a two-party contest.

The larger the win-set, the higher the number of potentially winning positions against the status quo. In other words, the larger the win-set, the higher the probability that an opposition party can win with an innovative package of policy proposals against the status quo, or incumbent, party.

Look at the figure again and observe that people voting in a multidimensional space may be relatively unsatisfied, while losing parties can have a lot of room for maneuver on the basis of that dissatisfaction. Imagine an election between parties SQ and X. Voter A votes for X because X is inside A's curve of indifference. But while X's position on issue 1 is closer to A's ideal point than the status quo (on the horizontal axis), X's position on issue 2 is more distant from A's ideal point than the status quo (on the vertical axis). Look at these distances on the two linear dimensions in the figure. Similar disparities occur with the other voters and with other pairs of competing parties, as you can also see in the figure.

This implies that in a multidimensional election, some voters have to vote for a party on the basis of their preferences on some issues but against their preferences on other issues. Some voters may have to accept a package of policy proposals on numerous issues even if they disagree on some of the proposals and prefer some of the status quo policies that will be defeated in the election, thanks, in part, to their votes. In our example, some voters may have to vote for a party offering a policy proposal on socioeconomic issues that they may like in comparison with the status quo, for instance in favor of free market, but also on one that they may dislike, for instance on family values. Or vice versa.

In order for such voters to accept a party's package of policy proposals, some of which they may disagree with, the voters' utility, or "closeness," to the party on some issues must be higher than the "distance" on other issues. The voter must be "more satisfied" with the first policy (e.g., free market) than "dissatisfied" with the second policy (e.g., family values). Note in the figure that the relative distance from voter A to the status quo and to X's proposal on issue 2, even though it is higher for X (on the vertical axis), is lower than the voter's relative distance to the two alternatives on issue 1 (on the horizontal axis). In other words, voter A's relative "closeness" to X on issue 1 makes him vote for X in spite of his "remoteness" to X on issue 2. For other voters, the choice may imply relative satisfaction and dissatisfaction on other combinations of issues.

There are two implications of this observation that we discuss later on:

• The degree of people's utility or satisfaction with the electoral outcome in a multidimensional election is lower than it would be in a set of elections or voting decisions dealing with each issue separately. This is so because in single, multidimensional voting, some voters have to vote for a party some of whose policies they do not like. In contrast, if different issues are voted on separately, each voter can vote for their preferred policy on every issue.

• Voters' dissatisfaction with some winning policies of the party they have voted for creates room for maneuvering for the losing party. The loser can offer better proposals on the issues the voters dislike about the winning party up to the point of compensating for their satisfaction with the winning party on other issues.

In our example, the losing party could now offer a more satisfactory proposal on moral issues able to compensate the voter's satisfaction with the winning party on socioeconomic issues, even if the losing party's proposal on socioeconomic issues may be less satisfactory than those of the winner, thus moving the voter to vote for the other party. A winning "package" relatively in favor of social spending and moral freedom, for instance, could be defeated by another more in favor of free market and moral freedom, but then this could be defeated by another leaning toward social spending and family values, and so on. The higher the number of issues in the packages, the larger the room for maneuvering by offering successive party packages. This may bring about uncertain electoral results, relatively frequent alternations of winning parties, and instability in policy making.

Party's Attraction Areas. Let us take an instantaneous or static photograph of party competition. Let us assume that party positions are given in a stable multidimensional space and cannot be modified. For a specific election, we can estimate the capability of each party to attract votes.

For this we can use a diagram such as that in Figure 11.3. Between each pair of party positions, the bisector line is drawn so to separate the voters' ideal points that are relatively closer to each of the two parties. Voters on either side of the line are closer and will bend toward a different party. As you can see, dividing lines—dotted in the figure—can be drawn for however many political parties there are. These lines define **the spaces of voters' ideal points that are closer to each party**. At the end, we have a set of areas of vote attraction for every party. They can be seen as "river basins" within each of which the "water," that is, the votes, go to the closer party.

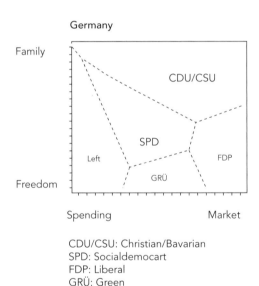

CDU/CSU: Christian/Bavarian
SPD: Socialdemocart
FDP: Liberal
GRÜ: Green
Left: Socialist

*Source: Adapted from Kenneth Benoit and Michael Laver,
Party Policy in Modern Democracies (2006).*

FIGURE 11.3 PARTIES IN A MULTIDIMENSIONAL SPACE
As an example of multidimensional distribution of votes, the main political parties of Germany are located in a two-dimensional space defined by socioeconomic and moral issues. The dotted lines indicate the areas of the policy space closer to each party. The font size indicates the relative size in votes for each party.

CASE 11.1   ELECTORAL COMPETITION IN THE UNITED STATES

Over time, the two major parties in the United States have changed their policy positions and chosen different issue dimensions over which to fight during elections. Two main dimensions in the policy-ideology space can be identified: economy and culture. Each dimension includes a number of issues with opposite stances, such as growth, industry versus agriculture, business versus labor, on the economic dimension and issues such as race, family, and immigration on the cultural dimension (as proposed by Gary Miller and Norman Schofield). See Figure 11.4 to identify the party candidates' basic positions: left and right on the economic dimension, and liberal and conservative on the cultural dimension.

Since the current two-party system was established, several periods can be distinguished. After 150 years of rotating clockwise, the two parties have almost completely traded their relative positions, as suggested here:

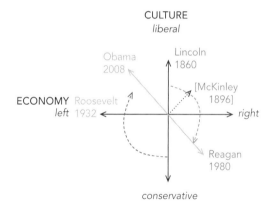

FIGURE 11.4   U.S. ELECTORAL COMPETITION

1860–1928

Major president and event: Republican Abraham Lincoln wins the Civil War.

Main issues and positions: Abolition of slavery (culture; liberal); industry development (economy; center).

In 1896 the economic issue becomes more salient, with the Republican Party taking a more pro-business position. The Democrats are electorally weakened by the Populists as a third party.

Record: Republicans win 80 percent of presidential elections and 67 percent of House elections.

End: Financial crash of 1929 and further economic depression break support for the Republicans on the economic dimension.

1932–1964

Major president and event: Democrat Franklin D. Roosevelt wins the Second World War.

Main issues and positions: State intervention (economy; left); racial segregation in the South (culture; conservative).

Record: Democrats win 77 percent of presidential elections and 97 percent of House elections.

End: Civil rights and sexual liberation movements break support for the Democrats on the cultural dimension. Split of pro-segregation Southern candidacies.

1968–2004

Major president and event: Republican Ronald Reagan wins the Cold War.

Main issues and positions: Financial market deregulation (economy; right); family values (culture; conservative).

Record: Republicans win 70 percent of presidential elections, although only 30 percent of House elections.

End: The financial crisis of 2008 erodes support for the Republicans on the economy dimension.

SOURCE 11.1   Multidimensional Instability

In the public debate, each party or candidate seeks to give salience to those issues on which it is more credible and expects to obtain electoral advantage.

It is old wisdom that single-issue decisions can produce stable outcomes, while multidimensional issue competition between single-party packages fosters instability.

It is a true thing that some divisions hurt the republic and some reinvigorate it. Hurting are those issues that are accompanied by sects and partisanship; invigorating are those which persist without sects or partisanship. Since no foundation for a republic can be provided without enmities, it should be provided at least that there were no sects.

Niccolò Machiavelli, Florentine Histories (1525)

The report of the Committee of the French Chamber notices "that a stable majority is possible only when an essential issue dominates." But essential issues do not exist or are not eternal or unique, and "when serious problems follow each other, majorities alternate at any moment." Also "established policy" has not the same sense as in the past, it cannot be applied anymore in an invariable form to the whole set of problems of national life. When the cleavages dividing

SOURCE 11.1

the nation were neat and simple, when all aspirations and all political and social tendencies were classified into two compartments, they came, on each side, from a master idea, corresponded to the same temperament, and implied the same spirit and the same line of behavior in their practical realization; any deviation showed incoherence, weakness of political character, even moral failure. Nowadays, with multiple and cross-cutting issues, the spirit of continuity can display itself only within the limits of a big problem or of some problems closely united by natural affinity.

Moisei Ostrogorski, *Democracy and the Organization of Political Parties* (1902)

There still seems to be a tendency in much of the formal literature dealing with majority rule over multidimensional policy spaces to view majority rule as a fairly well defined notion, which will generally force the social outcome towards "median" like alternatives...Rather, the usual situation will be that majority paths exist between any two points in the space...[*This*] seem to imply that there are essentially unlimited possibilities for agenda manipulation.

R. D. McKelvey, "General Conditions for Global Intransitivities in Formal Voting Models" (1979)

Do not forget that each "basin" defines an area of policy positions whose measure is not necessarily proportional to the number of people whose preferences are contained within it. If it is possible to estimate the number of voters' ideal points located within each "basin," then we will be able to predict the relative sizes in votes of each party. We can also observe the degree of variety of preferences of voters voting for the same party.

Quick Quiz

• What's the win-set?

Setting the Agenda

Forming the public agenda implies selecting issues on which elections and decisions will be held. While party competition in a multidimensional issue space likely leads to instability, as we saw in the previous section, if the agenda is formed by a series of single-issue decisions, there can be stable policy outcomes on each issue. When parties give salience to a few issues in the public debate and electoral campaigns, the voter may have the opportunity not to choose a big package of policy proposals on many issues at the same time, but rather to focus on only a few issues or a single issue. On each issue, a policy can be settled, typically to the advantage of the party with the best government record on that issue.

When, after World War II, the British Labour Party in government introduced a general system of social security, including universal health care, pensions for the elderly, and other safety nets, this was a very innovative policy, greatly distant from the status quo. It quickly won the support of broad layers of society, thus inducing the Conservative Party to adapt. Policy consensus on the issue existed for several decades in Britain, as in many other countries following similar experiences. But the British Labour and other social democratic parties were, generally, more broadly trusted by the public concerned with the issue than were conservative parties.

In another instance, the policy of balancing the budget—that is, equating public revenues with expenditure over the business cycle—was very innovative, and distant from the status quo, when it began to be introduced in the United States in the 1980s. Later on, in light of its universally beneficial effects for reducing inflation, the policy of near-balanced budgets was adopted by the European Union, and by the International Monetary Fund for low-income countries. Policy consensus was widely diffused. In this case, it worked to the political advantage of the conservatives, to which liberal, social-democrat, and other parties adapted.

Similar stories can be told for once-innovative policies, such as civil rights for ethnic minorities, transnational free trade, equal rights for women, re-privatization of state-owned industries producing private goods, suppression of compulsory military service, and international justice for crimes against humanity. When it was first formulated, each of these proposals was considered highly innovative and apparently "extreme" in relation to status quo policies. Eventually, policy consensus was built on these and other issues, after some success. Typically, it implied initiative by some parties and adaptation by others.

PARTY ADVANTAGE ON ISSUES

Generally, a party can choose an issue to be politicized. If a party gives salience to an issue, if it succeeds in making the issue highly relevant for voters' choice, and if its policy proposal on the issue is valued positively by most voters, thus including the median voter, that party will be the election winner. Even if the other parties adapt to and unilaterally "converge" on the winner's position, the party having first adopted the winning position may get credit for it and have an advantage before the public opinion when the issue takes salience in public debate. Logically, the losers can try to change the electoral outcome by giving salience to other issues on which they can hold more popular positions. Electoral equilibrium can therefore imply that two large parties adopt similar positions on an issue, as postulated by the median voter theorem. But each of the parties is likely to put different emphases on the issue in question—greater by the winning party and lesser by the others.

Not all policy issues can be the subject of the same degree of party manipulation. On some issues, different parties can indeed hold alternative policy proposals. But on certain other issues there can be broad consensus. Almost everybody, for instance, prefers economic prosperity to depression, and peace to war, and if a party ran in elections proposing general austerity or the launching of a war of aggression on innocent people, it would risk being widely rejected.

We can therefore distinguish between **position issues** and **valence issues**. The former, **position issues, imply competition between distant policy proposals**. Different parties can compete, for instance, by favoring either private schools or state schools. In contrast, **valence issues, are those on which there is broad consensus and which almost everybody wants more of**. It is assumed that the goal of government action should be the provision of valence issues—for example, prosperity or peace. Party competition on these issues consists of claiming credit or getting blamed for them, mostly on the basis of the parties' previous government record and the subsequent likelihood of performing well in the future.

A position issue can become a valence issue if parties converge in their positions and a new consensus is formed around a specific policy. For instance, broad support for not raising taxes can emerge after a long period of steady increase in government's fiscal resources. Conversely, a previously existing consensus can be broken after some shocks. A valence issue, such as peace by all means, can suddenly become a divisive issue if the country suffers an external attack.

Issues on which a policy is broadly recognized as desirable may appear as being temporarily "owned" by a party. **"Issue ownership" can result from the accumulation of positive policy performances by a party over time**. "Owned" issues are those in which a party has credit and is reckoned as more capable on a long-term basis. When an issue takes salience in the public's concerns, the party that "owns" the issue, if this is the case, has the advantage and is likely to obtain broad public and electoral support.

"Issue ownership" can be seen by voters as a form of "party identification," which we discussed in the previous chapter but limited to specific issues. Voters can vote for a party on the basis of the party's past performance rather than its current positions, but only when an issue on which the party has the advantage is prominent in the election.

For example, in the United States, Democrats have been well reputed on education, health care, and civil rights, while Republicans have had a broader following on national security, anti-crime, and tax issues. In other countries, labor and social democratic parties have a higher reputation on social policy issues; liberals are more credible when they emphasize individual rights; and conservatives are associated with better performance on the economy, defense, and security issues.

However, issue ownership can change. After a major policy failure, which can be caused by international, technological, or population innovations or by changes in people's values, voters can change their minds regarding which parties can be positively or negatively associated with an issue.

The controversial issue of race in the United States, for example, was given extremely high salience by the Republicans around the 1860s, in the specific form of proposing a ban on slavery in the South—a process that led to the Civil War. In contrast, about a century later, in the 1960s, it was the Democrats who responded positively to African American mobilizations by introducing new legislation on civil rights and affirmative action. In between, the race issue was largely dormant for several decades. In the long term, voters can realign with respect to political parties as a consequence of the introduction or reintroduction of certain issue dimensions in the public agenda.

ELECTORAL CAMPAIGNS

An issue may become salient in voters' perception if it is known that problems related to it deserve some policy action. The status quo policy might have become unsatisfactory, even if it has been stable for a long period. Lasting dissatisfaction can be the result of the fact that a single vote on a package of multiple policy issues may impede the implementation of policy positions on certain issues that are preferred by a majority of voters, as noted before. Dissatisfaction may also derive from changing circumstances, such as new technology migrations or other population changes, making a traditional policy produce new, unintended, undesirable effects, and from changes in values among the voters, perhaps as a consequence of the effects of new policies in other issues.

Electorally motivated leaders or candidates can be moved to give salience to a new issue by public demand, pressure from activists, or the threat that a new party heralding the issue may enter the competition. For a political party or entrepreneurial politician, giving salience to an issue implies adopting a new policy position on that issue in contrast to the presumably unsatisfactory status quo policy. Two additional actions are required to launch an electoral campaign:

- Selecting issues by talking about them and making them news with some effort investment—or **heresthetics**; and
- Framing the new position or policy proposal with some value or argument—or **rhetoric**.

Heresthetics.   This is the art of selecting issues. In electoral campaigns, parties devote much effort to persuading voters that some issue should be "salient" in their decision. The choice of what to talk about can be more important than what is said, since the message can be predicted from the party's previously established policy position on the issue.

Each party has a fixed endowment of "effort," measurable in terms of time, money, personnel, and organization, that can be distributed across issues. In addition, parties may also want to select candidates who are more competent on the issues they wish to emphasize, as a way of credibly committing to devote effort to a given issue.

The share of the effort devoted to an issue can determine the weight given by voters in evaluating the party's position on that issue. For many voters, salience suggests the commitment of the party, if it arrives in government, to dedicate the corresponding fraction of time and resources to that issue. It would be risky for a voter to vote for a party on the basis of an issue that is not salient in the campaign, even if the voter cares much about the issue, because it is likely that the party, once in government, will not pay much attention to it. It is less risky to expect that the party will spend more governmental effort on issues to which it has committed itself during the electoral campaign, although usually there is no guarantee of this.

In the public debate, campaign advertisements, and media messages, each party seeks to give salience to those issues on which it is more credible and expects to obtain voters' attention and votes. A skilful party or candidate can create opportune events, ranging from the typical town visits and press conferences to book presentations and artfully provoked international conflicts. It can also launch personal attacks or provocations on the rival party or candidate in order to divert its attention or put it on the defensive, and then fill the corresponding vacuum with the preferred message. But no party is in full control of the environment, in which other parties, interest groups, the media, and unexpected events contribute to shaping the public agenda.

Two types of campaign agendas can be distinguished, depending on whether they are endogenous to party competition or exogenous if imposed by external events, pressure groups, or independent media.

For **endogenous** formation of campaign agendas, two strategies can be distinguished:

- **"Dominance" criterion**. The party insists on an issue on which its proposal proves to be successful and gives the party an advantage. Typically, the other party abandons the issue and tries to change the subject of conversation.

- **"Dispersion" criterion**. The party abandons an issue when the party proposal fails to attract voters' attention or support. All parties abandon the issue when no party has a clear advantage on it.

British prime minister Winston Churchill once said, "A fanatic is one who cannot change his mind, and won't change the subject." Good advice for an electoral campaigner is not to be a fanatic: if a candidate cannot change his mind (that is, the policy proposal he is associated with), he should change the subject. Such party strategies produce electoral campaigns in which the parties do not engage in discussion with each other. In every election campaign, parties can fight on several dimensions at once by choosing different issues to emphasize—so they talk about different issues, and change the subject when explicitly challenged on an alternative issue. In successive campaigns, the agenda tends to shift to different issues.

In **exogenous** campaign agendas, an unexpected event—say, a sudden economic crisis, a big scandal, massive popular protests, a natural disaster, a terrorist attack, or an external war—may force a party to deal with a subject on which it has a disadvantaged position. A candidate caught in an unfavorable field may react with fervor, saying, "That's not an issue," which usually means it's not an issue about which the candidate wants to talk because he does not have an advantageous position on it. He can also try to deny the relevance of the event in question.

However, if the issue has received overwhelming weight in the news and in voters' perception, the best response for the disadvantaged party may be to give salience to the least unfavorable value within the issue. We discuss this tactic in the following paragraphs.

Rhetoric.   This is **the art of framing the party's position or policy proposal on an issue by means of persuasive values and arguments**. Values can include liberty, security, equality, efficiency, justice, peace and others. Two types of arguments exist: (1) "negative" arguments oriented at rejecting the status quo, which are likely to be given relatively high weight by voters; and (2) "positive" arguments for choosing new proposals, which may be accepted by default. Arguments can refer to authority, expertise, precedent, analogy, danger, fear, distrust, risk, disdain, or other available resorts.

The discussion of different values for an issue can create a new multidimensional value space. For instance, health care and abortion can be two issues to which different parties try to give salience in an election. If the issue of health care acquires greater salience in the public debate, media messages, and voters' attention, then a party may want to remark upon the quality of social investment for people's "well-being," while the other party may give salience to the implication that the health care policy proposed requires new "taxes." Thus a two-value dimension for the issue is created. If it is the abortion issue that becomes more salient, one party can give salience, within the issue, to the value of freedom of "choice," while another may try to make the value of

CASE 11.2   ELECTORAL ISSUES IN TELEVISION ADS

A review of TV ads in the U.S. presidential electoral campaigns during more than fifty years (1952–2004) shows that Democrats and Republicans give priority to different issues. The Republicans have managed to set the presidential agenda more times than the Democrats, inducing the latter to reply to the former's preferred issues on numerous occasions. The two issues with highest salience in a collection of 300 TV electoral ads are national security and taxes (the subject of 90 and 77 ads, respectively). Two thirds of the ads on national security were launched by Republican candidates. Most wars in which the United States was involved during the twentieth century were fought during periods with Democratic presidents. But when, in 1952, World War II hero General Dwight D. Eisenhower, after having been courted by the Democrats, became the presidential candidate of the Republican Party, it created an image that has prevailed ever since: voters have tended to find Republican candidates stronger and more experienced than Democrats on issues involving the military. For example, candidate Richard Nixon asserted explicitly in a TV ad in 1960 that "the communist threat is the most important issue." The Democrats were accused repeatedly of being weak and ineffective in ending war and establishing robust peace, especially since the Vietnam War. However, the Iraq War might have reversed this alignment.

The issue of reducing taxes was already given salience by Republican candidate Barry Goldwater in the 1964 election, with the lemma "to make the government the servant and not the master of us all," as formulated in TV. Democrats, in contrast, were portrayed as the "tax and spend" party, especially since 1980, when vice-president and presidential candidate Walter Mondale still promised to raise taxes in order to reduce the growing public deficit. Republican Ronald Reagan proposed cutting taxes in order to facilitate jobs and growth. The issue, however, backfired against Republican president George Bush, Sr., in 1992, when Democratic candidate William Clinton accused him of having broken his broadly aired promise, "Read my lips: no new taxes."

The Democrats have gained clear advantage on the issue of education, which they have emphasized regularly (23 ads). They have also given salience to civil rights (19 ads), which the Republicans have opposed sometimes, for example, in the 1972 campaign of Nixon against "busing" children to schools. However, the race issue weakened the Democrats' support in the South, where anti–civil rights candidates emerged, especially in 1948 and 1968.

The most controversial dimension involved welfare and family issues (raised in 10 Democratic and 11 Republican ads). Republicans opposed welfare policy as of 1972. But twenty years later, Democrat Clinton announced, "It's time to make welfare what it should be; a second chance, not a way of life" and "End welfare as we know it."

Source: Author's own elaboration, from classification and contents list of 300 TV ads for the period 1952–2004. American Museum of the Moving Image, "The Living Room Candidates: Presidential Campaign Commercials 1952–2004", available at www.living-roomcandidate.org.

"life" more salient. Parties may be forced to talk about the same issue, but by emphasizing different values related to that issue, no party will really enter into discussion with another.

CUMULATIVE POLICY MAKING

When a new issue is given salience through a new policy proposal in order to attract voters' attention and votes, three alternative outcomes may happen. First, the party may fail in its endeavor, never arrive in government, and not be able to implement the policy. Second, the party may win sufficient support to enter government and implement the policy, but this may produce unexpected or undesirable effects, making voters prefer again the previous status quo or a similar position. In these two occurrences, which both imply a policy failure, the previous status quo policy will

SOURCE 11.2   Political Arguments

By the name of fallacy, it is common to designate any argument employed, or topic suggested, for the purpose, or with a probability, of producing the effect of deception, of causing some erroneous opinion to be entertained by any person to whose mind such argument may have been presented...The classes of fallacies can be arranged in the order in which the enemies of improvement may be supposed to resort to them according to the emergence of the moment.

First, fallacies of authority: appeal to authority, to the wisdom of our ancestors, to irrevocable laws, to no-precedent, self-assumed authority, and laudatory personalities. The immediate object is to repress all exercise of the reasoning faculty.

Second, fallacies of danger: "no innovation!", distrust, "attack us, you attack government", and vituperative personalities (for bad design, bad character, bad motive, inconsistency, suspicious connections). The object is to repress altogether the discussion proposed to be entered on.

Third, fallacies of delay: "no complaint", "wait a little, this is not the time", "one thing at a time! not too fast! slow and sure!", artful diversion. The object is to postpone such discussion, with a view of eluding it altogether.

Fourth, fallacies of confusion: vague generalities (order, establishment, constitution, balance of powers, glorious revolution), allegorical idols (government, the law, the church), anti-rational fallacies ("utopian", "good in theory, bad in practice"...). The object is to produce, when discussion can no longer be avoided, such confusion in the minds of the hearers as to incapacitate them for forming a correct judgment on the question proposed for deliberation.

Jeremy Bentham, *The Book of Fallacies* (1824)

prevail. It is likely that the party having promoted salience for the new issue will either withdraw its policy proposal or be electorally weakened in future elections. It can then apply the "dispersion" criterion and shift salience to other issues.

In the third outcome, the new policy may be successful in the sense of its being satisfactory for the citizens, and this may reinforce the party's electoral support. In this occurrence, as the new policy can be implemented with wide popular acceptance, it is likely that the winning party will apply the "dominance" criterion and keep giving emphasis to the issue. Other parties may then adapt their positions on the issue to the new status quo. A new policy consensus may be created.

In any of these occurrences, it can be expected that the issue will lose salience in future contests. In the long term, therefore, whether new policy proposals fail or succeed, we should expect that an increasing number of settled issues will be successively discarded from the electoral contest. For advanced democracies, empirical analysis of policy making shows long periods of policy stasis interrupted episodically with bursts of rapid policy change.

Quick Quiz

• What's the difference between position issues and valence issues?
• What's the difference between heresthetics and rhetoric?

Conclusion

In two-party elections dealing with multiple issue dimensions at the same time, parties can manipulate the combination of policy proposals on different issues in their "packages." Due to the different degrees of voter satisfaction with different issues within the same party package, changing votes and alternation of parties in government can be expected. This may produce high policy instability over time. In contrast, if one or a few issues are chosen separately in every election, a policy may obtain broad support and remain stable.

This permits establishing the following *propositions* in political science:

- **Issue ownership.** In spite of parties' convergence in their policy positions on some issues, a party can keep advantage and "own" an issue if its past record in government has given it credit for policy making on the issue.

- **Non-debate campaigns.** In electoral campaigns, rival parties and candidates tend to choose to emphasize different issues, according to different issue ownerships and their expected relative advantage.

- **Policy consensus.** In the long term, broad policy consensus can be accumulated on an increasing number of issues. But in the short term, mediocre policies and incumbent parties with no good performance in government may survive for lack of a sufficiently popular alternative. ∎

Summary

In a multidimensional space of issues, the area including all the potential electoral winners is called the "win-set." The larger the win-set, the higher the number of potentially winning positions against the status quo, and thus the higher the potential policy instability.

In contrast to instability in multidimensional-issue party competition, if the agenda is formed by a series of single-issue decisions, there can be stable outcomes.

On position issues, parties compete with alternative policy proposals. On valence issues on which broad consensus has formed, party competition consists of claiming credit or getting blamed.

A party can have the advantage and "own" an issue on the basis of its previous record in government and its likelihood of performing well in the future.

Heresthetics is the art of selecting issues in the public agenda. Parties tend to change the subject of conversation and promote a series of different issues in successive campaigns.

Rhetoric is the art of framing the party's policy proposals on an issue by means of persuasive values and arguments. The discussion on different values for each issue can create a new multidimensional value space in which parties emphasize different values.

In the long term, there can be cumulative policy consensus among political parties on a succession of issues, broken only by periodical shocks.

Key Concepts

Agenda setting. Selecting the policy issues to be given salience in public debate or legislation.

Dispersion criterion. A criterion by which no party has clear advantage regarding an issue and all abandon that issue.

Dominance criterion. A criterion by which the party with advantage emphasizes an issue and other parties abandon it.

Heresthetics. The art of selecting policy issues.

Issue ownership. Party advantage on an issue from positive past performance.

Party's attraction area. The area of voters' ideal points closer to the party.

Position issue. Issue on which parties hold distant policy proposals.

Rhetoric. The art of framing a policy proposal with values and arguments.

Valence issue. Issue with broad consensus on which parties compete for credit.

Voter's curve of indifference. In a multidimensional space, the set of policy positions at equal distance from the voter's ideal point, as can be represented by a circumference.

Win-set. The area including all potential electoral winners against the status quo.

Questions for Review

1. Draw a two-dimensional space, the status quo point, a voter's ideal point, and the voter's curve of indifference.
2. Enunciate the dominance and the dispersion criteria in the selection of issues.
3. What's the difference between heresthetics and rhetoric?

Problems and Applications

1. Choose a political speech and analyze:
   a. The issue or issues it deals with.
   b. The values emphasized.
   Discuss possible alternative values and arguments on the same issues.
   You can find collections of interesting political speeches by searching for "political speeches" on your web browser. Or go to sites such as:
   www.historyplace.com/speeches/previous.htm or
   www.americanrhetoric.com/top100speechesall.html.

Quantitative measurements

2. Draw a two-dimensional space with positions from 0 to 10 on each dimension. Place the status quo in the space at SQ(4,4). Locate the following voters' ideal points: A(2,2), B(4,6), C(6, 4).
   a. Draw the indifference curves of each of the three voters, A, B, and C, with respect to the status quo, SQ. Identify the win-set, that is, the set of all possible winning positions against the status quo by any majority of 2 voters out of the 3.
   b. Is position X(5,5,) within the win-set?
   c. Calculate, by Pythagoras, the distances from each of the three voters A, B, and C, to SQ and to X. For which party will each voter vote?

Let us now assume that the new status-quo is located at SQ(5,5).

d. Is the previous SQ(4,4) within the win-set of SQ?

e. Is position Y(5,4) within the win-set of SQ?

f. Is position Z(4,5) within the win-set of SQ?

g. Is position W(6,6) within the win-set of SQ?

h. Calculate, by Pythagoras, the distances from each of the three voters, A, B, and C, to Y, to Z, to W, and to SQ.

3. Draw a two-dimensional space with positions from 0 to 10 on each dimension. Locate in the space the following parties' positions: X(4,6), Y(7,3), Z(7,8).

a. Draw the bisectors between each pair of party's positions and identify each party's attraction area.

b. For voter A(5,5), which is the closest party?

c. And for voter B(7,5)?

d. And for voter C(7,6)?

For a term paper

4. Choose an electoral campaign you can pay attention to, if you have the occasion. It can be any type of political election, including college/university elections, or any other electoral contest you can witness. Make an account of the main media messages during a few weeks of the campaign by concentrating either on front-page headlines of a couple of newspapers, or on TV news headlines of a couple of TV stations, or on a party or a candidate's TV ads, leaflets, or posters. Define well which sources you are going to analyze. For each piece of information, identify:

a. Who the party or candidate sending the message is.

b. What the issue is.

c. Whether it is a positive or a negative message.

Evaluate the expected impact of the messages reviewed on the electoral result.

5. Multidimensional spaces can be identified for real politicians, such as the members of the U.S. Congress. For possible further research, consider using the following analytical tool: Winset-CyberSenate: www.winset.com.

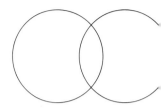

12

PARTY SYSTEMS

In This Chapter You Will

- Examine the differences between two-party and multiparty systems.
- Analyze what political ideology is.
- Reflect on the contents of the left-right ideological axis.
- Learn that few parties tend to develop high polarization, while multiple parties can facilitate consensus.

It is well known that, in the United States, only two major parties compete with reasonable expectations of winning government, that is, the Democrats and the Republicans. In a similar manner, in the United Kingdom, the Labourites and the Conservatives have alternated in government for several decades. But in India and Japan, for instance, while multiple parties compete in elections and win parliamentary seats, a single large party has been in government for most of the time since the mid-twentieth century, the Congress Party and the Liberal-democratic Party, respectively. In Germany, multiple parties are represented in parliament, but the two larger ones, the Christian-democrats and the Social-democrats, lead alternatively the formation of different multiparty governments in coalitions with the Liberals, the Greens, or other parties. In France and Italy, two multiparty blocs at the right and the left are usually confronted. In other countries, diverse coalition governments are formed with the chief executive belonging to any of three or four different parties, such as in Brazil, Finland, Israel, the Netherlands, and Switzerland.

As these examples suggest, different numbers of parties in a system can be related to the salience of different numbers of policy issues and the parties' relative policy and ideological positions. In the previous chapters, we studied the characteristics of electoral competition and agenda setting in two-party systems. In this chapter we address the relationship between different systems of parties and discuss the role of ideological positions along the "left-right" or similar ideological axis in shaping policy proposals. We will see how the number of parties competing in a political system matters to generate either broad policy consensus or sharp polarization. ■

Number of Parties

Certain authoritarian regimes try to organize control by means of a political party that excludes or strongly constrains others from competition, although many dictatorships do not even bother to organize such a thing. In contrast, in conditions of political freedom and open democratic elections, it is highly unlikely that only one political party will be formed. Regarding the numbers, party systems in a democracy can be distinguished for having either:

- **two parties**, or
- **multiple parties**.

Two-party System.   If only two sufficiently large political parties compete in elections, they will focus on one or a few issues in electoral competition, as we discussed in the previous chapters. If there are only two parties, one of them will typically obtain a majority of seats and be able to form a single-party government.

In the past, two-party systems focusing on few issues and forming single-party cabinets were considered a sound formula for effective and stable government. However, two-party systems are nowadays characteristic of only a few of the oldest democracies with well-established electoral and institutional rules, including the United States and, more imperfectly, the United Kingdom. In many other countries, the expansion of suffrage rights and the increasing complexity of political competition have created more opportunities for the development of multiple parties.

Multi-party System.   Electoral competition among a high number of political parties is indeed a typical feature of most democratic regimes. Multiple parties tend to politicize a high number of issues. In a multiparty competition, typically no party has a majority of votes. However, even if multiple parties are formed, run in elections, and obtain fair representation, a single party may be sufficiently large as to form government and become "dominant" for a relatively long period. For example, the Congress Party in India, the Christian-democratic Party in Italy, the Liberal-democratic Party in Japan, the Social-democratic Party in Sweden and Norway, were dominant single parties for long periods.

More frequently, two larger parties among many receive the most votes and are able to lead the formation of alternative multiparty governments. In Germany, for instance, as in Austria, Belgium, and the Netherlands, the Christian-democrats and the Social-democrats have alternated in leading the formation of governments, always in coalition with other parties. This configuration has been called a "two-and-a-half"-party system.

In contrast, when three or more parties have similar proportions of votes and seats, several multiparty coalition governments can be formed. In Finland, for example, the Agrarian (or center), Conservative, and Socialist parties have led governments in different coalitions that have included several other parties. In Switzerland, four parties—the Christian, the Radical, the Socialist, and the Populist—are usually included in the so-called "magic formula" of government, with alternating prime ministers from different parties.

NUMBERS OF ISSUES AND PARTIES

The number of political parties competing in elections is strongly linked to the number of policy issues that take salience in public debate and electoral campaigns. Certain politicized issues that have shaped some traditional parties are based on old social **cleavages**, which may have been produced by remote historical events and transformations. First, processes of nation-state building under the French model, especially in Europe, produced a state-church cleavage, since the state sought to absorb social tasks that were traditionally in the hands of the church. Subsequent politicized issues include the role of the church in the school, and a variety of family and sexual matters. Nation-state building also generated a center-periphery cleavage, since the state sought to centralize government control and homogenize the population across the territory. As a consequence, some politicized issues involve the distribution of public institutions and resources across a territory and the relations between people with different religious, racial or language characteristics.

In turn, industrial revolutions under the English model produced a land-industry cleavage, including issues such as public support for agriculture or industry, freedom of trade or the protection of local producers, and the protection of natural resources and the environment. Likewise, an owner-worker cleavage emerged due to the dominant role of industrial entrepreneurs; this includes controversies over who should pay taxes and how much; the validation of property rights; the perils of unemployment, and of inflation; the provision of health care coverage and elderly pensions. Conservative and liberal political parties were initially prominent in these processes by holding opposite stances, such as church versus state or agriculture versus industry, but new parties were also formed in many countries, including ethnic-territorial and socialist parties, defending peripheral populations and workers' interests, respectively.

However, in any society with a working government, the number of politicized issues and the emergence and relative strength of each party do not necessarily depend on the importance of old revolutions or the depth of cleavages associated with long-term social structures. Initiatives of politicization and party formation can encompass literally any aspect of human life that can be submitted to regulation by public and enforceable decisions for which some alternative to the status quo can be proposed.

A general relationship between the number of political issues and the number of relevant political parties is: **issues plus one equals parties**, or:

$$I + 1 = P$$

Where:
I: number of political issues; and
P: number of political parties.

The logic behind this relationship is that when a single issue is at stake, for instance, on socioeconomic matters, two parties proposing alternative policies define the dimension as a controversial one, around, say, pro-market and interventionist stand-points. Thus, the minimum values in democracy would be one issue with two party proposals: I = 1, P = 2. A second dimension, around moral issues, for example, can become salient if a third party takes the initiative of introducing new policy propos-als on those issues alternative to the status quo. The salience of a third dimension around, for instance, ethnic and territorial issues, would imply that a fourth party comes onto the scene, and so on.

New issues can create the occasion and motive for the formation of new parties, but they can also be developed inside old parties. For instance, the emergence of movements of African Americans, students, or women's liberation did not generate new political parties, but rather the incorporation of new demands and proposals by existing parties. Which of the two alternatives will occur depends partly on the restrictions imposed by the electoral and institutional system upon entry of new par-ties into political competition, as will be analyzed in other chapters of this book. Conversely, there can be more than two policy proposals (and corresponding parties) on an issue, and a new issue can give rise to the creation of not one, but two new par-ties with opposite standpoints. Due to these variants, the best empirical fit for the relationship just presented is: $I + 1 = P \pm 1$.

Quick Quiz

• What is the relationship between the number of issues and the number of parties?

Ideology

A political ideology can be defined as an encompassing set of a high number of economic, moral, ethnic, or other policy issues and values. If different political parties and citizens have correlated preferences on a number of issues, they can syn-thesize their messages or preferences in the form of a simple ideological position.

Assume that in a given community there is broad coincidence in political par-ties' policy proposals on different issues such as taxes, foreign trade, race, and family values. For instance, those in favor of high taxes and trade protection also promote affirmative action and give priority to individual moral freedom over family stability, while opposite positions are held by alternative parties and citizens. The former group can be called "left-wing," "liberal," or "progressive," and the latter "right-wing," or "conservative." Then all those issues will be synthesized into a single ideological axis, which can be called "left-right," "liberal-conservative," or other labels.

WHAT IS AN IDEOLOGY?

An ideology is a simplification. It usually implies labels used by political parties, such as conservatism, environmentalism, liberalism, nationalism, progressivism, social-ism, etcetera. Each "ism" can be argued with the help of some values, such as liberty, security, equality, efficiency, justice, or peace. Parties also use different symbols, such as colors, heroes, dates, animals, flags, banners, and badges, to distinguish themselves from one another. Each ideological label and its symbols entails a set of public policy proposals and values on a number of issues.

Why do we need ideologies? Basically, for communication purposes. On the demand side, a citizen may resort to a simplified ideological representation of a party's standpoints on many policy issues in order to save information costs. It may not be rational for a voter with very little influence on the electoral result to pay high costs to obtain detailed information about each party's standpoints on each issue, as we discussed in the first part of this book. General ideological and symbolic messages may provide sufficiently good hints and cues for a voter to make an electoral choice in favor of a party in accordance with his preferences or interests. When a citizen resorts to a party ideology to establish his or her preference, he or she stops thinking about the issue in question, since the ideology provides a given preference. Although this has certain intellectual risks, it saves time, that is information and deliberation costs.

On the supply side, parties also have to present their policy proposals within the restrictions imposed by a simplified ideological message, since this is the only way to obtain a broad audience. Communicational requirements may prevent parties from adopting disparate or apparently contradictory positions on different issues. A competitive party cannot afford to be "leftist" on one issue and "rightist" on another without risking being misunderstood by potential supporters and voters.

However, political communication through ideologies has significant drawbacks for electoral decision and policy making. First, parties' ideological consistency can produce cognitive dissonance among voters. This means that certain voters can find it hard to manage instances in which they agree with a party on some issues and disagree with the party on other issues. If voters embrace a given party's ideological position instead of thinking further and weighing the pros and cons on each issue when making their choice, they may be dissatisfied with regard to some issues with the party they choose.

Communication needs can also prevent parties from making dramatic changes in policy positions in order not to confuse their voters. Ideology forces parties to take rather predictable positions when a new issue emerges in order to be understood by the electors in argumentative consistency with the party's previous positions on other issues. The "stronger" the ideology—that is, the more both voters and parties rely on simplified ideological symbols—the more it will determine party policies.

Consider, for instance, the emergence of a new issue such as stem cell research, which may be politicized and take salience in the public debate. Parties have ideological restrictions on discussing different policy alternatives and adopting positions. Although ideologies may not give detailed guidance as to which position to take on the issue policy space, they do indicate the general policy "position," whether on the left or the right, that a party should occupy. If, for instance, a party has heralded strong family values on issues such as abortion, it might be inclined to resist public subsidies for stem cell research in order to be consistent with some of its previous arguments about when life begins, whereas the opposite may hold for other parties.

On all issues, parties tend to locate themselves on the same relative part of the ideological spectrum with respect to others, so they do not play "leap-frog" with the other parties. Parties recognize each other's spatial boundaries and, usually, cannot greatly change their relative positions to the left or right. Ideological inconsistency might confuse electors and erode credibility for the party that has repudiated its past commitments. But the need to maintain "ideological consistency" to keep their members together and communicate in simple ways with voters can limit parties' ability to fight successfully or innovate on certain issues because they cannot take the most popular position on them. Ideological consistency, therefore, condemns some parties to appearing disadvantaged on certain issues and therefore not interested in emphasizing or giving them salience.

THE LEFT-RIGHT IDEOLOGICAL AXIS

The most widely accepted ideological representation of political party positions is the "left-right" spatial axis. This representation started to be used as shorthand for political preferences during the French Revolution in the late eighteenth century. Before that, "up-down" was a better-established spatial representation of different political positions, typically implying that the king or emperor was "up" and different layers of subjects were placed along the road, "down." Through turbulent changes, the "up" position became "right" and the "down" position, "left." Specifically, at the Constitutional Convention held in Paris in 1789, aristocrats and defenders of the monarchy sat to the right of the speaker's tribune, while those in favor of a republic sat to the left. Grouping members of the assembly with similar stances facilitated counting votes, which were cast by the delegates' standing or remaining seated.

However, it was not until the second half of the nineteenth century that the "left" and "right" labels spread from France to the rest of continental Europe. By then, parties and politicians on the left promoted civil liberties and economic freedom, while

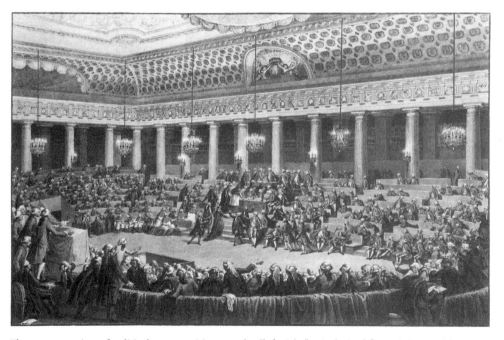

The representation of political party positions on the "left-right" axis derived from sitting positions at the Constitutional Convention during the French Revolution in the late 18th century.

Table 12.1   Parties on the Left-Right Axis

Political parties hold relatively consistent ideological positions in different countries, as shown in these examples.

LEFT	CENTER-LEFT		CENTER	CENTER-RIGHT		RIGHT
Chile						
Communist	Socialist	Democratic	Christian	National		Independent
PC	PS	PPD	PDC	RN		UDI
Czech Republic						
Communist	Socialist	Green	Christian	Civic	Liberal	
KSBM	CSSD	SZ	KDU-CSL	ODS	US	
Germany						
Left	Green	Socialdemocrat		Liberal	Christian	
L	Grü	SPD		FDP	CDU/CSU	
Japan						
Communist	Socialist		Democratic	Komeito	Liberal	Conservative
JCP	SDP		DP	Kom	LDP	NCP
United States						
	Democratic			Republican		

Sources: Adapted from data in Kenneth Benoit and Michael Laver, *Party Policy in Modern Democracies* (2007), Josep M. Colomer ed. *Comparative European Politics 3rd ed.* (2008), Josep M. Colomer and Luis E. Escatel, "La dimensión izquierda-derecha en América Latina" (2005).

the right defended the old hierarchical order and commercial protectionism. But during the twentieth century, "left" and "right" were associated respectively with government interventionism in the economy and the free market, thus implying reversed positions on some issues in comparison with the previous century.

The specific policy position contents of "left" and "right" or of "liberal" and "conservative" global ideological positions are accidental. There is, after all, no logical or inherent reason why support for peace, for instance, should be associated with government interventionism or homosexual marriage. The emergence of new politicized issues usually requires some collective discussion to make opposite standpoints adapt to the left-right labels. For instance, the emergence of the environmental issue in late twentieth century did not initially imply clear associations with positions along the left-right axis. In fact, "green" parties in different countries chose different ideological standpoints, including some "conservationists" of nature, until most of them converged toward the left side.

Even today, although the "left-right" label is the most common one across countries, it is not always the main reference. In certain countries, labels such as "liberal-conservative," "radical-moderate," or "softliner-hardliner" are more popular for identifying the position of political parties in a simplified manner. Consider the cases in Table 12.1 as expressing relatively consistent but not completely coinciding party positions with similar ideological labels in different countries.

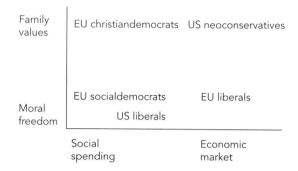

FIGURE 12.1 PARTIES ON TWO ISSUE DIMENSIONS
"Left" and "right" take on different meanings in different party systems depending on which issue is more important, as in the cross-cutting of the socioeconomic and moral issues in this figure.

Political parties can adopt apparently different ideological positions in different countries if they combine policy issues in different ways. To illustrate this, let us consider two issues: a socioeconomic one with opposite positions in favor of either economic market competition or social spending, and a moral one with opposite positions in favor of either moral freedom or family values. It could be argued that social spending and family values are alternative ways of providing safety nets: the lack of the two would maximize individual risks; the strength of both would be redundant. However, all four possible combinations of alternative policies on the two issues do exist as significant party programs. Specifically, economic market/moral freedom, the most individualistic combination, has traditionally been adopted by European

CASE 12.1 SWING POLITICAL PARTIES

Political parties can modify their relative ideological positions over time. The example of the United Kingdom shows how parties' relative distances on the left-right axis change. As shown in Figure 12.2, first, after the Second World War, the Labourites were innovative on the left by introducing social security and welfare programs. Then, during the 1950s and '60s, the Liberals and Conservatives adapted to and "converged" with the Labourites. But since the 1970s the Conservatives have moved toward the right by adopting more pro-free-market positions, eventually attracting the Labourites to their side.

Source: Adapted from Ian Budge, H-D. Klingemann, Andrea Volkens, and Judith Bara, *Mapping Policy Preferences* (Oxford University Press, 2001), and Judith Bara, "The 2005 Manifestos" (Journal of Elections, Public Opinion and Parties, 2006).

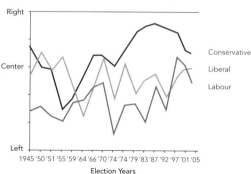

BOX 12.1   MEASURING PARTY SYSTEMS

The two dimensions of a party system, that is, the number of parties and their relative distances, can be measured quantitatively. With precise measurement, party systems in different countries and periods can be compared. Some variants of the measures presented here have been given for measuring ethnic variety in chapter 6, but party systems permit the use of the ideological left-right dimension.

Number of Parties

The number of parties in a system can be measured using either of these indices:

$$\text{Fragmentation: } F = 1 - \Sigma P_i^2$$

$$\text{Effective number: } N = 1 / \Sigma P_i^2$$

Where:
F: Fragmentation;
N: Effective number; and
P_i: Size of party i (in share of either votes or seats).

The fragmentation index has values between 0 and 1, where 0 corresponds to a single party with all votes or seats (likely not a democracy) and 1 corresponds to an infinite number of voters each voting for a different party (presumably for the voter himself). The effective number of parties has values from 1 upward, and higher the higher the number of parties of similar size. A conventional estimate is that multiparty systems exist when there are at least three "effective"

parties. In other words, there is still a two-party system, even if there are more than two parties collecting votes and seats, if two of the parties are sufficiently large (as happens, for instance, in the British House of Commons). The values of the two indices are strongly correlated, since N = 1 / (1−F).

Party Polarization

The degree of polarization in a two-party system can be measured with this index, which captures the weighted distance between the two parties:

$$\text{Polarization}_1: \text{Pol} = P_1X_1 - P_2X_2$$

Where:
Pol: Polarization;
P_i: Size of party i (in share of either votes or seats); and
X_i: Ideology position of party i

The polarization index has values from 0 up (depending on the scale used). The highest polarization is achieved when two parties are at highly distant positions.

For applied analyses, a quantitative measurement is needed of the ideology space and distances. Quantitative values can be provided by survey polls in which party positions are located on a scale from 0 to 10, where 0 represents the extreme left and 10 the extreme right, or other similar scales, which are available for some countries.

liberals; economic market/family values is heralded by American neoconservatives; social spending/moral freedom is typical of American liberals and European social-democrats; and social spending/family values, the most protective, is characteristic of European christian-democrats.

If the socioeconomic issue is most relevant, as usually happens in Europe, then those in favor of the market—that is, liberals in Europe and neoconservatives in America—would be located on the right; while those favoring social spending—that is, social-democrats and christian-democrats in Europe and liberals in America—would be on the left. But if the moral issue takes greater salience, as happened in the United States in recent times, then the liberals and social-democrats would be together on the left, while neoconservatives and christian-democrats would be placed on the right. See Figure 12.1 for a representation of this.

The different salience given to different issues, whether socioeconomic or moral, is the reason why the "liberal" label is usually associated with the right in Europe

SOURCE 12.1   Types of Party Systems

The study of party systems is as changing as the party systems themselves. Some classifications and typologies have been very influential for applied analysis and further discussion. Some implications, however, have been critically revised, as discussed in the text quoted here.

From the typology that I have developed at length elsewhere [*Parties and Party Systems, 1976*], let me derive three major systemic patterns: 1) two-party mechanics, i.e., bipolar single-party alternation in government; 2) moderate multipartism, i.e., bipolar shifts among coalition governments; 3) polarized multipartism, i.e., systems characterized by multipolar competition, unipolar center-located coalitions with peripheral turnover, and antisystem parties. In this typology the decisive variable is systemic polarization, defined as the distance (ideological or other) between the most-distant relevant parties.

Giovanni Sartori, "The Influence of Electoral Systems" (1986)

(where it refers above all to those in favor of the market), while it has become synonymous of "leftist" in the United States (referring to those in favor of moral freedom). Confusingly enough for the unlearned observer, Europeans call those favoring family values "neoliberals," while Americans call those favoring high public expenditure "liberals." You should be able now to understand why this is so.

This example shows that ideological labels are empty cans for stuffing and refilling. Whatever the combination of policy issues, however, it is convenient for a party to maintain predictable and relatively stable positions on each issue and on the encompassing ideology, in order to be able to offer understandable "packages" to the voters over time.

Quick Quiz

• What is the relation between a party's ideology and policy proposals?
• List several differences between "left" and "right" parties.

Polarization Versus Consensus

If parties compete for votes by adopting relatively close policy or ideology positions to each other, they may build "consensus." The introduction of issues on which their positions are more distant tends to create "polarization." There has been some discussion as to the propensity of systems with different numbers of political parties to promote either consensual or polarized electoral competition.

The degree of consensus or polarization can be estimated by the existence of two or multiple poles and a central balance. A party system can be relatively highly polarized if electoral competition is between, for example, laborites and conservatives, or two multiparty leftist and rightist blocs, or even more so if it is between distant "anti-system" parties, such as communists and fascists. The system may be relatively less polarized if the two poles are relatively close, for example, if they are democrats and republicans, or social-democrats and christian-democrats. Even higher consensus can be obtained if there is an intermediate balance between two distant parties, which can be provided by liberal, center, agrarian, ethnic, regional, or other parties.

More precisely, the degree of polarization in a party system is minimal when there is only one, internally compact party—that is, when all voters prefer the same policy and ideology—which is indeed a very rare occurrence in a democratic regime. By contrast, polarization can be maximal when the number of parties is two, if they are similarly large in size, and if they are located at a great distance from each other—the classic locus of "adversarial" politics. In multiparty systems, the higher the number of parties, the smaller each is likely to be, and thus the lower their relative distances (because there may be intermediate, relatively close parties) and the degree of polarization among them.

Thus, there can be an inverse correlation between the number of parties and the degree of party polarization in multiparty systems. A traditionally illustrative case is Switzerland, where there is a high number of parties and a very high degree of policy consensus among them. Some quantitative measurements confirm, for instance, that party polarization is higher in some two-party systems, such as the United Kingdom, where adversarial or confrontational politics tends to prevail, than in multiparty systems such as Germany, where broad policy consensus is built through multiparty coalition governments. Systematic empirical analyses have shown that, generally, high fragmentation, that is, a high number of parties, is associated with low polarization.

Quick Quiz

• Give examples of countries with two-party systems and countries with multiparty systems.

Conclusion

This chapter has discussed the relationship between the number of political parties in a system and the profile of electoral competition. In principle, the higher the number of political parties running, the higher the number of issues that are politicized by the introduction of new policy proposals. Parties, however, need simplifying ideologies, such as those using the "left" and "right" spatial representation, to deliver their messages to mass audiences, but this constrains their room for policy innovation.

In general, two-party systems tend to focus on a few issues or a strong ideology, while multiparty systems may favor larger public agendas, broader coalitions, and low policy polarization. A *proposition* in political science can be stated as follows:

• **Consensual pluralism**. There is an inverse correlation between the number of political parties and the degree of party polarization. High fragmentation is associated with low polarization. ∎

Summary

Political parties and electoral candidacies are based on the politicization of issues. Politicizing an issue implies proposing a new policy at some "distance" from the presumably unsatisfactory existing policy, called the status quo.

Approximately, the number of issue dimensions plus one equals the number of parties.

Certain politicized issues are based on old social cleavages, but political entrepreneurs may give salience to other issues not reflecting a preexisting social demand.

Ideologies are needed in politics to reduce information costs and deliver the parties' or the candidates' messages to mass audiences. But ideologies constrain policy innovation.

The "left-right" spatial axis is the most widely accepted ideological representation of political party positions, although not the only one.

In two-party systems, electoral competition tends to focus on a few issues, while in multiparty systems the public agenda is broadened.

There is an inverse correlation between party fragmentation and party polarization. Two-party systems can foster polarization, while multiparty systems can favor consensus.

Key Concepts

Fragmentation. Number of political parties weighted by their sizes; the opposite of "concentration."

Ideology. An encompassing simplification of a high number of issue policies.

Left-right. Ideological representation of party policy positions on a spatial basis.

Multiparty system. A system in which multiple parties obtain seats and share government.

Party system. Profile of electoral competition based on the number of parties and their ideological distance.

Polarization. Relative distances between parties weighted by their sizes.

Two-party system. A system in which only two parties compete for government.

Questions for Review

1. What is the relationship between the number of parties and the number of issues?
2. What is a political ideology?
3. What are the differences between two-party systems and multiparty systems?
4. What is the relationship between the number of parties and party polarization?

Problems and Applications

1. Search the names and symbols of ten parties from at least three different countries. Discuss the relation of party symbols with political ideologies.

Quantitative indices

2. Calculate the fragmentation index and the effective number of parties in this two-party system.

PARTY	PERCENTAGE OF VOTES	POSITION ON THE LEFT-RIGHT AXIS (1–10)
Socialist	48	3
Conservative	58	8

3. Calculate the fragmentation index and the effective number of parties in this multiparty system.

PARTY	PERCENTAGE OF VOTES	POSITION ON THE LEFT-RIGHT AXIS (1–10)
Green	20	2
Labour	35	4
Liberal	25	6
Popular	20	8

Data sources

Wikipedia political parties:
http://en.wikipedia.org/wiki/List_of_political_parties_by_country
Wikipedia, elections:
http://en.wikipedia.org/wiki/List_of_election_results_by_ country

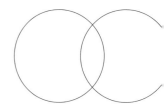

PART IV **GOVERNMENT**

Political institutions are the rules of the game. Typical institutional formulas for governments include a one-person office, such as a presidency or prime ministership, and multiple-person councils or assemblies. Different political regimes combine different procedures to select the rulers and different divisions of powers and relationship between one-person and multiple-person institutions, whether of mutual dependency or autonomy. But all institutional formulas have to face the fundamental problem for democratic governance, which is how to form a political majority giving power-holders sufficient support to make binding and enforceable collective decisions.

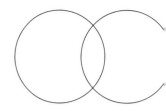

13

CHOOSING PRESIDENTS

In This Chapter You Will

- Consider the advantages and drawbacks of electing leaders by unanimous consent.
- Distinguish between "simple" majority and "relative" majority.
- Analyze diverse electoral procedures based on the majority principle.
- Discuss how different electoral rules are associated with different numbers of parties or candidates.

The election of the president of the United States in 2000 was won in the Electoral College by Republican George W. Bush against Democrat Al Gore, although Gore had obtained an advantage of 0.5 percent of popular votes, according to the official results (47.9 to 48.4 percent). Gore delayed his recognition of the winner, but five weeks after the election, upon a decision by the Supreme Court in favor of Bush, Gore conceded.

By contrast, the loser of the presidential election in Mexico in 2006 did not accept the result. Of the five candidates running, the new candidate, Felipe Calderon, of the incumbent conservative National Action Party (PAN), officially obtained 35.9 percent of popular votes, short of a majority. The second candidate, A-M. López-Obrador of the leftist Party of the Democratic Revolution (PRD) obtained 35.3 percent—that is, they were separated by a narrow margin of only 0.6 percent of votes. In Mexico, a president can be elected in spite of having only about one third of the votes, thanks to the plurality, or "relative" majority, rule enforced, which does not require more than half the votes to win, but only a higher number than any other candidate. The same rule is used in other countries and, for most elections to the Electoral College, in the United States.

López-Obrador fought by a vote-by-vote general recount, but the Electoral Tribunal accepted only a partial recount, after which Calderón was declared president-elect.

Then the loser and his supporters organized mass protests, marches, and encampments in the center of Mexico City. In a massive rally, López-Obrador rejected the "imposition" of Calderón, called for civil disobedience, and self-proclaimed the "legitimate" president. For the following years, the members of the PRD, including the mayor of Mexico City, did not recognize the winner of the election and blocked institutional cooperation with the presidency. In order to prevent minority winners and controversial results like these, many countries have adopted new electoral rules providing for a second round of voting between the two most voted candidates at the first round.

In this chapter we discuss different procedures for selecting presidents and other one-person leaders, such as mayors and governors, by means of voting and elections. Leaders can be chosen by unanimity, which implies broad consensus, but may also require difficult agreements. Alternatively, they can be selected by different rules and procedures based on the majority principle, such as those just mentioned. Majority rule is more effective at making decisions than unanimity, but as suggested with the examples just given, it can involve biases in the selection process and different degrees of people's satisfaction with the elected. ■

Unanimity

You may have had this kind of experience. If the community, organization, or group to which you are affiliated is united and has a clear purpose, a leader can be elected by silent acquiescence, murmurs in favor, shouts of commendation or acclamation, clapping and applause, clashing fists over a table, or other open expressions of agreement. But if the community is large and heterogeneous, the requirement of unanimity may make decision making difficult, induce paralysis, and provoke conflicts and splits.

UNANIMOUS CONSENT

Unanimity rule requires the agreement of all voters to choose a delegate or representative or to make an enforceable decision. If the community has a clear common interest and shares the same values and preferences, a leader can be chosen by acclamation or acquiescence. A variety of historical evidence suggests that already in ancient assemblies many decisions were made and leaders elected by virtual unanimity. Roman law, for instance, established the principle that "What concerns similarly all ought to be approved by all," which was adopted by the Christian Church as "He who governs all should be elected by all." In ancient and medieval Europe, consuls were elected by traders, bishops by priests and believers, and magistrates by citizens, all on the basis of broad agreements. Many regulations at the time established that institutional decisions should be made by "consensus and acclamation," "approval and consent," with "no discrepancy" or "no contradiction," by "free veto," and so on.

The formula of an electoral college—similar to the one currently used in the United States to choose the president—which typically required broad consensus, was already employed in the ancient Roman *comitia* and in numerous medieval cities around the Mediterranean to choose a single high magistrate, and by the Church to elect the pope. Medieval Frankish and Carolingian emperors, and Bohemian,

Hungarian, and Polish kings were elected by their peers gathered at colleges of electors at which unanimity was expected.

Unanimity rule has some good properties. Unanimous decisions correspond to the social efficiency criterion associated with the name of Italian economist Vilfredo Pareto. **A collective decision is said to be "Pareto-superior" if it increases the satisfaction of some participants or at least does not worsen any** in comparison with the previous situation. This criterion is guaranteed by unanimity rule because it gives every voter the possibility to veto any collective decision that may be considered unsatisfactory.

ADVANTAGE OF THE STATUS QUO

However, it may be impossible for unanimity decisions to be made if voters' preferences can be located along a single dimension, such as the left-right axis or any other issue or ideological dimension on which the participants have consistent preferences. Any voter can veto a move of the status quo away from his or her preference. In leader elections, advantaged voters or, in spatial terms, those whose preferences are "closer" to the incumbent, can consolidate their privileges. If the successor has to be elected by unanimity, the incumbent leader can remain in office in spite of the existence of alternative candidates able to reduce the aggregate distance from all individual voters' preferences, and thus increase collective satisfaction.

Unanimity decisions and elections may, therefore, require costly negotiations involving several issues and dimensions at the same time. While a candidate may be placed at a significant distance from some voters' preferences on one issue or value, say, economic policy, he can be closer on other issues or values, such as territoriality or personal skills, and therefore become globally satisfactory and acceptable. As a whole, everybody can accept a candidate for one reason or another. But a possible winner by unanimity will give different voters different degrees of satisfaction regarding their preferences on different issues or dimensions.

When unanimity rule is unable to produce satisfactory collective decisions, two alternatives usually emerge. One is the split of the community—call it divorce, schism, or secession. The other is a change of rule to less than unanimity, typically relying upon the principle of the majority, as we discuss in the following section.

Quick Quiz

• What does "Pareto-superior" mean?

Majority

You may be used to accepting that a decision made by the majority of the members of a community or group to which you are voluntarily affiliated must be obeyed and enforced. However, this may not be so obvious. In fact the introduction of majority rule to make collective decisions enforceable was one of the most innovative changes in human history. It implies nothing less than people accepting to comply with a decision that they do not share—something that nonhuman animals certainly do not do. Majority rule initially emerged, and is broadly accepted nowadays, as a criterion for

TABLE 13.1 Majority Rules

Absolute majority: 1/2	{	Qualified- or super-majority: 2/3, 3/5, 3/4, etc.
		Simple majority: 1/2
Relative majority or plurality	{	Qualified-plurality: 1/3, 2/5, etc. (less than 1/2)
		Simple plurality: the greatest number (even if less than 1/2)

making collective decisions mainly because unanimity rule is so ineffective and can create paralysis and discontent, as we have just discussed. As put by English political theorist John Locke in the seventeenth century, with this rule "the act of the majority passes for the act of the whole."

Majority rule, however, is not easy to implement. If there are only two candidacies to choose from, majority rule can produce relatively satisfactory outcomes. But with more than two candidacies, different decisions or different elected candidates can result, depending on the procedure used, even if all of them are based upon the majority principle, as we discuss in this chapter.

Let us begin with some clarifications. We should distinguish between **"relative" majority, also called "plurality,"** which gives the victory to the largest group, even if it encompasses less than half of the voters, and **"absolute" majority**, implying that more than half of the voters have to choose the same option. Within relative majority, or plurality, rules, it is possible to distinguish simple plurality from other rules requiring a minimum threshold below one half, such as one third or two fifths. Within absolute majority rules, we can have **"simple" majority**, which establishes the threshold for winning exactly at half the votes, and **"qualified," or "super," majorities**, which may require three fifths, two thirds, three quarters, or any other threshold beyond one half. When talking about a "majority," with no further specifications, we should assume that we are dealing with the rule of one half (simple absolute majority). Please note that "simple" majority is not the same as "relative" majority. See Table 13.1 for clarification.

THE MEDIAN VOTER'S MAJORITY

The majority principle has been praised for being the only system that satisfies the following criteria: (1) decisiveness, or the capacity to produce a result; (2) anonymity, or voter equality; (3) neutrality with respect to issues, so the status quo or the largest group does not have an advantage; and (4) monotonicity, or a positive response to changes in voters' preferences, as stated by mathematician Kenneth O. May.

However, majority rule can guarantee good results only if there are two candidates, parties, or policy proposals to choose from and if the voters' preferences are located along a single issue or ideological dimension, such as the left-right axis. In this case, majority rule will give victory to the candidate closer to the median voter's preference, as we discussed in a previous chapter. Remember that the median voter is the one whose preference is located in an intermediate position with fewer than half the voters on both sides, and thus is always necessary for the formation of a consistent majority

SOURCE 13.1   The Majority Is the Whole

The majority principle was invented to replace the unanimity principle, which in complex communities made decisions difficult. It implies that everybody must accept majority decisions as if they were shared by all.

What is done by two thirds of the sacred college [*of cardinals*], that is surely of the Holy Ghost, which may not be resisted.

Pope Pius II (1458)

The majority would naturally have the right and authority of the whole.

Hugo Grotius, De Jure Belli ac Pacis (1624)

The will and determination of the majority...passes for the act of the whole and determines, as having by the Law of Nature and Reason, the power of the whole.

John Locke, Two Treatises of Government (1689)

The law of majority voting is itself something established by convention, and presupposes unanimity, on one [*foundational*] occasion at least...The vote of the majority always binds the rest.

Jean-Jacques Rousseau, The Social Contract (1762)

The fundamental maxim of republican government...requires that the sense of the majority should prevail.

Alexander Hamilton, Federalist Papers (1787)

What is the Third Estate? It is the whole.

Emmanuel-Joseph Sieyès, "What Is the Third Estate?" (1789)

In political discussion, many scholars seem to have overlooked the central place that unanimity rule must occupy in any normative theory of democratic government. We have witnessed an inversion whereby majority rule has been elevated to the status which the unanimity rule should occupy. At best, majority rule should be viewed as one among many practical expedients made necessary by the costs of securing widespread agreement on political issues when individual and group interest diverge.

James M. Buchanan and Gordon Tullock, The Calculus of Consent (1962)

on a single dimension. Since the median voter's preference minimizes the sum of distances from all other individual preferences, it can be considered that the winner by majority rule in a two-candidate contest maximizes social utility. However, when there are more than two candidates, majority rule can be indecisive, that is, unable to produce a winner because no candidate may obtain more than half the votes.

MAJORITY RUNOFF

To try to make the majority principle operational, several electoral procedures have been invented. The one usually known as a majority with a second-round runoff or majority runoff, which is used for presidential elections in France and in many countries in Latin America, can guarantee a winner in every election. **It requires an** absolute majority of votes in the first round, but in a second round of voting, the choice can be reduced to the two most voted-for candidates in order to secure a majority support for one of them. Majority runoff with a second round permits multiparty competition in the first round and encourages the formation of two broad coalitions in the second round.

Remember that along a single issue dimension, the median voter's candidate is always able to form a majority against any other candidate. However, with the majority runoff procedure, the candidate preferred by the median voter may obtain fewer votes than two other, more extreme candidates in the first round, and thus be eliminated. This implies that the winner in the second round may not be the median voter's candidate. Thus, the winner by majority runoff could be defeated by another candidate (the one preferred by the median voter) by absolute majority if the choice between the two were available. This has been the case, for instance, in most presidential elections held by majority runoff in France since 1965, and in a number of presidential elections in Latin American countries since the 1980s.

The winner by majority runoff depends, therefore, on the number and characteristics of the candidates running in the first round, which can be decisive for selecting the two candidates going into the second round. For this reason it is said that the winner by majority runoff is **"dependent on irrelevant alternatives"**: the victory of a candidate may be an indirect consequence of the merge or split of candidacies that do not win but on which the selection of the winner may depend.

As an example, let us consider the case of the presidential election in France in 2007, as represented in Table 13.2. More than ten candidates ran in the first round. From left to right, they were: five leftist candidates (including a green, a communist, and several trotskyites) who shared about 11 percent of votes; the socialist Ségolène Royal, who obtained 26 percent of votes; the democrat François Bayrou, with 19 percent; the conservative Nicolas Sarkozy, with 31 percent; the far right Le Pen, with 11 percent, and other extreme-right runners, with 2 percent of votes altogether. Note that the median voter's candidate was Bayrou, since he had less than half the votes on either side of the left-right political spectrum (37 percent of voters voted for candidates to the left of him, and 44 percent, for candidates to his right). Bayrou would likely have won against any other candidate by absolute majority. But since he was

TABLE 13.2 A Majority Runoff Election

The example of the presidential election in France in 2007 shows that under majority rule with a second-round runoff, the median voter's candidate can be eliminated in the first round and lose the election, in spite of being the likely winner against any other candidate by absolute majority.

Ideology:	Left		Center		Right
Candidates:	5 leftists	Royal	Bayrou	Sarkozy	Le Pen, far right
% votes, 1st round:	1, 2, 2, 2, 4	26	19	31	11, 2
			Median voter		
% votes, 2nd round:			47	53	

the third in votes in the first round, he was eliminated from running in the second round.

PLURALITY

It may sound like common sense that the winner of an election must be the candidate who obtains the greatest number of votes. However, this is just an expedient for elections in which no candidate obtains an absolute majority of votes or broader support. "Relative majority," or "plurality," rule does not require any particular number, proportion, or threshold of votes to win an election; the winner is merely "the first past the post." This rule is, therefore, highly effective because it always produces a winner. But it can certainly imply strong biases in the selection of a winner. Used in England for long periods, plurality rule was exported to the United States and other former British colonies and has been used for direct presidential elections in a number of Latin American, East Asian, and African countries.

Plurality rule creates strong incentives for potential candidates to coordinate into only two candidacies in order to secure a majority support. A high level of coordination into only two candidates is usually achieved, in particular, in United States presidential elections, although it requires costly and long-term competition and negotiation among many preliminary and potential candidates (including primary elections, party conventions, and so on). In general, we should expect that, for presidential and

The President of the United States is chosen by an Electoral College largely based upon plurality rule, which permits the election of a candidate supported by a minority of popular votes.

other one-person office elections, plurality rule should work satisfactorily in settings dominated by a single party or with two balanced parties obtaining alternating victories in successive elections.

However, sometimes coordination fails and a minor candidacy can split a major candidate's support and indirectly give the victory to the major rival. Plurality rule may be highly dependent on irrelevant alternatives. It encourages tactics not only to "unite [ours] and win," but also to "divide [the others] and win." Imagine, for instance, that party Left wins by majority against party Right in a two-party election. If a new party, Far Left, enters competition and there is a sufficient number of voters preferring Far Left to Left, now the winner by plurality can be the party Right. The same electorate with the same preferences can make different plurality winners depending on the introduction or withdrawal of a new alternative, Far Left, which does not win—it is "irrelevant."

Although plurality rule is formally based on the majority principle, if there are more than two candidates it can give the victory to a candidate with minority support. In the United States almost half of the presidents elected by the Electoral College based largely upon plurality rule have obtained a minority of popular votes (seventeen of the thirty-six presidents since 1828); while in the nine Latin American countries having used plurality rule for democratic presidential elections since 1945, more than 70 percent of presidents have been elected with a minority of votes (forty-one of fifty-eight).

With more than two candidates, the winner by plurality can even be the most rejected candidate. The plurality winner can be an extreme candidate who is the last preference of a majority of voters who may have divided their votes among several other, relatively closer, defeated candidates. In other words, the winner by plurality can be a candidate who would have been defeated by majority by *every* other candidate in contests of two candidates each. An example is given in Box 13.

COMPARING MAJORITY RUNOFF AND PLURALITY RULES

As we have seen, no practical procedure for voting based on the majority principle can guarantee that the winner is the first preference of a majority of voters. Performance varies, however, for different rules. Let us compare the two rules just described, which are most widely used for democratic elections of presidents and for a number of mayoral, gubernatorial, and other one-person offices: majority runoff and plurality. We have seen that neither of these guarantees that the median voter's candidate, able to attract majority support against any other candidate, will win the election. This is due to the fact that the winner by either of the two procedures can be dependent on irrelevant candidacies splitting other candidates' votes. But the two rules operate in different ways.

On the one hand, plurality rule encourages candidates' coordination and the formation of a few broad candidacies for the single round. However, this coordination has to be based on expectations of votes for each candidacy rather than actual support. In contrast, majority rule with a second-round runoff tends to defer potential agreements among candidacies. Minor candidates can run independently in the first round with the expectation of obtaining sufficient votes and of negotiating their support for one of the two front-runners for the second round on the basis of votes in the first round. We should thus expect more candidates to run in the first round of elections by majority runoff than in those by plurality rule, which may make the outcome of the first round more hazardous under the runoff procedure.

BOX 13.1   **THE "IMPOSSIBILITY" TO BE FAIR**

No voting or decision rule can guarantee outcomes fulfilling some apparently simple requirements of fairness. For example, the winner by simple plurality rule among three candidates may be the one most rejected by an absolute majority of voters having split their votes among the other two candidates. In fact all voting rules may produce inefficient results and are to some extent vulnerable to unstable outcomes or to manipulation by voters and leaders.

The "impossibility theorem," as initially formulated by Nobel Prize–winning economist Kenneth Arrow, proposes a set of normative conditions to make a collective decision acceptable. They include: (i) monotonicity, or the requirement of a consistent relation between citizens' preferences and the collective choice; (ii) independence of the collective choice from individual preferences regarding irrelevant alternatives that cannot win the voting contest; and (iii) "no dictatorship," or the inexistence of an automatically decisive actor. No decision rule can fulfill all these conditions all the time.

However, certain conditions regarding citizens' preferences have been identified as guaranteeing efficient and stable decisions with some voting procedures. Duncan Black introduced, as a sufficient condition for preventing some major paradoxes, the concept of "single-peakedness" of individual preference curves—which is formally equivalent to the condition that voters' preferences can be ordered along a single linear dimension. These and other contributions suggest the advantages of relatively harmonic societies in producing stable and consistent collective decisions, even with potentially manipulatable procedures.

Actually, different voting rules perform differently to satisfy citizens' preferences. The "impossibility" theorems tell us that it is impossible to guarantee efficient and stable collective choices with any rule. But it is indeed "possible" to obtain stable and efficient choices with some rules in communities with relatively harmonious distributions of preferences. A relevant point is that certain rules produce inefficient choices more than others, as we discuss throughout this book.

On the other hand, the probability of the median voter's candidate winning is double under majority rule than under plurality rule. This is due to the fact that if the median voter's candidate is present at the second round, that candidate can be expected to win by majority against any other rival. Remember that in a two-candidate contest the median voter's candidate can always form a majority by attracting votes to his or her "side." Thus, the probability of the median voter's candidate winning by majority runoff is equal to the probability of that candidate's being one of the two most voted-for candidates in the first round, which, a priori, is double the probability of his being the single most voted-for candidate in the only round by plurality.

The two consequences of majority runoff rule—higher number of candidacies in the first round and advantage of the median voter's candidate in the second—somehow counteract each other. Empirical observations of 111 presidential elections in 18 Latin American countries during current democratic regimes show that the median voter's candidates have won the presidency in about two thirds of elections by plurality rule and in three fourths of elections by second-round rules. The better performance of majority runoff is apparently due to some coordination among candidates already for the first round. For the United States, it can be estimated that in the presidential elections by the Electoral College system mostly based on plurality rule during the period 1948–2008, more than 80 percent of winners were the median voter's candidates (in thirteen out of sixteen elections, the exceptions being Kennedy in 1960, by a very tiny margin, Clinton in 1992, and Bush in 2000, in all cases due to the role

BOX 13.2 MAJORITY PROCEDURES

Several Christian philosophers and Enlightened academics invented voting procedures based on the majority principle that have become references for evaluating results in real elections. The thirteenth-century Catalan philosopher Ramon Llull and the eighteenth-century French marquis de Condorcet almost coincided in proposing variants of pair-wise comparisons. By these procedures, an election requires multiple rounds of voting between all possible pairs of candidates. In Llull's version, the winner is the candidate having won the greatest number of pair-wise comparisons, while in Condorcet's version, a candidate is required to win all pair-wise comparisons— that is, the winner is the candidate able to win by majority against every other candidate. When the candidates are perceived by the voters as ordered along a single linear dimension, such as the left-right axis, the winner by Condorcet procedure is always the one preferred by the median voter. The "Condorcet winner" can be considered highly satisfactory for the electorate and can be used as a positive reference for comparison with other procedures. However, in multidimensional spaces, such a candidate may not exist.

Another sophisticated procedure, known as rank-order count, was devised independently by both the fifteenth-century German cardinal Nicholas of Cusa and the eighteenth-century French academic Jean-Charles de Borda. This procedure requires that the voter order all the candidates and award them 1, 2, 3, etc. points, ranking them from the least to the most preferred. The winner is the candidate having collected the highest sum of points. The "Borda winner" can also be considered highly satisfactory for the electorate and can be used as a normative reference. But this voting procedure can be manipulated because some voters can award lower points to rival candidates than would actually correspond to their sincere preferences, in order to prevent their victory. For this reason, Cusanus warned that electors should "act according to conscience," and Borda remarked that his procedure was conceived "only for honest men."

To understand how these procedures work, examine the example as represented in the following table. Three groups of voters, A, B, and C,

respectively with 40, 35, and 25 voters each (100 in total), prefer candidates X, Y, and Z in different orders, respectively, X > Y > Z, Y > Z > X, and Z > Y > X, always in consistent manner with the alphabetical order (which can be considered to be the single "dimension" in this case).

First, let us apply the Llull-Condorcet procedure. In the comparison between the pair of candidates X–Y, candidate Y wins by majority with the votes of B and C, who both prefer Y to X (25 + 35 = 60), against those of A, who prefers X to Y (40); in the pair X–Z, candidate Z wins by a majority with the votes of B and C (25 + 35 = 60) against those of A (40); and in the pair Y–Z, candidate Y wins by majority with the votes of A and B (40 + 25 = 65) against those of C (35). Thus, candidate Y is the only one able to win by majority against every other candidate and is the Condorcet winner. The most rejected candidate—that is, the one who loses all comparisons by pairs, X—is the Condorcet loser.

Let us now apply the Cusanus-Borda procedure. According to the voters' preferences, candidate X receives 3 x 40 = 120 points from A, 1 x 25 = 25 from B, and 1 x 35 = 35 from C, that is, 180 in total; candidate Y receives 2 x 40 = 80 points from A, 3 x 25 = 75 from B, and 2 x 35 = 70 from C, that is, 225 in total; and candidate Z receives 1 x 40 = 40 points from A, 2 x 25 = 50 from B, and 3 x 35 = 105 from C, that is, 195 in total. The Borda winner with the highest score is thus Y. (The total number of points is now 300, that is, 100 times the number of candidates, 3).

Please note that the winner by both procedures, candidate Y, is not the one with the highest number of first preferences (which is X, with 40 from A), but the one with the lowest number of first preferences, only 25 from B. Not only would Y not be the winner by plurality rule, but she would not even go through to the second round, were this procedure applied. However, Y is the least rejected candidate (observe that she is not the last preference of any voter) and can thus be considered the most widely accepted. Y's victory by pair-wise comparisons or by rank-order count can reflect a broad majority support. In contrast, the winner by plurality rule, X, is the most rejected candidate (the Condorcet loser and the one with lowest score by Borda count).

BOX 13.2

Voters:	A-40	B-25	C-35
First preference	X	Y	Y
	Y	Z	Y
Least preference	Z	X	X

Borda procedure:	A -40	B-25	C-35	
X:	3 x 40+	1 x 25+	1 x 35	= 180
Y:	2 x 40+	3 x 25+	2 x 35	= 225
Z:	1 x 40+	2 x 25+	3 x 35	= 195
Winner: Y				

Condorcet procedure: X (40) < Y (25 + 35);
X (40) < Z (25 + 35);
Y (40 + 25) > Z (35).
Winner: Y

of third candidates). The relatively good record for the United States corresponds, of course, to the prevalence of two-party competition in most elections. However, in the nineteenth-century, with more volatile party systems, electoral results were more comparable to those reported for Latin America.

More important, majority runoff rule can prevent the victory of the "worst" possible candidate. The winner in the second round cannot be the least preferred candidate for an electoral majority, in contrast to relatively likely occurrences of this in presidential elections by plurality rule, as we have mentioned. In the worst of the cases, the winner in the second round will be considered a lesser evil by many of the voters.

THE CHOICE OF MAJORITY RULES

Elections of one-person offices by majority rule tend to be unpredictable and risky. After all, it is never easy to aggregate many people's varied interests and values into a single winner. In a single-office election by majority rule, the winner takes all and all the other candidates get nothing, whatever their popular support may have been.

Different electoral procedures based on the majority principle can be chosen on the basis of their expected results. Specifically, in settings dominated by a single party or with two evenly balanced parties expecting to obtain alternating victories in successive elections, plurality rule may be chosen and maintained by the dominant party or parties, as happens in the United States. With the emergence of new parties, however, the large parties' votes can split and make the elections riskier, which can move the participants to adopt majority runoff or other rules permitting multiparty competition, as happened in most countries in Latin America in the last few decades. Over time, for presidential elections in democratic countries, electoral colleges have been replaced by plurality rule, and plurality rule by majority or other rules with a second round. Table 13.3 shows the numbers.

Quick Quiz

• What is the difference between "simple" majority and "relative" majority?
• When does the victory of a candidate depend on "irrelevant alternatives?"

CASE 13.1   DIVIDE AND WIN IN BLACK AND WHITE

Elections by plurality rule, since they enable winning with only a minority of votes, encourage the tactics of merging potential candidacies and dividing rivals. Most mayors in the United States are elected by plurality rule. During the second half of the twentieth century, a number of American cities were polarized along racial lines, when African Americans migrated en masse to large cities and promoted strenuous civil rights campaigns. In the 1970s and '80s, a number of black mayors were elected for the first time, including in the four largest U.S. cities: New York, Los Angeles, Chicago, and Philadelphia. All of these places were evenly divided in racial terms, with the white population encompassing between 45 and 55 percent, and for a candidate to win the mayoral office by plurality, concentrating or dividing ethnic votes played a major role. Specifically, a black candidate could win by mobilizing black voters, attracting sufficient Hispanics and Jews to some kind of "rainbow" coalition, and dividing the whites, while the whites usually needed to concentrate their support on a single candidate regardless of party line.

Highly segregated Chicago is a case in point. As an overwhelmingly Democratic city, the Democratic primary election usually delivered the winner of the general election. In 1983, for the first time a black candidate, Harold Washington, surprisingly won the Democratic mayoral primary election by plurality with a minority of 36 percent of votes, while the white voters split between two candidates, the incumbent

mayor, Jane Byrne, and the son of a famous former mayor of the same name, Richard Daley, Jr. (with 34 and 30 percent of votes, respectively). Washington would likely have lost by majority against either of the other two candidates in a second round. In the general election, the white Republican candidate obtained the highest support ever, including from many lifelong Democrats who abandoned the party for the sole purpose of voting against the black candidate, but Washington won narrowly, with 51 percent of votes, including nearly unanimous support from highly mobilized blacks, three fourths of Hispanics, and one third of Jews. Four years later, Washington was reelected against two white candidates, one for the Republican Party and a former Democrat running for the Illinois Solidarity Party.

But Washington soon died in office. The later Democratic primary in 1989 displayed the opposite scene: the blacks were now divided between two candidates, the incumbent acting mayor, Eugene Sawyer, and the heir to Washington's legacy, Timothy Evans, this time in front of a unified white bloc around Richard Daley, Jr., who won. Evans, nevertheless, ran in the general election as the candidate of a new Harold Washington Party, with the aim of dividing the white vote again, as Washington had done twice before. But this time the Republicans presented an irrelevant candidate to facilitate Daley's victory. White Daley was successively reelected, as his father had been, for more than twenty years.

TABLE 13.3   Presidential Electoral Rules

In democratic countries with separate election of president, electoral colleges have been replaced by direct elections by plurality rule and in turn by majority and other rules with a second round.

Electoral rule	1874	1922	1960	2010
Electoral college	6	4	3	1
Plurality	–	4	9	10
Second round	–	6	4	38
Preferential vote	–	–	1	2
Total number of countries	6	14	17	51

Conclusion

In this chapter we have discussed several rules and procedures for electing mayors, governors, presidents, and other one-person offices. Unanimity rule is associated with high consensus, but it may also induce the stability of some unsatisfactory decision or incumbent ruler. In contrast, majority rule is more effective in decision making and permits more changes. But the majority principle must be applied through specific procedures. The most common rules for mayoral, gubernatorial, and presidential elections are simple plurality rule and majority runoff with a second round (or some variants), which do not guarantee the victory of the candidate most preferred by a majority of voters.

Different electoral rules are associated with different configurations of party competition. A well-established *proposition* in political science is as follows:

- **Majority bipartism**. For presidential and other one-person elections, plurality rule is associated with single-party dominance or a balance between two parties. In contrast, majority runoff is associated with higher multiparty competition in the first round and two blocs in the second round. ■

Summary

Unanimity rule produces highly consensual winners in homogeneous communities with a clear common interest.

A unanimous decision is "Pareto-superior" because it can increase the satisfaction of some participants, or at least not worsen any.

Unanimity rule favors the stability of the status quo or the continuation of the incumbent ruler, even if some alternative is preferred by many voters.

Majority rule produces good results if there are only two candidates by giving the victory to the median voter's preference.

Majority runoff with a second round permits multiparty competition in the first round and encourages the formation of two broad coalitions in the second.

By majority runoff, the median voter's candidate can be eliminated in the first round. The victory of a candidate may be an indirect consequence of the merge or split of irrelevant candidacies.

Plurality or relative majority rule creates strong incentives for potential candidates to coordinate into only two candidacies to secure majority support.

However, plurality rule is highly dependent on irrelevant alternatives. It encourages tactics such as "merge and win" and "divide and win."

With multiple candidates, the plurality winner can be the candidate most rejected by a majority of voters.

Key Concepts

Absolute majority. More than half the votes.
Dependence on irrelevant alternatives. The winner depends on candidacies that do not win.
Majority runoff. Absolute majority in the first round with a second round between the two most voted-for candidates.

Pareto criterion. A decision is efficient if it increases the satisfaction of some voters or at least does not worsen any.

Plurality, or relative majority. The highest number of votes, even short of a majority.

Representation. The election of people to act in the voters' interests.

Simple majority. Just one more than half the votes.

Super, or qualified, majority. Two thirds, three fourths, or some other threshold beyond half.

Unanimity rule. The agreement of all voters is required.

Questions for Review

1. What's the Pareto criterion?
2. What's the difference between absolute majority and relative majority?
3. Which rules can encourage the tactics of "divide and win"?

Problems and Applications

1. Search a standard data source and list the presidents of the United States (by giving name and year of election) who were elected with a minority of popular votes.

2. Search for results in a sports tournament that you may like (e.g., football, basketball, motor racing, baseball).
   a. Has the winner of the championship won all the matches?
   b. How could one team win the championship by winning fewer matches than some other team?

3. Look at the following electorate, which is distributed uniformly (so the probability of having a voter on each position along the axis is the same). A moderate left candidate, X, is located at a point to the left of which 25 percent of voters lie; a near-center candidate, Y, is located at 40 percent point; and an extreme-right candidate, Z, is located at 90 percent (so only 10 percent of voters lie to his right). Each voter chooses the candidate who is closer to his or her preference.
   a. Which candidate wins by plurality rule?
   b. Any comment?

Candidates:		X	Y	Z	
Voters:	Left 0	25	40	90	100 Right

4. Look at the distribution of voters' preferences in this electorate:
The election is held by absolute majority rule, with a second-round runoff between the two most voted-for candidates, if necessary.
   a. Who wins?

Number of voters:	8	7	6
First preference	X	Z	Y
	Y	Y	X
Least preference	Z	X	Z

Let's now assume that, in the next election, candidate X gains support and candidate Z loses support among voters, so that now the three groups of voters are formed by 10, 5, and 6 voters respectively (from left to right in the figure).

b. With the same electoral rule, who wins?

    c. Comments

5. Given the following distribution of voters' preferences, identify the winner by each of the following voting rules:

    a. Plurality rule.

    b. Majority runoff.

As explained in Box 13.2:

    c. Condorcet pair-wise comparisons.

    d. Borda rank-order count.

Number of voters:	3	2	1	1
First preference	X	Y	Z	W
	Z	W	W	Y
	W	V	V	Z
	V	Z	Y	V
Last preference	Y	X	X	X

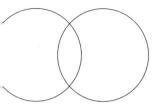

14

ELECTING ASSEMBLIES

In This Chapter You Will

- Consider how large democratic assemblies can be.
- Ponder the benefits of personal representation and party representation.
- Analyze different rules and voting procedures for proportional representation.
- Examine the relationship between assembly size, district magnitude, and the number of parties.
- Learn what the "micro-mega rule" is.

Why does such a large and varied country like the United States keep small electoral districts in which a single representative is elected? Why, in contrast to many other democracies, has it not adopted electoral rules of proportional representation, permitting multiple parties to obtain seats? The answer seems to be that in large countries such as the United States, as well as in Australia, Canada, France, India, and the United Kingdom, a large assembly and, in most cases, federalism or regional decentralization, can be sufficiently inclusive of the territorial variety of the representatives. By contrast, in smaller democratic countries such as Denmark, Estonia, Finland, Hungary, Israel, the Netherlands, Norway, and Sweden, precisely because they are relatively small, the assembly has few seats, they have a unitary, non-federal structure, and, as a consequence, the variety of interests and tastes in the society favors the development of multiple political parties and the adoption of more inclusive electoral rules. A relevant implication for institutional design is that the emergence of new parties is the key factor in producing a change in the electoral system.

In this chapter we analyze the main elements of the different electoral systems for democratic representative assemblies. They are: the number of seats in the assembly, or assembly "size," which is correlated to the size of the population; the number of seats for election in each district or constituency, or district "magnitude," which can be equal to one or larger than one; the "formula" for the allocation of seats to political parties on the basis of votes, based either on the majority or the proportionality principles; and the "ballot" or vote form to select individual representatives. As we will see, different electoral rules are associated with different systems of political parties and different personal qualities of the representatives. ∎

Assembly Size

How large can a democratic assembly be? Of course, its size can vary with the size of the community. As you may expect if you think about the question for just a moment, large countries tend to have large assemblies, while small countries tend to have small assemblies. The higher the number of people and the more varied their interests, values, and preferences, the more representatives may be required to account for them. Indeed, the number of seats in an assembly or parliament greatly depends on the number of inhabitants in the community it intends to represent.

LARGE COUNTRIES, LARGE ASSEMBLIES

The smallest democratic assemblies exist nowadays in micro-countries, such as some small islands in the Caribbean, including Barbados, Grenada, or St. Lucia, whose parliaments have fewer than thirty members. The largest democratic assemblies are the European Parliament, with more than seven hundred seats, and the British House of Commons, the German Bundestag, and the Italian Chamber of Deputies, with more than six hundred members each. As population grows in most countries, the number of seats in democratic assemblies tends to go up, although updating may come with significant delays.

The size of the assembly has a serious influence on the work of each individual representative. On the one hand, interactions between representatives and voters can be facilitated by relatively high numbers of seats, which may induce each representative to address just a few voters. But in an assembly with many members, the costs of talking, listening, transmitting and sharing information, discussing proposals and arguments, and negotiating and bargaining among members may be too high. For each member of parliament, the costs of interacting with voters counteract those of interacting with the other parliamentarians. Thus, most countries have assemblies of an intermediate size, which increases with the population, but less than proportionally, in order to allow the members of parliament to develop collective work with moderate costs. The assemblies of most democratic countries have between one hundred and three hundred members. Consistently, some nondemocratic countries have enormous assemblies (such as China, with three thousand members), which produces both a fictitious impression of participation and real internal paralysis.

As an average value for all democratic countries, the best fit seems to be that assembly size equals the cube root of population, as represented with the formula:

$$Pop^{1/3} = S$$

Where:
Pop: Population; and
S: Size or number of seats of the assembly.

For instance, in Mexico, whose population has about 110 million inhabitants, the Chamber of Deputies has 500 seats ($110m^{1/3} = 479$), and in Spain, with about 44 million inhabitants, the Congress of Deputies has 350 seats ($44m^{1/3} = 353$). As a country's population varies continuously, the size of the assembly can be adjusted at some moments more than others. Specific countries can deviate more significantly from the formula. The British House of Commons, for instance, with 646 seats, is larger than predicted by the formula, while the United States House of Representatives, whose size of 435 has not been updated to the growth of the population for about one hundred years, is now relatively small.

SEAT APPORTIONMENT

All the members of an assembly can be elected in a single district, as happens, for instance, in Israel (with about 120 seats) and the Netherlands (with about 150 seats). However, to choose such a long list of candidates may prevent voters from knowing their representatives and may make them incapable of selecting individual candidates. More commonly, the members of an assembly are elected in several districts. There can be as many electoral districts as assembly seats if every district has only one seat, as in the United States, Britain, France, or India; or some other number if there are multi-seat districts, as in Brazil, Germany, Japan, or Sweden.

In order to achieve fair representation of the community, every district should have a similar number of inhabitants. But in many instances, electoral districts correspond to previously existing counties, provinces, regions, or other political or administrative division, which may create imbalances in representation. Seats must be apportioned among different districts according to some mathematical rule of proportionality, as we will discuss in a later section.

Quick Quiz

• What is the relationship between assembly size and a country's population?

Persons and Parties

If you have ever voted in elections of student delegates or representatives, neighborhood associations, condominium meetings, or comparable clubs or organizations, it is likely that you have used a standard electoral system that is very old and popular in small groups and local governments the world over. If you have had that kind of experience, the following pages offer you the opportunity to remember how you voted, for how many candidates, and how the winner was selected, or to make sense now of what you did possibly thinking that it was a "natural" way of voting.

COMMUNITY VOTING

A simple, traditional electoral system is composed of the following elements:

1 Several delegates or representatives are elected, or the district magnitude is larger than one, **M>1**;
2 the most voted-for candidates win; that is, some **majority rule** is applied; and

3   each voter can vote for as many candidates as there are posts to be filled, without restrictions of lists, in an **open ballot**.

An interesting variant is **approval voting**, which permits the choice of as many candidates as the voter wants, from one on up, not necessarily in the same number as there are representatives to elect. As every voter may vote for only those candidates he or she considers acceptable, the winners are likely to obtain broad consensus and low rejection.

In professional associations, clubs, and unions, as in small towns, typically, political parties do not play a very significant role, if they play any role at all, and can even be disdained as divisive factions. The type of electoral system just described produces personal representation, that is, it permits the choice of individual representatives with no party constraints, because, in general, such communities or organizations are highly harmonious and their members have clearly identifiable common interests and priority collective goods to obtain. In this kind of communities, the election of representatives or delegates is understood as a procedure for choosing the best persons to realize the community's goals. Such community voting may be compatible with voting by show of hand, oral voting, or secret ballots. Although majority or plurality rules can be used, the election of several representatives tends to be rather consensual and acceptable.

Although the traditional electoral rules just mentioned are able to produce satisfactory representation, they can also create incentives for self-interested would-be political leaders to coordinate the formation of candidacies and voting. For ambitious candidates, forming or joining a coordinated candidacy may increase the prospects of winning additional votes and seats. Also, in some historical settings it was the increasing complexity of the society, especially during the process of building or renewing local community institutions for large states, that generated the formation of political parties. The choice of individual representatives and personal representation can be effective in promoting the preferences of the community, if these are well defined. But political parties can be necessary for selecting the most relevant issues in the public agenda and for designing public policy when different interests are in conflict and people have significantly different policy preferences.

Under the traditional type of electoral system just described, the formation of factions or parties tends to induce voting "in bloc" for a closed list of candidates (also called "the general ticket"), which may change election results drastically. Political party competition tends to result in a party sweep. The biases identified in the previous chapter for majority rule one-person offices are aggravated, because now it is a group of candidates running "in bloc" who "take all," that is, all the offices or posts to be elected. Especially in professional organizations, clubs, small towns, and other homogeneous communities with broadly common interests, the introduction of party competition and the subsequent biases in the selection of personal representatives can generate dissatisfaction among community members. The very same idea of personal representation of the community as a whole may be hindered.

SINGLE-SEAT DISTRICTS

The traditional system of elections by majority rule in multi-seat districts, as just reviewed, is still used in a significant number of local government elections in which it can be presumed that citizens share some clearly identified, broad common interest. However, for large state assemblies and parliaments in some more varied and heterogeneous countries, multi-seat districts have been largely replaced by smaller, single-seat districts. **The district "magnitude" is the number of seats to be elected in each district.**

Reestablishing Community Voting. The introduction of elections in single-seat districts reestablished in each district the traditional sense of community voting in small, homogeneous units and the subsequent personal representation of the community's interests. Single-seat districts were diffused during processes of building or reforming large-scale parliaments in large states, in parallel with the disbanding of traditional compact communities brought about by modern economic changes, and accompanying the broadening of suffrage rights.

Specifically, single-seat districts were widely introduced in Scotland and Wales, and in lower proportions in England, during the eighteenth century, and by the end of the nineteenth century they had become the norm for the British House of Commons. They were also introduced in the U.S. state of Vermont in the late eighteenth century, and by the mid-nineteenth century had expanded to the rest of the country, especially for the election of the House of Representatives. In Canada, single-seat districts became the only formula for all seats in the House of Commons only by the late twentieth century. France's National Assembly oscillated between multi-seat districts and single-seat districts during long periods since the nineteenth century, and leaned toward the latter by the second half of the twentieth century. In India, some multi-seat districts were still used in the first couple of elections after independence, in the mid-twentieth century, before adopting single-seat districts for all of Lok Sabha, the lower chamber of parliament.

With elections in multiple single-seat districts, a candidate who would have been defeated by a party sweep in a large multi-seat district may be elected as a representative for a small district. Smaller communities can therefore elect their representatives with broad consensus and without strong partisan bias. This depends, however, on how the district boundaries are drawn. "Districting" or "redistribution", may help or hinder this purpose.

The typical American expression "gerrymandering" refers to Elbridge Gerry, an eighteenth-century governor of Massachusetts, and to the "salamander" shape of some electoral districts in his state. There has been "gerrymandering" in the United States since the initial carving of territories into states, but the districts for the House of Representatives are redrawn every ten years, following each census, usually at the same time as the districts for state legislatures. Districting can be used to identify groups of people with similar economic or cultural interests, and to create areas dominated by an ethnic group, such as African Americans or Hispanics, who are minorities at the federal level but are strongly concentrated in certain neighborhoods, as particularly happens in California, Texas, and the U.S. South.

Also in Britain, Canada, and other countries, districting may be used to give members of different economic, religious, or language minority groups the opportunity to elect representatives with broad support. Actually, in many electoral districts for the U.S. House of Representatives, and for the British and Canadian houses of commons, seats are won by relatively large margins, which suggests relatively high levels of homogeneity in the electorate at the district level. Specifically, in the United States, more than three fourths of the House seats are won by more than 60 percent of votes, most of them reelect the same representative for long periods, and some seats are uncontested.

Minority Majorities.   When the voter can vote for only one candidate, and only one candidate is elected in a small district, personal representation merges with party representation in the voter's choice. But the aggregation of individual representatives into large parliamentary parties may produce some drawbacks. In the United States, one-party dominance at the district level is relatively frequent, but some local parties are not strongly aligned with the federal parties; as was noted by its speaker, Thomas P. O'Neill, in the House of Representatives "all politics is local." Although one party may be dominant in each district on the basis of the district's relatively high homogeneity, the parties can be different in different districts and produce multiparty systems in the large country or federal assembly. In most British, Canadian, and Indian districts, only one or two parties compete successfully. But multiple parties exist in the British and the Canadian houses of commons and in the Indian Lok Sabha, each with unequally distributed broad support in different parts of the country.

In assembly elections based on multiple single-seat districts, even if the winner in each district obtains an absolute majority of votes (which is not always the case), a party can receive an absolute majority of seats in the assembly by gaining only "a majority [of votes] of the majority [of districts], who may be, and often are, but a minority of the whole," as observed by nineteenth-century English political economist and politician John Stuart Mill.

In fact, in certain countries using single-seat districts and plurality rule, most times a party receives an absolute majority of seats in the assembly on the basis of a minority of popular votes in the whole country. In the United States, which has an attuned two-party system, this has happened in 30 percent of elections since 1828 (twenty-seven of ninety-one elections). But in Britain it has happened in 63 percent of the cases since 1885 (twenty-six of forty-one elections); in Canada, in 50 percent since 1878 (eighteen of thirty-six elections); in New Zealand, in 65 percent between 1890 and 1993 (twenty-two of thirty elections); and in India, in 71 percent since 1952 (ten of fourteen elections). Of course, this is at the expense of smaller candidacies; for example, the British Liberal Party has obtained 13 percent of votes, as an average, in all national elections since 1931, but has received only an average of 3 percent of seats in the House of Commons.

It may also happen that one party receives more popular votes than another but is allocated fewer seats. Due to different degrees of homogeneity of electoral districts, if a party wins by a very large margin in some districts and another party wins by a hairsbreadth in a few more districts, as a consequence of a system in which "the winner takes all," the latter party may gain more seats than the former in spite of having obtained fewer votes in total. This has happened, in particular, in the U.S. House of Representatives ten times (and at least three times in the presidential Electoral College); in Britain, six times; in Canada, three; and in New Zealand, four. Only if all districts enclose populations with similar degrees of economic, cultural, and ethnic homogeneity and produce winners with large vote majorities can it be guaranteed that

BOX 14 .1   PROPORTIONAL QUOTAS

It is not commonly known that several mathematical formulas for the proportional allocation of seats were first devised and discussed by eighteenth-century U.S. statesmen and Constitution makers George Washington, secretary of state (and later president) Thomas Jefferson, and treasury secretary Alexander Hamilton. The same formulas were rediscovered by several European lawyers and politicians in the late nineteenth century. For the former, the problem was the apportionment of seats in the House of Representatives among the previously independent states on the basis of population, while the latter were looking for formulas to allocate seats to different political parties on the basis of votes received. But the basic formulas concur.

For the two different aims just mentioned, American Alexander Hamilton and Englishman Thomas Hare coincided in proposing the "simple" quota, which is the quotient of the total number of inhabitants or votes divided by the total number of seats, that is, $1/M$ (where M is the magnitude or number of seats). This formula is quite intuitive from the notion of proportionality. However, as the votes received by the parties usually do not come in exact multiples of the quota, only a fraction of the total number of seats can be allocated with this criterion. The remaining seats have to be allocated by using some other supplementary formula, such as the "largest remainders" of inhabitants or votes or "any other crotchet which ingenuity may invent, and the combinations of the day given strength to carry," as Thomas Jefferson critically remarked.

Another formula, the "highest average," was conceived by both the aforementioned Jefferson and Belgian civil law professor Victor d'Hondt, to allocate all the seats by a single, "sufficient" quota. Logically, to fulfill its aim of allocating all the seats, this quota must be smaller than the "simple" quota. It can be calculated by trial and error, by a series of divisors, or by lowering the simple quota until it fits.

The Hamilton-Hare quota can produce high proportionality between inhabitant or vote shares and seat shares. The smaller Jefferson-d'Hondt quota can give some overrepresentation to the states or parties larger than the average, which can have more multiples of the quota.

To understand how these procedures work, examine the following example, as represented in the table that follows. Let us focus on the allocation of seats to parties (although the calculations would be the same for apportioning seats among electoral districts). In the example, four parties, W, X, Y, and Z, obtain 40, 30, 20, and 10 votes, respectively (100 in total); the district magnitude, M, or seats to be allocated, is six.

Let us first apply the Hamilton-Hare quota. The quota is $100/6 = 16.7$. On the basis of the quota, party W receives ($40/16.7 =$) 2 seats (and retains $40 - 16.7 \times 2 = 6.7$ votes); party X receives ($30/16.7 =$) 1 seat (and retains $30 - 16.7 = 13.3$ votes); party Y receives ($20/16.7 =$) 1 seat (and retains $20 - 16.7 = 3.3$ votes); and party Z receives ($10/16.7 =$) 0 seats, (and retains all its 10 votes). The initial allocation is thus W: 2, X: 1, Y: 1, and Z: 0, for a total of 4 seats. The other two seats up to six can be allocated to the parties with the largest remainders of votes, which are X with 13.3 remaining votes, and Z with 10 remaining votes. So the complete allocation is W: 2, X: 2, Y: 1, and Z: 1.

Let us apply now the Jefferson-d'Hondt quota. We divide the number of votes of each party by the series of divisors 1, 2, 3, etc., to obtain a series of quotients until the M-th (in this case the sixth) highest quotient, or "highest average," which will be the distributive quota. As marked in the table that follows, of the six highest quotients, W has 3, X has 2, Y has 1, and Z has 0. Remember that the lowest of the six highest quotients is the distributive quota, 13.3 (which is smaller than the Hamilton-Hare quota, 16.7). Note that the allocation of seats to the parties corresponds to the multiples of this quota: W: $40/13.3 = 3$; X: $30/13.3 = 2$; Y: $20/13.3 = 1$; and Z: $10/13.3 = 0$.

As you can observe, the two quotas produce different allocations of the six seats among the four parties. The Hamilton-Hare quota gives seats to all the four parties (2, 2, 1, 1), while the Jefferson-d'Hondt quota gives higher number of seats to the largest party, W, and no seats to the smallest party, Z (3, 2, 1, 0). Try to decipher the following table to learn how to apply these rules.

BOX 14.1

HAMILTON-HARE, OR "SIMPLE QUOTA"						JEFFERSON-D'HONDT, OR "HIGHEST AVERAGE"						
Parties:	W	X	Y	Z	Total	Parties:		W	X	Y	Z	Total
Votes:	40	30	20	10	100	Votes:		40	30	20	10	100
M = 6						M = 6						
Quota: 100/6 = 16.7						Divisors:	1	40	30	20	10	
Allocation:	40/16.7	30/16.7	20/16.7	10/16.7			2	20	15	10	5	
Quotas	2	1	1	0	4		3	13.3	10	6.7	3.3	
Remainders	6.7	13.3	3.3	10			4	10	7.5	5	2.5	
	–	1	–	1		Quota: 6th quotient: 13.3						
Seats:	2	2	1	1	6	Allocation:		40/13.3	30/13.3	20/13.3	10/13.3	
						Seats:		3	2	1	0	6

the parties formed with those individual winners will gather a total number of seats in the federal assembly proportional to their total number of votes in the country.

PROPORTIONAL REPRESENTATION

As just discussed, traditional elections by majority rule have been widely used in contexts of simple communities with rather homogeneous electorates dealing with local issues. But the creation of new parties trying to politicize new issues and the emergence of new political demands in newly complex societies made results with majority rule increasingly dissatisfactory for both voters and candidates. With increasing political and social pluralism, the "winner takes all" character of majority rule tended to produce actual minority winners. As we have seen, the most usual procedures in elections based on the majority principle do not guarantee that the winner has, in practice, majority support, or at least not a majority of voters' first preferences.

With the development of political parties, proportional representation rules were invented with the aim of including varied minorities in the assembly and facilitating the formation of an effective political majority to legislate and rule. In a number of countries, the introduction of proportional representation rules in the early twentieth century ran parallel to the expansion of suffrage rights and the subsequent demands by different social, political, and ethnic groups for representation.

In order to establish fair representation of political parties, each party may be given a portion of seats corresponding to its votes. **In elections in multi-seat districts with proportional representation rules, seats are allocated to multiple parties competing in the election on the basis of the votes received.** In order to distribute seats among parties, each proportional representation formula defines a quota of votes worth a seat. As many times the votes received by a party are multiples of the quota, as many seats the party is allocated. See Box 14.1 for the most commonly used formulas of proportional representation in current democracies.

In some sense, party representation implies the building of new non-territorial communities of people with homogeneous political preferences, which may obtain fair representation. In complex societies, even if individual voters sharing some relevant economic, cultural, or ethnic interests and akin policy inclinations do not live in contiguous neighborhoods or within the same electoral district, they can vote for the same political party and be rewarded with the corresponding number of seats. In the absence of traditional local communities with homogeneous characteristics, political parties can act as a kind of politically constructed new community attracting people with similar traits. With the vanishing of small districts and traditional community voting in which people's preferences were pretty transparent, elections by proportional representation among differentiated neighbors usually imply written ballots and secret voting.

Electoral Representation

Electoral rules have significant political consequences. The most direct effects can be seen at three stages: the formation of candidacies, the citizens' vote, and the allocation of seats to political parties.

Let us remember some of the effects of plurality rule in single-seat districts:

• First, at the stage of presenting candidacies, plurality rule encourages the "coordination" of potential candidates on a small number of candidacies in order to reduce the risk of becoming an absolute loser.

• Second, if in spite of this there are more than two candidates running, some voters may choose to vote for a candidate who is one of the largest and more likely to win, even if they would prefer one of the smaller candidacies, thus reducing the variety of votes. Then it is said that there is some "strategic," or non-sincere, voting.

• Finally, a single winner takes all, even if short of a majority.

In contrast, proportional representation rules can give seats to several groups. Specifically:

• They encourage multiple parties to run separately according to their own profile, that is, not to withdraw or merge. Women's and minorities' candidates tend to run in relatively high proportions.

• Voters are given more choices and tend to choose sincerely their most preferred candidacies, even if they are small, because they will receive representation according to their votes. Turnout tends to be higher than in elections in single-seat districts.

• After the election, different minorities can be included in the assembly and influence collective decision making on the basis of their popular support. An aggregative majority is usually formed.

These mechanisms are relevant because they have consequences for some important features of political systems: the number of political parties receiving representation; the degree of correspondence between parties' shares of votes and seats received; the characteristics of the legislative and government majorities formed after the election; and the quality of the people elected. We review these in the following pages.

PARTY REPRESENTATION

Different electoral rules can be associated with different party systems. Specifically, we can establish a relationship between the number of parties in parliament, P, and

BOX 14.2   **MEASURING PROPORTIONALITY**

The proportionality of the allocation of seats to political parties relative to the votes received by the parties can be measured using several indices, including the following:

$$\text{Proportionality: Prop} = 1 - \tfrac{1}{2} \Sigma \, |V_i - S_i|$$

$$\text{Least squares: LSq} = 1 - [\tfrac{1}{2} \Sigma \, (V_i - S_i)^2]^{1/2}$$

Where:
Prop: Proportionality index;
LSq: Least squares index;

V_i: share of votes for each party i; and
S_i: share of seats of each party i.

In the versions presented here, in which deviations from proportionality are subtracted from 1, both indices have values between 0 and 1, where 0 corresponds to a situation in which no party with seats has votes and no party with votes has seats (which would be nondemocratic) and 1 corresponds to every party having exactly the same proportion of seats as proportion of votes. The values of the two indices are strongly correlated.

two basic elements of any electoral system: the total number of seats in the assembly, S, and the average number of seats in all districts, M. In general, the larger the assembly and the larger the district magnitude, the more parties may be represented. More precisely, the best fit seems to be the formula of the "seat product," as given by Johan Skytte Prize–winning political scientist Rein Taagepera. It is:

$$(SM)^{1/4} = P$$

For instance, the British House of Commons has a size of 650 seats (S = 650) and is elected by plurality rule in single-seat districts (M = 1). According to the "seat product" formula, between five and six parties in Parliament should be expected; in fact, there are the Conservative, the Labour, the Liberal-Democrat, the Scottish, and the Welsh parties (plus the parties elected in Northern Ireland by another electoral system). In Norway, the Chamber of Deputies has a size of 169 seats (S = 169) and is elected by proportional representation in multi-seat districts with an average of 9 (M = 9). According to the formula, there should be more than six parties with seats; in fact, after the election in 2005, there were seven parties. However, in the United States, the values of the variables S = 435 and M = 1 would predict more than four parties, which again calls our attention to the aggregative effort and internal divisions implied by the two "large tent" or "umbrella" parties in the country.

Logically, elections in large districts by proportional representation rules produce more "proportionality" between the vote shares and the seat shares of the parties than elections in single-seat districts, just as they intend. In general, **the degree of proportionality is higher the larger the district magnitude**.

The proportionality between votes and seats for each party produced by different rules can be measured with several indices, which are all strongly correlated (see Box 14.2). With conventional measures, proportionality may take values from as high as over 98 percent, as in Germany, with proportional representation in a very large single nationwide district, to less than 80 percent, due to overrepresentation in favor of the larger parties and underrepresentation of the smaller parties, as in the plurality

CASE 14.1   PROTECTIVE PROPORTIONAL REPRESENTATION

Proportional representation has been promoted by new, emerging parties with few opportunities to receive seats in single-seat districts in which the winner takes all. Typical promoters of proportional representation include new radical and ethnic parties against old conservative and liberal domination in the nineteenth century, new socialist and christian parties in the early twentieth century, and other minor parties with uncertain prospects in new democracies in different places and at different moments. However, changing expectations can change parties' preferences for electoral rules. In particular, when some previously dominant parties feel threatened by newly growing parties, they can favor introducing proportional rules, while successful new parties may also turn coats on the issue. For example, the British Labourites were in favor of proportional representation in the early twentieth century, but when they became one of the two largest parties in votes, together with the Conservatives, they abandoned such a demand, while the relegated Liberals adopted it ever since.

Proportional representation would give every group protection against the class legislation of others, without claiming the power to exercise it in their own.

John Stuart Mill, Radical member of the British House of Commons (1861)

Our party would derive great advantages from the introduction of this electoral system...Under the present electoral system the greater part of our votes is lost—whereas under proportional representation our strength in parliament would be doubled or tripled.

Wilhelm Liebknecht, leader of the German Social-democratic Party (1890)

This will kill that. So is the formula of voting in district. These will kill those. So is the formula of voting by list without proportional representation. These and those will have their fair share. So is the formula of voting by list with proportional representation.

Jean Jaurès, leader of the French Socialist Party (1903)

With universal suffrage and elections in single-seat districts, the time will not be distant when the interests of the farmers here and there in the country will not be well represented in elected bodies . . . [With proportional representation] the danger of a shift in the direction now indicated is very greatly diminished. Even if farmers are no longer in a majority, agriculture should nevertheless have a chance to enjoy its fair share of representation.

Arvid Lindman, Swedish Conservative Prime minister (1907)

rule system with single-seat districts and multiple parties in Britain. However, in plurality rule single-seat districts in the United States, the degree of proportionality tends to be about 95 percent, thanks to successful coordination into only two parties.

Party Government and Policy Making. While elections in single-seat districts favor single-party government, proportional representation is characteristically associated with multiparty coalition governments. As we discussed, plurality rule can typically fabricate a single party's absolute majority of seats on the basis of a minority of popular votes, as in the emblematic case of Britain. In contrast, multiparty coalition governments are usually based on a majority of seats and popular votes, as, for instance, in Germany, as in most other European countries. In practice, electoral systems based on majority rule often create governments with minority electoral support, while proportional representation rules, which are able to include minorities, tend to produce parliamentary governments with majority electoral support.

SOURCE 14.1   The Chicken or the Egg

Whether it is the electoral systems that generate the formation of political parties and shape party systems or the parties that choose electoral systems to consolidate their positions has been discussed at length among political scientists. Some early students of the consequences of electoral systems hinted at the latter relation, as shown in these quotes.

I expressed [*the electoral system*] effects in 1946 [*L'influence des systèmes électoraux sur la vie politique*] in the formulation of three sociological laws: (1) a majority vote on one ballot is conducive to a two-party system; (2) proportional representation is conducive to a multiparty system; (3) a majority vote on two ballots is conducive to a multiparty system, inclined toward forming coalitions...The brutal finality of a majority vote on a single ballot forces parties with similar tendencies to regroup their forces at the risk of being overwhelmingly defeated...In a system of proportional representation, the situation is quite different. Since every minority, no matter how weak it may be is assured of representation in the legislature, nothing prevents the formation of splinter parties, often separated only by mere shades of opinion...It is also clear that the relationship between electoral and party systems is not a one-way phenomenon; if a one-ballot vote tends toward a two-party system, a two party system also favors the adoption of a single ballot voting system.

Maurice Duverger, "Factors in a Two-Party and Multiparty System" (1972)

In fact, in most cases it makes little sense to treat electoral systems as independent variables and party systems as dependent. The party strategists will generally have decisive influence on electoral legislation and opt for the systems of aggregation most likely to consolidate their position, whether through increases in their representation, through the strengthening of the preferred alliances, or through safeguards against splinter movements.

Seymour M. Lipset and Stein Rokkan, "Cleavage Structures, Party Systems, and Voter Alignments" (1967)

When an assembly of S seats is elected in districts of M seats, the most likely number of seat-winning parties (N_o) is

$$N_o = (MS)^{1/4}$$

This means that, with a large number of cases, we expect one-half of them to fall above and one-half below the value N_o.

Rein Taagepera, *Predicting Party Sizes: The Logic of Simple Electoral Systems* (2007)

The number of parties and the largeness of electoral support for the winners have consequences on policy making. Elections in small districts are prone to focusing on local issues, while in multiparty elections, each party can deal with a different set of issues, globally enlarging the public agenda and the political debate.

Also, the degree of stability or change in public policies may depend on the electoral system. In plurality rule electoral systems, a small change in the total number of

BOX 14.3 ASSEMBLY ELECTORAL SYSTEMS, 1870–2009

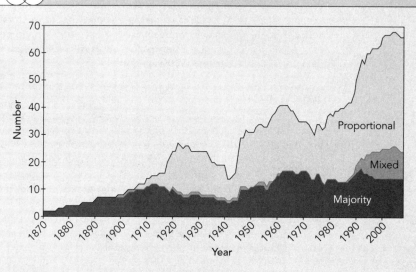

FIGURE 14.1 ASSEMBLY ELECTORAL SYSTEMS

In democratic countries, indirect assembly elections decreased and virtually disappeared in the early twentieth century. The appeal of majority rule, which was the basic formula in the few electoral democracies existing in the late nineteenth and early twentieth centuries, was replaced by proportional representation, especially after the First World War. This trend has intensified in recent democratization processes. Mixed systems of majority and proportional representation have also spread most recently, mainly as a result of changes from nondemocratic regimes or majority rule. Nowadays, the vast majority of democratic countries with more than one million inhabitants use electoral systems with proportional representation rules.

Sources: Author's own elaboration for sixty-four democratic countries with more than one million inhabitants with update of data in Josep M. Colomer, *Handbook of Electoral System Choice* (Palgrave-Macmillan, 2004).

popular votes can bring about a complete alternation of the party in government and in subsequent policies. In contrast, with proportional representation, since several parties may have opportunities to share power, they may have to reach compromises producing relatively more policy continuity in the long term.

The Micro-Mega Rule. In general, political parties tend to choose electoral rules, just as they choose other institutions, in the expectation that they will give them some advantage to promote their aims. Specifically, the choice of electoral systems tends to follow the "micro-mega rule," by which **the large prefer the small and the small prefer the large**. A few large parties tend to prefer small assemblies, small district magnitudes (the smallest being one), and rules based on small quotas of votes for allocating seats (the smallest being simple plurality, which does not require any specific threshold), in order to exclude others from competition. Likewise, multiple small parties tend to prefer large assemblies, large district magnitudes, and large quotas (like those of proportional representation), which are able to include them within.

More clearly: if there are only a few parties, the one or two larger parties can expect to become absolute winners under majority rule. Consequently, they tend to multi-seat districts and proportional representation is usually favored in multi-party systems, both by traditional incumbents, such as conservatives or liberals, under threat of losing their dominant position, and by minority but growing opposition parties, as was historically the case of socialist, christian, ethnic, and other parties.

Nowadays, single-seat districts with plurality or majority rules are used for assembly elections basically in a number of democratic regimes in former British colonies. Proportional representation rules began to be used in the early twentieth century in relatively small, but socially or ethnically complex countries in Western Europe, especially when they introduced establish or maintain single-seat districts with majority rule. But if the number of parties increases, under majority rule, in which the winner takes all, any party can risk becoming an absolute loser, and so they may prefer to move to systems using proportional representation rules likely to secure them a fair share of seats.

In fact, single-seat districts have been supported in countries with a single dominant party or with two parties frequently alternating in power, typically a conservative and a liberal party (or a Republican and a Democrat, as in the United States) or, in more recent times, a conservative and a socialist party (as in Britain). In contrast, multi-seat districts and proportional representation is usually favored in multiparty systems, both by traditional incumbents, such as conservatives or liberals, under threat of losing their dominant position, and by minority but growing opposition parties, as was historically the case of socialist, christian, ethnic, and other parties.

Nowadays, single-seat districts with plurality or majority rules are used for assembly elections basically in a number of democratic regimes in former British colonies. Proportional representation rules began to be used in the early twentieth century in relatively small, but socially or ethnically complex countries in Western Europe, especially when they introduced new regulations of universal male suffrage. Today they are used in most democratic regimes across the world, as shown in Box 14.3.

Quick Quiz

• What is the relationship between district magnitude and the number of parties?
• What is the micro-mega rule?

PERSONAL REPRESENTATION

The personal quality of individual representatives has been a traditional concern for the quality of representative democracy. Blaming the decline of the political class has become a common topic of conversation in many countries in recent times. But already in nineteenth-century England, for instance, John Stuart Mill referred to the "grade of intelligence in the representative body," complaining that "it is becoming

CASE 14.2   SINGLE-SEAT AND MULTISEAT BALLOTS

		VOTE FOR ONE CANDIDATE ONLY	
Counterfoil	1	**BHATT** Atull Kumar Bhatt, 52 Doveldale Road, Sunderland Independent	
Election for the Fulwell Ward of the City of Sunderland on Thursday 16th day of September 1993	2	**DODDS** Brian Doods 264 Leechmore, Road, Sunderland The Labour Party, candidate	
Polling District	3	**FRYETT** David Brian Fryett 159 Sea Road, Fulwell, Sunderland Liberal Democrat	
No. on Register.	4	**STOREY** Dorreen Storey 82 Torver Crescent, Seaburn Dene, Sunderland Conservative	

Britain

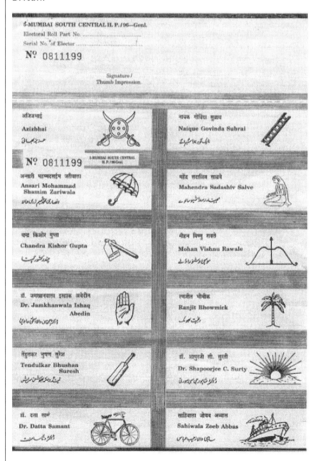

India

Dominique
BERTINOTTI

Maître de conférences
Conseillère de Paris • 4ème arrondissement

Suppléant
Pierre SCHAPIRA
Chirurgien-Dentiste • Conseiller de Paris, 2em arrondissement

La candidate du changement

Présentée par le Parti Socialiste, soutenue par le Parti Radical Socialiste, le Parti Communiste Français, le Mouvement des Citoyens, Les Verts et les forces de la Gauche Alternative et Écologiste

France 1

République Française
Elections législatives des 25 mai et 1er juin 1997
Ière circonscription de Paris

Laurent
DOMINATI

Député sortant

Suppléant : Jean-François LEGARET

"MAJORITÉ PRÉSIDENTIELLE
Union UDF-RPR"

France 2

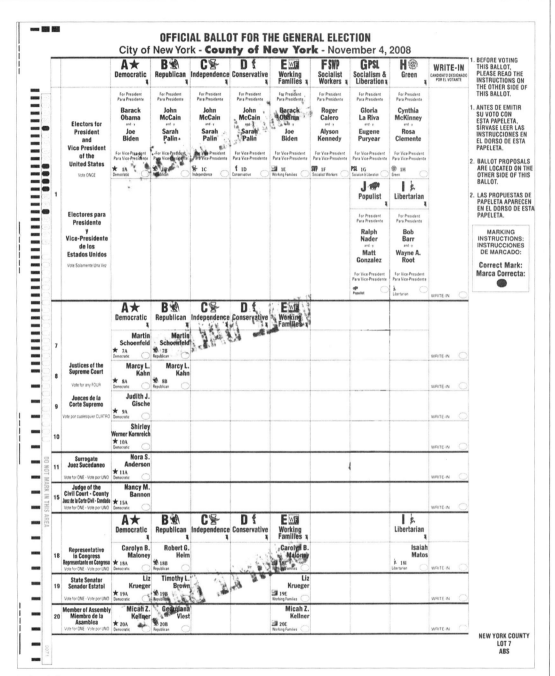

United States

FIGURE 14.2A SINGLE-SEAT BALLOTS

Britain, India, France, and the United States. All seats are filled on the basis of voters' preferences for individual candidates, but personal representation and party representation merge into a single voter's choice.

Continued

CASE 14.2 *Continued*

Stimmzettel

für die Bundestagswahl im Wahlkreis 18 Bergedorf am 3 Oktober 1976

Sie haben 2 Stimmen

hier 1 Stimme	hier 1 Stimme
für die Wahl	für die Wahl
eines Wahlkreisabgeordneten	einer Landesliste (Partei)
(Erststimme)	(Zweitstimme)

1 Schmidt, Helmut — Bundeskanzler — Hamburg 62, Neuberger weg 80 — **SPD** Sozialdemokratische Partei Deutschlands	◯	◯ **SPD** Sozialdemokratische Partei Deutschlands — Schmidt, Wehner, Dr Apel, Glombig, Dr Meinecke **1**
2 Dr. Reimers, Stephan — Theologe — Hamburg 52, Tönninger Str 50 — **CDU** Christlische Demokratische Union Deutschlands	◯	◯ **CDU** Christlich Demokratische Union Deutschlands — Blumenfeld, Ruhe, Dr. Reimers, Damm, Francke **2**
3 Bodelt, Wolfgang — Oberfahnrich a D — Hamburg 60, Cesar-Klein-Ring 4 — **F.D.P.** Freie Demokratische Partei	◯	◯ **F.D.P.** Freie Demokratische Partei — Frau Schuchardt, Kirst, Weber, Bodelt, Czerwonka **3**
4 Peemüller, Hans-Heinz — Rentner — Hamburg 72, Meierstraße 7 — **AUD** Aktionsgemeinschaft Unabhängiger Deutscher	◯	◯ **AUD** Aktionsgemeinschaft Unabhängiger Deutscher — Frau Johannsen, Paasch, Frau Peemüller, Dr.-Ing. Heydt, Frau Benter **4**
5 Hetzer, Hans — Schornsteinfeger — Hamburg 28, Horner Weg 47a — **DKP** Deutsche Kommunistische Partei	◯	◯ **DKP** Deutsche Kommunistische Partei — Enlebach, Wenecke, Hoff, Frau Luth, Sturmann **5**
		◯ **EAP** Europäische Arbeiterpartei — Hellenbroich, Frau Hopf, Frau Tannen, Bernel **6**
		◯ **GIM** Gruppe Internationale Marxisten — Hackbusch, Gless, Zamory, Lierow **7**
		◯ **KPD** Kommunistische Partei Deutschlands — Lenze, Stamer, Wachmann, Heide **8**
		◯ **KBW** Kommunistischer Bund Westdeutschland — Plumer, Frau Oberkampf, Dene, Rocnatz, Schween **9**
6 Prien, Hans — Geschaftsführer — Hamburg 28, Klov 114, Parz 502 — **NPD** Nationaldemokratische Partei Deutschlands	◯	◯ **NPD** Nationaldemokratische Partei Deutschlands — Sabrautzky, Timmermann, Frau Rahtf, Dr. Dr. Ohnesorge, Müller **10**

Germany

FIGURE 14.2B MULTI-SEAT BALLOTS

In Germany, with double vote, the voters have the opportunity to select both a party and some of the candidates to be elected. In Spain, closed party lists do not permit the voters to select any individual candidate. In Denmark, with open lists, the voters choose individual candidates within party lists. In Ireland, preferential vote permits voters to select and rank individual candidates for all the seats to be elected.

ELECCIONES A CORTES GENERALES 2000
ELECCIONS A CORTS GENERALS 2000

DIPUTADOS
DIPUTATS

CONVERGÈNCIA I UNIÓ

BARCELONA

Doy mi voto a la candidatura presentada por:
Dono el meu vot a la candidatura presentada per:

**CONVERGÈNCIA I UNIÓ
(CIU)**

XAVIER TRIAS i VIDAL DE LLOBATERA   (CDC)
HERIBERT PADROL i MUNTÉ   (CDC)
Ma. MERCÈ PIGEM i PALMÉS   (CDC)
JOSEP SÁNCHEZ i LLIBRE   (UDC)
JORDI JANÉ i GUASCH   (CDC)
CARLES CAMPUZANO i CANADÉS   (CDC)
IGNASI GUARDANS i CAMBÓ   (CDC)
MANEL J. SILVA i SÀNCHEZ   (UDC)
JORDI MARTÍ i GALBIS   (CDC)
IMMACULADA RIERA i REÑÉ   (CDC)
ANTONI ABAD i POUS   (CDC)
MARIA JOSEP ATIENZA i GUERRERO   (UDC)
CARLES AGUSTÍ i HERNÁNDEZ   (CDC)
PERE OMS i PONS   (CDC)
LLUÍS ARBOIX i PASTOR   (CDC)
JOSEP Ma. FORNÉS i CALLIS   (UDC)
ROSA REBOREDO i CIVEIRA   (CDC)
CECÍLIA BOSCH i NURI   (CDC)
MARIA FRANCISCO i CODINACH   (CDC)
MARTA ALSINA i TEIXIDÓ   (UDC)
XAVIER ESCRIBÀ i VIVÓ   (CDC)
RAMON BONASTRE i BERTRAN   (CDC)
JOSEP VIDAL i BARTOLÍ   (CDC)
JOAN CAPDEVILA i ESTEVE   (UDC)
MARIA BERTRAN i BASCOMPTE   (CDC)
Ma. LLUÏSA PUIG i MARIGOT   (CDC)
RICARD CABALLÉ i CABALLÉ   (CDC)
ORIOL VILA i CASTELLÓ   (UDC)
AGUSTÍ GALLART i TEIXIDÓ   (CDC)
JOAN QUERALTÓ i IBÀÑEZ   (CDC)
JOSEP Ma. CARBONELL i VILARÓ   (CDC)

Suplentes - *Suplents*

JOAN MARTÍN i TORIBIO   (UDC)
ANNA MORELL i ARIMANY   (CDC)
MANEL ABRIL i ROSELL   (CDC)

Spain

more and more difficult for anyone who has only talents and character to gain admission into the House of Commons," and remarking on the importance of voting procedures, together with internal party rules, in the selection of electoral candidates.

In order to fulfill the classic aspiration to be "governed by the best," democracy requires that talented and skilled people should run in elections. Running for election can depend on the potential candidate's opportunity costs, as we discussed in

Nordjyllands amts 2. kreds

Folketingsvalget 1990

A. Socialdemokratiet
Ole Stavad
Martin Glerup
Holger Graversen
Ilse Hansen
Arne Jensen
Frank Jensen
J. Risgaard Knudsen
Bjarne Laustsen
Kaj Poulsen

B. Det Radikale Venstre
Lars Schönberg-Hemme
Bent Bundgaard
Marianne Jelved
Bent Jørgensen
Hans Larsen-Ledet
Axel E. Mortensen
Lars Lammert Nielsen
Ove Nielsen
Preben Pedersen

C. Det Konservative Folkeparti
Karsten Frederiksen
Niels Ahlmann-Ohlsen
H. P. Clausen
Suzanne Kogsbøll
Jørgen Lund
Allan Nygaard
Gerda Thymann Pedersen
Per Seeberg
Søren Pflug

D. Centrum-Demokraterne
Peter Duetoft
Gregers Folke Gregersen
Bodil Melgaard Haakonsen
Anton Jepsen
Tove Kattrup
Hartvig Kjeldgaard
Bent V. Villadsen

E. Danmarks Retsforbund
Knud Christensen
Aase Bak-Nielsen
Jane Dyrdal
Karen Hansen
Ejnar Pedersen
Ole Thielemann
Egon Thomsen

Denmark

TREORACHA

1. Féach chuige go bhfuil an marc oifigiúil ar an bpáipéar.
2. Maircáil an figiúr 1 sa bhosca le hais ghriangraf an chéad iarrthóra is rogha leat, maircáil an figiúr 2 sa bhosca le hais ghriangraf an iarrthóra do dhara rogha, agus mar sin de.
3. Fíll an páipéar ionas nach bhféadfaí do vóta a fheiceáil. Taispeáin cúl an pháipéir don oifigeach reachtála agus cuir sa bhosca ballóide é.

INSTRUCTIONS

1. See that the official mark is on the paper.
2. Mark 1 in the box beside the photograph of the candidate of your first choice, mark 2 in the box beside the photograph of the candidate of your second choice, and so on.
3. Fold the paper to conceal your vote. Show the back of the paper to the presiding officer and put it in the ballot box.

AHERN — FIANNA FÁIL
(BERTIE AHERN of 'St. Lukes', 161 Lower Drumcondra Road, Dublin 9 Taoiseach)

COSTELLO — THE LABOUR PARTY
(JOE COSTELLO OF 66 Aughrim Street Dublin 7, Public Representative)

FITZPATRICK — FIANNA FÁIL
(DR. DERMOT FITZPATRICK of 80 Navan Road, Dublin 7 Medical Doctor and Public Representative)

GREGORY — NON PARTY
(TONY GREGORY of 5 Sackville Gardens, Ballybough, Dublin 3 Full Time Public Representative)

KEHOE — SINN FÉIN
(NICKY KEHOE of 50 Fintan Road Cabra, Dublin 7, Bricklayers)

MITCHELL — FINE GAEL
(JIM MITCHELL of Leinster House, Dublin 2, Full-Time Public Representative)

O'DONNELL — NON PARTY
(PATRICK NOEL O'DONNELL of 14 Cliftonville Road, Glasnevin, Dublin 9)

O'LOUGHLIN — COMHAR CRÍOSTAÍ CHRISTIAN SOLIDARITY PARTY
(PAUL THOMAS O'CONNELL of Flat 4 255 North Circular Road, Phibsborough, Dublin 7; Shop Assistant)

PRENDINVILLE — NON PARTY
(TOM PRENDENVILLE of 52 Goldbraith Street Phibsborough, Dublin 7, News Reporter)

SIMPSON — GREEN PARTY COMHAONTAS GLAS
(TOM SIMPSON of 3 Hempstead Avenue Glasnevin, Dublin 9; FÁS Instructor)

Specimen

Ireland

chapter 4, and the party's internal procedures, which may require more or less competition, as discussed in chapter 9.

From the sole point of view of citizens' participation, the electoral ballot also has some influence. **Different ballot forms give different opportunities to voters to participate in the selection of individual candidates**.

Several procedures can be used. Each voter can select and rank all candidates, as in the form of the preferential ballot used in the British- and Irish-style formula of the "single transferable vote." Alternatively, voters can select a number of candidates within a party list, who will be preferably elected for the party's seats, as in the open lists used in a number of countries in central and northern Europe. The double vote permits the voter to select both a closed party list and a single individual candidate (who may or may not be from the same party), as used in Germany and New Zealand. In the so-called mixed systems, some seats in the assembly are elected in single-member districts by majority rule, and some seats are elected by proportional representation. All these procedures usually result in a combination of candidates selected by the party leadership and others selected by the voters. Only closed lists (which are a form of voting "in bloc") restrict the voter's choice to a party label and do not permit any modification in the selection of candidates as given by the party.

Conclusion

In this chapter we have discussed different formulas for electing a representative assembly on the basis of their capacity to produce satisfactory personal representation and party representation. Regarding the personal characteristics of representatives, we have considered the hypothesis that they depend partly on the opportunities given to voters to participate in the selection of individual candidates, especially in the ballot form.

Regarding party representation, we have discussed the relationship between the total number of seats, or assembly size, the number of seats for election in each district, or district magnitude, and the number of parties with representation.

Some findings can be summarized as two *propositions* in political science:

- **More seats, more parties.** For assembly and parliamentary elections, the larger the size of the assembly and the higher the district magnitude with proportional representation, the higher the number of political parties.

- **Micro-mega rule.** Large parties prefer small assemblies and small district magnitudes by plurality rule, while small parties prefer large assemblies and large districts with proportional representation.

- **Small assemblies, large districts.** The development of multiple parties favors the adoption of large multi-seat districts with proportional representation rules. In the long term, proportional representation rules have been increasingly adopted. But in very large countries, a large federal assembly can be elected with different electoral rules, including small single-seat districts. ■

Summary

The number of seats or the size of a democratic representative assembly, S, is related to the population of the country, Pop, with a cube root: $S = Pop^{1/3}$.

Traditional small and local communities may use multi-seat districts, majority rule, and open ballot, which permit homogeneous community voting and personal representation.

With the emergence of political parties, elections in single-seat districts tend to reestablish the traditional sense of community voting. Personal representation and party representation merge into a single voter's choice.

However, an assembly elected in multiple single-seat districts may give a party an absolute majority of seats on the basis of a minority of popular votes, or even more seats than another party with more votes.

Parties can receive seats on the basis of votes by proportional representation rules. Each proportional representation formula defines a quota of votes worth a seat; as many times the votes received by a party are multiples of the quota, as many seats the party is allocated.

The number of parties, P, may depend on the assembly size, S, and the district magnitude, M, as captured by the formula: $(SM)^{1/4} = P$.

Single-seat districts favor single-party government, while proportional representation is usually associated with multiparty coalition governments.

Larger parties prefer small districts and small quotas such as plurality, while smaller parties prefer large districts and large quotas of proportional representation.

Over time, increasing numbers of countries tend to adopt proportional representation rules.

The personal quality of representatives depends partly on the opportunities for voters to choose individual candidates for either all seats, as in preferential voting or primary elections; only some, as with open lists, the double vote, and mixed systems; or none, as with closed lists.

Key Concepts

Apportionment, or districting. Distribution of seats among different electoral districts.

Assembly size. Total number of seats in an assembly.

Ballot. Form of voting to select parties and individual candidates.

Magnitude. Number of seats to be elected in a district.

Majority rule. First past the post, or the winner takes all.

Micro-mega rule. Large parties prefer small districts and small parties prefer large districts.

Mixed electoral system. Some seats are elected by majority rule and others by proportional representation.

Multi-seat district. A district with a magnitude larger than one.

Proportional representation. Allocation of seats to parties on the basis of quotas of votes.

Single-seat district. A district with a magnitude equaling one.

Questions for Review

1. What's the relationship between assembly size and country population?
2. What's "gerrymandering?"
3. What's the relationship between district magnitude and the number of parties?
4. What's the micro-mega rule?

Problems and Applications

1. Search for the results of a recent election in Israel. Compare the shares of votes for each party and the shares of seats received. Discuss.

Data sources

Wikipedia, Elections: http://en.wikipedia.org/wiki/List_of_election_results_by_country
ACE, the Electoral Knowledge Network: www.aceproject.org/

Quantitative measurements

2. In the following election, allocate six seats among the four parties by each of the following rules of proportional representation (as explained in Box 14.1):
   a. Simple quota (Hamilton-Hare) plus largest remainders
   b. Highest average (Jefferson-d'Hondt)
   c. Discuss.
3. In the following election, allocate six seats among the four parties by each of the following rules of proportional representation (as explained in Box 14.1):
   a. Simple quota (Hamilton-Hare) plus largest remainders
   b. Highest average (Jefferson-d'Hondt)
   c. Discuss.

PARTIES	VOTES
W	23
X	14
Y	30
Z	33
Total	100

4. Look back at the allocations of seats to the parties in the two previous problems. For each election, which is more proportional? Consult Box 14.2.

PARTIES	VOTES
Green	60, 000
Liberal	50, 000
Conservative	38, 500
National	12, 500
Total	161, 000

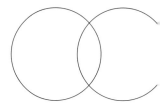

15

DIVISION OF POWERS

In This Chapter You Will

- Reflect on how traditional kings were either suppressed or replaced.
- Distinguish between a parliamentary regime and a presidential regime.
- Discuss the advantages and disadvantages of fusion of powers and division of powers.
- Learn what "unified government" and "divided government" mean.
- Discuss the effects of institutional deadlock.

The United States government "shut down" for several weeks in late 1995 and early 1996 as a result of a conflict between Democratic President William Clinton and the Republican-controlled Congress led by Newt Gingrich. Usually the President and the majority of Congress can cooperate to advance legislation. However, when the president's party does not have a majority of congressmen, a legislative "deadlock" can occur. If the disagreement between the President and the Congress is over the annual budget bill, the government may have to paralyze some of its activities for lack of funding. On the occasion mentioned, the Republicans wanted additional cuts in health care, education, environmental controls, and a refundable income tax credit in order to balance the budget, which President Clinton and most Democratic legislators considered unnecessary. Thus, major portions of the federal government became inoperative, including the national institutes of health, parks, museums, monuments, the processing of visas and passports, and other "nonessential" services, implying that about 284,000 federal employees were placed in a non-duty, non-pay status for a while.

The situation is different in parliamentary regimes. As the prime minister is usually appointed by a majority of parliament, the cabinet and the legislators' majority can easily work together. However, when the government's support is formed by a multiparty coalition, it may also fail. For example, Italian center-left Prime minister Romano Prodi lost the support of one of his coalition partners in parliament, due partly to disagreement over a proposed law on same-sex couples, in 2008, less than two years after having been sworn in. As a consequence, he dissolved the parliament and called a new anticipated parliamentary election, which was won by the center-right opposition, led by Silvio Berlusconi, who became the new prime minister. This kind of exit cannot be implemented in a regime with separate elections for the congress and the presidency.

In this chapter we analyze a few basic institutional configurations of democratic regimes. In parliamentary regimes, the parliament and the government are mutually dependent. In presidential regimes, the two institutions are elected separately. Interinstitutional relations are also shaped by the political party system, whether based on two or multiple parties. Different institutional and party formulas favor different ways of making decisions on policies and laws. ■

Assemblies and Presidents

Virtually all the political regimes in world history have been based on a dual formula: a one-person office combined with multiple-person offices. The rationale for this dualism is that while a one-person institution may be highly effective at decision making and implementation, a multiple-person institution may be more representative of the different interests and values in the society. Even traditional kings, emperors, and popes consulted with councils and assemblies before making certain major decisions, including declaring war and peace, raising certain taxes, or making doctrinal changes.

In the past in some European countries, a balanced relationship between the non-elected monarch and the elected assembly created a mixed formula. This type of separation of powers was established by both the English Revolution in the late seventeenth century and the French Revolution in the late eighteenth century by forcing the incumbent king to accept new rules. It was somehow replicated in other European kingdoms during the nineteenth century. A one-person, non-elected monarch with executive powers faced a multiple-person, elected assembly with legislative and fiscal powers. In this framework, on the one hand, the king or queen could appoint his or her ministers without constraints. On the other, the monarch had to rely upon a parliamentary majority in order to approve bills, although typically the monarch could also veto legislative initiatives of the parliament. Separate institutions contained and controlled each other. Similar formulas still exist in a few Arab countries such as Jordan or Morocco.

However, this is not usually a long-term, durable formula. With the development of parliamentary political parties promoting broadening suffrage and democratization, the elected assembly's powers tend to expand to include calling and dissolving the assembly, developing full legislation, and controlling executive ministers. In parallel, the powers of the non-elected monarch tend to be reduced. With these processes, two basic democratic models have developed:

- In one model the monarch's powers were curbed in favor of the parliament.
- In the other, the monarch was replaced with an elected president.

PARLIAMENTARY REGIME

One of the two democratic formulas that can result from the process of enhancing the role of the elected assembly and limiting the monarch's powers is the so-called parliamentary regime. In the English experience, the Parliament became the sovereign institution by depriving the monarch of the power of vetoing bills and assuming the power of appointing and dismissing ministers, while the monarch became a ceremonial although non-accountable figurehead. Nowadays, there are parliamentary regimes in about half of the democratic countries in the world. Some of these regimes are British-style monarchical variants, such as those in Australia, Belgium, Canada, Denmark, Japan, the Netherlands, New Zealand, Norway, Spain, and Sweden. Others have, instead of a monarch, a ceremonial, but nonhereditary and accountable president of the republic, such as Austria, Czech Republic, Estonia, Finland, Germany, Greece, Hungary, India, Ireland, Italy, Latvia, Slovakia, Slovenia, South Africa, and Switzerland.

In a parliamentary regime, the one-person institution that becomes most relevant is not the monarch or president, but **the prime minister, that is, the chief executive,** who forms his or her own cabinet and whose power is based on the support of a majority of members of parliament. The dual formula in this model is organized around the one-person prime minister and the multi-person parliament. Both make decisions on the basis of the same political party or coalition majority, producing a fusion of powers between the two institutions.

PRESIDENTIAL REGIME

In the other democratic formula, which originated in the United States in the late eighteenth century, it is not only the multi-person legislative assembly that is popularly elected but also the one-person chief executive. **The non-elected monarch was replaced with an elected president** with significant powers similar to those of traditional monarchs, including vetoing legislation and appointing and dismissing the cabinet members. This model of political regime implies, therefore, separate elections and divided powers between the chief executive and the legislative branch. In the original U.S. version, it contains a complex system of "checks and balances," or mutual controls, between separately elected or appointed institutions, including the Presidency, the House of Representatives, the Senate, and the Supreme Court. In other countries the balance of powers tends toward one side or the other, as we will see later in this chapter.

It is worth noting that the initial design of the U.S. institutional regime was based on some misunderstanding of the British model and on an error in calculation. First, the authors of the U.S. Constitution thought they were adapting the traditional British model of separation of powers, and thus gave to the presidency the powers of the traditional monarch, but at the time, the British model had already been transformed in favor of parliament, as we mentioned. The American constituents did not adopt the British-type parliamentary system because they were not aware of its recent existence.

Second, when it was established that the president would be indirectly elected by the Electoral College, it was widely expected that no presidential candidate

BOX 15.1 **THREE ASSEMBLIES**

The shape of some democratic chambers can inform on the functioning of institutions and party systems, as shown in these examples:

In the British House of Commons, the government's party and the opposition sit in separate trenches, one facing the other, suggesting polarization and alternation.

In the United States Senate, individual senators are notably independent from party lines in some of their votes and decisions.

In the German Bundestag, multiple political parties become compact, disciplined parliamentary groups, which form multiparty majority coalitions.

would obtain a majority of electors and so presidential selection would pass to the House of Representatives. However, as a consequence of each state of the union voting in bloc for a single presidential candidate and the development of large-scale political parties and electoral campaigns, presidential candidates became able to win by majority in the Electoral College, thus out of control of the House. The separation of powers between the executive presidency and the legislative assembly was consolidated, each institution with separate powers and elections. The basic formulas of the U.S. Constitution have been replicated in a number of Asian countries under American influence, including Indonesia, South Korea, the Philippines, and Taiwan. Table 15.1 summarizes the institutional relations in the two models just presented.

TABLE 15.1   Two Models of Political Regime

In a "parliamentary" regime, voters elect the assembly or parliament, which indirectly elects the prime minister, who appoints the cabinet. In a "presidential" regime, voters elect separately the assembly and the president, who appoints the cabinet.

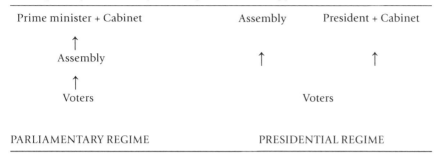

Quick Quiz

• How is the chief executive elected in a parliamentary regime?
• And in a presidential regime?

Parliamentary Regime

In a Parliamentary Regime, the Parliament and the Cabinet Led by the Prime Minister have Relations of Mutual Dependence.   On one side, parliament elects and can overthrow the prime minister. On the other, the prime minister can dissolve parliament and call a new parliamentary election. These powers of mutual destruction usually work as threats, inducing preventive cooperation between the two institutions. The prime minister and the majority of parliament cooperate with each other in order to prevent the removal of the former or the dissolution of the latter.

The Parliament Elects the Prime Minister.   If a party has an absolute majority of seats in parliament, then a single-party cabinet can be formed. Otherwise, the candidate for prime minister may have to negotiate a multiparty majority to obtain support and be voted for in parliament. Usually, the majority supporting the prime minister and forming the cabinet remains a legislative majority to pass bills and annual budgets. The parliament can also depose the prime minister and, in some cases, individual ministers or cabinet members. Hence the "fusion" of powers in a parliamentary regime, which in fact takes place within a political party structure.

The Prime Minister Can Dissolve Parliament.   On the other side, the prime minister (or the chief of state at the prime minister's proposal) can dissolve parliament and call a new election before term, typically with some time restrictions, so as not to do so too close to the previous election. Official parliament terms usually last for three, four, or five years. But, for example, as a consequence of anticipated elections in Britain and Canada, where the parliament term is five years, an election has been called in average every three years and four months and every three years and nine months, respectively, since World War II. The capacity of the prime minister to shape the electoral calendar is considered as giving parliamentary regimes some flexibility to react to unexpected crises. For instance, Japanese prime minister Koizumi dissolved the House of Representatives in 2005, two years before term, after bills to privatize the postal system were voted down in the upper house, and he neatly won the following election. But if the calendar is manipulated for political maneuvering—for instance, to make an election coincide with a good moment in the economic cycle or other governmental success, and prevent it from coinciding with adverse events—the decision to call an early election can backfire. A decision to call an early election can reveal government incompetence to the public.

SINGLE-PARTY PARLIAMENTARISM

In England, the development of parliamentary political parties, the expansion of Parliament's powers, and the limitation of those of the monarch transformed the political regime from a system of checks and balances between separate institutions into a parliamentary regime. But it is one with a high concentration of power. In the seventeenth and eighteenth centuries, England, with the type of mixed formula we have just sketched out, was considered the model of division of powers to prevent an absolute monarchy and to guarantee freedom to its subjects. In John Locke's observation, "the legislative and executive powers come often to be separated," while in Montesquieu's analysis, "the legislative body...is restrained by the executive power, as the executive is by the legislative...[although] there is no liberty if the judiciary power be not separated from the legislative and executive."

However, in the nineteenth century, constitutional analyst Walter Bagehot identified "the efficient secret of the English constitution" in the opposite stance, that is, in "the close union, the near complete fusion, of the executive and legislative powers." In the twentieth century, the United Kingdom was considered indeed the democratic model of concentration of power by most constitutional lawyers and political scientists.

The key of this evolution is the formation of parliamentary parties and the predominance of the House of Commons, in which two major parties predominate and a single party can form the cabinet with majority support in Parliament. The tendency toward concentration of power is self-reinforcing. If a single political party controls both a parliamentary majority and the cabinet, the most concentrated institution tends to prevail. Specifically, the one-person office of prime minister prevails over the collective cabinet (whose members the former has appointed) and even more over the multi-member parliament.

This can be explained with the theory of collective action that we studied in chapter 2, which, as you should recall, highlights the advantages of small groups over large groups. A one-person prime minister or a small organization such as a cabinet can decide more quickly than a large organization, such as a parliamentary group or a parliament, for reasons of unity of purpose and the time required to collect information, share that information with others, bargain, and vote, even if all or a majority of the organizations' members share similar political or ideological preferences.

Please note that under a system of political party representation, the relative power of the institutions does not depend only on their formal relations as defined at the beginning of this chapter. In spite of the parliament having appointed the prime minister, the latter prevails on the basis of his or her higher capacity for decision making. When mutually dependent institutions, such as parliament, the cabinet, and the prime ministership, fall under the control of the same political party, not only do they behave as a single actor, but the most concentrated, or "smallest," unit prevails. On the basis of this tendency toward increasingly concentrated power, conservative politician Lord Hailsham called the British political system, somewhat exaggeratedly, an "elective dictatorship." In fact, a multiple-person parliament can balance its relationship with the one-person or a few-person executive only when the latter has no majority in the former, that is, when a multiparty system exists.

MULTIPARTY PARLIAMENTARISM

In most parliamentary regimes in the world, there are multiparty systems that induce the formation of multiparty coalition cabinets. Let us take the example of Germany. The seats in the lower chamber of parliament are allocated to political parties by proportional representation, so that each party gets about the same proportion of seats in parliament as votes received in the election. No single party has ever obtained an absolute majority of votes, and thus no absolute majority of parliamentary seats either. All German cabinets formed since the end of World War II have been multiparty coalitions. The chancellor or prime minister has always been either a Christian-democrat or a Social-democrat, but government coalitions include several formulas: rightist Christian-democrats (always with their allies, the Bavarian Social-Christians) with center-right Free-democrats, center-left Social-democrats with Free-democrats, Social-democrats with left Greens, and the so-called "grand coalition" of Christian-democrats and Social-democrats. All these governmental formulas have had majority support in terms of both popular votes and parliamentary seats. Due to the long-term participation of a few parties in government and other institutional mechanisms, the degree of stability in major public policies in Germany is very high.

Multiparty coalition cabinets in parliamentary regimes tend to induce a more balanced relationship between institutions. As political parties need to bargain and reach agreements in order to make policy decisions and pass bills, they learn to share power and develop negotiation skills. Members of different groups in parliament need to exchange initiatives and give each other mutual support in order to build a legislative majority. Cabinet members from different parties need to cooperate as well. The prime minister cannot prevail over the cabinet or the assembly as much as when leading a single-party government because, even if he or she is a member of one of the parties involved, he or she has to negotiate with the other parties and keep the coalition united. In a parliamentary regime the institutional role of the parliament thrives when no party has an absolute majority of seats.

Quick Quiz

• What does "fusion of powers" mean?

CASE 15.1 CEREMONIAL CHIEF OF STATE

In the framework of a parliamentary regime in which the two main institutions are the parliament and the prime minister, the chief of state becomes a secondary figure. In most parliamentary regimes, especially in Europe and in a number of former British colonies, the chief of state, whether a monarch or a republican president, formally keeps some functions previously in the hands of traditional monarchs. In particular, he or she may appoint the candidate to prime minister, dissolve the parliament, and ratify legislation with his or her signature. However, this is just a legal or customary remnant of an obsolete institutional formula. In fact, these functions are exerted in accordance with electoral results and a parliamentary political majority, and thus they only help the regular institutional process to run on. As is often said, in a parliamentary regime, the monarch (or the president) reigns, but does not rule.

In order to be able to play an arbitral or intermediary role among the other institutions, the chief of state in a parliamentary regime must be neutral among political parties. To choose a dynasty for a long period implies a great, though infrequent, risk of choosing the wrong family. In contrast, periodical elections or negotiations among political parties to build a broad consensual majority in favor of a president of the republic imply less risk although more frequent decisions. Among the twenty-seven member states of the European Union, seven have parliamentary monarchs (including, Britain, Holland, Spain, and Sweden), while in thirteen republics the president is directly elected (as in Austria, France, Ireland, and Poland), and in seven, he or she is appointed by parliament (as in Germany, Hungary, and Italy). Among the members of the British Commonwealth, some keep the queen of England as their monarch (including Australia, Canada, and New Zealand), while others are republics (including India, Namibia, and South Africa).

Presidential Regime

In a presidential regime, the chief of state is also the chief of government, able to appoint the cabinet, just as traditional monarchs do. But in contrast to monarchs, the new president depends on a popular election. Thus there are **separate elections for the presidency and the assembly** (or congress), which can produce different political party configurations.

The situation in which **the president's party has a majority of seats in the assembly is called "unified government."** It tends to occur when a single party is strongly dominant or when the elections for the two institutions concur in time and the presidential campaign wins and pulls voters toward voting for the same party for all the institutions. In a situation of unified government, the president tends to be the arch-dominant figure, in analogy to the role of the prime minister with a single-party government majority in parliament, which we discussed in the previous section. In the United States, in particular, certain "imperial" presidents with concentrated powers have been accused of expanding their authority, especially in foreign policy to capture the decision to go to war, and in domestic affairs. Again, under single-party dominance, the one-person institution tends to prevail.

In contrast, when presidential and assembly elections produce different winners and **the president's party does not have a majority of seats in the assembly, it is said that there is "divided government."** This tends to be a relatively frequent situation in regimes with division of powers. It may bring about a stalemate and interinstitutional conflict, but it can also induce different actors and different political parties to look for bridges and possible agreements on some issues on which they may have to make joint decisions, as we will analyze in the next chapter.

CHECKS AND BALANCES

In the original United States version, the "presidential" regime includes a complex system of **"checks and balances," or mutual controls between the Presidency, the House of Representatives, the Senate, and the Supreme Court.**

Mutual Controls. Both the Congress and the President control each other to some extent. On the one hand, the U.S. Congress can impose some limits on the President's powers and decisions:

- While the members of Congress can be reelected indefinitely (the actual average for both representatives and senators is nearly ten years), the President can be elected for only two terms (with a total of eight years, as established since the mid-twentieth century).

- The Senate must ratify and can reject certain presidential appointments for executive positions, including several members of the cabinet, and international treaties.

- The Congress appoints a number of officers and controls administrative agencies (including, for instance, the U.S. Agency for International Development, or USAID, and the National Aeronautics and Space Administration, or NASA).

On the other hand, the President can limit Congress's powers, especially by means of:

- The presidential veto over congressional legislation (somehow adapted from a traditional monarch's power in past times).

Finally:

- The Supreme Court submits legislation to judicial revision.

Counter-balancing mechanisms between institutions with different political orientations, such as those just mentioned, play in favor of power sharing and as equivalent devices to super-majority rules for decision making. For different bodies, such as the Presidency, the House, and the Senate, in which different political parties may prevail, to be able to make a joint decision they have to aggregate the different political majorities in each institution into a single, broader majority. The political support necessary for making certain decisions in a system of division of powers lies beyond the requirement of a simple majority in each institution. The effort of aggregating different preferences is similar to that which would be required in a single institution making decisions by some qualified majority rule.

Policy Deadlock. Joint decisions by separate institutions whose members represent different interests or preferences can hardly be innovative. Some authors have remarked that the obstacles introduced by numerous institutional checks may stabilize socially inefficient status quo policies. Separate elections and divided governments can create a "dual legitimacy" prone to **"deadlock,"** also called "stalemate" or "gridlock," that is, **legislative paralysis and interinstitutional conflict.**

With similar analytical insight but a different evaluation, others observe that those institutional mechanisms also guarantee that the most important decisions are made by broad majorities able to prevent the imposition of the will of a small or minority group. As U.S. Constitution co-author Alexander Hamilton argued, "It may perhaps be said that the power of preventing bad laws includes that of preventing good ones; and may be used to the one purpose as well as to the other. But this objection will have little weight with those who can properly estimate the mischiefs of that inconstancy and mutability in the laws…because it is favorable to greater stability in the system of legislation."

PRESIDENTIALISM

A variant of a political regime with separate elections for the presidency and the assembly, which is usually called "presidentialism," has emerged in almost all republics in Latin American since the mid- or late nineteenth century, and in a few countries in Africa since the mid-twentieth century. New independence leaders in those countries tried to create strong government as a substitute for weak states, in the sense that they lacked control of the territory, were unable to extract taxes, and lived in the midst of persistent violence and frequent interstate border conflicts. But they mistakenly sought to strengthen the government by concentrating powers in the hands of a single individual, the president. A number of constitution makers, especially in nineteenth-century Latin American countries such as Argentina, Brazil, Mexico, and Venezuela, claimed to be imitating the U.S. Constitution. But, in contrast to the preventions against one person's expedient decisions introduced in the United States, which we mentioned in the previous section, some of them looked farther back to the absolutist monarchies preceding any division of powers and mixed regimes and aimed at having "elected kings with the name of presidents," in Simón Bolívar's words.

Presidential dominance in regimes of formal division of powers has been attempted through the president's veto power over legislation and his control of the army, both of which exist in the United States, supplemented with long presidential terms and reelections, unconstrained powers to appoint and remove members of the cabinet and other highly placed officers, legislative initiative, the capacity to dictate legislative decrees, fiscal and administrative authority, discretionary emergency powers, suspension of constitutional guarantees, and, in formally federal countries, the right to intervene in state affairs. The other side of this same coin is weak congresses, which are frequently constrained by short session periods and lack of resources, and are not usually given control over the cabinet. In contrast to expectations, presidentialist concentration of power tends to create a small, weak, and contentious government, which also further weakens the state.

In recent processes of democratization or redemocratization in Latin America, some of these features have been softened. A presidential single-party majority in congress has become an infrequent occurrence. Accordingly, most presidential cabinets in the region nowadays are multiparty coalitions, which may favor interinstitutional cooperation and consensual decisions. But some recent institutional reforms have tended to provide the president with decree powers or with the ability to initiate urgency bills, which may induce him to try to rule on his own and overpass an adverse congress, with extended reelections. As a case of increasing concentration of power in the presidency, Hugo Chávez's Venezuela stands out: the president initially elected in 1999 introduced a series of constitutional reforms extending the presidential term length and permitting indefinite reelection, while the assembly was reduced to one chamber and its members were limited to reelection for two terms.

SEMI-PRESIDENTIALISM

Another variant of division of powers, usually called a "semi-presidential" regime, was experimented with in Finland and Germany after World War I and more consistently shaped in France since the mid-twentieth century. Institutional formulas of this sort also exist in a few countries in Eastern Europe, including Lithuania, Poland, Romania, and Russia, and in a few countries in Africa, sometimes in transition from dictatorships to parliamentary regimes.

With the semi-presidential formula, the presidency and the assembly are elected separately, as in a checks-and-balances regime. But it is the assembly that appoints and can dismiss a prime minister, as in a parliamentary regime. At the same time, the president has some reserved executive powers and can dissolve the assembly, in spite of having been elected separately. In this type of regime, the multiple-person office is, of course, the assembly. But two one-person offices, **the president and the prime minister, share executive powers** in "governmental diarchy," in the words of Maurice Duverger.

Table 15.2 summarizes these relationships. Please compare this table with Table 15.1 earlier in this chapter and consider whether we are dealing with an intermediate alternative between the two basic models previously analyzed.

The semi-presidential regime works very differently depending on whether the president's party has a majority in the assembly. If the president enjoys a compact party majority in the assembly, he or she can concentrate many powers. The prime minister becomes a secondary figure under the president's control. The French president in a situation of unified government can become even more powerful than in classic presidential regimes such as in the United States, because he has the additional power of dissolving the assembly. He is also more powerful than British-style prime ministers because, in practice, he accumulates the latter's powers plus those of the monarch.

TABLE 15.2 Semi-presidential Regime

Voters elect separately the assembly, which indirectly elects the prime minister, who appoints the cabinet, and the president with some executive powers.

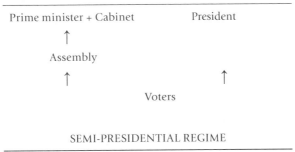

BOX 15.2　　　　CONCENTRATION OF POWER

ONE PERSON'S POWERS:	CHIEF OF STATE	CHIEF EXECUTIVE	MAJORITY PARTY LEADER	EXAMPLES
1. Presidential or semi-presidential, unified	x	x	x	United States, B. Obama, 2009– France, N. Sarkozy, 2007–12
2. Parliamentary, single-party	–	x	x	United Kingdom, A. Blair 1997–07 Australia, K. Rudd, 2007–10
3. Presidential, divided	x	x	–	United States, W. Clinton, 1995–01 Brazil, L. I. da Silva, 2003–11
4. Semi-presidential, divided	x	dual	–	France, J. Chirac, 1995–2001
5. Parliamentary, multiparty	–	coalition	–	Germany, A. Merkel, 2005–09 Netherlands, J. P. Balkenende, 2006–10

Different political regimes can be classified according to higher to lower degrees of concentration of power. An estimate of the degree of concentration of power is whether a single person can accumulate three crucial positions:

- chief of state,
- chief of government, and
- leader of the majority party in the assembly.

Look at the following classification and ensure that it is consistent with what you have understood from the previous discussion. Note that types 2 and 5 correspond to the classical category of "parliamentary" regime, here drastically split for different party systems, while types 1, 3, and 4 are variants of the classical category of "presidential" regime as discussed before.

In contrast, if the development of multipartism forces the president to face a prime minister, a cabinet, and an assembly majority with a different political orientation, power sharing is more effective. The French call this situation **"cohabitation."** The president usually retains significant powers, including some executive appointments, and partial vetoes over legislation, depending on the specific rules in each country. This makes the president certainly more powerful than any ceremonial monarch or republican president in parliamentary regimes and confirms the expected executive dualism.

Quick Quiz

• What is a "deadlock?"

Conclusion

Let us try to summarize the main findings in this chapter. Different institutional regimes framing different ways of decision-making are shaped by formal relations between one-person and multi-person offices, and by different political party systems. On the one side, an extreme form of fusion of institutional powers is the concentration

BOX 15.3 ⬭ **POLITICAL REGIMES, 1870–2009**

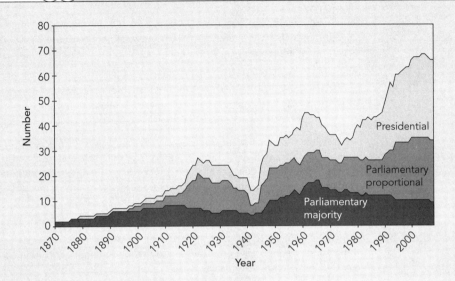

FIGURE 15.2 TYPES OF DEMOCRATIC REGIME

The British model of parliamentary regime with a majority rule electoral formula favoring single-party governments was appealing during the first wave of democratization. However, after the Second World War, most experiences in new democracies with this model favoring the concentration of power into a single group failed, especially in former British colonies in Africa and Asia with plural ethnic composition.

In contrast, parliamentary regimes with proportional representation formulas favoring multiparty coalition governments have consolidated since the mid-twentieth century, especially in Europe. Presidential and semi-presidential formulas have also surged. In spite of some controversy, direct presidential elections were reestablished in Latin America during the processes of redemocratization in the late twentieth century and have also been adopted by some newcomers to democracy in Eastern Europe, Africa, and Asia. By the early twenty-first century, of all democratic regimes in countries with more than one million inhabitants, only one sixth are parliamentary regimes with majority electoral rules, while one third are parliamentary regimes with proportional representation, and one half are presidential or semi-presidential regimes.

Sources: Author's own elaboration for sixty-four democratic countries with more than one million inhabitants, with update of data in Josep M. Colomer, *Political Institutions* (Oxford University Press, 2001).

of power in a single-party government. On the other, division of powers truly exists if several parties have to share collective decisions.

On the basis of the previous discussion we can state the following *proposition* in political science:

 • **Institutional "deadlock."** Single-party government promotes high concentration of power, which may foster effectiveness in decision making. In contrast, separate elections and division of powers may produce divided government, "deadlock," and policy stability.

SOURCE 15.1   The Presidentialist Temptation

Reinforcing the power of the president has been a permanent temptation for constitution makers in search of effectiveness, although it has usually created arbitrariness and conflict.

The accumulation of all powers, legislative, executive, and judiciary, in the same hands, whether of one, a few, or many, and whether hereditary, self-appointed, or elective, may justly be pronounced the very definition of tyranny.

James Madison, president of the United States, *Federalist Papers* (1787)

That unity is conducive to energy will not be disputed. Decision, activity, secrecy, and dispatch will generally characterize the proceedings of one man in a much more eminent degree than the proceedings of any greater number, and in proportion as the number is increased, these qualities will be diminished.

Alexander Hamilton, *Federalist Papers* (1787)

In the republics, the executive must be the strongest figure...If all means are not made available to the executive, it falls inevitably into nullity, anarchy, usurpation and tyranny...The president of the republic is in our constitution like the sun that, firm in the center, gives life to the universe.

Simón Bolívar, "Address to the Congress of Venezuela in Angostura" (1819)

The separation of powers, instead of providing for a stable equilibrium, almost everywhere...produced the exaggerated form of presidentialism, known in the local coloration of Latin America as *caudillismo*.

Karl Loewenstein, "The Presidency Outside the United States" (1949)

The chief executive in Latin American politics has often been a presidential dictator or "democratic caesar"...the more unrestricted and uncontrolled is political power, the greater is the tendency toward violation of moral and legal principles.

William S. Stokes, *Latin American Politics* (1959)

The indivisible authority of the state is entirely given to the President by the people who elected him. There exists no other authority, neither ministerial, nor civil, nor military, nor judicial that is not conferred or maintained by him.

Charles de Gaulle, president of France (1964)

Summary

Different political regimes can be defined by formal relations between institutions and the political party system.

In a parliamentary regime, the prime minister and the parliament are mutually dependent. The parliament elects the prime minister and can depose him by means of a motion of censure or "confidence," while the prime minister can dissolve parliament.

Mutual threats of destruction between the prime minister and parliament induce cooperation. Decisions are made on the basis of the same political party majority producing fusion of powers.

With a single-party parliamentary government there is high concentration of power. The prime minister prevails over the cabinet and the parliament. With multiparty coalition cabinets there is a more balanced relationship between institutions.

In a presidential regime, there are separate elections for president and for the assembly, and divided powers between the two institutions.

If the president's party has a majority of seats in the assembly, there is "unified government;" otherwise there is "divided government."

In the U.S. version of separation of powers, there is a system of checks and balances between institutions. Mutual controls among institutions can produce deadlock, that is, legislative paralysis and interinstitutional conflict, but it can also prevent minority government.

Presidential dominance can be promoted for the sake of effectiveness, but it tends to produce interinstitutional conflict and arbitrariness in decision making.

In a semi-presidential regime, the presidency and the assembly are elected separately, the assembly appoints and can dismiss a prime minister, and the president can dissolve the assembly.

The highest concentration of power can be found in presidential regimes with unified government and in parliamentary regimes with a single-party government, while more diffusion of power is produced in situations of divided government and with multiparty coalition cabinets.

There is a trade-off between effectiveness in decision making, which is expected in situations with fusion of powers, and the prevention of arbitrary decisions and minority government by the prevalence of checks and balances among institutions.

Key Concepts

Checks and balances. Mutual controls among institutions, especially the president, the chambers of congress, and the judiciary.

Cohabitation. In a semi-presidential regime, the president and the prime minister belong to different parties.

Deadlock. Legislative paralysis and interinstitutional conflict.

Divided government. The president's party does not have a majority in the assembly.

Parliamentary regime. Mutual dependence between the prime minister and the parliament.

President. Chief of state, which in some regimes also implies chief executive.

Presidential regime. Separate elections and powers between the presidency and the assembly.

Presidentialism. Executive dominance and high concentration of powers in the president.

Prime minister. Chief executive, also called president of the council of ministers, president of government, chancellor.

Semi-presidential regime. Dual executive between the elected president and the prime minister accountable to the assembly.

Unified government. The president's party has a majority of seats in the assembly.

Questions for Review

1. How is the chief executive elected in a parliamentary regime and in a presidential regime?
2. What does "fusion of powers" mean?
3. Define "checks and balances."
4. What is the difference between "unified government" and "divided government?"
5. What is "deadlock?"
6. What is "cohabitation?"

Problems and Applications

1. Define the following political regimes:
   a. Parliamentary.
   b. Presidential.
2. Name, as examples, three countries for each type of political regime mentioned in question 1.
3. Discuss the consequences for policy making in:
   d. Single-party governments.
   e. Division of powers.
   f. Multiparty coalition governments.

Data sources

Inter-Parliamentary Union: www.ipu.org/parline-e/parlinesearch.asp
Constitution Finder, University of Richmond: www.confinder.richmond.edu

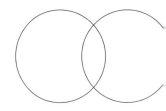

16

PARTY GOVERNMENT

In This Chapter You Will

- Study how governments are appointed.
- Learn what "minimum winning coalition" and "minimal connected winning coalition" mean.
- Consider the relation between the number of parties in the cabinet and its duration.
- Analyze the party conditions in which either the president or the congress can prevail.
- Discuss the degree to which institutional deadlock depends on the number of parties.

After the presidential and congressional elections in Chile in 2005, a situation of divided government was created. Michelle Bachelet was elected president, but her Socialist Party obtained only one eighth of seats in congress. Law making, however, was not that difficult, because the central party in the Chilean congress, the Christian-democratic Party, was an ally of the Socialists, and of two more center-left parties, in the "Coalition for Democracy" that regularly supported one single candidate in the presidential election—Bachelet, in this case. Although the four parties ran separately in the congressional election, their electoral coalition for the presidential race also became a legislative coalition facilitating interinstitutional cooperation and governability.

The circumstances were different after the presidential and congressional elections in Mexico in 2006. Felipe Calderón was elected president, and his National Action Party received only about 40 percent of seats in the congress. But in contrast to the situation in Chile just described, in order to form a legislative majority, the president had to deal with the former long-term ruling and rival Revolutionary Institutional Party (PRI). Adversarial politics prevailed, keeping major structural reforms and legislation paralyzed.

In this chapter we analyze how political parties can be the unifiers of separate institutions. First, we analyze how the "fusion" of powers between the parliament and the cabinet in a parliamentary regime, to which we referred in the previous chapter, is built by political parties. If no party has a majority of seats, multiple political parties can form a majority coalition in parliament and give successful support to the cabinet. Second, we discuss the conditions for interinstitutional cooperation in a regime with different elections for the congress and the presidency, as in the United States and in Latin American countries such as those just mentioned. ■

Single-Party and Multiparty Government

In almost all democratic countries in the world today, governments are formed by political parties. If institutions are the rules of the game, parties are the main players. An analogy can be drawn with competition in sports. Different sports, like different types of regimes, imply different rules of the game. Within a single regime, although all teams or individual players play within the same rules, they can use different strategies to win.

We began to discuss this topic in the previous chapter, where we remarked that, in parliamentary regimes, the "fusion" of powers between the government and the parliament takes place within a political party structure. But whether a parliamentary cabinet is formed of a single political party or multiple parties can make a significant difference for the government's policies and the citizens' subsequent wellbeing.

Specifically, if a party has an absolute majority of seats in parliament, then a single-party cabinet can be formed, as in Britain. Otherwise, the candidate for prime minister may either have to negotiate a multiparty majority to obtain support and be voted into parliament, as in Germany and the Netherlands, or form a minority cabinet, as frequently happens in some Scandinavian countries. Usually, the majority supporting the prime minister and forming the cabinet remains a legislative majority to approve bills and annual budgets, while in minority situations, the prime minister may have to negotiate legislative support on an issue-by-issue basis with different opposition parties.

Each of these options can change the government's agenda and policy decisions. In this section we pay attention to different institutional procedures for forming government in a parliamentary regime, and to different formulas for multiparty coalition government, and some of their consequences.

APPOINTING THE GOVERNMENT

A prime minister can also be called chancellor, president of the council of ministers, president of the government, or other titles, depending on the country. There are different procedures for appointing and dismissing such a figure in parliamentary regimes, which can influence the type of government that is formed.

In some countries, the leader of the party with the highest number of seats is appointed prime minister immediately after the election. In other cases, a formal **investiture of the prime minister by a majority of the members of parliament** is required. If the candidate's party is short of a majority of seats, he or she may have to negotiate with other parties for further parliamentary support or form a multiparty coalition government.

The parliament can also depose the prime minister and, in some cases, individual ministers or cabinet members. A number of members of parliament can present a motion of **censure or no-confidence to be voted on in the chamber**. If a parliament majority supports the motion, either a new majority is formed, able to appoint a new prime minister, or the parliament is dismissed and a new election is called. For example, Canadian liberal prime minister Paul Martin, Jr., was defeated in 2005 by a motion, presented by the conservative party, which obtained the support of the new democratic and Quebecois parties also in the opposition. Alternatively, the prime minister can present a motion of **confidence** to confirm parliamentary support, or challenge it with the threat of dissolution.

OFFICE AND POLICY

Consider the parliamentary election held in Poland in 2007, as presented in Table 16.1. The incumbent rightist party Law and Justice came in second in number of votes and seats. Its two former junior coalition partners in government, the League of Polish Families and Self-Defense of the Republic of Poland, failed to cross the 5 percent electoral threshold and thus lost all their seats and made the previous majority coalition no longer feasible. The center-right party called Civic Platform, until then in opposition, received the highest number of seats, but fell short of a majority. Three other parties obtained seats, the Left-Democrats, the agrarian Peasants' Party, and the small German Minority. After the election, Law and Justice leader Jarosław Kaczynski stepped down from office, and the Civic Platform leader, Donald Tusk, was appointed prime minister. The Civic Platform formed a new majority coalition government with the Peasants' Party, gathering total support from 240 of the 460 seats in parliament.

Confirm that the new prime minister's party was the largest party and the median party in parliament in Table 16.1. We will see that the new government coalition had the minimum size necessary to win a majority. The parties in the coalition were also ideologically connected on the left-right axis.

Politicians are frequently accused of seeking only the tenure of public office and the benefits and perks derived therefrom. The ambition of power is certainly an important motivation for entering and staying in politics. But as we have discussed in previous chapters regarding leadership and political parties, politicians also need to be committed to certain public policies and show some ideological consistency. For some people active in politics, the pursuit of some policy or value may be a personal driving force. But even for the most opportunistic, to deliver policy according to

TABLE 16.1 A Government Coalition

The example of Poland in 2007 shows the formation of a government coalition between two parties, the Civic Platform and the Peasants' Party, which is both minimum in size and ideologically connected along the left-right dimension.

Ideology:	Ethnic	Left	Center-left	Center	Right		
Parties:	German	Left-Democrats	Peasants'	Civic-Platform	Law & Just	Total	Majority
Seats:	1	53	31	209	166	460	231
Government coalition:			**Peasants' + Civic Platform**				

previous promises and citizens' expectations can be a condition for obtaining votes and gaining access to office in further elections.

Both the search for office and the search for policy or ideology goals are, therefore, realistic and legitimate motivations of political party leaders. At the time of forming government, the interest of members of parliament in enjoying as much **power** as possible translates into the aspiration to accumulate as many government **portfolios** or ministries as possible for their party. This becomes a criterion for forming a coalition of the minimum viable **size**. The explanation for this is that if a government is formed of a multiparty coalition without superfluous members, it can give each party a relatively high share of power to exert and enjoy. Coalition politics driven by only a criterion of size can "make strange bedfellows," in the words of a William Shakespeare character seeking common shelter with a monster.

In contrast, for those with a stronger interest in **policy**, a relevant criterion for choosing potential partners in government is their relative "closeness," or **"distance,"** in policy or ideology. "Close" parties, for example along the left-right axis, can be more amenable to establishing some common policy and compatible goals in a coalition government. Different types of governments derive from these motivations and criteria.

Minimum Winning Coalitions.   For political parties interested in power, the attainment of a high share of portfolios in the cabinet requires forming **as large a parliamentary coalition as necessary to win, but as small as possible to exclude superfluous partners**. This coalition is "minimal" in the sense that it does not include any party that is not necessary in order to win. A party will have a higher power share if it resists the inclusion of unnecessary parties in the coalition, as their presence would reduce its share of portfolios in the cabinet. In a minimum winning coalition, each of its party members is pivotal, in the sense that the loss of a party would render the coalition no longer a winning coalition.

Of course, in the particular case of party having an absolute majority of seats in parliament, the minimum winning "coalition" is the majority single-party government without additional partners. According to systematic analyses of government formation in parliamentary democratic regimes throughout the world, minimum winning coalitions are more likely to form than either surplus majority coalitions or minority cabinets.

An additional criterion can be the minimization of the number of parties in the coalition. If, for example, a party in a parliament can belong to two different minimum winning coalitions, one with two parties and another with three parties, the former may be preferred because it can lower the costs of negotiation and bargaining and diminish the probability that the coalition might split.

Minimal Connected Winning Coalitions.   For parties interested in policy, a criterion for selecting potential partners in a government coalition is the minimization of policy/ideology distance. Specifically, parties may try to form a coalition with "connected" parties, for example on the left-right dimension, that is, **with parties that are contiguous to their positions**, and thus devoid of unnecessary parties. For policy-seeking parties, it should be relatively easy to form and maintain a coalition with parties holding close policy positions on relevant issues, since closeness can facilitate

BOX 16.1 ⬤⬤ **FORMING A WINNING COALITION**

The formation of a majority multiparty coalition in parliament may follow different criteria, which are captured by different models. Let us examine the following example, as presented in the table. Four parties, W, X, Y, and Z, have 25, 30, 10, and 35 seats, respectively (100 in total); the required majority to appoint a prime minister is 51; alphabetical order defines a policy-ideology dimension.

The first column on the left lists all possible winning coalitions gathering at least 51 seats. Note that a majority coalition can be formed by either two, three, or four parties (the so-called "total" coalition). The second column lists the minimum winning coalitions, that is, only those not including any superfluous member. Finally, the third column lists the minimal connected winning coalitions, that is, those formed of parties with contiguous positions on the alphabetical axis and devoid of any superfluous partner. Please note that the set of minimally connected winning coali-

tions is not a subset of the minimum winning coalitions (neither is it the opposite).

Ideology:	Left	Center-left	Center-right	Right
Parties:	W	X	Y	Z
Seats:	25	30	10	35
Total seats:	100			
Majority:	51			

WINNING COALITIONS	SEATS	MINIMUM WINNING COALITIONS	MINIMALLY CONNECTED COALITIONS
W-X	55	W-X	W-X
W-X-Y	65		
W-X-Y-Z	100		
W-X-Z	90		
W-Y-Z	70		
W-Z	60	W-Z	
X-Y-Z	75		X-Y-Z
X-Z	65	X-Z	

the negotiation of a government program and diminish internal policy conflicts within the coalition. For instance, social-democratic, leftist, and green parties are more likely to form coalitions with each other than with liberal, christian-democratic, or conservative parties, which in turn can be prone to unite in some governmental coalition. However, some center, agrarian, ethnic, liberal, or democratic parties may be located in a central place able to form coalitions, at different moments, with either the parties on their left or those on their right.

A minimal connected winning coalition with more than two parties may include some superfluous partners in terms of size if they are located on intermediate ideological positions and are thus necessary to maintain the ideological connection between its members. But also in a minimal connected winning coalition, each party is pivotal because the loss of a party would render the coalition either no longer winning or no longer connected.

On a single-dimension policy space such as the left-right axis, the median party will always be included in a connected winning coalition. Remember that the median is the position having less than half the positions on each side and is thus necessary for forming a consistent majority along the issue space. Empirical analyses show that government coalitions containing the median party in parliament are more likely to form.

Please note that we are distinguishing between:

- Party members' **motivation**, which can basically be summed up as power and policy;

- **criteria** to form coalitions, which are size and distance, corresponding respectively to the two motivations just mentioned; and
- coalition **models**, which include minimum winning as well as minimal connected winning coalitions, according to the motivations and criteria just presented.

Thus:

MOTIVATION		CRITERION		COALITION MODEL
Power	→	Size	→	Minimum winning
Policy	→	Distance	→	Minimal connected winning

POWER DISTRIBUTION

When different winning coalitions can be formed in a parliament, the party composition of the government may depend on the bargaining power of each party and the presence, or not, of a dominant party. Different parties also have different policy preferences for different portfolios in charge of different issues. All this can explain which parties enter government and which portfolios or ministries each party receives. We have several tools for analyzing these points.

Measuring Bargaining Power.   At forming a coalition, different political parties may have bargaining power that does not correspond to their numbers of seats. A relatively minor party that is "pivotal" for forming a majority, that is, a party able to contribute with the necessary number of seats to make a coalition winning, may have relatively high power to negotiate cabinet membership or policy decisions. In contrast, a relatively large party whose contribution can be easily replaced with that of a smaller party may have relatively low bargaining power. An example of disproportionate bargaining power of small parties frequently occurs in the Knesset, the multiparty parliament of Israel, where a few small religious parties may be necessary for forming a majority coalition. The two larger parties can avoid giving them much power only by forming a National Unity coalition.

A party's bargaining power in parliament can be measured by the proportion of potential winning coalitions in which that party is pivotal. There are several "power indices" available for measuring a party's bargaining power. They differ slightly in their assumptions regarding actors' criteria, coalition models, and decision rules, but most of them produce similar results.

To illustrate how bargaining power can be measured, let us take the very simple example of a parliament formed by three parties in which none of them has an absolute majority of seats. In order to form a majority coalition, two parties are necessary and sufficient. Let us assume that any pair of parties is equally valid for forming such a majority.

There can be the following distribution of seats: X: 40, Y: 40, Z: 20. In order to form a majority of more than fifty seats, three coalitions are possible: X-Y (with 80 seats), X-Z (60 seats), and Y-Z (60 seats). Note that the minor party, Z, is pivotal in two of these potential winning coalitions, as is each of the two larger parties, and thus as powerful as either of them. The power of each party can be expressed as the number of its pivotal positions out of the total number of pivotal positions in all viable coalitions, so that the power index (usually symbolized with a Greek letter) of party X equals 2 out of 6 pivotal positions, $\Phi(X) = 2/6$, as $\Phi(Y) = 2/6$, and $\Phi(Z) = 2/6$. In other words, the three parties have equal bargaining power in spite of the big differences in their numbers of seats. One of the possible readings of this result is that the three parties have, a priori, equal probability of being members of a coalition government.

The Dominant Party.   In certain configurations, the largest party in parliament, even if it does not have a majority of seats, can be dominant to the extent that it is **able to block any coalition cabinet** and take all portfolios. In other words, a party is dominant if it can form a winning coalition with some partners but the other parties cannot form a winning coalition without that party.

Consider the example of the Swedish Social-democratic Party, which has formed single-party minority governments most of the time since the 1930s. Table 16.2 presents the 2002 election, which was the latest in a long series of elections producing similar situations. The largest party, the Social-democrats, led by incumbent prime minister, Göran Persson, obtained 144 seats out of the 349 in parliament (about 41 percent of seats, short of a majority). The parties on its right, the Center, Liberal, Christian, and Moderate parties, did not gather a majority of seats, and neither did the parties on its left, the Green and Left parties. As the four parties on the right were incompatible with the two parties on the left, which were located at excessive policy and ideological distances, no winning coalition could be formed without the Social-democratic Party, which was thus "dominant." After the election, the Social-democrats, helped by the absence of investiture requirement, rebuffed the Left and Green parties' proposals to enter a government coalition and formed, as in numerous previous occasions, a single-party minority cabinet. The Social-democratic Party governed alone with varied legislative support, especially from the left parties on domestic policy and from parties on its right on foreign affairs.

In the case just discussed, the nondominant parties were unable to form a majority coalition due to their ideological distance. In this case, the dominant party can block any coalition and form a minority cabinet. **Minority cabinets of a dominant**

TABLE 16.2 A Viable Minority

This example presents the Social-democratic party of Sweden in 2002 as the largest and dominant party, which, in spite of not having a majority of seats, can block any coalition and form a single-party minority government.

Ideology:	Left		Center-left			Center-Right		Right			
Parties:	Left	Green	**Social-Democratic**	Center	Liberal	Christian	Moderate	Total	Majority
Seats:	30	17	144 Dominant party	22	48	33	55	349	175

party are viable and are more likely to form the greater the policy-ideology divisions and the smaller the size of the parties in the opposition.

Portfolio Allocation.   The discussions just presented deal mainly with the question of which parties are more likely to enter a coalition cabinet. Within the cabinet, however, a further question is the allocation of ministries to the parties. It has been widely observed that the distribution of cabinet portfolios among coalition parties tends to be proportional to the number of seats controlled by each party, that is, with its contribution to making a coalition winning.

However, different parties have preferences for different portfolios depending on the policy issues they emphasize the most, which may produce varied allocations. The prime minister's party usually controls most of the portfolios in charge of major policy domains, especially economy, defense, and interior. Other cabinet portfolios can be allocated to parties with a strong profile on certain issues on which they tend to campaign and attract citizens' votes, such as social policy for laborites or socialists, education for christian-democrats, finance for liberals, and agriculture for agrarians.

Consider the case of Germany, where all cabinets since World War II have been multiparty coalitions. The Christian-democrats (together with the Bavarian Social-Christians) and the Social-democrats, in that order, have held the highest proportions of governmental portfolios because they have been the two largest parties in votes and seats and the only ones leading governments. But the minor Free-democratic Party has held a higher proportion of governmental portfolios than its proportion of parliamentary seats, due to the fact that it has been able to form coalitions with both the Christian-democrats and the Social-democrats at different periods.

Different coalition agreements have been built largely upon parties' preferences for different portfolios. While the Christian-democrats need to make some concessions in policy making to allocate certain portfolios to the Free-democrats, especially the ministry of Foreign Affairs, the Free-democrats fit well with the Christian-democrats when the latter hold the ministry of Economy in a free-market orientation. In contrast, while the Social-democrats may be relatively close to liberal positions on foreign and other policies of the Free-democrats, the latter have found themselves too distant from the former's more interventionist economic policy. Over time, the Free-democrats have therefore tended to choose the Christians as priority partners. In response, the Social-democrats moved to choose the Greens as a new governmental partner to lead a coalition government.

CABINET DURATION

Regular parliamentary elections are usually scheduled at intervals of three, four, or five years, depending on the country. But a significant number of parliamentary cabinets do not last as long as they legally could. There are anticipated dissolutions of parliament and elections, which, as we have mentioned, can usually be called by the prime minister, as there are resignations by prime ministers, successful motions of censure, and defeated motions of confidence. Several factors can explain the diverse duration of parliamentary cabinets.

CASE 16.1   THE IMPORTANCE OF BEING NOT TOO MANY

Political parties in parliament may prefer not to share power with too many partners and form a "minimum winning" government in order to enjoy a higher share of portfolios and not have to perform too much. In one of his novels, Benjamin Disraeli, a conservative prime minister of Britain in the nineteenth century, attributed the following reflections to a fictional politician involved in recruiting parliamentary support and forming government, which are obviously based on his own experience.

"We are too strong," prophetically exclaimed one of the fortunate cabinet, which found itself supported by an inconceivable majority of three hundred [members of parliament]…It is evident that the suicidal career of what was then styled the Liberal Party had been occasioned and stimulated by its unnatural excess of strength…It was not feasible to gratify so many ambitions, or to satisfy so many expectations…No government can be long secure without a formidable opposition. It reduces their supporters to that tractable number which can be managed by the joint influences of fruition and of hope. It offers vengeance to the discontented and distinction to the ambitious; and employs the energies of aspiring spirits, who otherwise may prove traitors in a division or assassins in a debate.

Benjamin Disraeli, *Coningsby, or The New Generation* (1844)

Cabinet Durability.   The rules for appointing and dismissing a parliamentary cabinet and the party structure of coalitions can significantly influence a cabinet's durability. If the formal investiture of the prime minister is required, which brings about explicit support, the cabinet can be relatively enduring. In contrast, the absence of formal investiture and the possibility of a motion of censure, which may make the cabinet

The United Kingdom has been an egregious example of single-party parliamentary government, led by its powerful prime minister.

vulnerable to a parliamentary majority in opposition or lead to an anticipated election, tend to shorten the duration of cabinets.

Regarding the party composition of cabinets, it is well established that **single-party majority cabinets tend to last longer** than multiparty coalition or minority cabinets. For coalition cabinets, the higher the number of parties and the broader the ideological distance between them, the less durable the cabinets are and the more vulnerable they are to splits and departures.

Critical Events.   Under favorable institutional and political conditions, such as those just mentioned, unanticipated events able to modify public opinion about the government record can trigger cabinet crises and falls. Public opinion shifts can be produced by policy shocks, that is, bad performance of certain government policies, which may force parties to take new positions on some issues, and by agenda shocks, implying new gains or losses in the salience of certain issues in voters' concerns. Diverse unexpected events can produce these shocks, including technological innovations, migrations and other population changes, economic recession, foreign conflicts, and personal scandals. These changes can alter parties' electoral expectations. Party leaders and members will choose to remain in a coalition government depending on how they expect its performance will influence voters' behavior at the next election. The peril of losing votes may be critical for a political party to altering its strategy regarding government membership.

Under these kinds of pressures, several responses are possible. In single-party governments, conspiracies among party members to replace the incumbent prime minister are relatively likely, especially if party members expect to have better electoral prospects with a new candidate. In contrast, in multiparty coalition governments, internal party cohesion tends to increase, while coalition partners are more willing to work against the incumbent formula. This kind of event is relatively frequent in parliamentary regimes. Among fifteen countries in Western Europe since the Second World War, about one sixth of parliamentary governments have not concluded their term due to a change of prime minister or the party composition of the government coalition, or the dissolution of parliament and the call for an early election.

Quick Quiz

- Define a minimum winning coalition.
- Define a minimal connected winning coalition.

Unified and Divided Government

Whether separate institutions such as the presidency and the assembly cooperate or enter into relations of mutual hostility and conflict can make a significant difference for policy making and the citizens' subsequent wellbeing. In most countries in the Americas, the presidency and the assembly, usually called congress, are elected separately, as we studied in the previous chapter. But political parties can build bridges between institutions and facilitate joint decisions. **Political parties can be the unifiers of the separate powers.**

Specifically, if the president's party has an absolute majority of seats in congress, that is, if there is "unified government," the two institutions usually work together, under the direction of the president. In contrast, with different political party majorities in support of the president and in the congress, that is, with "divided government," interinstitutional cooperation is not guaranteed. Certain procedural rules and political party configurations can create different opportunities and incentives for either cooperation or conflict. We review this problem in the following paragraphs.

DIVIDED ELECTIONS

Let us start with the fact that separate presidential and congressional elections can produce different winners. This is due to different factors related to the conditions in which elections are held, basically: division of powers, separate electoral campaigns, and electoral rules.

Divided Powers.   First of all, people may prefer different parties for different policy domains. Indeed, separate elections are likely to focus on different issues. Usually presidential electoral campaigns pay more attention to broad interest public goods and foreign and security policy, while assembly or congressional elections tend to deal with domestic policies and local issues. Different parties' candidates can be appropriate for the different issues at stake.

Note that the higher the number of separate offices—including, for instance, the presidency, two chambers in the assembly, and regional and local assemblies and governors and mayors—the fewer the issues corresponding to each of them. The fewer the number of relevant issues in each electoral campaign, the more simplified the election, and thus the more predictable and stable the outcome will be. In contrast, in a single election dealing with multiple issues at the same time, the outcomes can be unforeseeable, as we will discuss in chapter 16.

As an alternative motivation, certain voters may prefer to have power divided between different parties rather than a high concentration in a single party. In some cases, this can be due to a preference for small government and broad private freedom. But certain moderate or "centrist" voters interested in a more active government can also expect power sharing between different parties to produce intermediate compromise and moderate policy decisions relatively close to their preferences, and thus they can vote for divided government on purpose.

Separate Elections.   Elections for different institutions can be held at different times. Typically, the president and the congress have different mandate lengths, of between four and six years for the former and two and four years for the latter. They also have fixed terms, as mentioned, so that the electoral calendar is established a priori and cannot be changed. Thus, depending on the respective calendars, some elections can be concurrent in time for both institutions and some may be separate. If they are concurrent, it is more likely that a single party will attract unified votes for all the party's candidacies. In contrast, in nonconcurrent elections, it is easier for voters to identify specific issues for each institution and distinguish the advantages of different parties for different issues, and vote against the incumbent party in order to facilitate divided government, if this is what they want.

Different Electoral Rules. Finally, presidents and assemblies are chosen by different electoral systems. Any president, as any other one-person office, must be elected by some rule based on the majority principle. In contrast, the assembly or congress can be elected by either some majority rule, but always in multiple districts, which may not fit the presidential election, or by proportional representation, as is the case in most countries with division of powers. Diverse electoral rules can produce different winners, even in concurrent elections with similar distributions of votes, as we studied in chapters 13 and 14.

Considering all together—different issues for different offices, separate elections, different electoral rules—we can understand that elections for separate institutions are likely to produce different winners, that is, a different political party configuration in each institution.

LEGISLATIVE PROCESS

After the president and the congress are elected separately and with different electoral rules, they have to cooperate to advance legislation. The typical legislative procedure in a regime of division of powers includes the following steps:

1. The congress can approve a bill by simple majority. We can presume that the median legislator or the median party, that is, the one that, thanks to its central position, is necessary for forming a consistent majority, as we have discussed in previous chapters, is likely to be at an advantage and manage to attract a majority in favor of its proposal.

2. The president may either approve or veto the bill.

3. In the latter case, the congress can override the presidential veto by some defined rule, usually some qualified majority, for instance two thirds. If the presidential veto is overridden by the congress, the bill is approved. In contrast, if the president does veto the congressional bill and opposition legislators do not have sufficient votes to override the veto, the bill is cancelled and the previous status quo or existing policy remains.

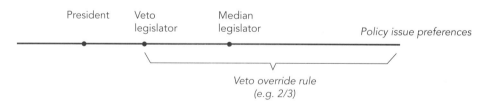

FIGURE 16.1 PIVOTAL ACTORS FOR LEGISLATION
In a regime with separation of powers, the decisive actors in the legislative process are the median legislator in congress able to approve a bill, the president able to veto the congressional bill, and the veto legislator able to either confirm or override the presidential veto.

16.2.A <u>Presidential government</u>

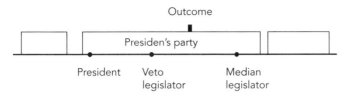

16.2.B <u>Divided government</u>

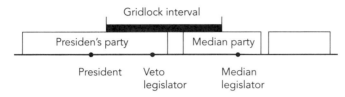

16.2.C <u>Congressional government</u>

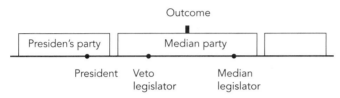

FIGURE 16.2 INTERINSTITUTIONAL RELATIONS
In the legislative process with division of powers, there can be presidential dominance, strongly divided government, or congressional dominance, depending on the political party system.

These rules create three "pivotal" actors on whom legislative decisions depend. They are:

1. The **median legislator** or the median congressional party, which, due to its intermediate position with less than half of legislators on each side, is likely to gather a legislative majority around it;
2. The **president**, with powers to ratify and veto bills; and
3. The **veto legislator** or the veto party, which, by tipping on the side of either the presidential veto or the congressional majority, can either confirm the veto or make the congress successfully override it.

Let us consider for a moment the figure of the veto legislator. If the preferences of the members of congress on the issue in question can be ordered along a single dimension, the veto legislator should have a number of members of congress on the president's side equal to one minus the override rule, that is to say, under the two-thirds override rule, the veto legislator is the one with one third of legislators on the president's side. His or her vote will be decisive in giving the congress sufficient support to override the president's veto.

Note that the assumption of a single policy dimension is used for each legislative decision. As we discussed in chapter 10, in general elections, a single ideological dimension, such as the left-right axis, may try to synthesize multiple issues with disperse voters' preferences over a multidimensional space. However, the present model refers to legislative decisions on one issue at a time, which facilitates simplicity of legislators' preferences. For clarification, see Figure 16.1 (which is a simplification of the model initially proposed by political scientist Kenneth Krehbiel).

PRESIDENTIAL AND CONGRESSIONAL DOMINANCE

With the notions just provided, we can analyze more precisely the conditions and consequences of situations of "unified" government and "divided" government. Three basic configurations can be distinguished: presidential dominance, strongly divided government, and congressional dominance. As we have mentioned previously, these different interinstitutional relations depend partly on the configuration of the political party system. To start with, have a look at Figure 16.2.

Presidential Dominance. Single-party dominance in the federal government has existed in the United States during several periods, and it reached a peak in the 1930s and early '40s, during the presidency of Democrat Franklin D. Roosevelt. It is also a common feature in a number of states in the union, especially in the South, thus facilitating the prevalence of the governor over the state legislature. This type of situation had become relatively less frequent in recent times, but it was reproduced with the election of Democratic president Barack Obama in 2008.

In a number of Latin American countries, there were also dominant presidential parties able to maintain some degree of stability, together with a high concentration of power in the president. These included the National Revolutionaries in Bolivia and in Mexico, the Liberals in Colombia, the Social-democrats (PLN) in Costa Rica, and the Colorados in Uruguay for some periods.

In this type of situation, the president's party may include both the veto and the median legislators, that is, a single party may include all pivotal actors in the process, as illustrated in Figure 16.2.A. This certainly happens when the president's party has an absolute majority of seats in congress and sufficient internal discipline to vote in bloc on major issues, which is the situation usually referred to as **"unified government."**

But it can also be the case that the president's party is sufficiently large and appropriately located around the "center" of the policy space to include all the pivotal actors, even if it does not control an absolute majority of seats, in which case a "quasi-unified" government may have about the same implications, that is, single-party control of legislation. The latter situation is in some manner similar to that of a dominant party able to form a minority government in a parliamentary regime, which we have just discussed. With a **dominant presidential party** there can be interinstitutional cooperation, although it will be under the dominance of the president, the one-person institution that typically takes advantage of this type of situation.

In the United States Congress, it frequently happens that the President's party has not a majority of seats, thus creating "divided government."

Divided Government. In the United States, different party majorities in support of the president and in the Congress have resulted in over 40 percent of the elections since 1832 and in most elections since 1945 (in 18 of 32). Also, about 60 percent of states in the U.S. had different parties in the governorship and in the majority of the legislature by the early twenty-first century. Similarly, the president's party

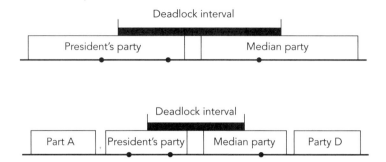

FIGURE 16.3 LEGISLATIVE DEADLOCK AND PARTY SYSTEMS
The deadlock interval or set of stable policies is larger with two parties than with multiple parties.

has not had a majority in the Congress in two thirds of elections in nineteen Latin American countries (excluding Cuba) in democratic periods since 1979 (in 78 of 114 elections).

In this situation, the president's party does not have a majority of seats in congress, thus does not include the median legislator, but it does include the veto legislator, as illustrated in Figure 16.2.B. This is the most typical situation of "divided government," which may hinder interinstitutional cooperation and effective law making. However, different opportunities can exist.

Imagine, for example, that the existing status quo policy on some issue is highly unsatisfactory for all actors because it is located, for instance, at an extreme position to the far right of the policy spectrum. Then, a bill approved with support of the median legislator, which in the example implies moving the status quo from the far right toward the center, will be "closer" to the president's preference. Thus, the president may not veto it but approve it, even if he or she would have preferred a more drastic reform. Some degree of interinstitutional cooperation can exist.

In contrast, if the status quo policy is located in the "space" in between the president's and the median party's preference, cooperation between the two institutions may be difficult. This situation implies that the issue is divisive, since the median party in control of congress prefers a policy alternative to one side of the spectrum and the president prefers a policy to toward the other side. The president may veto any change towards the median party's preference and away from the presidential one.

The distance between the policy preferences of the presidential party and the median party can be called the **"equilibrium set,"** or the **"deadlock interval,"** that is, **the set of policy decisions that can be stable despite both the president and the majority of congress favoring policy change**. The larger the interval, as marked in black in Figure 16.2.B, the higher the likelihood that a policy can remain in place, even if change is supported by a majority of voters or a majority of congressmen.

"Divided government" may provoke legislative paralysis and interinstitutional tensions. But it can also induce the actors involved to look for connections and possible agreements on other issues on which to make joint decisions. In the U.S. Congress,

BOX 16.2   **GOVERNMENT PARTIES, 1945–2005**

Number of chief
executives

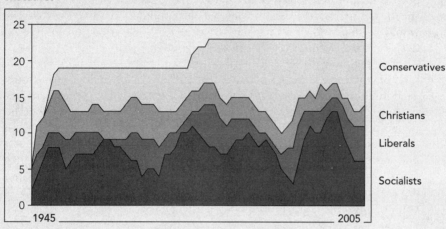

FIGURE 16.4   PARTY GOVERNMENT, 1945–2005

Different parties win elections and lead the formation of government in democracy. No long-term ideological trend has been found in a review of the party and ideology orientation of chief executives (prime ministers or presidents) in twenty-three stably democratic countries during the sixty-year period 1945 to 2005. Labor or social-democratic chief executives were more than half of the total in the late 1950s, the early 1970s, and the late 1990s (their peak moment), while conservatives and christian-democrats, if counted together, were more than half in the 1960s, the late 1980s, early 1990s (a peak moment for the conservatives alone), and the early 2000s.

Note: "Socialist" parties include socialists, social-democrats, laborites, and the Italian Left-Democrats; "Liberal" parties include liberals, agrarians, centrists, and the U.S. Democrats; "Christian-democrats" are also called populars; "Conservatives" include conservatives, the Japanese Liberals, the Portuguese Social-democrats and Centrists, and the U.S. Republicans.

Sources: Author's own elaboration for 366 elections in 23 countries: Australia, Austria, Belgium, Canada, Denmark, Finland, France, Germany, Greece, Ireland, Israel, Italy, Japan, Netherlands, New Zealand, Norway, Portugal, Spain, Sweden, Switzerland, Turkey, United Kingdom, United States, during the period 1945–2005. Data from Budge, Ian, Hans-Dieter Klingemann, Andrea Volkens, and Judith Bara, *Mapping Policy Preferences*, Oxford University Press, 2001, and Klingemann, Hans-Dieter, Andrea Volkens, Judith Bara, and Ian Budge, *Mapping Policy Preferences II*. New York: Oxford University Press, 2006.

the exchange of votes between individual representatives on different issues is called logrolling. It basically means that "you scratch my back and I'll scratch yours," as crudely put by Simon Cameron, President Lincoln's secretary of War. With relative frequency, the president can also gather a congressional majority or adapt to congressional initiatives by negotiating local issues, "pork barrel" or redistributive decisions in favor of different territories. Logrolling favors legislative productivity, although it may induce legislators to focus on disparate local issues and produce laws with sincere support from only a minority of congressmen.

Congressional Dominance.   As a variant of divided government, a minority, extreme president's party can be neither the veto nor the median party, as illustrated in Figure 16.2.C. The likelihood of this situation may depend heavily on the differences between the rules for electing the president and the congress. This type of "congressional government" might produce legislative decisions coinciding with the preferences of the median party, in a similar way to a parliamentary regime. But then the presidency would be deprived of all legislative influence, since it could not veto congressional decisions (presidential vetoes can be overridden.)

In a regime with separation of powers and popular election of the president, this kind of government may provoke a sense of **"dual legitimacy"** prone to conflict. Then each institution may try to rule on its own. Especially if the president has the authority to issue decrees with immediate force or other legislative powers, he or she can be tempted to legislate independently from the congress. In certain Latin American countries, in particular, a number of presidents with non-party or eccentric allegiance and extremely small legislative support below the veto rule have ended in institutional conflict with the congress, either being impeached or illegally dissolving congress or resigning. Multiparty coalitions, nevertheless, can prevent interinstitutional conflict, promote cooperation, and facilitate governance.

MULTIPARTY PRESIDENTS

The opportunities for a single party to control all pivotal actors in the legislative process greatly depend on the number of parties in the system. With one dominant party, as we have mentioned, the presidency and the congress can work together and make effective decisions on laws and policy.

In contrast, with two balanced, disciplined parties, divided government and the subsequent stalemate are relatively probable. Indeed policy making in the United States is more difficult and unsatisfactory when party discipline increases than when individual congressmen run more on their own.

Finally, the flourishing of multiple parties may facilitate agreements between the president's party and pivotal actors in congress to make legislative decisions feasible, depending on the institutional inducements, as tends to happen, for instance, in Brazil or Chile, to mention two cases.

It seems clear that if there are only two large political parties, the likelihood of having divided government is high. The president's party may not have a majority of seats in congress. If the two parties have high internal discipline and their members in congress vote in bloc, the two policy preferences to deal with can be significantly distant from each other and the legislators "entrenched" around them. In a congress with only two disciplined parties, decisions require unanimity agreements, which are characteristically hard to win in a democratic regime. Indeed decision making can be relatively contentious and can inflict significant bargaining and other transaction costs on legislators and executive officers. With a strong two-party system, it is difficult for the president to work out deals with the opposition, and adversarial politics and deadlock may burgeon.

In contrast, the situation can be relatively more fluid with a multiparty system, since the distance between the president's party and the median party in the congress can be relatively small. Note in Figure 16.3 that, with the same positions for the hypothetical preferences of the president, the veto legislator and the median legislator, the distance that defines **the "deadlock interval" is shorter with multiple parties than with only two parties**. In certain countries with a system of division of powers there has been bipolar confrontation and conflict, as in Argentina and Colombia. With multiparty systems, in contrast, minority presidents tend to be able to manage multisided negotiations to reach broad agreements and push their initiatives ahead in congress.

The situation can be even more favorable to flexible agreements if the members of congress have no strong party discipline and can take individual positions on policy issues. Even if there are officially only two large parties, the power of members of congress to take different individual positions can enlarge the actual range of preferences in congress and facilitate the formation of sufficient majorities among relatively close ones.

High freedom for individual legislators to vote on their own is linked to elections with strong personal representation, that is, with electoral systems based on single-seat districts or with high intra-party competition among individual candidates, as happens, most remarkably, in the United States. In contrast, party discipline is usually associated with strong party representation and, particularly, with elections in which representatives are selected from party lists. The preceding discussion does not imply a generally favorable judgment of party indiscipline. While a congress dominated by individuals' preferences and voting decisions is likely to focus on local issues or private favors, responsive parties may provide relatively more consistent policy proposals. But, in a context of bipartism, party indiscipline can be the grease that oils the wheels of divided government.

Conclusion

We have discussed how political parties can unify separate institutions and gather sufficient support for the chief executive to make governance feasible. In parliamentary regimes the key strategy is to form a multiparty coalition in support of the cabinet or prevent the opposition from forming an alternative majority. In division of power regimes, interinstitutional decision making requires cooperation between the presidency and the pivotal actors in the congress.

The following *propositions* can summarize the most solid findings available:

• **Minimum coalitions.** Political parties in parliament tend to form minimum-size winning coalitions and prefer partners located on contiguous positions along the policy-ideology space. The distribution of cabinet portfolios among coalition parties tends to be proportional to the number of seats controlled by each party.

• **Cabinet duration.** Single-party majority cabinets tend to last longer than multiparty coalition or minority cabinets.

• **Two-party stalemate.** In a system with division of powers between the presidency and the congress, the "deadlock interval" or range of stable policies is relatively short with multiple parties and with individual members of congress' freedom to vote. In contrast, a two-party system with strong party discipline favors confrontation and interinstitutional stalemate. ■

Summary

Political parties are the unifiers of separate powers between the executive and the legislative.

Parties and politicians seeking power tend to form minimum-size winning coalitions without superfluous partners in order to maximize their shares of portfolios.

Parties and politicians motivated by policy tend to form minimally connected winning coalitions with parties located on contiguous positions along the policy-ideology space. A connected majority coalition always includes the median party.

A party's bargaining power can be measured by the proportion of potential winning coalitions in which the party is pivotal.

A party is dominant if it can block any coalition and form a single-party minority cabinet.

The distribution of cabinet portfolios among coalition parties tends to be proportional to the number of seats controlled by each party. Coalition agreements can be built upon parties' preferences for the allocation of different portfolios.

Single-party majority cabinets tend to last longer than multiparty coalition or minority cabinets.

Unexpected events can alter parties' electoral expectations and provoke a reshuffling in government, the replacement of the incumbent coalition, or the dissolution of the parliament.

In a regime with separation of powers, the pivotal actors in the legislative process are the median legislator, the president, and the veto legislator.

Unified government implies that the dominant presidential party has a majority of seats in congress, including both the median and the veto legislators.

There is divided government when the president's party does not have a majority of seats in congress. If the president's party does not control the veto legislator, conflict between the presidency and the assembly is likely to arise.

The "deadlock interval," or set of stable policies, is shorter with multiple parties than with two parties, and even shorter with low party discipline and individual representatives' freedom to vote.

Key Concepts

Censure. The majority of the parliament can overthrow the prime minister.

Confidence. The prime minister can check his or her own support in the assembly.

Deadlock interval. A set of stable policies located between the preferences of the president and those of the median legislator.

Dominant party. The largest party able to block any coalition and form a single-party minority cabinet.

Government. In its strict sense, the collective executive body, also called the cabinet.

Investiture. A requirement of majority voting in support of the prime minister in parliament.

Logrolling. The exchange of votes between different groups of legislators on different policy issues.

Median legislator. The pivotal actor able to attract a congressional majority in favor of his proposal.

Minimal connected winning coalition. A coalition formed of parties located on contiguous positions along the policy-ideology space.

Minimum winning coalition. Majority coalition without superfluous partners.

Veto legislator. The pivotal actor able to either confirm or override the presidential veto.

Questions for Review

1. Define minimum winning coalition.
2. Define minimal connected winning coalition.
3. Which type of parliamentary cabinets tends to last longer?
4. Define the median legislator.
5. Define the veto legislator.
6. What's the "deadlock interval?"

Problems and Applications

1. In the parliament that follows there are five parties ordered from left to right alphabetically and with the distribution of seats indicated.
   a. List all possible winning coalitions (WC).
   b. List all possible minimum winning coalitions (MWC).
   c. List all possible minimally connected winning coalitions (MCWC).

Ideology:	Left	Center-left	Center	Center-right	Right
Parties:	V	W	X	Y	Z
Seats:	20	15	10	25	30
Total seats:	100				
Majority:	51				

2. Look at the distribution of seats between parties in the parliament of Norway elected in 2005.
   a. List all possible minimum winning coalitions (MWC).
   b. List all possible minimally connected winning coalitions (MCWC).
   c. Discuss the characteristics of the so-called "Red-Green" coalition government that was formed. Led by the Labor Party (DNA), it included the Socialists (SV) and the Center-Agrarians (SP, considered "greens").
   d. Discuss the viability of other alternative majority coalitions.

Ideology:	Left	Center-left	Center	Center-right		Right	
Parties:	Socialist	Labor	Agrarian	Christian	Liberal	Progress	Conservative
	SV	DNA	SP	KRF	V	FRP	H
Seats:	15	61	11	11	10	38	23
Total seats: 169							
Majority: 85							

Data sources

World Bank Database of Political Institutions: www.go.worldbank.org/2EAGGLRZ40
Interactive websites and calculators:
Computer Algorithms for Voting Power Analysis: www.warwick.ac.uk/~ecaae/
Indices of Power: www.uni-konstanz.de/FuF/Verwiss/koenig/
Voting Power and Power Index Website: www.powerslave.val.utu.fi/calculate.html

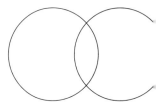

FINAL THOUGHTS

After reading and studying this book, you may be persuaded that politics is a noble science and can be a less dismal activity than some people believe. In the light of our analyses, politics is not always good, but it is not always bad, either. Sometimes governments are able to solve collective problems and provide public goods. Sometimes they may distort citizens' lives and waste collective resources. Governments are not always philanthropic, but they are not always ogres, either—more or less like the markets. Indeed, markets sometimes provide private goods and collective prosperity; sometimes they are unable to allocate resources in an efficient manner, and therefore provoke misery and misuse. Both politics and the economy—through governments and markets—work satisfactorily if they develop within good institutional formulas, and if people behave according to the expectations created by the incentives and opportunities available. Otherwise they may not.

There is, however, a fundamental difference between politics and the economy. While individuals may be able to produce, exchange, and consume private goods, they have trouble providing **public goods**. This is a key concept for understanding the fundamentals of politics, which we studied in the first chapter of this book. Public goods are not divisible into private parts, and so they can be used by multiple individuals, even by those who do not contribute to their provision and maintenance. Security, justice, currency, means of transport, schools, the environment, among many others, are blatant examples of public goods.

As we reviewed in the first part of the book, the provision of public goods is not always achieved to the extent desired by the citizens because it does not depend on the costs of the goods, but on the costs of collective action for the goods' provision. However, people can learn to cooperate among themselves through sustained interactions within a stable setting and by learning lessons from failures and conflicts. Collective action can also be promoted by means of **leadership**. This is another key concept for understanding politics. Leaders do not necessarily share all the interests and demands they serve. But citizens can give them their support in exchange for making the provision of public goods effective.

The most fundamental problem in politics is with whom everybody is ready to form a **community**; that is, with whom make decisions for the provision of public goods, share burdens, including taxes and other duties, and comply with the rules even when one finds oneself in a minority or as a loser in a collective choice. This is the problem of building cities, nations, states, empires, and federations, as well as of migrations. It basically requires the establishment of boundaries for a population or a territory in which enforceable collective decisions can be made.

As we studied in the second part of the book, individuals in small or relatively consistent communities are more likely to have harmonious policy preferences, and thus better able to engage themselves in collective action, make consensual decisions, and comply with the others. But people also share interests and preferences with those living at remote distances, with whom they may have differences. Public goods have different territorial scales—from security to currency, from communications networks to transport, from schools and hospitals to personal assistance. The efficient provision of these goods may require multiple-level institutions and both large- and small-scale processes of decision making involving different sets of people within different territories.

Democracy, another key concept in this book, is just a procedure to make enforceable collective decisions based on freedom, people's right to participate, and elections between alternative candidates and political parties. Whether a community is able to seek the public good by democratic means may depend on its degree of internal harmony and its capacity to identify priority issues and make decisions with broad support, and on the specific institutional formulas and procedures adopted to make those decisions. Key elements for good democratic governance are temperance of redistributive conflicts and inclusive institutional design.

The most widely diffused democratic system for selecting leaders and developing exchanges between leaders and citizens in modern times is through political parties and competitive elections, which we studied in the third part of this book. Elections help to solve the problem of **representation**—one more crucial concept—of diverse individual preferences. Multiparty elections select leaders and rulers and contribute to setting the public agenda.

Generally, complex institutions may prevent, tame, or channel potential conflicts and favor broad agreements. But different institutional formulas, as we saw in the fourth part of the book, give varied responses to the problem of citizens' representation in government. While **institutions**—a key concept indeed—are the rules of the game, political parties are the players. Parties are agents for the formation of majority coalitions, and bridges that unify separate powers. The concentration of power into a single political party can be effective for making expedient decisions, but the diffusion of power among separate institutions and multiple parties can foster broad acceptance of collective decisions and consensual results. Democratic decision making requires the formation of a political majority to give support to legislative, governmental, and other policy decisions. When favorable conditions like those summarized here are present, politics tends to be rather good—an activity worthy of studying scientifically, and getting involved in.

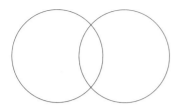

BIBLIOGRAPHY

If you have enjoyed this political science course, you may wish to read some of the basic sources for this book. In the following list I include both a few relatively old, seminal works, and more recent contributions that have made scientific progress. This summer you may wish to choose one topic in which you have been most interested and try reading some of the pieces listed here. If you have chosen political science as your major field of study, you may want to make a point of reading or at least taking a serious look at all these one hundred or so readings by the time of your graduation.

General

Annual Review of Political Science (Nelson W. Polsby, founding ed.). Palo Alto, Calif.: Annual Reviews, since 1998.

The Encyclopedia of Political Science (George T. Kurian, general editor). 5 vols. Sage, 2010.

International Encyclopedia of Political Science (Bertrand Badie, Dirk Berg-Schlosser, and Leonardo Morlino, general editors), 8 vols, Sage, 2011.

Oxford Handbook of Political Science (Robert Goodin, general editor). 10 vols. New York: Oxford University Press, 2006–2009.

Political Science: The State of the Discipline. 1st ed. 1983 (Seymour M. Lipset, ed.), 2nd ed., 1993 (Ada Finifter, ed.), 3rd ed., 2002 (Ira Kaznetson and Helen Milner, eds.). Washington, D.C.: American Political Science Association.

I. Action

CHAPTER 1. THE PUBLIC GOOD

Buchanan, James. 1965. "An Economic Theory of Clubs," *Economica* 32.

Coase, Ronald H. 1988. *The Firm, the Market, and the Law.* Chicago: University of Chicago Press.

Hardin, Garret. 1968. "The Tragedy of the Commons," *Science* 162.

Ostrom, Elinor. 1990. *Governing the Commons: The Evolution of Institutions for Collective Action.* Cambridge, UK: Cambridge University Press.

Samuelson, Paul A. 1954. "The Pure Theory of Public Expenditure." *The Review of Economics and Statistics* 36.

———. 1955. "Diagrammatic Exposition of a Theory of Public Expenditure." *The Review of Economics and Statistics* 37.

CHAPTER 2. COLLECTIVE ACTION

Aldrich, John H. 1993. **"Rational Choice and Turnout."** *American Journal of Political Science* 37, 1.

Hardin, Russell. 1982. *Collective Action*. Baltimore, Md.: Johns Hopkins University Press.

Hirschmann, Albert O. 1970. *Exit, Voice, and Loyalty*. Cambridge, Mass.: Harvard University Press.

Olson, Mancur (1965). 1971. *The Logic of Collective Action: Public Goods and the Theory of Groups*. Cambridge, Mass.: Harvard University Press.

Sandler, Todd. 2004. *Global Collective Action*. Cambridge, UK: Cambridge University Press.

CHAPTER 3. COOPERATION AND CONFLICT

Axelrod, Robert (1984). 2006. *The Evolution of Cooperation*. New York: Perseus.

Brams, Steven J., and Alan D. Taylor. 2000. *The Win-Win Solution: Guaranteeing Fair Shares to Everybody*. New York: W.W. Norton.

Nash, John F. 1950. "The Bargaining Problem." *Econometrica* 18.

———. 1951. "Noncooperative Games." *Annals of Mathematics* 54.

Poundstone, William. 1993. *Prisoner's Dilemma: John von Neumann, Game Theory, and the Puzzle of the Bomb*. New York: Doubleday.

Rapoport, Anatol, and M. A. Guyer. 1966. "A Taxonomy of 2x2 Games." *General Systems* 11.

Von Neumann, John, and Oskar Morgenstern. 1944. *Theory of Games and Economic Behavior*. Princeton, N.J.: Princeton University Press.

CHAPTER 4. LEADERSHIP

Burns, James McGregor. 1978. *Leadership*. New York: Harper and Row.

Colomer, Josep M. 1995. "Leadership Games in Collective Action." *Rationality and Society* 7, no. 2.

Frohlich, Norman, Joe A. Oppenheimer and Oran R. Young. 1971. *Political Leadership and Collective Goods*. Princeton, N.J.: Princeton University Press.

Marwell, Gerald, and Pamela Oliver. 1993. *The Critical Mass in Collective Action*. Cambridge, UK: Cambridge University Press.

Nye, Joseph S., Jr. 2008. *The Powers to Lead*. New York: Oxford University Press.

Schelling, Thomas C. 1978. *Micromotives and Macrobehavior*. New York: Norton.

Weber, Max. 1922. "Types of Domination." In Max Weber. 1978. *Economy and Society*. Berkeley: University of California Press.

II. Polity

CHAPTER 5. COMMUNITY

Alesina, Alberto, and Enrico Spolaore. 2003. *The Size of Nations*. Cambridge, Mass.: MIT Press.

Colomer, Josep M. 2007. *Great Empires, Small Nations*. London: Routledge.

Finer, Samuel. 1997. *The History of Government from the Earliest Times*. New York: Oxford University Press.

Rokkan, Stein. (1973). 1999. *State Formation, Nation-Building, and Mass Politics in Europe*. (Edited by Peter Flora, with S. Kuhnle and D. Urwin.) New York: Oxford University Press.

Service, Elman R. 1975. *Origins of the State and Civilization: The Process of Cultural Evolution*. New York: Norton.

Tilly, Charles, ed. 1975. *The Formation of National States in Western Europe*. Princeton, N.J.: Princeton University Press.

Van Creveld, Martin L. 1999. *The Rise and Decline of the State*. Cambridge, UK: Cambridge University Press.

CHAPTER 6. FEDERATION

Dahl, Robert A., and Edward Tufte. 1973. *Size and Democracy*. Palo Alto, Calif.: Stanford University Press.

Elazar, Daniel J. 1987. *Exploring Federalism*. Tuscaloosa: University of Alabama Press.

Filippov, Mikhail, Peter C. Ordeshook, and Olga Shvetsova. 2004. *Designing Federalism: A Theory of Self-sustainable Federal Institutions*. Cambridge, UK: Cambridge University Press.

North, Douglass C., and Barry W. Weingast. 1989. "The Evolution of Institutions Governing Public Choice in Seventeenth-Century England." *Journal of Economic History* 49.

Ostrom, Vincent. 1987. *The Political Theory of a Compound Republic: Designing the American Experiment*. Lincoln: University of Nebraska Press.

Riker, William H. (1964 adapted). 1987. *The Development of American Federalism*. Norwell, Mass.: Kluwer.

CHAPTER 7. DICTATORSHIP

Colomer, Josep M. 2000. *Strategic Transitions: Game Theory and Democratization*. Baltimore, Md.: Johns Hopkins University Press.

Gandhi, Jennifer. 2008. *Political Institutions Under Dictatorship.* Cambridge, UK: Cambridge University Press.

Laitin, David. 2007. *Nations, States, and Violence.* New York: Oxford University Press.

Linz, Juan J. (1975). 2000. *Totalitarian and Authoritarian Regimes.* Boulder, Co.: Lynne Rienner.

O'Donnell, Guillermo, and Philippe C. Schmitter, eds. 1986. *Transitions from Authoritarian Rule.* Baltimore, Md.: Johns Hopkins University Press.

Olson, Mancur. 2000. *Power and Prosperity: Outgrowing Communist and Capitalist Dictatorships.* New York: Oxford University Press.

Przeworski, Adam. 1991. *Democracy and the Market.* Cambridge, UK: Cambridge University Press.

Skocpol, Theda. 1979. *States and Social Revolutions: A Comparative Analysis of France, Russia, and China.* Cambridge, UK: Cambridge University Press.

CHAPTER 8. DEMOCRACY

Acemoglu, Daron, and James A. Robinson. 2006. *Economic Origins of Dictatorship and Democracy.* Cambridge, UK: Cambridge University Press.

Almond, Gabriel, and Sidney Verba (1963). 1989. *The Civic Culture: Political Attitudes and Democracy in Five Nations.* Thousand Oaks, Calif.: Sage.

Dahl, Robert A. (1971). 1989. *Democracy and Its Critics.* New Haven, Conn.: Yale University Press.

Lipset, Seymour M. 1960. *Political Man: The Social Bases of Politics.* New York: Doubleday.

Przeworski, Adam, Mike Alvarez, José Antonio Cheibub, and Fernando Limogi. 2000. *Democracy and Development: Political Institutions and Material Well-being in the World, 1950–1990.* Cambridge, UK: Cambridge University Press.

Putnam, Robert D. 1993. *Making Democracy Work: Civic Traditions and Modern Italy.* Princeton, N.J.: Princeton University Press.

Russett, Bruce. 1993. *Grasping the Democratic Peace: Principles for a Post–Cold War World.* Princeton, N.J.: Princeton University Press.

Sen, Amartya. 1999. *Development as Freedom.* New York: Alfred A. Knopf.

III. Election

CHAPTER 9. POLITICAL PARTIES

Aldrich, John. 1995. *Why Parties? The Origin and Transformation of Political Parties in America.* Chicago: University of Chicago Press.

Duverger, Maurice. (1951). 1954. *Political Parties: Their Organization and Activity in the Modern State.* New York: John Wiley.

May, John D. 1973. "Opinion Structure of Political Parties." *Political Studies* 21, 2.

Michels, Robert. 1911. *Political Parties: A Sociological Study of the Oligarchical Tendencies of Modern Democracy.* Glencoe, Ill.: Free Press.

Weber, Max. (1918–19). 2004. *The Vocation Lectures: Science as a Vocation, Politics as a Vocation.* Indianapolis, Ind.: Hackett.

CHAPTER 10. ELECTORAL COMPETITION

Davis, Otto A., Melvin J. Hinich, and Peter C. Ordeshook. 1970. "An Expository Development of a Mathematical Model of the Electoral Process." *American Political Science Review* 64, 2.

Downs, Anthony. 1957. *An Economic Theory of Democracy.* New York: Addison-Wesley.

Erikson, Robert S. 1971. "The Advantage of Incumbency in Congressional Elections." *Polity* 3, 3.

Hinich, Melvin J., and Michael C. Munger. 1996. *Ideology and the Theory of Political Choice.* Ann Arbor: University of Michigan Press.

———. 1997. *Analytical Politics.* Cambridge, UK: Cambridge University Press.

Shepsle, Kenneth. 1991. *Models of Multiparty Electoral Competition.* New York: Routledge.

CHAPTER 11. AGENDA FORMATION

Jones, Bryan. 1995. *Reconceiving Decision-Making in Democratic Politics: Attention, Choice, and Public Policy.* Chicago: University of Chicago Press.

McKelvey, Ricard D. 1976. "Intransitivities in Multidimensional Voting Models and Some Implications for Agenda Control." *Journal of Economic Theory* 12.

Miller, Gary, and Norman Schofield. 2003. "Activism and Partisan Realignment in the United States." *American Political Science Review* 97, no. 2.

Petrocik, J. R., W. L Benoit, and G. Hansen. 2002. "Issue Ownership and Presidential Campaigning, 1952–2000." *Political Science Quarterly* 118, no. 4.

Poole, Keith T. 2005. *Spatial Models of Parliamentary Voting.* Cambridge, UK: Cambridge University Press.

Riker, William H. 1986. *The Art of Political Manipulation.* New Haven, Conn.: Yale University Press.

———, ed. 1993. *Agenda Formation.* Ann Arbor: University of Michigan Press.

Stokes, Donald E. 1963. "Spatial Models of Party Competition." *American Political Science Review* 57, no. 2.

CHAPTER 12. PARTY SYSTEMS

Benoit, Kenneth, and Michael Laver. 2007. *Party Policy in Modern Democracies.* New York: Routledge.

Lipset, Seymour M., and Stein Rokkan, eds. 1967. *Cleavage Structures, Party Systems and Voter Alignments: Cross-national Perspectives.* Glencoe, Ill.: Free Press.

Sartori, Giovanni. 1976. *Parties and Party Systems.* Cambridge, UK: Cambridge University Press.

Taagepera, Rein, and Bernard Grofman. 1985. "Rethinking Duverger's Law: Predicting the Effective Number of Parties in Plurality and PR Systems: Parties Minus Issues Equals One." *European Journal of Political Research* 13.

III. Government

CHAPTER 13. CHOOSING PRESIDENTS

Brams, Steven. (1979) 2007. *The Presidential Election Game.* Natick, Mass.: A. K. Peters.

Buchanan, James, and Gordon Tullock. 1962. *The Calculus of Consent: Logical Foundations of Constitutional Democracy.* Ann Arbor: University of Michigan Press.

McGann, Anthony. 2006. *The Logic of Democracy.* Ann Arbor: University of Michigan Press.

McLean, Iain, and Arnold Urken, eds. 1995. *Classics of Social Choice.* Ann Arbor: University of Michigan Press.

Manin, Bernard. 1997. *The Principles of Representative Government.* Cambridge, UK: Cambridge University Press.

May, Kenneth O. 1952. "A Set of Independent, Necessary, and Sufficient Conditions for Simple Majority Decision." *Econometrica* 20.

Negretto, Gabriel L. 2010. *Making Constitutions. Presidents, Parties, and Institutional Choice in Latin America.* Cambridge, UK: Cambridge University Press.

CHAPTER 14. ELECTING ASSEMBLIES

Balinski, Michel L., and H. Peyton Young (1982). 2001. *Fair Representation: Meeting the Ideal of One Man, One Vote.* Washington, D.C.: Brookings Institution Press.

Carey, John M., and Matthew S. Shugart. 1995. "Incentives to Cultivate a Personal Vote: A Rank Ordering of Electoral Formulas." *Electoral Studies* 14.

Colomer, Josep M. ed. 2004. *Handbook of Electoral System Choice.* London: Palgrave-Macmillan.

Cox, Gary W. 1997. *Making Votes Count: Strategic Coordination in the World's Electoral Systems.* Cambridge, UK: Cambridge University Press.

Grofman, Bernard, and Arend Lijphart, eds. 1986. *Electoral Laws and Their Political Consequences.* Edison, N.J.: Agathon.

Taagepera, Rein. 2007. *Predicting Party Sizes: The Logic of Simple Electoral Systems.* New York: Oxford University Press.

CHAPTER 15. DIVISION OF POWERS

Bryce, James (1888, 1910). 1995. *The American Commonwealth.* City: Liberty Fund.

Colomer, Josep M. 2001. *Political Institutions.* Oxford: Oxford University Press.

Cox, Gary W. 1987. *The Efficient Secret: The Cabinet and the Development of Political Parties in Victorian England.* Cambridge, UK: Cambridge University Press.

Grofman, Bernard, and Donald Wittman, eds. 1989. *"The Federalist Papers" and the New Institutionalism.* Edison, N.J.: Agathon.

Hammond, Thomas H., and Gary J. Miller. 1987. "The Core of the Constitution." *American Political Science Review* 81.

Miller, Nicholas R. 1983. "Pluralism and Social Choice." *American Political Science Review* 21.

Shugart, Matthew S., and John M. Carey. 1992. *Presidents and Assemblies.* Cambridge, UK: Cambridge University Press.

CHAPTER 16. PARTY GOVERNMENT

Krehbiel, Kenneth. 1998. *Pivotal Politics: A Theory of U.S. Lawmaking.* Chicago: University of Chicago Press.

Laver, Michael, and Kenneth Shepsle. 1997. *Making and Breaking Governments.* Cambridge, UK: Cambridge University Press.

Laver Michael, and Norman Schofield (1990). 2003. *Multiparty Government.* New York: Oxford University Press.

Lijphart, Arend. 1999. *Patterns of Democracy.* New Haven, Conn.: Yale University Press.

Powell, G. Bingham. 2000. *Elections as Instruments of Democracy.* New Haven, Conn.: Yale University Press.

Riker, William H. 1962. *Theory of Political Coalitions.* New Haven, Conn.: Yale University Press.

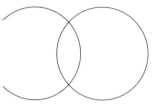

KEY CONCEPTS

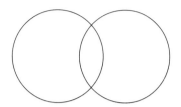

REFERENCES FOR QUOTES

Acemoglu, Daron, and James A. Robinson. 2006. *Economic Origins of Dictatorship and Democracy.* New York: Cambridge University Press.

Alesina, Alberto, and Enrico Spolaore. 2003. *The Size of Nations.* Boston: The MIT Press.

Arendt, Hannah. (1951) 1973. *The Origins of Totalitarianism.* Orlando, Fla.: Hartcourt.

Bara, Judith. 2006. "The 2005 Manifestos: A Sense of Déjà vu?" *Journal of Elections, Public Opinion and Parties* 16, no. 3.

Benoit, Kenneth, and M. Laver. 2007. *Party Policy in Modern Democracies.* London: Routledge.

Buchanan, James M., and Gordon Tullock. 1962. *The Calculus of Consent: Logical foundations of constitutional democracy.* Ann Arbor: University of Michigan Press.

Budge, Ian, Hans-Dieter Klingemann, Andrea Volkens, and Judith Bara. 2001. *Mapping Policy Preferences: Estimates for Parties, Electors, and Governments, 1945–1998.* Oxford: Oxford University Press.

Burns, James MacGregor. 1978. *Leadership.* New York: Harper and Row.

Colomer, Josep M. 2001. *Political Institutions.* Oxford: Oxford University Press.

———, ed. 2004. *Handbook of Electoral System Choice.* London: Palgrave-Macmillan.

———. 2007. *Great Empires, Small Nations.* London: Routledge.

———, ed. 2008. *Comparative European Politics.* 3rd ed. London: Routledge.

Colomer, Josep M., and Luis E. Escatel. 2005. "La dimension izquierda-derecha en America Latina," *Desarrollo Economico* (Buenos Aires) 44, no. 177.

Dahl, Robert A., and Edward Tufte. 1973. *Size and Democracy.* Stanford, Calif.: Stanford University Press.

Davis, Otto A., Melvin J. Hinich, and Peter C. Ordeshook. 1970. "An Expository Development of a Mathematical Model of the Electoral Process." *American Political Science Review* 64, no. 2.

Democracy and Development: Political Institutions and Well-being in the World, 1950–1990. New York: Cambridge University Press.

Downs, Anthony. 1957. *An Economic Theory of Democracy.* New York: Addison-Wesley,

Duverger, Maurice. 1972. "Factors in a Two-Party and Multiparty System." In *Party Politics and Pressure Groups.* New York: Thomas Y. Crowell.

Elazar, Daniel J. 1987. *Exploring Federalism*. Tuscaloosa: University of Alabama Press.

Friedrich, Carl, and Zbigniew Brzezinski. 1956. *Totalitarian Dictatorship and Autocracy*. New York: Praeger.

Frohlich, Norman, Joe A. Oppenheimer, and Oran R. Young. 1971. *Political Leadership and Collective Goods*. Princeton, N.J.: Princeton University Press.

Hardin, Garrett. 1968. "The Tragedy of the Commons." *Science* 162.

Huber, Evelyn, Dietrich Rueschemeyer, and John D. Stephens. 1993. "The Impact of Economic Development on Democracy." *Journal of Economic Perspectives* 7, no. 3.

Huber, John D., and G. Bingham Powell, Jr. 1994. "Congruence Between Citizens and Policy Makers in Two Visions of Liberal Democracy." *World Politics* 46, no. 3.

Klingemann, Hans-Dieter, Andrea Volkens, Judith Bara, and Ian Budge. 2006. *Mapping Policy Preferences II: Estimates for Parties, Electors, and Governments in Central and Eastern Europe, European Union and OECD 1990–2003*. Oxford: Oxford University Press.

Lijphart, Arend. 1994. "Presidentialism and Majoritarian Democracy." In Juan J. Linz and Arturo Valenzuela eds. *The Failure of Presidential Democracy*. Baltimore, Md.: Johns Hopkins University Press.

Linz, Juan J., and Alfred Stepan. 1996. *Problems of Democratic Transition and Consolidation: Southern Europe, South America, and Post-Communist Europe*. Baltimore, Md.: Johns Hopkins University Press.

Lipset, Seymour M. 1960. *Political Man: The Social Bases of Politics*. New York: Doubleday.

Lipset, Seymour M., and Stein Rokkan. 1967. *Cleavage Structures, Party Systems, and Voter Alignments*. New York: Free Press.

Loewenstein, Karl. 1949. "The Presidency Outside the United States: A Study in Comparative Political Institutions." *The Journal of Politics* 11, no. 3.

MacDougall, Terry Edward. 1988. "Yoshida Shigeru and the Japanese Transition to Liberal Democracy." *International Political Science Review* 9, no. 55.

McKelvey, Richard. 1979. "General Conditions for Global Intransitivities in Formal Voting Models." *Econometrica* 47, no. 5.

Maddison, Angus. 2003. *The World Economy: Historical Statistics*. Paris: Organisation for Economic Co-operation and Development (updated at www.ggdc.net/maddison).

May, John D. 1973. "Opinion Structure of Political Parties." *Political Studies* 21, no. 2.

Miller, Gary, and Norman Schofield. 2008. "The Transformation of the Republican and Democratic Party Coalitions in the U.S." *Perspectives on Politics* 6, no. 3.

Moore, Jr., Barrington. 1966. *Social Origins of Dictatorship and Democracy*. Boston: Beacon Press.

Morgenstern, Oskar. 1976. "The Collaboration Between Oskar Morgenstern and John von Neumann on the Theory of Games." *Journal of Economic Literature* 14, no. 3.

Nye, Jr., Joseph S. 2008. *The Powers to Lead*. New York: Oxford University Press.

Olson, Mancur. (1965). 1971. *The Logic of Collective Action: Public Goods and the Theory of Groups*. Cambridge, Mass.: Harvard University Press.

Ostrom, Vincent. 1971. *The Political Theory of a Compound Republic. Designing the American Experiment*. Lincoln: University of Nebraska Press.

Paxman, Jeremy. 2002. *The Political Animal*. London: Penguin.

Przeworski, Adam, Michael E. Alvarez, José A. Cheibub, and Fernando Limongi. 2000.

Riker, William (1964). 1987. *The Development of American Federalism*. Boston: Kluwer.

Rokkan, Stein. 1999. *State Formation, Nation-Building, and Mass Politics in Europe*. Edited by Peter Flora, with S. Kuhnle and D. Urwin. Oxford: Oxford University Press.

Russell, Bertrand. 1959. *Common Sense and Nuclear Warfare*. New York: Simon and Schuster.

Samuelson, Paul A. 1954. "The Pure Theory of Public Expenditure." *The Review of Economics and Statistics* 36.

Sartori, Giovanni. 1986. "The Influence of Electoral Systems: Faulty Laws or Faulty Method?" In Bernard Grofman and Arend Lijphart, eds. *Electoral Laws and Their Political Consequences*. New York: Agathon.

Schumpeter, Joseph A. 1942. *Capitalism, Socialism, and Democracy*. New York: Harper.

Stokes, William S. 1959. *Latin American Politics*. New York: Thomas Y. Crowell.

Taagepera, Rein. 2007. *Predicting Party Sizes: The Logic of Simple Electoral Systems*. Oxford: Oxford University Press.

Tanzi, Vito, and Ludger Schuknecht. 2000. *Public Spending in the Twentieth Century: A Global Perspective*. New York: Cambridge University Press.

Wills, Garry. 1994. *Certain Trumpets: The Call of Leaders*. New York: Simon and Schuster.

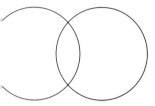

NAME INDEX

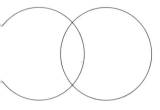

SUBJECT INDEX

Note: Information in figures and tables is indicated by *f* and *t*.